Hugging Face in Action

Hugging Face in Action

WEI-MENG LEE

MANNING
SHELTER ISLAND

brief contents

contents

preface

When I started exploring Hugging Face, I was struck by how accessible and powerful its tools were. Models that once required specialized knowledge and massive compute resources were now available to anyone with a laptop and Python. I spent countless hours experimenting—running pretrained models, fine-tuning them on my own datasets, and trying to figure out how to integrate them into real applications. That journey was exciting, but I quickly realized that learning to use models was only part of the story. The real challenge—and the real fun—comes from building AI systems that can act, interact, and solve real-world problems.

This book is the result of that journey. It's designed to take you from the basics of navigating Hugging Face to building end-to-end AI applications—from natural language processing (NLP) and computer vision tasks to autonomous agents, interactive web interfaces, and locally running models. Along the way, I explore advanced concepts such as multimodal models, LangChain for AI workflows, retrieval-augmented generation (RAG) for querying documents, and the Model Context Protocol (MCP) for connecting AI systems to tools and data. My goal is to give you not just code examples but also a framework for thinking about AI applications—how to design them, extend them, and make them useful in the real world.

Each chapter is hands-on and practical. You'll find exercises, examples, and tips drawn from real projects so you can learn by doing. I hope this book helps you move beyond experimenting to building intelligent systems that can learn, reason, and interact; I hope it inspires you to explore new possibilities with AI.

Whether you're a developer, data scientist, or AI enthusiast, my hope is that this book becomes a companion on your own journey, helping you turn curiosity into skill, and skill into impactful applications.

acknowledgments

Writing this book was a journey made possible by the support, guidance, and inspiration of many people. First, I'd like to thank the team at Manning Publications for their encouragement, patience, and valuable feedback throughout the writing and editing process.

In particular, I'm grateful to all the Manning staff, especially Dustin Archibald, my development editor, for his thoughtful guidance and detailed suggestions, and Jonathan Gennick, my acquisitions editor, for believing in this project and helping bring it to life. Their support helped shape this book into a practical, hands-on guide that I hope will be useful to developers and AI enthusiasts alike. Thanks also to the production team, whose behind-the-scenes work helped make this book what you see.

I'm deeply grateful to the Hugging Face community, whose open source contributions, forums, and resources have been invaluable sources of learning and inspiration. The work of the developers, researchers, and engineers behind Hugging Face models and tools made the ideas in this book possible.

Special thanks to friends and students who provided feedback on early drafts, tested examples, and shared insights from their own experiences. Your questions, challenges, and curiosity helped refine the explanations and examples in this book.

In addition, thanks to all the reviewers: Abhijeet Rajwade, Ankur Padia, Astha Puri, Baskar Sikkayan, Bonny Albo, David Yakobovitch, Dhirendra Kumar Choudhary, Georgerobert Freeman, Giovanni Alzetta, Justin Reiser, Lokeshwar Reddy Vangala, Madiha Khalid, Manish Jain, Marco Massenzio, Marco Seguri, Michael Bright, Ninoslav Čerkez, Parmanand Sahu, Paul Silisteanu, Rahul Raja, Ritobrata Ghosh, Robert Rozploch, Saurabh Aggarwal, Sriram Selvam, Stefano Priola, Steven Edwards, Subhash Chandra Bose Naripeddy, Sukanya Moorthy, Todd Jobson, Vignesh Govindarajan

Ravichandran, Vikram Kulothungan, Vinod Goje, Vinod Veeramachaneni, and Yilun Zhang. Your suggestions helped make this book better.

Finally, I want to thank my family for their patience and encouragement. Your support made the long hours of writing and experimentation not only possible but also truly enjoyable.

To all of you, this book is a reflection of your inspiration and contributions. Thank you.

about this book

Artificial intelligence is no longer confined to research labs; it's becoming a tool that anyone can use to build intelligent, interactive real-world applications. This book is your gateway to the Hugging Face ecosystem, guiding you step by step from understanding pretrained models to creating fully functional AI applications. You'll learn how to harness the power of transformers for NLP; explore computer vision models; fine-tune models on your own datasets; and even work with multimodal models that handle text, images, and more.

But this book goes beyond simply using models; it also shows you how to make AI work for you. You'll discover how to build autonomous agents that can make decisions, interact with tools, and retrieve information; create web-based interfaces that allow others to experience your AI; run models locally for privacy and speed; and connect AI to the real world through protocols such as MCP.

With hands-on examples, practical projects, and clear explanations, this book equips you to move from experimentation to building intelligent end-to-end AI systems—applications that can learn, adapt, and interact in meaningful ways. By the end of this book, you won't just understand Hugging Face; you'll also have the skills to build AI-powered solutions that solve real problems, automate tasks, and engage users in entirely new ways.

Who should read this book

This book is for developers, data scientists, and AI enthusiasts who want to move beyond simply calling APIs and start building end-to-end AI applications using the Hugging Face ecosystem and related frameworks. If you're curious about how to use pretrained models for NLP and computer vision tasks, fine-tune them for your own datasets, or integrate them into real-world applications with interactive UIs, this book is for you. No deep learning expertise is required, though a working knowledge of Python will be helpful.

This book is designed for readers with varying levels of expertise in NLP and machine learning. It caters to both beginners and intermediate practitioners who are interested in harnessing the capabilities of Hugging Face's platform. The content covers a wide range of topics, from using the Transformers library for NLP tasks to performing computer vision tasks such as object detection in images and videos. It also explores building applications with large language models (LLMs) using LangChain and Langflow. The target audience includes those who are looking to prototype visually, create LLM-based chat applications with private data, and build user interfaces using Gradio. Overall, this book serves as a comprehensive guide for anyone who wants to use Hugging Face for diverse NLP and machine learning applications.

Prerequisites

Before you begin, it's important to ensure that you have the necessary background knowledge and tools to follow the material covered in this book effectively. The following prerequisites will help you get the most out of this book. You should already be comfortable with programming in Python and working with essential data-analysis libraries. In addition, familiarity with Jupyter Notebooks is required because many of the exercises and demonstrations are conducted in that environment.

- *Python (intermediate)*—
  - Fluency with basic Python language constructs
  - Familiarity with data structures such as lists, tuples, dictionaries, and sets
  - Familiarity with intermediate concepts such as iterables and generators
  - Ability to work with various data formats, such as CSV and Microsoft Excel
  - Ability to create an independent Python program and run it in Terminal or Anaconda Prompt
- *NumPy and pandas (intermediate)*—
  - Experience using NumPy's array to manipulate data
  - Experience using the pandas Series and DataFrame data structures to manipulate structured data
  - Familiarity with the various functions and methods in NumPy and pandas
  - Basic knowledge of data analytics
- *Jupyter Notebooks*—
  - Creating environments in, and starting and loading Jupyter Notebooks
  - Ability to save and load Jupyter Notebooks
  - Familiarity with Markdown syntax for documentation
  - Ability to find documentation for functions and methods within Jupyter Notebooks

How this book is organized: A road map

The book is designed as a hands-on, practical guide. Each chapter introduces key concepts and then walks you through examples and code that you can adapt for your own projects. You'll begin with the foundations of Hugging Face and progress toward building full-fledged applications powered by LLMs.

The chapters are structured to be read sequentially, with later chapters building on earlier ones. If you're already familiar with the basics of Hugging Face, however, you can jump directly into the sections that interest you, such as fine-tuning models, building LangChain agents, or creating user interfaces with Gradio. Each chapter is self-contained, with runnable examples and explanations. By the end of the book, you'll be able to do the following:

- Use Hugging Face models for NLP and computer vision tasks.
- Fine-tune and customize models for your own datasets.
- Build applications powered by LLMs using LangChain, Langflow, and LlamaIndex.
- Design autonomous AI agents that integrate with tools and services.
- Create web interfaces for your models with Gradio.
- Run lightweight LLMs locally with GPT4All.
- Extend your applications to the real world using MCP.

This book will equip you with the knowledge and practical skills to take advantage of the latest developments in AI, from pretrained models to agentic systems and beyond. Here is a brief overview of the chapters:

- *Chapter 1, Introducing Hugging Face*—A high-level overview of Hugging Face, its role in democratizing AI, and the ecosystem of tools it provides
- *Chapter 2, Getting started*—Setting up your environment and learning how to use Hugging Face resources such as the Hub and model repositories
- *Chapter 3, Using Hugging Face transformers and pipelines for NLP tasks*—Applying pretrained models to text classification, translation, summarization, and more
- *Chapter 4, Using Hugging Face for computer vision tasks*—Exploring image classification, object detection, and other vision tasks using Hugging Face models
- *Chapter 5, Exploring, tokenizing, and visualizing Hugging Face datasets*—Learning to prepare, tokenize, and explore datasets for NLP and computer vision tasks
- *Chapter 6, Fine-tuning pretrained models and working with multimodal models*—Training models on your own data and experimenting with models that handle multiple input types, such as text and images
- *Chapter 7, Creating LLM-based applications using LangChain and LlamaIndex*—Building applications that augment LLMs with tools, memory, and data retrieval

- *Chapter 8, Building LangChain applications visually using Langflow*—Designing and deploying AI workflows without writing code, using a visual programming interface
- *Chapter 9, Programming agents*—Exploring agent-based architectures in which models make autonomous decisions and interact with external tools
- *Chapter 10, Building a web-based UI using Gradio*—Creating user-friendly interfaces to showcase and interact with your AI models
- *Chapter 11, Building locally running LLM-based applications using GPT4All*—Running lightweight, open-source LLMs on your own machine without relying on the cloud
- *Chapter 12, Using LLMs to query your local data*—Applying RAG to answer questions about your files, databases, and knowledge bases
- *Chapter 13, Bridging LLMs to the real world with the Model Context Protocol*—Connecting LLMs with real-world tools, APIs, and services for more practical and integrated applications

What's required to use this book

To follow along, you'll need

- A computer with Python 3.11 or later installed
- Access to the internet for downloading models and datasets and using Hugging Face Hub
- (Optional) A GPU for training and fine-tuning tasks, though most examples can be run on a CPU or in cloud-hosted environments such as Google Colab

About the code

This book contains many examples of source code both in numbered listings and inline with normal text. In both cases, source code is formatted in a `fixed-width font` `like this` to separate it from ordinary text. Sometimes, code is also **in bold** to highlight changes from previous steps in the chapter, such as when a new feature adds to an existing line of code.

In many cases, the original source code has been reformatted; we've added line breaks and reworked indentation to accommodate the available page space in the book. In rare cases, even this was not enough, and listings include line-continuation markers (➥). Additionally, comments in the source code were removed from the listings when the code is described in the text. Code annotations accompany many of the listings, highlighting important concepts.

You can get executable snippets of code from the liveBook (online) version of this book at https://livebook.manning.com/book/hugging-face-in-action. The complete code for the examples in the book is available for download on the Manning website at https://www.manning.com/books/hugging-face-in-action and on GitHub at https://github.com/weimenglee.

liveBook discussion forum

Purchase of *Hugging Face in Action* includes free access to liveBook, Manning's online reading platform. Using liveBook's exclusive discussion features, you can attach comments to the book globally or to specific sections or paragraphs. It's a snap to make notes for yourself, ask and answer technical questions, and receive help from the author and other users. To access the forum, go to https://livebook.manning.com/book/hugging-face-in-action/discussion. You can also learn more about Manning's forums and the rules of conduct at https://livebook.manning.com/discussion.

Manning's commitment to our readers is to provide a venue where meaningful dialogue between individual readers and between readers and authors can take place. It is not a commitment to any specific amount of participation on the part of the author, whose contribution to the forum remains voluntary (and unpaid). We suggest you try asking the author some challenging questions lest his interest stray! The forum and the archives of previous discussions will be accessible on the publisher's website as long as the book is in print.

about the author

WEI-MENG LEE is a technologist and the founder of Developer Learning Solutions (http://calender.learn2 develop.net), a company specializing in helping companies adopt the latest IT technologies. Wei-Meng provides consultancy services to companies on adopting blockchain and AI solutions for their businesses.

about the cover illustration

The caption for the illustration on the cover of *Hugging Face in Action* is "Chiosgchi, musicien, turc jouant du Chiosq," or "Turkish drummer," taken from an album of Turkish costumes in the British Museum collection.

   In those days, it was easy to identify where people lived and what their trade or station in life was by their dress alone. Manning celebrates the inventiveness and initiative of the computer business with book covers based on the rich diversity of regional culture centuries ago, brought back to life by pictures from collections such as this one.

Introducing Hugging Face

This chapter covers

- What Hugging Face is known for
- The Hugging Face Transformers library
- The various models hosted by Hugging Face
- The Gradio library

Hugging Face is an AI community that promotes the building, training, and deployment of open source machine learning models. It has state-of-the-art models designed for different problem domains, such as natural language processing (NLP) tasks, computer vision tasks, and audio tasks. Besides providing tools for machine learning, Hugging Face provides a platform for hosting pretrained models and datasets. With AI at its peak, Hugging Face is at the epicenter of the AI revolution because

- It unleashes a new wave of applications that capitalizes on the large amount of data available.
- Many complementary technologies are being developed, such as prototyping tools for large learning model (LLM)–based applications.

- Instead of focusing on the fundamentals (such as building neural networks from scratch or learning machine learning algorithms), developers can focus on building AI-based apps to solve their problems immediately. AI is now a tool that developers can use directly rather than having to build it from scratch.

- Hugging Face's philosophy is to promote open source contributions. It is the hub of open source models for NLP, computer vision, and other fields in which AI plays vital roles.

This book highlights some of the key services and platforms provided by Hugging Face. You get a glimpse of the kinds of applications we will be building throughout the book. Hugging Face is best known for its Transformers library for developing NLP applications, its platform for sharing machine learning models and datasets, Hugging Face Spaces for hosting user-developed machine learning apps, and the Gradio Python library for rapid UI creation. In the next few sections, I introduce some of the features available through the Hugging Face Hub. Later in this book, I cover advanced topics such as the following:

- Building your own LLM-based applications using the LangChain framework
- Visually prototyping your LLM-based application with Langflow
- Exploring alternatives to OpenAI's generative pretrained transformer (GPT) models, such as GPT4All
- Developing LLM-based applications without compromising the privacy of your data
- Creating agents that integrate tools such as search engines and code interpreters
- Using the Model Context Protocol (MCP) to connect AI assistants to external data sources

1.1   *Hugging Face Transformers library*

The *Transformers library* is a Python package that contains open source implementations of the Transformer architecture models for text, image, and audio tasks. It provides APIs for developers to download and use for pretrained models. By using pretrained and state-of-the-art models, developers don't have to spend time and resources building models from scratch. As an example, consider the following code snippet (I explain the code in more detail and show you how to install the libraries in chapters 2 and 3):

```
from transformers import pipeline

classifier = pipeline('text-classification',
        model = 'distilbert-base-uncased-finetuned-sst-2-english',
        revision = 'af0f99b')
```

In this code snippet, I use the pipeline() function from the transformers package to perform a text-classification task. In particular, I want to create an application to detect the sentiments in a particular paragraph of text. The code specifies that I want to use this model, `'distilbert-base-uncased-finetuned-sst-2-english'`, and its version, `'af0f99b'`. That's it! I don't need to know how text classification works; neither do I need to know how to train a model to perform this task.

In Hugging Face's Transformers library, a *pipeline* is a high-level, user-friendly API that simplifies building and using complex NLP workflows. It makes it easy to perform a sequence of NLP tasks (text classification, named entity recognition, translation, summarization, and so on) with a few lines of code. You will learn more about transformers and pipelines in chapter 3.

To put this code to the test, I call the `pipeline` object and pass it a paragraph of text. The object returns this result:

```
import pandas as pd

text = '''
I thought this was a wonderful way to spend time on a too hot summer
weekend, sitting in the air conditioned theater and watching a
light-hearted comedy. The plot is simplistic, but the dialogue is
witty and the characters are likable (even the well bread suspected
serial killer). While some may be disappointed when they realize
this is not Match Point 2: Risk Addiction, I thought it was proof
that Woody Allen is still fully in control of the style many of us
have grown to love.<br /><br />This was the most I'd laughed at one
of Woody's comedies in years (dare I say a decade?). While I've never
been impressed with Scarlet Johanson, in this she managed to tone
down her "sexy" image and jumped right into a average, but spirited
young woman.<br /><br />This may not be the crown jewel of his career
, but it was wittier than "Devil Wears Prada" and more interesting
than "Superman" a great comedy to go see with friends.
'''

result = classifier(text)
pd.DataFrame(result)
```

This paragraph of text comes from the Internet Movie Database (IMDb) dataset (https://huggingface.co/datasets/stanfordnlp/imdb), a binary sentiment-analysis dataset consisting of 50,000 reviews from the IMDb website labeled positive or negative. The result returned by the `pipeline` object is formatted nicely as a pandas DataFrame (see figure 1.1), which shows that the sentiment is positive.

	label	score
0	POSITIVE	0.99919

Figure 1.1 The result of the sentiment analysis

As you can see from this code snippet, you can perform a relatively complex task of sentiment analysis in a couple of statements by using the Transformers library and the pipeline API from Hugging Face.

1.2 Hugging Face models

The Hugging Face Hub's Models page (https://huggingface.co/models; see figure 1.2) hosts many pretrained models for a wide variety of machine learning tasks. All the pretrained models are stored in repositories, and Hugging Face makes exploring the details of the models easy.

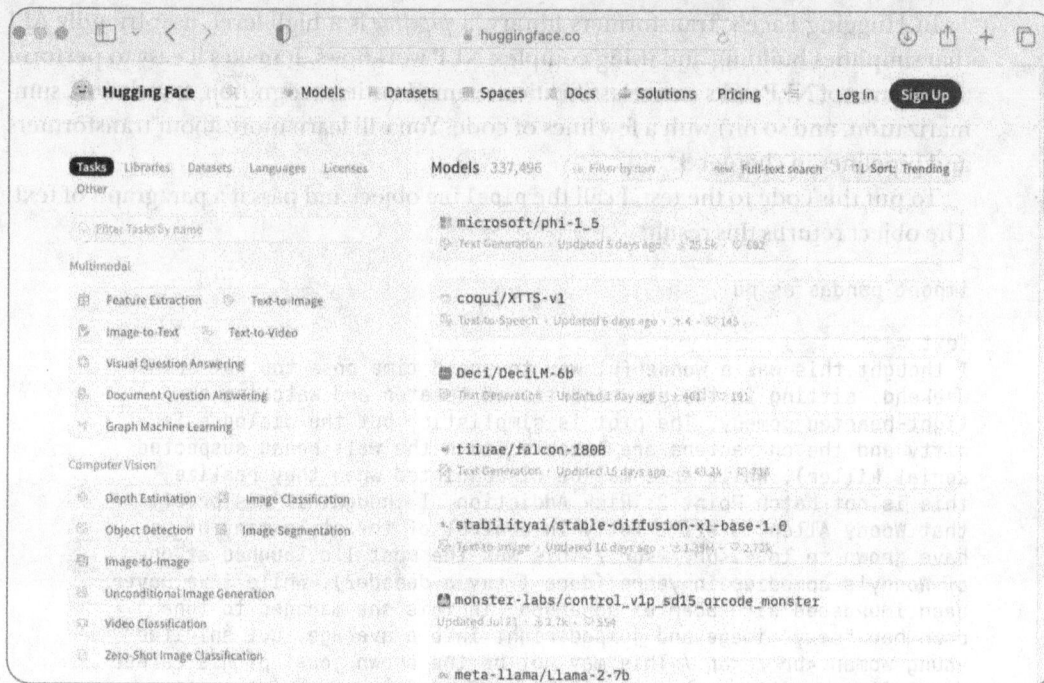

Figure 1.2 Exploring the pretrained models hosted at Hugging Face Hub

Many models have a widget that allows you to test them directly by running inferences in the web browser. To demonstrate, search for a pretrained model named `facebook/detr-resnet-50`. This Detection Transformer (DETR) model was trained end-to-end using the Common Objects in Context (COCO) 2017 object detection dataset (118 KB annotated images for training and 5 KB images for validation). COCO is a large-scale object detection, segmentation, and captioning dataset.

You can use the `facebook/detr-resnet-50` model to detect objects in an image. You can read more about this model on Hugging Face's website at https://huggingface.co/facebook/detr-resnet-50 (see figure 1.3). More important, Hugging Face provides the Hosted Inference API, which allows you to test the model directly in your web browser.

The Hosted Inference API enables developers to test and evaluate (for free) more than 150,000 publicly accessible machine learning models or their own private models via simple HTTP requests, with the fast inference hosted on Hugging Face's shared infrastructure.

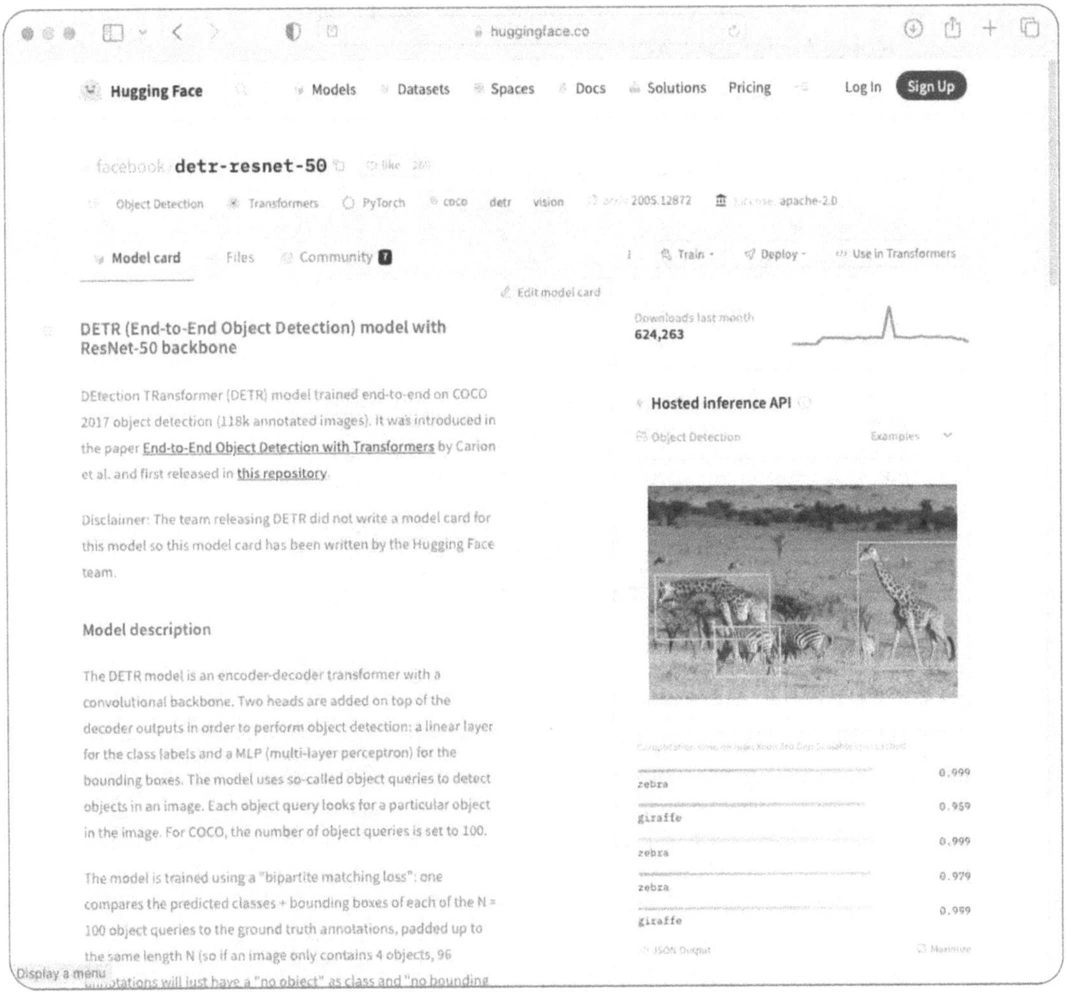

Figure 1.3 You can test the model directly on Hugging Face Hub using the Hosted Inference API

As an example, I dragged an image (see figure 1.4) to the Hosted Inference API section of the page for the facebook/detr-resnet-50 model on the Hugging Face website. The objects detected in the image are shown automatically, with the level of confidence displayed next to each object's name.

In addition, you can use this model for your own Python code. To do so, first click the Use This Model button (see figure 1.5); then, on the menu, click the Transformers button. In figure 1.6, you see code samples that show how to use the model.

You will learn more about using the Transformers library with various models for object detection in chapter 4.

⚡ **Hosted inference API** ⓘ

🔲 Object Detection   Examples   ∨

Computation time on Intel Xeon 3rd Gen Scalable cpu: 1.862 s

truck	0.942
truck	0.964
truck	0.938
truck	0.981
person	0.998
person	0.998
truck	0.928
truck	0.963
airplane	0.998
person	0.997

</> JSON Output   ⛶ Maximize

Figure 1.4   Performing object detection using my uploaded image (image: CC BY-SA 3.0)

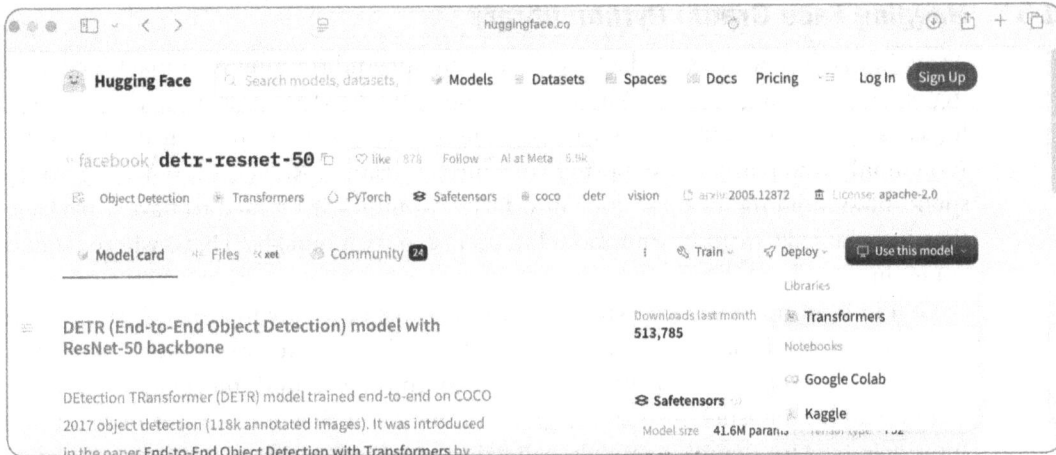

Figure 1.5   Locating the Use This Model button

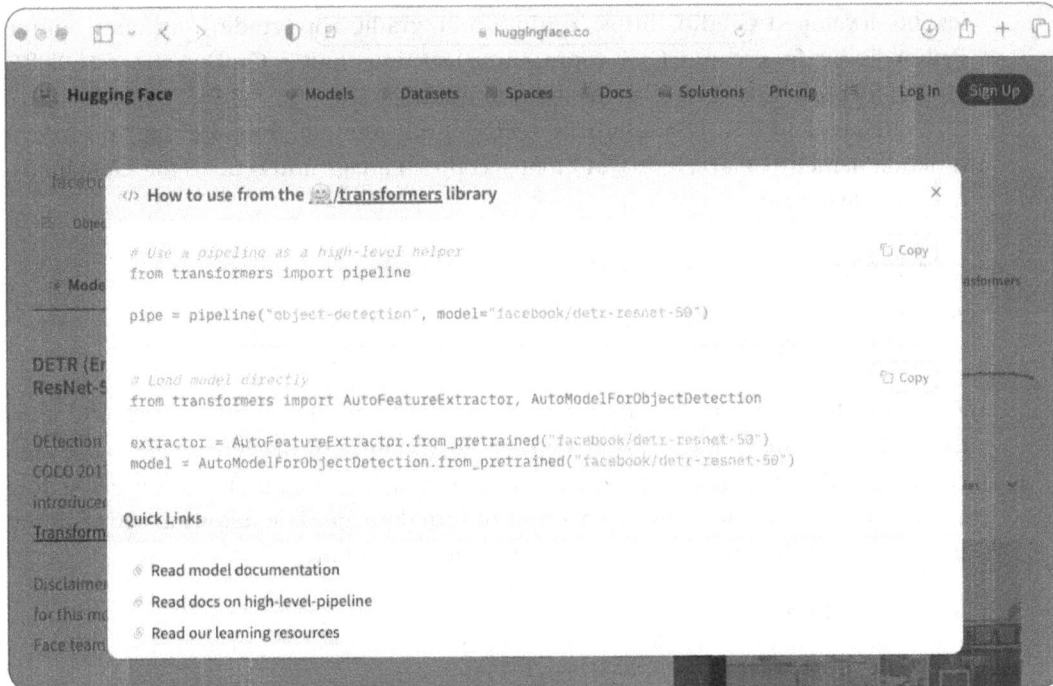

Figure 1.6   Using the model with the Transformers library

1.3   Hugging Face Gradio Python library

As an AI developer, you spend a lot of time building and training your machine learning or deep learning models. When your model is trained to your satisfaction, the next logical step is to let your users try it. Typically, this means building your dedicated UI (commonly, a web app) or exposing your models using a REST API, but you have to spend time building all these user interfaces. Wouldn't it be nice to have a package that automatically exposes your model so users can try it quickly? This is where Gradio comes in.

Gradio is an open source Python library that makes it easy to create customizable user interfaces for machine learning models and data science workflows. With a few lines of code, you can wrap your model in a simple web-based interface where users can upload inputs (such as text, images, or audio) and view the outputs in real time. It's widely used for demoing models, collecting user feedback, and building interactive machine learning applications. Gradio also integrates seamlessly with Hugging Face Spaces, allowing developers to share their apps with the community.

Gradio was founded by Abubakar Abid, a PhD student at Stanford University, who was focusing on deep learning applied to medical images and videos. During his studies, he developed Gradio (https://github.com/gradio-app/gradio), an open source Python library for creating GUIs for machine learning models. On December 21, 2021, Hugging Face announced its acquisition of Gradio.

To understand how Gradio works, consider an example. Suppose that you have a function named `transform_image()` that accepts an image and returns the same image in grayscale format:

```
from skimage.color import import rgb2gray

def transform_image(img):
    return rgb2gray(img)
```

To try this function, you must write your own UI to accept an image from the user; then, when the image is converted to grayscale, you must display the image to the user. Gradio greatly simplifies the process: it creates a web-based UI that allows users to drag and drop an image and then displays the converted image. The following code snippet shows how Gradio binds to the `transform_image()` function:

```
import gradio as gr

demo = gr.Interface(fn = transform_image,
                    inputs = gr.Image(),
                    outputs = "image")
demo.launch()
```

When you run this code, Gradio hosts your code on the local machine and creates a UI (see figure 1.7).

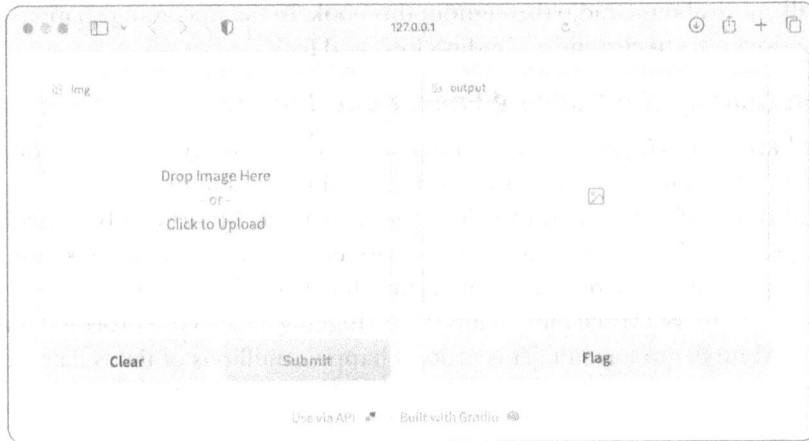

Figure 1.7   Gradio provides a customizable UI for your machine learning projects.

Drop an image on the left side of the page, and click the Submit button to send the image to the transform_image() function. The result is displayed on the right side of the page. Figure 1.8 shows my image after conversion to grayscale.

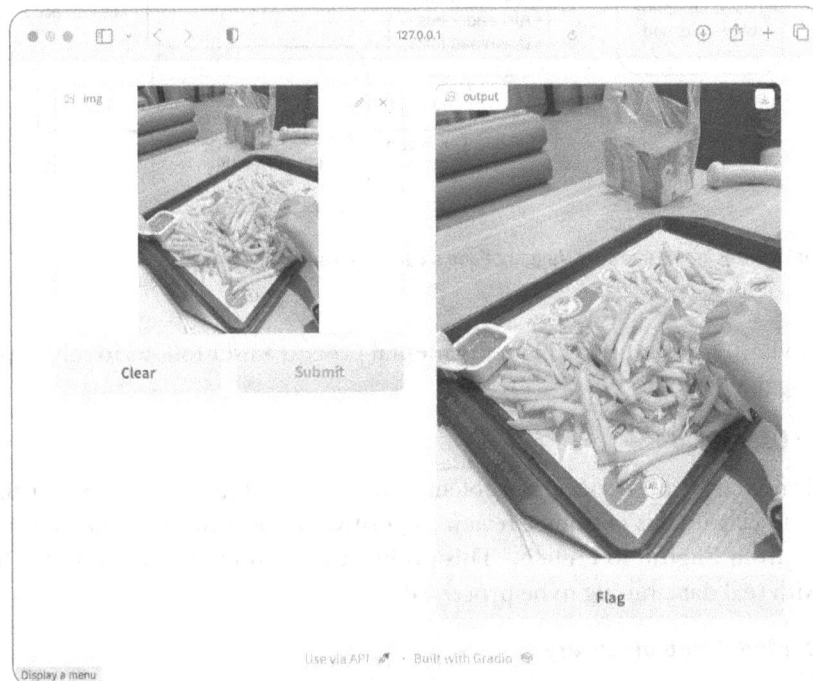

Figure 1.8   Viewing the result of the converted image

I will talk more about Gradio throughout this book. In the upcoming chapters, you will learn various ways to customize Gradio's look and feel.

1.4   *Understanding the Hugging Face mental model*

As you have seen, Hugging Face isn't just a model repository. It's also a complete AI pipeline that systematically moves users from problem to solution.

Think of Hugging Face as the world's largest AI model library combined with an execution platform. Every day, millions of developers, researchers, and businesses follow this basic pattern to go from having an AI problem to getting results.

Figure 1.9 shows a visual mental model of Hugging Face's core process: taking users from an AI model to a result. This process happens millions of times daily across the platform.

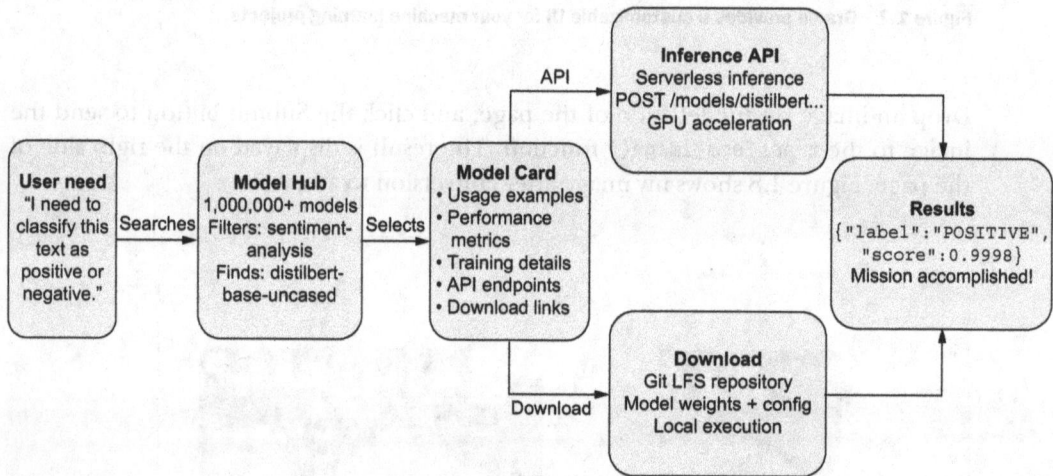

Figure 1.9   **A visual mental model showing Hugging Face's core process**

In the following sections, I explain the mental process a user follows to solve a problem with Hugging Face.

1.4.1   *Step 1: User need*

Everything starts with a specific problem. A developer sits at their computer thinking, "I need to classify this customer review as positive or negative" or "I need to translate this text from English to French." This problem isn't abstract; it's a concrete business need with real data waiting to be processed.

1.4.2   *Step 2: Model Hub discovery*

The user heads to Hugging Face's Model Hub, which contains more than 1 million pretrained models. This hub isn't a dumping ground; it's a sophisticated search and filtering system. Users can search by task (such as sentiment analysis, translation, or image classification), model architecture (such as BERT, GPT, or ResNet), language, or performance metrics. The platform guides users from "I have a problem" to "Here's the specific model that solves it."

1.4.3   Step 3: Model card

This step is where Hugging Face shines. Every model comes with a detailed model card that serves as both documentation and gateway. The card contain use examples (such as copy-and-paste code snippets), performance benchmarks, training details, and information about using the model. The model card is the bridge between discovery and implementation.

1.4.4   Step 4: Two execution paths

At this point, users choose their adventure:

- *Path A: Hosted Inference API*—This option is the faster route. Users can send HTTP requests directly to Hugging Face's servers, which host the models in graphics processing unit (GPU) clusters. No setup is required; send your text in a `POST` request and get JSON results. This path handles millions of API calls daily and autoscales based on demand.
- *Path B: Direct download*—This option is for users who want to run models locally or integrate them into their own infrastructure. Behind the scenes, this path uses Git Large File Storage (LFS) to handle multigigabyte model files. Users download the model weights and configuration files and run them using the Transformers library.

1.4.5   Step 5: Results delivered

Both paths converge where the user gets their answer. The sentiment classifier returns `{"label": "POSITIVE", "score": 0.9998}`, and the user's problem is solved. Mission accomplished.

Summary

- Hugging Face is a complete AI problem-solving pipeline that systematically moves users from problem to solution.
- The Transformers library is a Python package that contains open source implementation of the Transformer architecture models for text, image, and audio tasks.
- In Hugging Face's Transformers library, a pipeline is a high-level, user-friendly API that simplifies the process of building and using complex NLP workflows.
- The Hugging Face Hub's Models page hosts many pretrained models for a wide variety of machine learning tasks.
- Gradio is a Python library that creates a web UI you can use to bind to your machine learning models, making it easy to test your models without building the UI.

Getting started

2

In chapter 1, you saw some of the exciting projects you will be creating throughout this book using the Hugging Face pretrained models and services such as Auto-Train. The main programming language you'll be using is Python, and you'll also be using my favorite IDE, Jupyter Notebook. Jupyter Notebook is an open source web application that allows you to create and share documents containing live code, equations, visualizations, and narrative text. It's widely used in data science, scientific research, machine learning, and education due to its interactive and exploratory nature. In the following sections, you'll learn how to set up Jupyter Notebook and create a virtual environment to work with all the examples in this book.

2.1 Downloading Anaconda

The easiest way to install Jupyter Notebook is to download Anaconda, a distribution of Python and R programming languages that comes with a set of preinstalled libraries and tools commonly used in data science, machine learning, and scientific computing. It includes the `conda` package manager, which simplifies package management and environment creation. Jupyter Notebook is one of the core components of Anaconda. Therefore, installing Anaconda gives you access not only to Jupyter Notebook but also to many commonly used packages.

To obtain Anaconda (free for personal use), go to https://www.anaconda.com/download/success. Then click the download icon for your operating system (see figure 2.1). When the installer is downloaded, double-click the installer, and follow the onscreen instructions to install Anaconda on your computer.

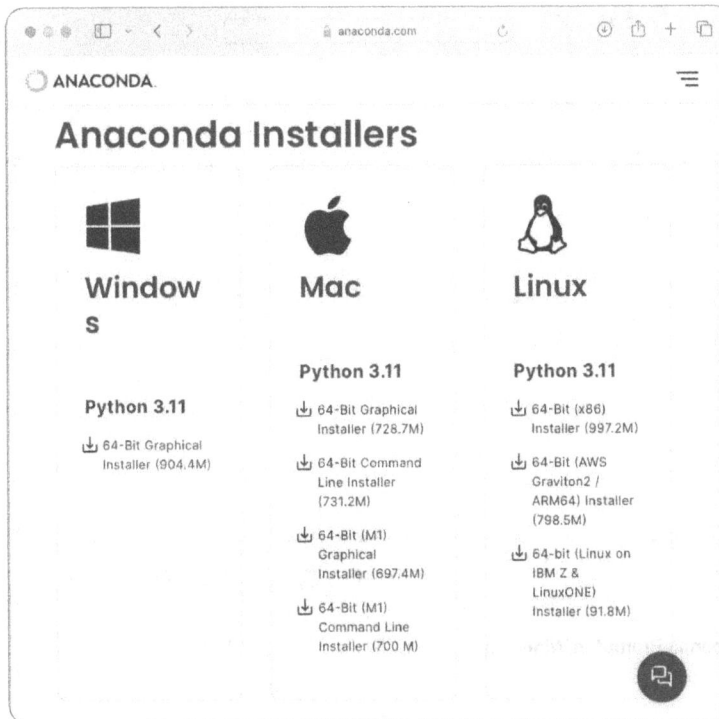

Figure 2.1   Downloading Anaconda for the three major platforms: Windows, macOS, and Linux

2.1.1 Creating virtual environments

With Anaconda downloaded and installed, you are ready to start using it. But before you launch Jupyter Notebook and start writing code, I recommend that you create a *virtual environment*—a self-contained environment that allows you to install and manage Python packages separately from your systemwide Python installation. It's a useful tool for isolating dependencies and managing different project requirements.

To create a virtual environment, launch Terminal (macOS) or Anaconda Prompt (Windows). Figure 2.2 shows how to launch Anaconda Prompt in Windows.

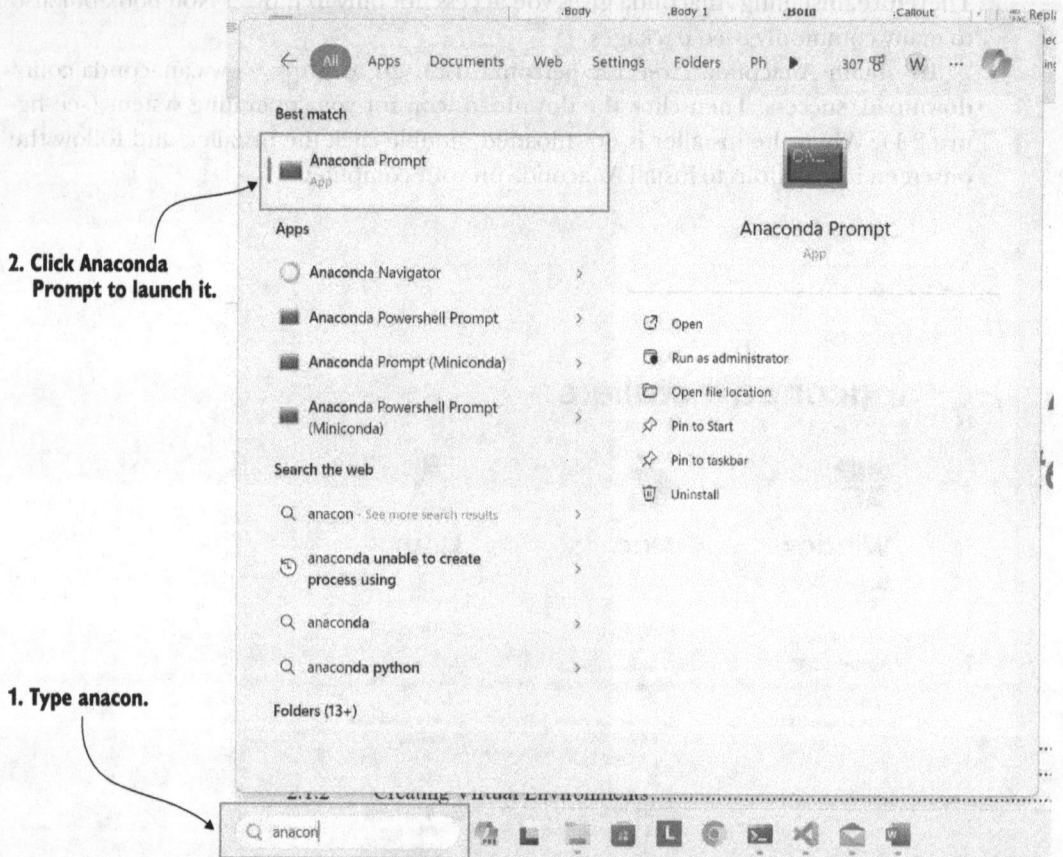

Figure 2.2   Launching Anaconda Prompt in Windows

Anaconda Prompt vs. command prompt

For Windows users, Anaconda Prompt looks just like the usual command prompt. In fact, they are the same, with one notable exception: Anaconda Prompt has the Anaconda environment variables and paths already set up. This means that when you open Anaconda Prompt, it's ready to use the Python interpreter, conda package manager, and other tools without additional configuration.

Next, use the conda command to create a new virtual environment, as follows:

```
$ conda create -n HuggingFaceBook python=3.11 anaconda
```

This command creates a virtual environment named HuggingFaceBook in Python 3.11. It also includes the Anaconda distribution. You'll be prompted to install the various packages (see figure 2.3). Type Y, and press Enter.

```
weimenglee — python ‹ conda create -n HuggingFaceBook python=3.11 anaconda — 94×27
webencodings        pkgs/main/osx-arm64::webencodings-0.5.1-py311hca03da5_1
websocket-client    pkgs/main/osx-arm64::websocket-client-0.58.0-py311hca03da5_4
werkzeug            pkgs/main/osx-arm64::werkzeug-2.2.3-py311hca03da5_0
whatthepatch        pkgs/main/osx-arm64::whatthepatch-1.0.2-py311hca03da5_0
wheel               pkgs/main/osx-arm64::wheel-0.41.2-py311hca03da5_0
widgetsnbextension  pkgs/main/osx-arm64::widgetsnbextension-3.5.2-py311hca03da5_1
wrapt               pkgs/main/osx-arm64::wrapt-1.14.1-py311h80987f9_0
wurlitzer           pkgs/main/osx-arm64::wurlitzer-3.0.2-py311hca03da5_0
xarray              pkgs/main/osx-arm64::xarray-2023.6.0-py311hca03da5_0
xlwings             pkgs/main/osx-arm64::xlwings-0.29.1-py311hca03da5_0
xyzservices         pkgs/main/osx-arm64::xyzservices-2022.9.0-py311hca03da5_1
xz                  pkgs/main/osx-arm64::xz-5.4.6-h80987f9_0
yaml                pkgs/main/osx-arm64::yaml-0.2.5-h1a28f6b_0
yapf                pkgs/main/osx-arm64::yapf-0.40.2-py311hca03da5_0
yarl                pkgs/main/osx-arm64::yarl-1.9.3-py311h80987f9_0
zeromq              pkgs/main/osx-arm64::zeromq-4.3.5-h313beb8_0
zfp                 pkgs/main/osx-arm64::zfp-1.0.0-h313beb8_0
zict                pkgs/main/osx-arm64::zict-3.0.0-py311hca03da5_0
zipp                pkgs/main/osx-arm64::zipp-3.17.0-py311hca03da5_0
zlib                pkgs/main/osx-arm64::zlib-1.2.13-h5a0b063_0
zlib-ng             pkgs/main/osx-arm64::zlib-ng-2.0.7-h80987f9_0
zope                pkgs/main/osx-arm64::zope-1.0-py311hca03da5_1
zope.interface      pkgs/main/osx-arm64::zope.interface-5.4.0-py311h80987f9_0
zstd                pkgs/main/osx-arm64::zstd-1.5.5-hd90d995_0

Proceed ([y]/n)? Y
```

Figure 2.3 Creating a new virtual environment and installing all the required packages

Anaconda distribution

The Anaconda distribution is a comprehensive package manager, environment manager, and Python distribution designed to simplify package management and deployment of Python and R data science and machine learning applications. It includes popular libraries such as NumPy, pandas, Matplotlib, scikit-learn, TensorFlow, PyTorch, and Jupyter Notebook.

When the installation is done, activate (switch to) the virtual environment using the conda activate command:

```
$ conda activate HuggingFaceBook
```

This command activates the `HuggingFaceBook` virtual environment. When you have switched to a particular virtual environment, Terminal or Anaconda Prompt prefixes the prompt with the environment name (see figure 2.4).

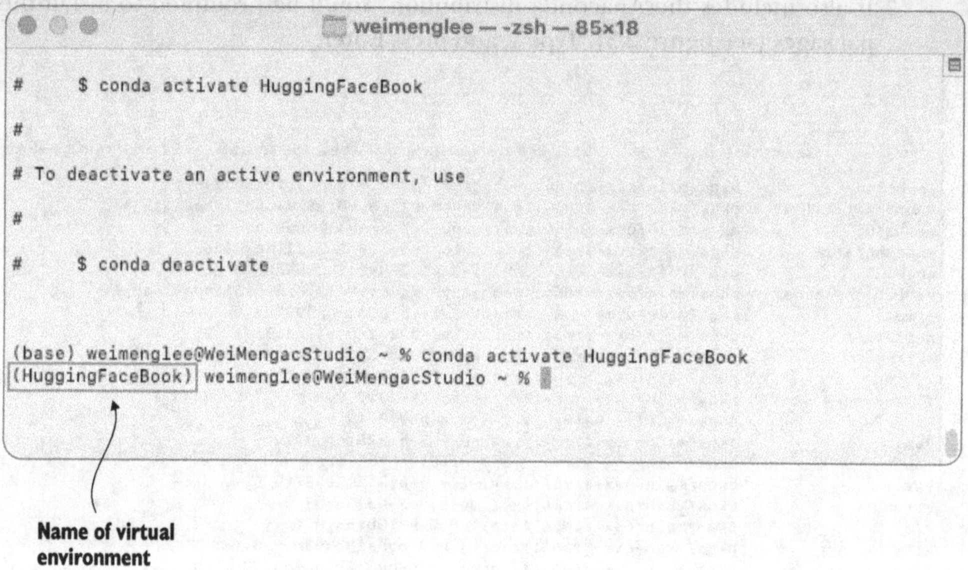

```
● ● ●                       🖳 weimenglee — -zsh — 85×18

#     $ conda activate HuggingFaceBook

#

# To deactivate an active environment, use

#

#     $ conda deactivate


(base) weimenglee@WeiMengacStudio ~ % conda activate HuggingFaceBook
(HuggingFaceBook) weimenglee@WeiMengacStudio ~ %
```

Name of virtual
environment

Figure 2.4   The virtual environment name prefixes the prompt.

2.1.2 *Starting Jupyter Notebook*

After you create a virtual environment, you are ready to launch Jupyter Notebook. I prefer to launch it via Terminal or Anaconda Prompt.

In Terminal, start by creating a folder in which you want to save your projects. Let's call this folder `HF_Projects`:

```
(HuggingFaceBook) weimenglee@WeiMengacStudio ~ % mkdir HF_Projects
```

Then change the current directory to the new one:

```
(HuggingFaceBook) weimenglee@WeiMengacStudio ~ % cd HF_Projects
```

To launch Jupyter Notebook, type `jupyter notebook`:

```
(HuggingFaceBook) weimenglee@WeiMengacStudio HF_Projects % jupyter notebook
```

The web browser launches and displays Jupyter Notebook's main page (see figure 2.5).

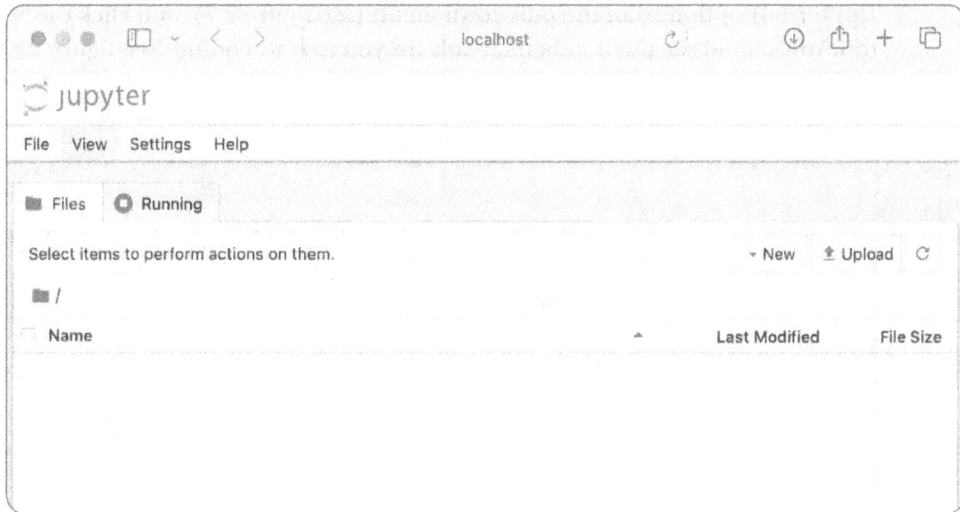

Figure 2.5   The web browser displays Jupyter Notebook's main page.

To create a notebook, click the New button and then click Notebook on the menu (see figure 2.6).

1. Click New.

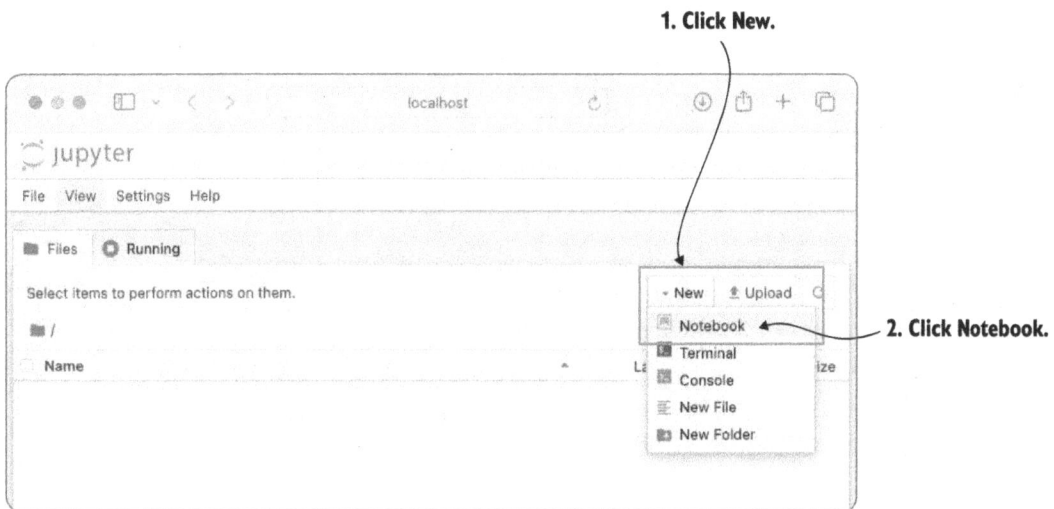

2. Click Notebook.

Figure 2.6   Creating a notebook

A new Untitled tab appears. (If you don't see it, your web browser may be blocking pop-up windows; clicking the address bar should reveal the tab.) Choose the Python 3 (ipykernel) option from the pull-down menu (see figure 2.7), and click the Select button. You should see the notebook, ready for you to start coding (see figure 2.8).

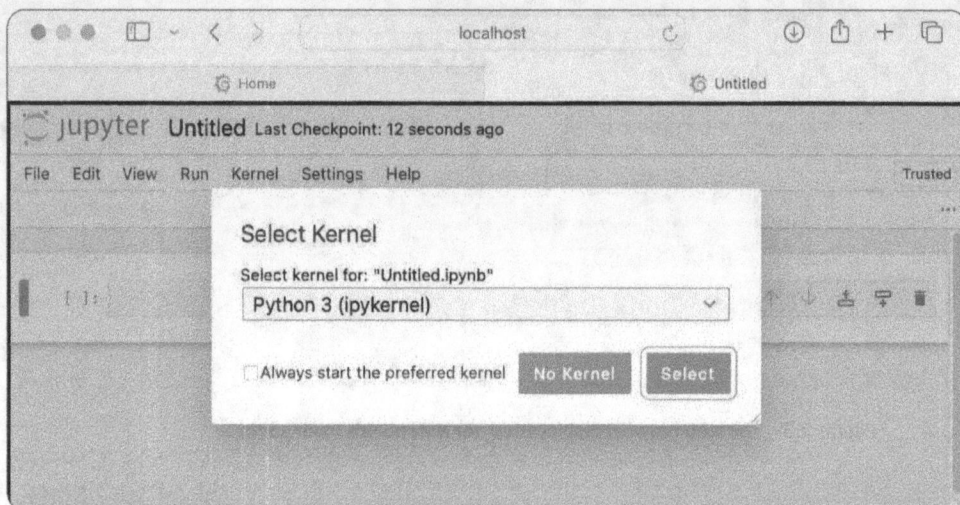

Figure 2.7   Selecting a kernel for your notebook

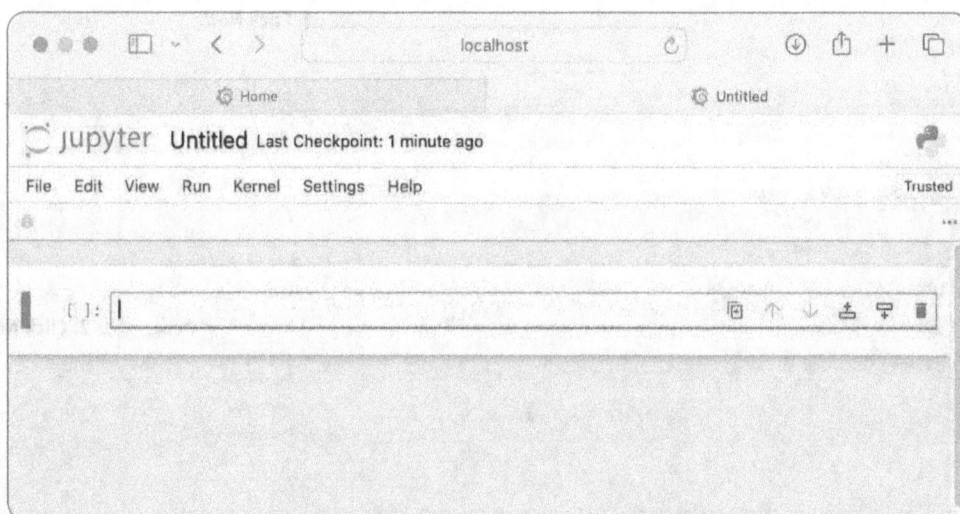

Figure 2.8   The notebook is ready to use.

TIP   If you are new to Jupyter Notebook, I suggest that you check out the official documentation at https://mng.bz/eB4P.

Finally, rename the notebook by clicking the default filename and entering a new name for your notebook in the Rename File dialog box (see figure 2.9). For this example, enter Chapter 2.ipynb. Click Rename when you're done. The Chapter 2.ipynb file is saved in the HF_Projects directory.

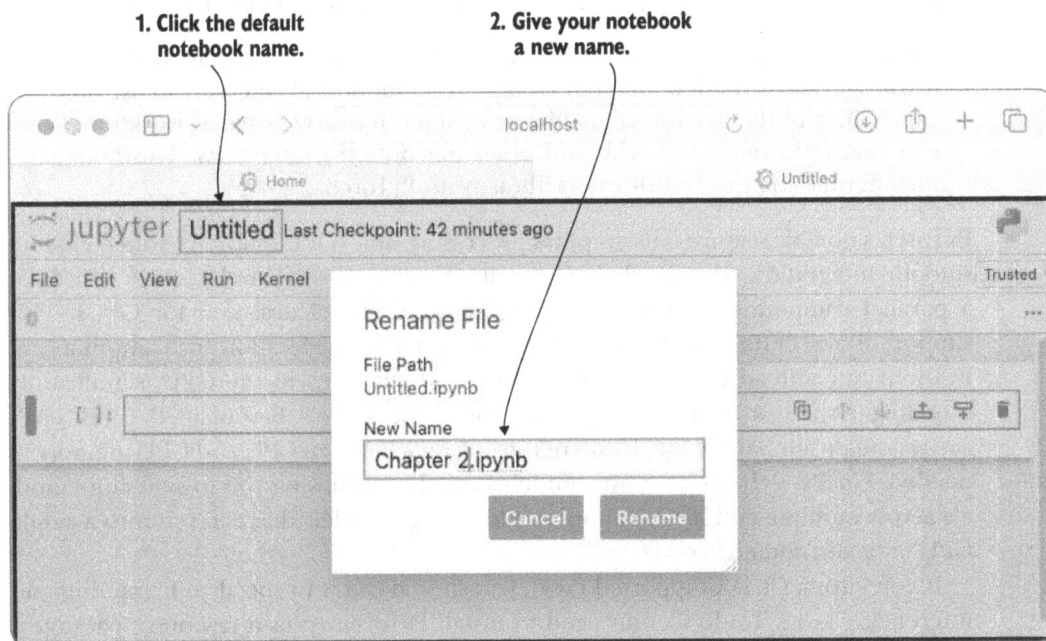

Figure 2.9 Renaming your notebook

2.2 *Installing the Transformers library*

In this book, you will use the Hugging Face Transformers library extensively. The Transformers library, an open source library developed by Hugging Face, provides an easy-to-use interface for working with state-of-the-art pretrained models for various natural language processing (NLP) tasks such as text classification, named entity recognition (NER), text generation, and question answering. In chapter 3, I discuss the Transformers library in more detail. For now, it's a good idea to install it. You can install the transformers Python package directly in Jupyter Notebook using the following statement:

```
!pip install transformers
```

If you prefer, you can install it in Terminal or Anaconda Prompt using the following command:

```
$ pip install transformers
```

2.2.1 *Support for GPU*

In Hugging Face, you use the Transformers library to perform various machine learning tasks such as NLP and image recognition. Behind the scenes, the library is primarily built on PyTorch, a popular deep learning framework developed primarily by Facebook AI Research (FAIR). It uses PyTorch's capabilities to build neural network architectures, train models, and optimize performance on tasks related to NLP.

> **NOTE** The Transformers library also supports TensorFlow, a widely used deep learning framework developed by Google. This support allows users to use the capabilities of the Transformers library in their TensorFlow-based workflows, enabling tasks related to NLP and other machine learning tasks. This book focuses on using the Transformers library with PyTorch.

PyTorch's notable feature is its graphics processing unit (GPU) support, which enables smooth integration with Nvidia's Compute Unified Device Architecture (CUDA), a parallel computing platform and programming model designed for GPUs. This support allows PyTorch to use CUDA to enable GPU acceleration for computations. PyTorch can offload tensor operations and computations to the GPU, significantly speeding training and inferencing for deep learning models. Best of all, PyTorch's API can automatically handle the details of moving data between CPU and GPU memory as needed. Finally, PyTorch supports model parallelism, allowing you to split large models across multiple GPUs. This support allows large models that can't fit into a single GPU to be distributed across GPUs.

If you have a CUDA-supported GPU, you should use it to speed your training and inferencing tasks. To do so, you need to install PyTorch (plus a few other packages) from a location that contains the PyTorch wheels compatible with CUDA. The following command installs the torch (PyTorch), torchvision, and torchaudio packages from https://download.pytorch.org/whl/cu121:

```
$ pip install torch torchvision torchaudio
--index-url https://download.pytorch.org/whl/cu121 -U
```

When the packages are installed, you can test them to see whether your GPU is supported. In Jupyter Notebook, you can use the following statements to check whether CUDA is available on your system:

```
import torch
print(torch.cuda.is_available())
```

If you get a True response, your system supports CUDA. The following code listing prints more information about the GPU you have in your system.

Listing 2.1 Using the torch package to find details on your GPU

```
import torch
use_cuda = torch.cuda.is_available()
```

```
if use_cuda:
    print('__CUDNN VERSION:', torch.backends.cudnn.version())
    print('__Number CUDA Devices:', torch.cuda.device_count())
    print('__CUDA Device Name:', torch.cuda.get_device_name(0))
    print('__CUDA Device Total Memory [GB]:',
          torch.cuda.get_device_properties(0).total_memory/1e9)
```

On my laptop, which is equipped with an Nvidia RTX 4060 GPU, the preceding code produces this result:

```
__CUDNN VERSION: 8801
__Number CUDA Devices: 1
__CUDA Device Name: NVIDIA GeForce RTX 4060 Laptop GPU
__CUDA Device Total Memory [GB]: 8.585216
```

You can also use the `GPUtil` package to find details about your GPU, such as total number of GPUs, utilization load, temperature, and memory used. First, install `GPUtil` with the `pip` command:

```
!pip install GPUtil
```

The following statements get the number of available GPUs on your system via the `getAvailable()` method:

```
import GPUtil

GPUtil.getAvailable()
```

For my system, which has one GPU, this code returns the following result:

```
[0]
```

You can retrieve information about each GPU in your system by using the `getGPUs()` method. Iterate through GPUs to fetch details such as name, utilization, memory use, temperature, and total memory, as shown in the following listing.

Listing 2.2 Using the `GPUtil` package to get details on each GPU

```
import GPUtil

gpus = GPUtil.getGPUs()

for gpu in gpus:
    print("GPU ID:", gpu.id)
    print("GPU Name:", gpu.name)
    print("GPU Utilization:", gpu.load * 100, "%")
    print("GPU Memory Utilization:", gpu.memoryUtil * 100, "%")
    print("GPU Temperature:", gpu.temperature, "C")
    print("GPU Total Memory:", gpu.memoryTotal, "MB")
```

2.2.2   Using GPU in the pipeline object

For the pipeline object to use the GPU, you need to explicitly specify the device parameter when calling the pipeline() function. The following code snippet shows the pipeline() function using the first (or single) GPU in your system:

```
from transformers import pipeline
question_classifier = pipeline("text-classification",
                               model="huaen/question_detection",
                               device = 0)
```

> **Transformers pipeline**
>
> In Hugging Face's Transformers library, a *pipeline* is a high-level, user-friendly API that simplifies the process of building and using complex NLP workflows. A pipeline makes it easy to perform a sequence of NLP tasks—such as text classification, NER, translation, and summarization—in a few lines of code.
>
> The preceding code sample creates a pipeline object that performs question classification. It takes in a string and returns a result indicating whether the string presented is a question.

Besides specifying a number for the device parameter to specify that you want to use the GPU for processing, you can set it to a string. You could rewrite the preceding statement this way:

```
question_classifier = pipeline("text-classification",
                               model="huaen/question_detection",
                               device = "cuda:0")
```
cuda:0 refers to the first GPU in your system.

On a Mac, you can accelerate Hugging Face pipelines by using Apple's Metal Performance Shaders (MPS) for faster inference on Apple silicon. Set device to "mps:0":

```
question_classifier = pipeline("text-classification",
                               model="huaen/question_detection",
                               device = "mps:0")
```

Table 2.1 shows the values you can use for the device parameter.

Table 2.1   Values for the device parameter in the pipeline() function

Numeric value	String value	Description
-1	"cpu"	Uses the CPU for processing. The CPU is the default device to use for the pipeline() function.
0	"cuda" "cuda:0"	Uses the single/first GPU in your system.

Table 2.1 Values for the `device` parameter in the `pipeline()` function (*continued*)

Numeric value	String value	Description
1	`"cuda:1"`	Uses the second GPU in your system.
n	`"cuda:n"`	Uses the (n+1)th GPU in your system.
0	`"mps:0"`	Refers to the MPS backend in PyTorch, which allows machine learning models to run on Apple's built-in GPU (M1, M2, and M3 chips).

If you're not sure whether your `pipeline` object uses the CPU or GPU, you can print it by using the `device.type` attribute:

```
print(question_classifier.device.type)
```

A reliable approach to selecting the optimal inference device is to check for CUDA or MPS support. If neither is available, the system defaults to the CPU. The following listing demonstrates how to implement this approach.

Listing 2.3 Autodetecting CUDA, MPS, or CPU for PyTorch Inference

```
from transformers import pipeline
import torch

if torch.cuda.is_available():
    device = "cuda"
elif torch.backends.mps.is_available():
    device = "mps"
else:
    device = "cpu"

question_classifier = pipeline("text-classification",
                               model="huaen/question_detection",
                               device=device)
print(f"Using device: {device}")
```

2.3 Installing the Hugging Face Hub package

The Hugging Face Hub (https://huggingface.co; see figure 2.10) is the go-to place for all things related to Hugging Face: pretrained models, demos, datasets, and more.

Although you can use a web browser to visit the Hugging Face Hub, you can interact with the Hub directly by using the `huggingface_hub` command-line package. With this package, you can perform tasks such as the following:

- Managing project repositories
- Uploading and downloading files
- Fetching models

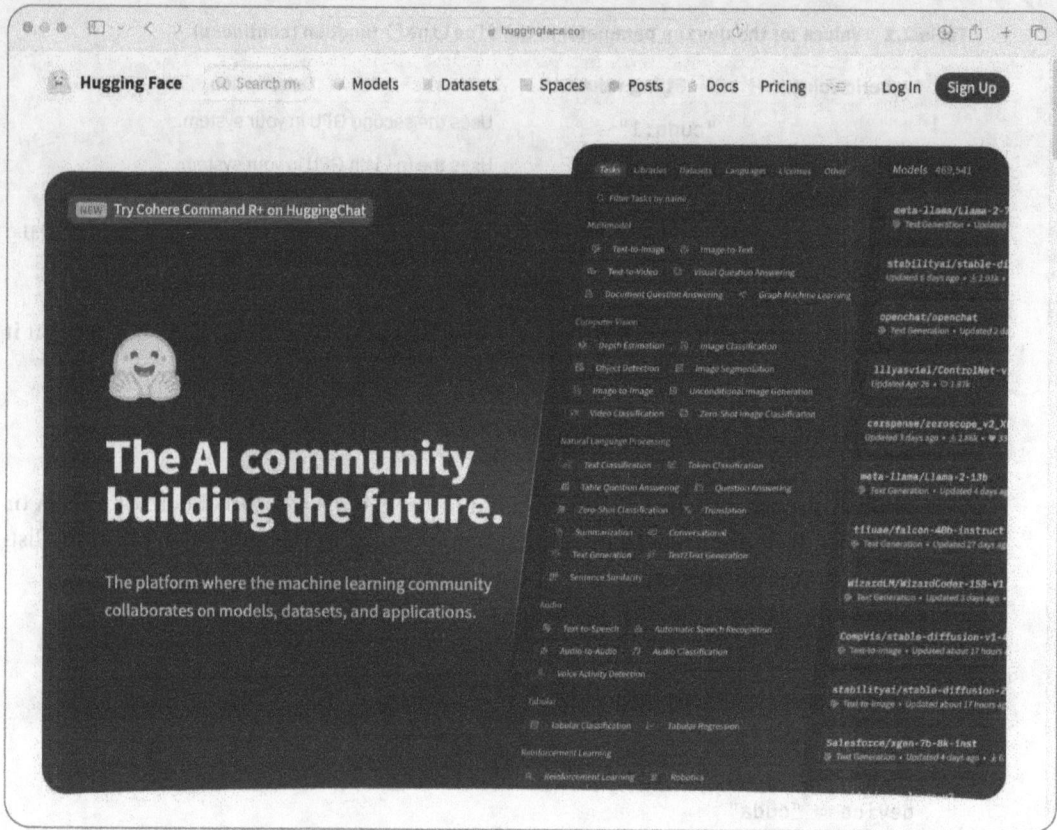

Figure 2.10   The Hugging Face Hub

To install the `huggingface_hub` package, use the `pip` command:

```
!pip install huggingface_hub
```

2.3.1 *Downloading files*

On the Hugging Face Hub, you'll find many pretrained models that you can freely use. Often, when you use a model for the first time, the Transformers library automatically downloads the files associated with the model and stores them locally on your computer. At times, however, it's more useful to download the files you need manually so that you can run your code offline.

To download a file from the Hugging Face Hub, go to the model's page and click the Download button. Consider the model named `google/pegasus-xsum` (https://mng.bz/gmXx), for example. On the model's page, if you want to download the `config.json` file, click its download icon (see figure 2.11).

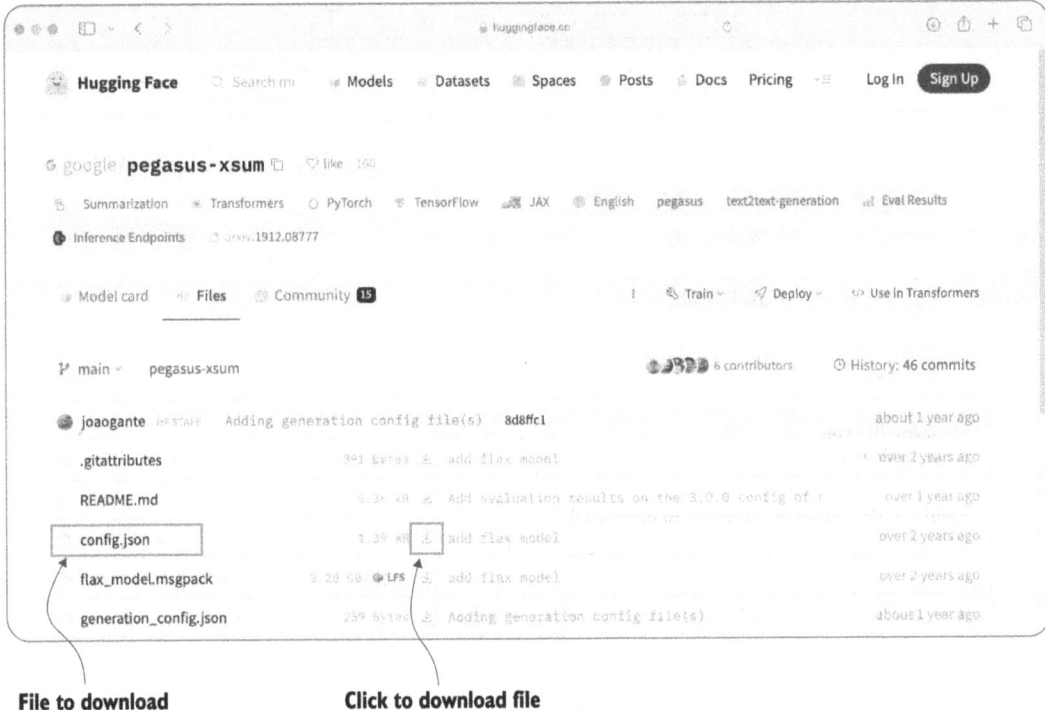

File to download   Click to download file

Figure 2.11 Downloading a file directly from a model's page

If you're using the huggingface_hub package, you can download the file programmatically using the hf_hub_download() function:

```
from huggingface_hub import hf_hub_download

hf_hub_download(repo_id="google/pegasus-xsum",
               filename = "config.json")
```

The config.json file is downloaded to the following directory:

```
<home_directory>/.cache/huggingface/hub/
models--google--pegasus-xsum/snapshots/
8d8ffc158a3bee9fbb03afacdfc347c823c5ec8b/
```

By default, the latest version of the file from the main branch is downloaded. In some cases, however, you want to download a particular version of the file (e.g., from a specific branch, pull request (PR), tag, or commit hash). To do so, first click the file you want to download (see figure 2.12).

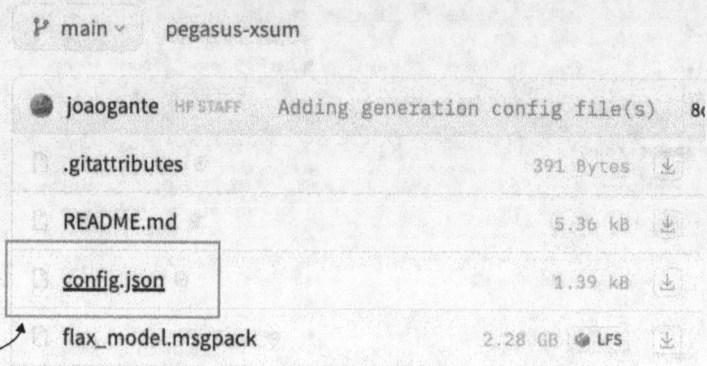

Click the file you
want to download.

Figure 2.12 Selecting the file to download

Then click the file's history link (see figure 2.13).

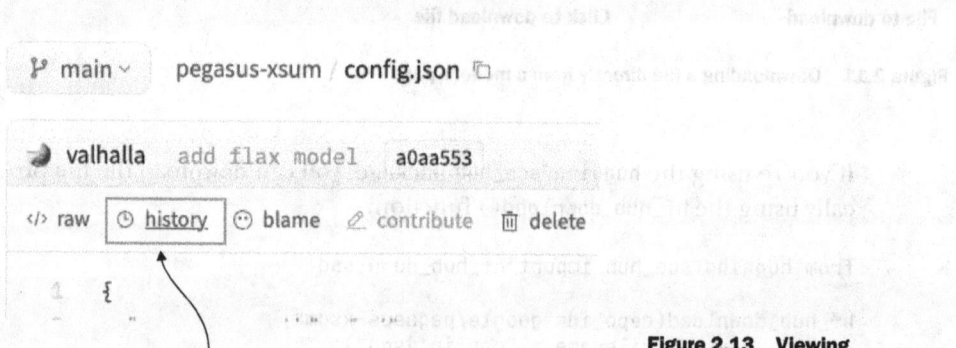

Click to view the
history of the file.

**Figure 2.13 Viewing
the historical commits
for a project**

Finally, copy the commit hash of the specific version of the file you want to download
(see figure 2.14).

When you've copied the commit hash of the file you want to download, you can set it
as the value for the revision parameter in the hf_hub_download() function:

```
hf_hub_download(
    repo_id="google/pegasus-xsum",
    filename="config.json",
    revision="a0aa5531c00f59a32a167b75130805098b046f9c"
)
```

Model card ᷄᷄ **Files and versions** Community **15**

⅄ main ˅ pegasus-xsum **config.json** ⎗

🕐 **Commit History**

Click to copy the
commit hash.

add flax model a0aa553 ⎗

⬡ **valhalla** committed on Sep 14, [Copy full commit hash to clipboard]

upload model ef6460f ⎗

⬡ **patrickvonplaten** committed on Jan 11, 2021

Update config.json 48d7b60 ⎗

system HF STAFF committed on Sep 14, 2020

Update config.json 4d33b01 ⎗

system HF STAFF committed on Aug 9, 2020

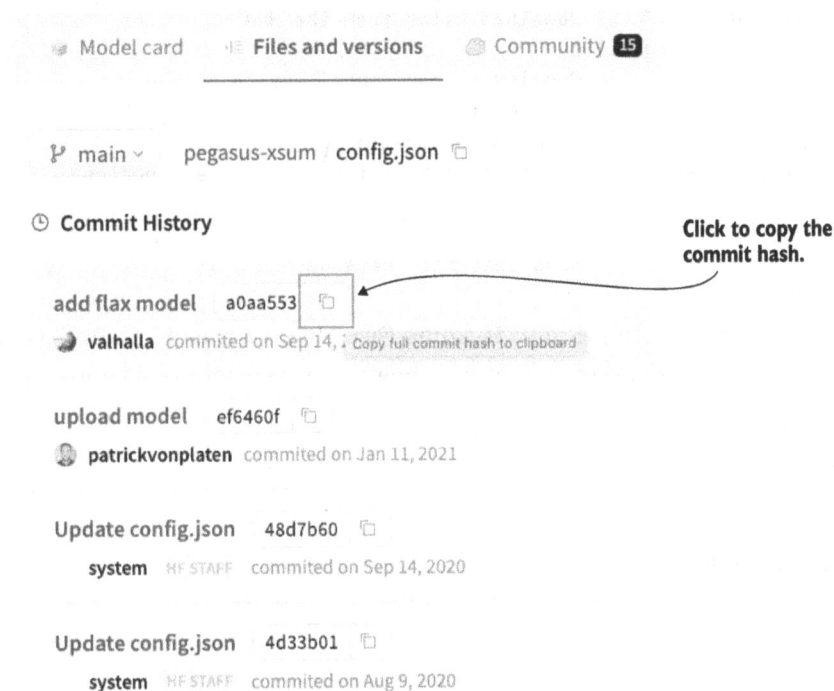

Figure 2.14 Copying the commit hash for a file

2.3.2 Using the Hugging Face CLI

The huggingface_hub package also includes the Hugging Face CLI, a command-line-interface tool that allows you to authenticate your applications using tokens. In Terminal or Anaconda Prompt, type huggingface-cli to view the various options you can use:

```
$ huggingface-cli
usage: huggingface-cli <command> [<args>]

positional arguments:
  {env,login,whoami,logout,repo,upload,download,
   lfs-enable-largefiles,lfs-multipart-upload,
   scan-cache,delete-cache}
                        huggingface-cli command helpers
    env                 Print information about the environment.
    login               Log in using a token from
                        huggingface.co/settings/tokens
    whoami              Find out which huggingface.co account
                        you are logged in as.
    logout              Log out
    repo                {create} Commands to interact with
                        your huggingface.co repos.
    upload              Upload a file or a folder to a repo on the Hub
```

```
download                  Download files from the Hub
lfs-enable-largefiles
                          Configure your repository to enable
                          upload of files > 5GB.
scan-cache                Scan cache directory.
delete-cache              Delete revisions from the cache directory.

options:
  -h, --help              show this help message and exit
```

Using the CLI, you can log in to Hugging Face Hub programmatically. First, though, you need to create an account at https://huggingface.co/join (see figure 2.15).

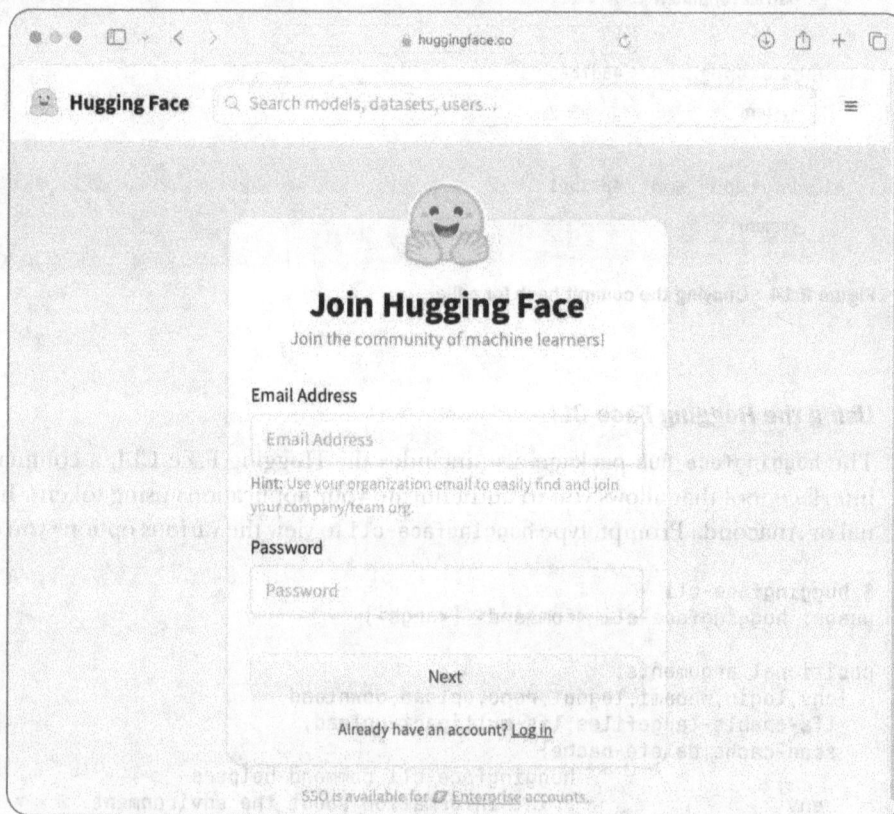

Figure 2.15   Signing up for a Hugging Face account

Hugging Face uses access tokens to authenticate users who need to download private repositories, upload files, create PRs, and so on. After you sign up as a Hugging Face user, you should create an access token for yourself at https://huggingface.co/settings/tokens. Then you can log in to Hugging Face Hub using the following command:

```
$ huggingface-cli login
```

```
    _|        _|    _|        _|        _|_|_|      _|_|_|    _|_|_|   _|          _|      _|_|_|
   _|_|_|_|     _|_|           _|_|_|   _|_|_|_|
    _|        _|    _|        _|    _|            _|                  _|      _|_|      _|  _|
    _|              _|        _|    _|            _|
   _|_|_|_|   _|        _|    _|   _|_|   _|   _|_|      _|        _|  _|   _|   _|  _|_|
    _|_|_|     _|_|_|_|   _|              _|_|_|
    _|        _|    _|        _|    _|        _|    _|      _|        _|      _|_|   _|      _|
    _|              _|        _|    _|            _|
    _|        _|        _|_|           _|_|_|      _|_|_|    _|_|_|   _|          _|      _|_|_|
    _|              _|        _|    _|_|_|   _|_|_|_|
```

```
        A token is already saved on your machine. Run `huggingface-cli
        whoami` to get more information or `huggingface-cli logout` if
        you want to log out.
    Setting a new token will erase the existing one.
        To login, `huggingface_hub` requires a token generated from
        https://huggingface.co/settings/tokens .
Enter your token (input will not be visible): <HuggingFaceAccessToken>
Add token as git credential? (Y/n) n
Token is valid (permission: read).
Your token has been saved to /Users/weimenglee/.cache/huggingface/token
Login successful
```

Note that when you type your token (or, more likely, paste it from your clipboard), you'll see no feedback onscreen. The token you entered is saved in the file named token, located in the *<home_directory>* /.cache/huggingface/ directory. To see which account you've signed in to, use the whoami option:

```
$ huggingface-cli whoami
```

You see the name of the user account you used to sign in. Another way to log in to Hugging Face Hub is to use the login() function in Python:

```
from huggingface_hub import login

login()
```

The login() function displays the UI, as shown in figure 2.16. Enter your token and then click the Login button.

> **NOTE** If you encounter an error related to ipywidgets in Jupyter Notebook, you should be able to fix it by updating ipywidgets to the latest version:

```
!pip install -U ipywidgets
```

Copy a token from your Hugging Face tokens page and paste it below.

Immediately click login after copying your token or it might be stored in

plain text in this notebook file.

Token: [   ]

☑ Add token as git credential?

Login

Pro Tip: If you don't already have one, you can create a dedicated

'notebooks' token with 'write' access, that you can then easily reuse for all

notebooks.

Figure 2.16   Logging in to Hugging Face Hub from Jupyter Notebook

Summary

- The Anaconda package comes with the `conda` package manager, which simpli-fies package management and environment creation. It also comes with Jupyter Notebook.
- Creating virtual environments allows you to install and manage Python packages separately from your systemwide Python installation. Virtual environments are useful for isolating dependencies and managing project requirements.
- The easiest way to start Jupyter Notebook is to launch it from Terminal or Anaconda Prompt.
- The Transformers library is built on PyTorch, a popular deep learning frame-work primarily developed by FAIR.
- PyTorch supports GPU, enabling smooth integration with CUDA, a parallel com-puting platform and programming model designed for GPUs.
- The Hugging Face Hub package allows you to download files, upload files, and perform authentication using the CLI.

Using Hugging Face transformers and pipelines for NLP tasks

This chapter covers

- Understanding the transformer architecture
- Using the Hugging Face Transformers library
- Using the `pipeline()` function in the Transformers library
- Performing NLP tasks using the Transformers library

You've had a glimpse of the Hugging Face Transformers library and seen how to use it to perform object detection using one of the pretrained models hosted by Hugging Face. Now we will go behind the scenes to learn about the transformers package: the transformer architecture and the various components that make it work. The aim of this book is not to dive into the detailed workings of the transformer model, but I want to discuss it briefly so that you have some basic understanding of how things work.

Next, we will use the `pipeline()` function that ships with the transformers package to perform various natural language processing (NLP) tasks such as text classifications, text generation, and text summarization.

NOTE   When I talk about *Transformers*, I'm referring to the open source library created by Hugging Face that provides pretrained transformer models and tools for NLP tasks. *Transformer*, on the other hand, refers to the neural network architecture discussed in section 3.1.

3.1   *Introduction to the transformer architecture*

The transformer architecture, introduced in the paper "Attention is All You Need" by Ashish Vaswani et al. (https://arxiv.org/pdf/1706.03762.pdf), has become the foundation for many state-of-the-art models in NLP. It relies heavily on the self-attention mechanism to process input data in parallel, making it more efficient and effective for many tasks compared with previous neural network architectures, such as recurrent neural networks (RNNs) and long short-term memory networks (LSTMs). Figure 3.1 shows the transformer architecture taken from the "Attention Is All You Need" paper.

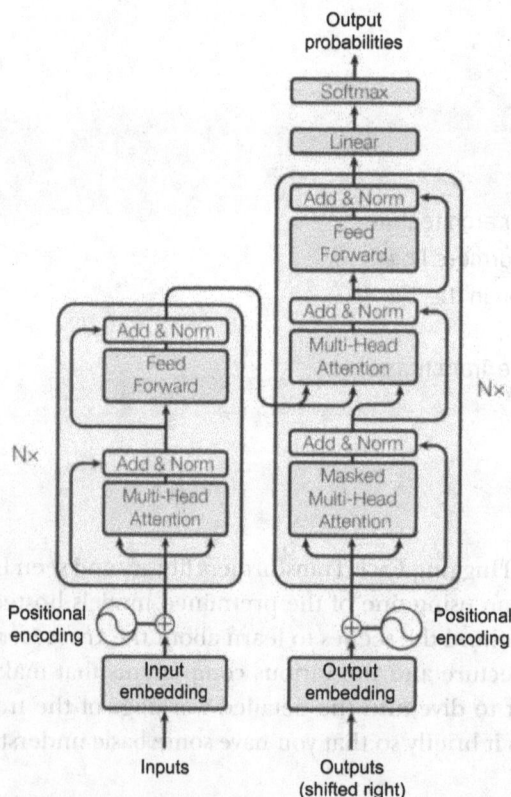

Figure 3.1   The transformer architecture (Source: "Attention Is All You Need" paper)

DEFINITION   The *self-attention mechanism* is a crucial component of the transformer architecture. It enables the model to weigh the importance of different words in a sequence when encoding a particular word, allowing the model to capture dependencies and relationships between words irrespective of their distance in the sequence. This mechanism allows transformers to handle long-range dependencies and parallelize the processing of input sequences effectively.

At a high level, the transformer architecture consists of two main blocks: Encoder and Decoder (see figure 3.2).

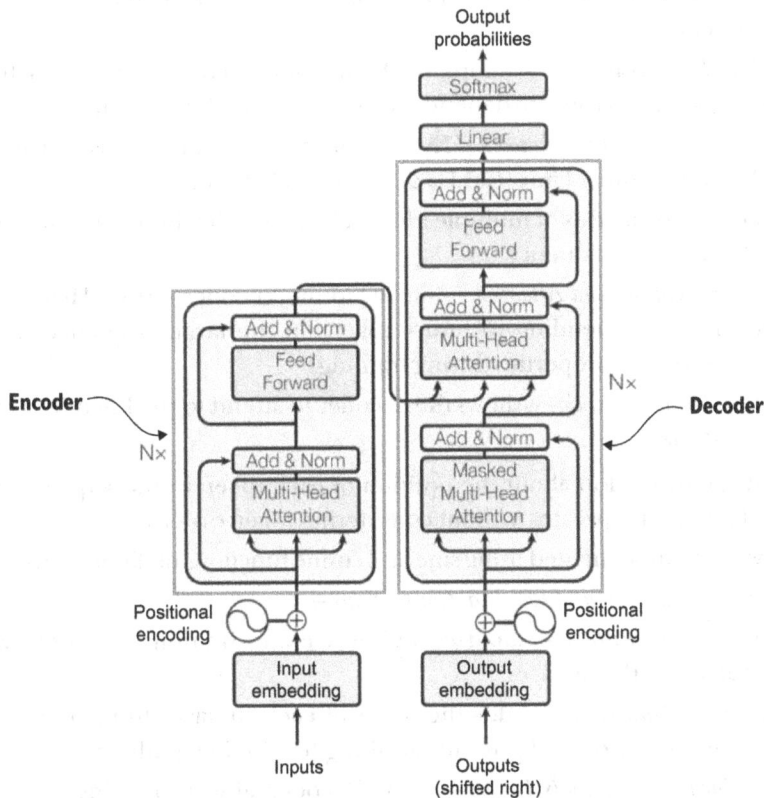

Figure 3.2 A transformer model contains an Encoder and a Decoder.

The Encoder gets the inputs and builds a representation of them. The Decoder uses the Encoder's representation, along with other inputs, to generate a target sequence (the outputs' probabilities). One intriguing aspect of this model is that each component can function independently. You can use a model solely featuring the Encoder component, for example. This model is beneficial for tasks such as sentence classification and named entity recognition (NER), in which comprehension of the input is paramount. Conversely, models that employ only the Decoder are suitable for tasks such as text generation. Furthermore, models incorporating both the Encoder and Decoder are well suited to endeavors such as text summarization and text translation.

Following are some of the key components of the transformer architecture:

- *Input Embedding*—
  - Converts input tokens to dense vectors of fixed size.
  - Adds positional encodings to retain information about the order of the tokens because the model processes input in parallel and lacks inherent sequential information.
- *Encoder*—Comprises multiple identical layers, each containing two main components:
  - *Multi-Head Attention*—Computes the attention scores between each pair of input tokens to capture dependencies regardless of their distance.
  - *Feed-Forward Neural Network (FFN)*—Comprises two linear transformations with a Rectified Linear Unit (ReLU) activation in between.
- *Decoder*—Also consists of multiple identical layers with additional components to handle the target sequence:
  - *Masked Multi-Head Attention*—Similar to the Encoder's Multi-Head Attention but prevents attending to future tokens in the target sequence (to ensure autoregressive properties during training).
  - *Multi-Head Attention*—Allows the decoder to attend to the Encoder's output.
- *Positional Encoding*—
  - Adds information about the position of each token in the sequence because self-attention operates without considering token order.
  - Typically implemented using sine and cosine functions of different frequencies.
- *Layer Normalization and Residual Connections*—
  - *Layer Normalization*—Stabilizes and accelerates training by normalizing the input across the features.
  - *Residual Connections*—Adds the input of each sublayer to its output to help with gradient flow and prevent vanishing/exploding gradients.
- *Final Linear and Softmax Layers*—In the Decoder, after processing the sequence through multiple layers, a final linear transformation followed by a Softmax layer is used to produce probabilities for the next token.

3.1.1   *Tokenization*

In the context of NLP and machine learning, a *token* is a chunk of text that a model processes as a single unit. A token can represent an individual word, punctuation mark, or other linguistic element, depending on the specific tokenization strategy employed. *Tokenization* is the process of converting a text document or sentence to smaller units. Generally, there a few types of tokenization strategies:

- *Word tokenization*—Splits text into individual words based on whitespace or punctuation characters. Figure 3.3 shows how the sentence "I love cats" is tokenized into three tokens.

- *Subword tokenization*—Breaks text into smaller linguistic units such as prefixes, suffixes, or root words. This strategy is commonly used for languages with complex morphology or tasks like machine translation. Figure 3.4 shows how the word *unhappiness* is tokenized into three tokens. Subword tokenization enables the model to encompass a broad, varied vocabulary while circumventing the constraints imposed by a rigid word-level vocabulary. This technique is especially useful for comprehending and generating text across diverse contexts, languages, and domains, enhancing the model's capability to accommodate linguistic variations and diminish vocabulary dimensions.

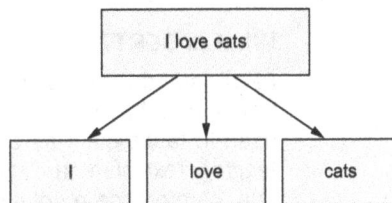

Figure 3.3   Tokenizing a sentence into three tokens using the word tokenization technique

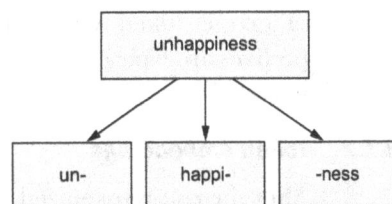

Figure 3.4   Tokenizing a sentence into three tokens using the subword tokenization technique

- *Character-level tokenization*—Segments text into individual characters, including letters, digits, and punctuation marks. Figure 3.5 shows how the word *Hello* is tokenized into five tokens. Character-level tokenization is ideal for tasks that require meticulous analysis at the character level, particularly when you're handling languages with intricate word structures (such as Chinese). Nonetheless, this strategy entails a larger vocabulary and may result in reduced interpretability at advanced linguistic levels.

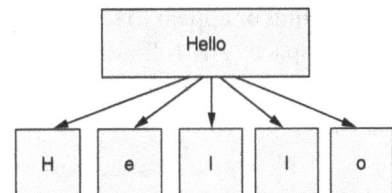

Figure 3.5   Tokenizing a sentence into five tokens using the character-level tokenization technique

Here is an example of subword tokenization using the BERT model:

```
from transformers import AutoTokenizer          Loads a pretrained tokenizer

tokenizer = AutoTokenizer.from_pretrained("bert-base-uncased")
input_text = "What is unhappiness?"
tokens = tokenizer.tokenize(input_text, return_tensors="pt")

print(f"{tokens = }")
                                                 Tokenizes input text
```

This code snippet prints the following tokens:

```
tokens = ['what', 'is', 'un', '##ha', '##pp', '##iness', '?']
```

> ### What is BERT?
>
> *BERT* stands for *Bidirectional Encoder Representations from Transformers*, a transformer-based machine learning model designed for NLP tasks. It is commonly used in tasks such as question answering, text classification, NER, part-of-speech tagging, text summarization, sentiment analysis, language translation, text generation, coreference resolution, paraphrase detection, semantic search, textual entailment, and dialogue systems.

The ## prefix attached to some tokens in the output indicates that the token is a continuation of the previous one in the original word. It signifies that the tokens are part of a larger token. When these tokens are decoded back into the original text, the ## prefixes are typically removed, and the tokens are combined to reconstruct the original word.

3.1.2   *Token embeddings*

After the text is tokenized, the next step is performing *token embeddings*, which convert tokens to numerical vectors. These embeddings capture semantic and syntactic information about the tokens, enabling machine learning models to understand the underlying meanings of and relationships between words in natural language text.

The embeddings are learned based on the co-occurrence and contextual relationships between words in the training corpus. As a result, words that have similar meanings or appear in similar contexts tend to have similar representations in the embedding space. The following code listing shows how you can perform token embedding on a paragraph of text.

Listing 3.1   Performing token embeddings on a paragraph of text

```
from transformers import BertTokenizer, BertModel        Loads pretrained BERT
import torch                                              tokenizer and model

tokenizer = BertTokenizer.from_pretrained("bert-base-uncased")
model = BertModel.from_pretrained("bert-base-uncased")

input_text = '''
After a long day at work, Sarah decided to relax by taking her
dog for a walk in the park. As they strolled along the
tree-lined paths, Sarah's dog, Max, eagerly sniffed around,
chasing after squirrels and birds. Sarah smiled as she watched
Max enjoy himself, feeling grateful for the companionship and
joy that her furry friend brought into her life.'''

tokens = tokenizer(input_text, return_tensors="pt")

with torch.no_grad():                      Generates token
    outputs = model(**tokens)              embeddings

last_hidden_states = outputs.last_hidden_state      Extracts token embeddings
                                                    from the last layer
```

```
print("Token embeddings:")
for token, embedding in zip(tokens["input_ids"][0],
                           last_hidden_states[0]):          ◄── Prints the token
    word = tokenizer.decode(int(token))                          embedding for each word
    print(f"{word}: {embedding}")
```

In this example, we tokenized the input text using the BERT model and then extracted the token embeddings from the last layer of the model's outputs. Finally, we print the embedding for each word, as shown in the following listing.

Listing 3.2   The embeddings for each word in the paragraph

```
Token embeddings:
[ C L S ]: tensor(
        [ 5.1886e-03, -1.3432e-01,  -6.8117e-01, -5.0901e-02, -1.3148e-01,
         -2.2708e-01,  4.2620e-01,   7.9117e-01, -3.0209e-01, -6.5137e-02,
        ...
         -9.4111e-02, -4.7972e-01,   9.1932e-02, -3.9814e-01,  4.3560e-02,
          1.8024e-01,  7.4798e-01,   2.8064e-01])
a f t e r: tensor(
        [-3.1720e-01, -3.1491e-01,   1.3892e-01,  3.9379e-01,  1.3412e-01,
          4.2373e-01,  4.9870e-01,   7.1422e-01,  1.0452e-01, -7.0356e-01,
        ...
```

It would be useful to plot the token embeddings on a graph so that you can visualize how the tokens are related. Because the embeddings are in very high dimensions, however, first we need to reduce their dimensionality to two dimensions so we can visualize them effectively. One common technique for dimensionality reduction and visualization is t-Distributed Stochastic Neighbor Embedding (t-SNE). We can use t-SNE to project the high-dimensional embeddings into a 2D space. The next listing shows how.

Listing 3.3   Using t-SNE to project high-dimensional embeddings into a 2D space

Reduces dimensionality using t-SNE with lower perplexity,
a parameter controlling nearest neighbors—higher for
larger datasets but always less than the sample count

```
from sklearn.manifold import TSNE
import matplotlib.pyplot as plt

tsne = TSNE(n_components=2, perplexity=5, random_state=42)
embeddings_tsne = tsne.fit_transform(last_hidden_states[0])

plt.figure(figsize=(10, 8))
plt.scatter(embeddings_tsne[:, 0],
            embeddings_tsne[:, 1], marker='o')           Plots the
for i, word in enumerate(tokenizer.convert_ids_to_tokens(    embeddings
    tokens["input_ids"][0])):                                on a 2D graph
    plt.annotate(word, xy=(embeddings_tsne[i, 0],
                          embeddings_tsne[i, 1]),
                fontsize=10)
```

```
plt.xlabel('t-SNE Dimension 1')
plt.ylabel('t-SNE Dimension 2')
plt.title('t-SNE Visualization of Token Embeddings')
plt.show()
```

Figure 3.6 shows the graph grouping the various tokens according to their embeddings.

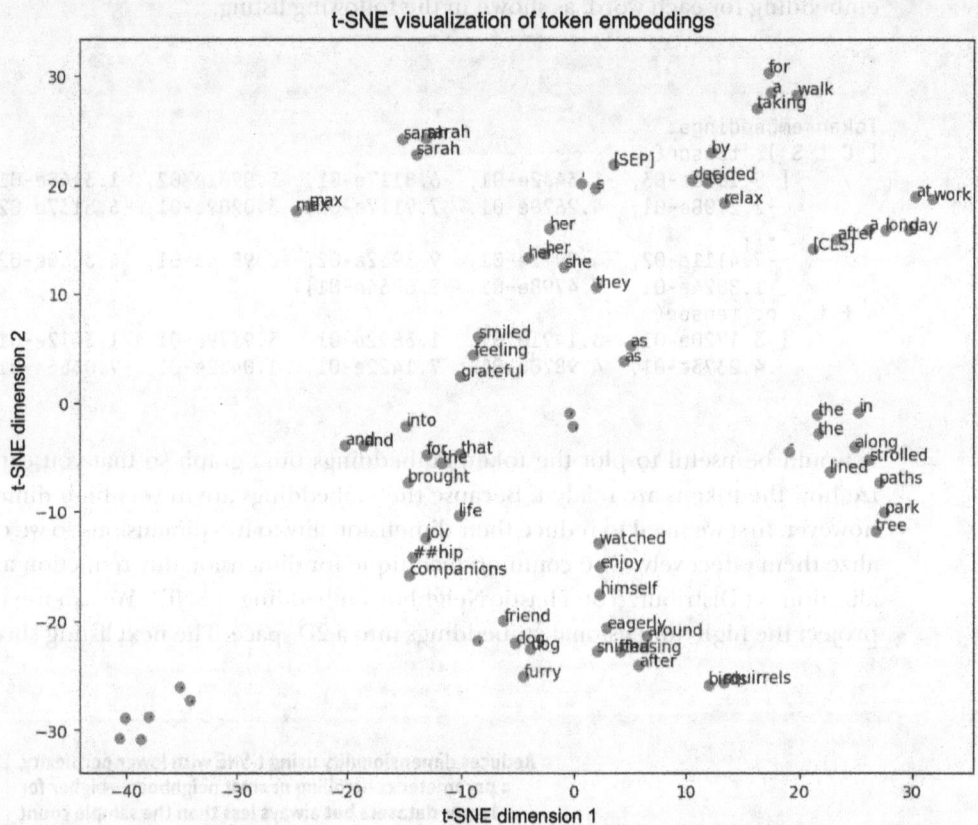

Figure 3.6   The visualization of token embeddings for the various words in a paragraph in 2D space

In short, word embeddings allow you to see which words are often used together. This technique captures semantic relationships between words based on their usage patterns in large text corpora. Here are two examples:

- The vectors for *king* and *queen* are closer to each other than to unrelated words like *train* and *buildings*.
- The vectors for words such as *bread* and *butter* are close to each other because they often co-occur in text.

3.1.3   Positional encoding

Positional encoding plays a crucial role in transformer-based models by imparting essential positional information about the order of tokens within a sequence. This positional context is vital for enabling the model to grasp the meaning and context of the input accurately. When we incorporate positional encoding into token embeddings, we give the model the ability to discern between tokens based on their positions in the sequence. Without this encoding, the model would struggle to differentiate between tokens based solely on their sequential positions, significantly impairing its performance on tasks that require a nuanced understanding of sequences, such as language modeling, machine translation, and text generation.

Positional encoding is typically added to token embeddings before they are input into the transformer model. The following code listing shows how you can extract the positional embeddings from a paragraph of text.

> **Listing 3.4   Printing the positional encoding for each token**

```
from transformers import BertTokenizer, BertModel
import torch

tokenizer = BertTokenizer.from_pretrained("bert-base-uncased")
model = BertModel.from_pretrained("bert-base-uncased")

input_text = '''
After a long day at work, Sarah decided to relax by taking her
dog for a walk in the park. As they strolled along the
tree-lined paths, Sarah's dog, Max, eagerly sniffed around,
chasing after squirrels and birds. Sarah smiled as she watched
Max enjoy himself, feeling grateful for the companionship and
joy that her furry friend brought into her life.'''

tokens = tokenizer(input_text, return_tensors="pt")
embeddings = model.embeddings
positional_embeddings = embeddings.position_embeddings.weight
position_ids = torch.arange(tokens['input_ids'].size(1),
                            dtype=torch.long).unsqueeze(0)
input_positional_embeddings = positional_embeddings[position_ids]

print("Positional embeddings shape:", input_positional_embeddings.shape)
print("Positional embeddings for each token:")

for token_id, pos_embedding in zip(tokens['input_ids'][0],
                                   input_positional_embeddings[0]):
    token = tokenizer.decode([token_id])
    print(f"{token}: {pos_embedding}")
```

Accesses the embeddings layer directly

Extracts the positional embeddings

Gets the positional encodings for the input tokens

Extracts the position IDs from the input tokens

In the BERT model, positional encodings are already integrated into the model architecture and are added to the input embeddings automatically, so, in this example, we're simply extracting the positional embeddings for each token. The following listing shows the output of the code.

```
Positional embeddings shape: torch.Size([1, 77, 768])
Positional embeddings for each token:
[CLS]: tensor([ 1.7505e-02, -2.5631e-02, -3.6642e-02, -2.5286e-02,  7.9709e-03,
        -2.0358e-02, -3.7631e-03, -4.6880e-03,  6.2253e-03, -3.8342e-02,
         1.3103e-02, -3.7083e-03, -2.1014e-02,  1.1626e-02, -3.9546e-02,
        ...
         4.0483e-03, -3.4331e-02,  1.0333e-02, -1.0450e-02, -1.4161e-02,
         3.3437e-05,  6.8312e-04,  1.5441e-02], grad_fn=<UnbindBackward0>)
after: tensor([ 7.7580e-03,  2.2613e-03, -1.9444e-02,
-1.7131e-02, -1.3234e-02, 1.4102e-02, -3.7121e-03,
-1.0888e-02,  6.2255e-03, -3.4778e-02, -7.7945e-03,
-1.4488e-02, -1.1725e-02,  1.0181e-02, -5.9442e-03,
        ...
```

In short, positional encodings provide information about the positions of words within a sequence. It allows models to understand the order of words in a sentence. Following are two examples:

- The sentence "The cat sat on the sofa" has a different meaning from "The sofa sat on the cat."

- Positional embeddings allow you to differentiate between "Tom loves Susan" and "Susan loves Tom."

3.1.4   *Transformer block*

At the heart of the transformer architecture is the Transformer block, which is the key component responsible for encoding and decoding information across multiple layers. The Transformer block contains the following components:

- *Self-Attention Mechanism*—The Transformer block uses *self-attention*, also known as *scaled dot-product attention*. This mechanism allows the model to weigh the importance of different words (tokens) in a sequence based on their relationships with each other. It computes attention scores for each pair of words in the sequence and uses these scores to construct context-aware representations of each word.

- *Feed-Forward Neural Networks*—After the self-attention mechanism, the Transformer block applies FFNs to process each word's representation independently and in parallel. FFNs typically consist of two linear transformations separated by a nonlinear activation function like ReLU.

- *Residual Connections and Layer Normalization*—To facilitate effective gradient flow and ease training, residual connections are employed around each sub-layer (self-attention and FFNs) of the Transformer block. Additionally, layer normalization is applied to stabilize training and improve the speed and convergence of the model.

3.1.5 Softmax

The last component of the transformer architecture is *Softmax*, a mathematical function that converts a vector of numbers to a probability distribution in which the probability of each element is proportional to the exponentiation of that element's value relative to the sum of all the exponentiated values in the vector. In the context of neural networks, Softmax is often used as the final activation function in classification tasks.

Figure 3.7 shows an example of using the Softmax function. On the left are the values for the output layer of a neural network. To transform the values into probabilities that the model can interpret, you use the Softmax function to generate the probability distribution. The probabilities generated sum up to 1. Each value in the probabilities represents the probability of a class or category.

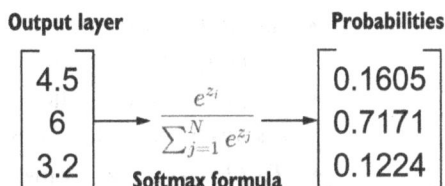

Output layer **Probabilities**

$$\begin{bmatrix} 4.5 \\ 6 \\ 3.2 \end{bmatrix} \longrightarrow \frac{e^{z_i}}{\sum_{j=1}^{N} e^{z_j}} \longrightarrow \begin{bmatrix} 0.1605 \\ 0.7171 \\ 0.1224 \end{bmatrix}$$

Softmax formula

Figure 3.7 Using the Softmax function to generate a set of probabilities based on the values of the output layer of a neural network

3.2 Working with the Transformers library

Now that you have a clearer idea of how the transformer architecture works, it's time to focus our attention on the key subject of this book: the Hugging Face Transformers library. As its name implies, the library is an open source library and platform developed by Hugging Face. Its aim is to provide an easy-to-access interface for working with state-of-the-art transformer-based models. Figure 3.8 illustrates the use of the library.

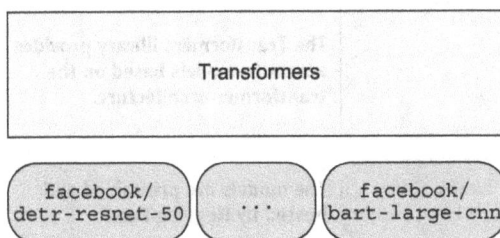

Transformers

The Transformers library provides access to models based on the transformer architecture.

```
facebook/          ...          facebook/
detr-resnet-50               bart-large-cnn
```

The models are pretrained and hosted by Hugging Face.

Figure 3.8 The role of the Hugging Face Transformers library

3.2.1 What are pretrained transformers models?

In this section, you learn how to use the Transformers library and its various pretrained models and how to use pipelines to simplify the process. *Pretrained transformer models* are transformer-based neural network models that have been pretrained on vast amounts of text data. These models are trained using an unsupervised learning technique, such as language modeling or masked language modeling, on large text corpora to learn the statistical properties of natural language. The following list describes several examples of pretrained transformer models, which serve as powerful building blocks for various NLP applications and have significantly advanced the state of the art in the field:

- *BERT*—Introduces bidirectional training for transformers, capturing context from both directions of a word
- *GPT* (Generative Pretrained Transformer)—Focuses on language generation tasks by predicting the next word in a sequence
- *RoBERTa* (Robustly Optimized BERT Approach)—Optimized version of BERT with improved training strategies and larger datasets
- *DistilBERT*—A smaller, faster variant of BERT, suitable for deployment in resource-constrained environments
- *T5* (Text-To-Text Transfer Transformer)—Trained on a unified framework in which all tasks are treated as text-to-text transformations

3.2.2   What are transformers pipelines?

To make the Transformers library easier to use, Hugging Face provides the convenient, user-friendly `pipeline()` function (also known simply as a *pipeline*) that shields the lower-level details from the developer. Figure 3.9 illustrates the role of the `pipeline()` function.

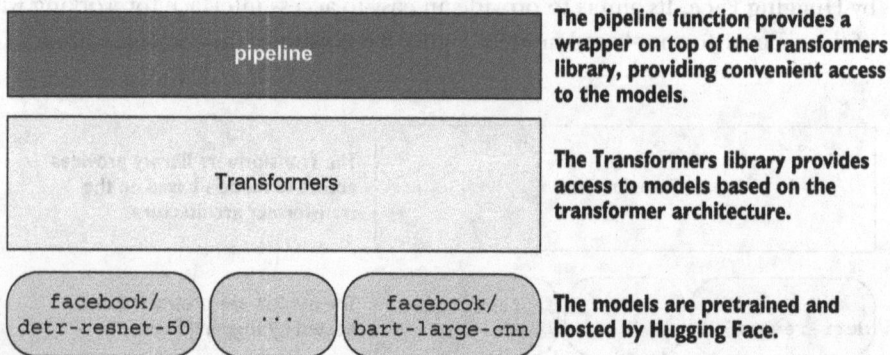

Figure 3.9   Pipelines are high-level APIs that use the transformer models provided by the Transformers library.

Consider the `distilbert/distilbert-base-uncased-finetuned-sst-2-english` model, a pretrained DistilBERT model that has been fine-tuned on the Stanford Sentiment Treebank (SST-2) dataset for sentiment analysis in English.

What is DistilBERT?

DistilBERT is a lighter, smaller, faster version of BERT, (a popular transformer-based model for NLP. It was introduced by Hugging Face researchers in a paper titled "Distil-BERT, a distilled version of BERT: smaller, faster, cheaper and lighter" by Victor Sanh et al. (https://arxiv.org/abs/1910.01108).

On the Hugging Face web page for this model (https://mng.bz/a96o; see figure 3.10), you can click the </> Use in Transformers button to see how to use this model.

Figure 3.10   Learning how to use the model using the Transformers library

Figure 3.11 shows two ways to use the model:

- Go through the transformers pipeline.
- Use the model directly.

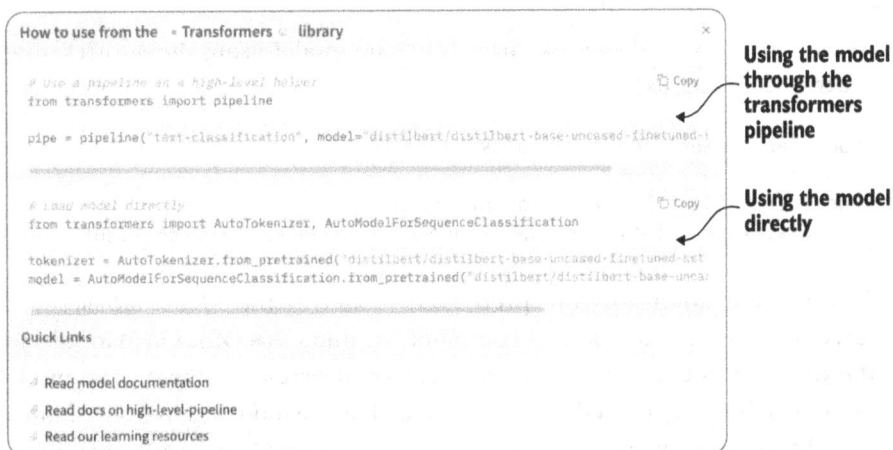

Figure 3.11   Two ways to use the pretrained model

I find using the model through the pipeline easier than the other option. Table 3.1 shows various reasons for using both approaches.

Table 3.1   Reasons for using a model directly or through a pipeline

Using a model directly	Using a model through a pipeline
Fine-grained control—You have more control of input preprocessing, tokenization, model inference, and postprocessing steps.	*Simplicity*—Pipelines provide a high-level, user-friendly interface for using the model without requiring you to understand the underlying complexities of model loading, input processing, and inferencing.
Flexibility—You can easily experiment with different model architectures, hyperparameters, and input formats.	*Rapid prototyping*—With pipelines, you can work with models with only a few lines of code.
Better understanding—Working directly with the model allows you to better understand how the model works.	*Preconfigured settings*—Pipelines come with preconfigured settings and default parameters optimized for common use cases. These settings can save you time and effort in selecting the appropriate model, fine-tuning hyperparameters, and handling input/output formats.

3.2.3   Using a model directly

In this section, you learn how to use models directly by working with the `distilbert/distilbert-base-uncased-finetuned-sst-2-english` model. You'll use this model to perform sentiment analysis on a piece of text.

> **DEFINITION**   *Sentiment analysis* is an NLP technique that determines the sentiment expressed in a piece of text. It involves analyzing textual data to categorize the sentiment as positive, negative, or neutral, indicating the overall emotional tone or polarity of the text.

As the first step, load the tokenizer from the model using the `AutoTokenizer.from_pretrained()` method:

```
from transformers import AutoTokenizer

tokenizer = AutoTokenizer.from_pretrained(
    "distilbert/distilbert-base-uncased-finetuned-sst-2-english")
```

This method downloads the pretrained model to the `~/.cache/huggingface/hub/` directory of your machine (for computers running macOS). On Windows machines, the directory is `C:\users\<user_name>\.cache\huggingface\hub\`. The model will be saved in a directory named after the model. For the model we're using in this section, the directory is named `models--distilbert--distilbert-base-uncased-finetuned-sst-2-english` (see figure 3.12).

chroma
gdown
gpt4all
huggingface
lm-studio
tooling
torch
whisper

hub

models--distil...-sst-2-english

blobs
refs
snapshots

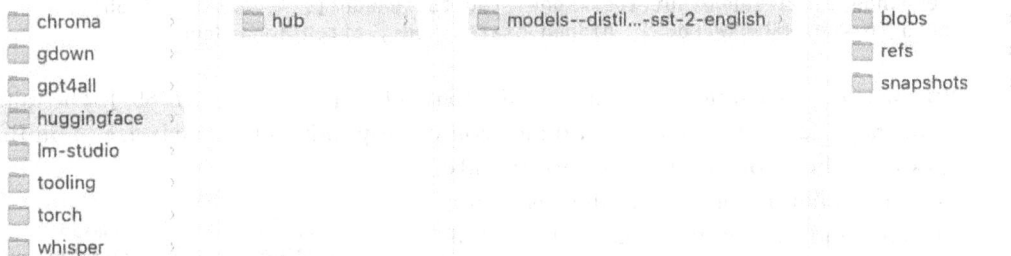

Figure 3.12 The directory containing the downloaded model

Next, load the model using the `AutoModelForSequenceClassification.from_pretrained()` method:

```
from transformers import AutoModelForSequenceClassification

model = AutoModelForSequenceClassification.from_pretrained(
    "distilbert/distilbert-base-uncased-finetuned-sst-2-english")
```

Before you can use the model to perform sentiment analysis on a paragraph of text, you need to tokenize it using the `tokenizer` object:

```
import torch

text = "I loved the movie, it was fantastic!"

inputs = tokenizer(text, return_tensors = "pt")        ◀──── Tokenizes the text
print(inputs)
```

The `tokenizer` object returns a dictionary containing the tokenized representation of the input text, suitable for consumption by a PyTorch model (indicated by the pt value):

```
{'input_ids': tensor([[  101,  1045,  3866,  1996,  3185,  1010,
2009,  2001, 10392,   999, 102]]), 'attention_mask': tensor([[1,
 1, 1, 1, 1, 1, 1, 1, 1, 1, 1]])}
```

Then the result of the `tokenizer` object is passed into `model` for inferencing:

```
outputs = model(**inputs)        ◀──── Performs inference
print(outputs)
```

In the preceding statements, you are giving the model the token IDs (stored in `input_ids` key) and optionally other tensors, such as the attention mask (stored in the `attention_mask` key). Then the model performs inference on these inputs, generating predictions or other relevant outputs depending on the specific model and task. You see the following output:

```
SequenceClassifierOutput(loss=None, logits=tensor([[-4.3428,  4.6955]],
grad_fn=<AddmmBackward0>), hidden_states=None, attentions=None)
```

In particular, take note of the values in the logits key: [[-4.3428, 4.6955]]. The value is of shape (1,2), where the first dimension corresponds to the batch size (1, in this case) and the second dimension corresponds to the number of classes (2, in this case: 0 for negative and 1 for positive). Each element in the tensor represents the model's confidence score for a particular class. In this example, the model outputs [-4.3428, 4.6955], which suggests that the model assigns a higher confidence score to the second class than to the first class (see figure 3.13).

Class 0 (negative)	Class 1 (positive)
-4.3428	4.6955

Figure 3.13   The confidence score for each class

Based on the interpretation of the result, you can extract the class with the higher confidence score and determine the class of the result:

> Gets the predicted label (0 for negative, 1 for positive)

```
predicted_label = torch.argmax(outputs.logits)
sentiment = "positive" if predicted_label == 1 else "negative"

print("Predicted sentiment:", sentiment)
```

You get the following output:

```
Predicted sentiment: positive
```

3.2.4   *Using a transformers pipeline*

Now that you've seen how to use a model directly, it's time to learn to use a transformers pipeline. The simplest way to use a pipeline is to specify the task you want to perform. But what tasks are supported in the first place? An easy way is to specify a task that is *not* supported and view the error message, which also shows a list of supported tasks:

```
from transformers import pipeline
try:
    dummy_pipeline = pipeline(task="dummy")
except Exception as e:
    print(e)
```

This code snippet prints the following error message, which includes supported tasks:

```
"Unknown task dummy, available tasks are ['audio-classification',
'automatic-speech-recognition', 'conversational', 'depth-estimation',
'document-question-answering', 'feature-extraction', 'fill-mask',
'image-classification', 'image-feature-extraction',
'image-segmentation', 'image-to-image', 'image-to-text',
```

```
'mask-generation', 'ner', 'object-detection', 'question-answering',
'sentiment-analysis', 'summarization', 'table-question-answering',
'text-classification', 'text-generation', 'text-to-audio',
'text-to-speech', 'text2text-generation', 'token-classification',
'translation', 'video-classification', 'visual-question-answering',
'vqa', 'zero-shot-audio-classification', 'zero-shot-classification',
'zero-shot-image-classification', 'zero-shot-object-detection',
'translation_XX_to_YY']"
```

Let's use the `distilbert/distilbert-base-uncased-finetuned-sst-2-english` model that we used in section 3.2.3. This model falls under the `text-classification` task. How would you know? In figure 3.11 earlier in this chapter, the code sample specified the task:

```
from transformers import pipeline

pipe = pipeline("text-classification",
    model="distilbert/distilbert-base-uncased-finetuned-sst-2-english")
```

Alternatively, you can view the model's page on the Hugging Face website and find the task that this model is trained for (see figure 3.14).

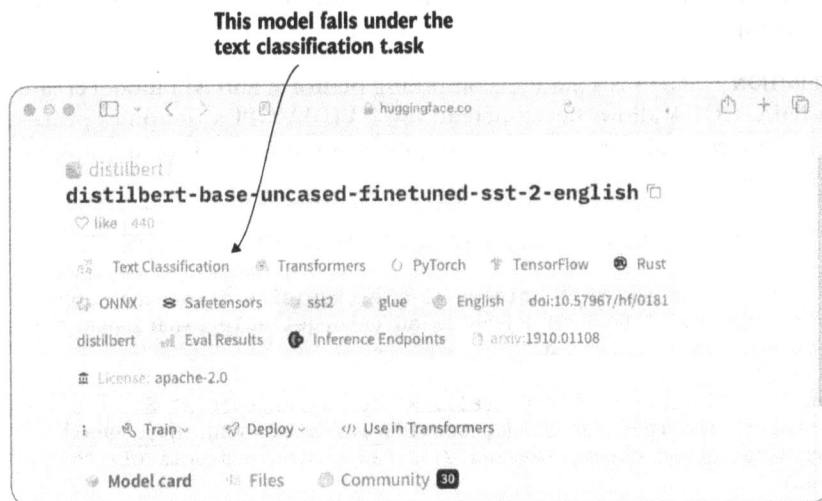

Figure 3.14   Finding the type of task a model falls under

Note that you can simply specify the tasks in the `pipeline` method and leave out the model you want to use. The `pipeline` method will use the default model and revision (version) for that task:

```
pipe = pipeline("text-classification")
```

This approach is not recommended, however, because the default model to use might change in the next release of the `pipeline()` method. It's better to specify the `model` parameter explicitly:

```
from transformers import pipeline

classifier = pipeline(task = 'text-classification',
    model = 'distilbert/distilbert-base-uncased-finetuned-sst-2-english')
```

If you've already identified the model you want to use, you don't have to specify the task parameter. Specify only the model, like this:

```
classifier = pipeline(
    model = 'distilbert/distilbert-base-uncased-finetuned-sst-2-english')
```

In addition, if you have a Compute Unified Device Architecture (CUDA)-compliant GPU on your computer, you can specify that the pipeline be allocated to run on the GPU:

```
classifier = pipeline(
    model = 'distilbert/distilbert-base-uncased-finetuned-sst-2-english',
    device = "cuda")
```

By default, `device` is set to `"cpu"`, which allows you to run a model using only the CPU of your computer.

> **DEFINITION**   CUDA is a parallel computing platform and API model created by NVIDIA. CUDA allows developers to use NVIDIA GPUs (graphics processing units) for general-purpose processing in addition to traditional graphics rendering tasks.

Let's define two blocks of text containing reviews of two restaurants:

```
review1 = '''From the warm welcome to the exquisite dishes and impeccable
 service, dining at Gourmet Haven is an unforgettable experience that
 leaves you eager to return.'''

review2 = '''Despite high expectations, our experience at Savor Bistro
 fell short; the food was bland, service was slow, and the overall
 atmosphere lacked charm, leaving us disappointed and unlikely to
 revisit.'''
```

We can use the `pipeline` object (`classifier`) to perform a sentiment analysis on the first review:

```
print(classifier(review1))
```

You see the following output, indicating that the review contains positive sentiment:

```
[{'label': 'POSITIVE', 'score': 0.9998437166213989}]
```

You can also pass in multiple blocks of text using a list, like this:

```
print(classifier([review1, review2]))
```

The preceding statement returns the following output:

```
[{'label': 'POSITIVE', 'score': 0.9998437166213989},
 {'label': 'NEGATIVE', 'score': 0.9997773766517639}]
```

When contrasting using the model directly with employing the pipeline, the simplicity and straightforwardness of pipelines become apparent. Simply by initializing a `pipeline` object with the desired task and model, you enable data to flow seamlessly through for inference, yielding immediate outputs. In some instances, however, direct model use is essential for finer control. In this book, I prefer using pipelines whenever feasible and use the model directly when precise control is required.

3.3 Using transformers for NLP tasks

The primary tasks the Transformers library was created for include NLP tasks, computer vision, audio, and reinforcement learning. In this section, we discuss the various NLP tasks you can perform using the Transformers library:

- Text classification
- Text generation
- Text summarization
- Text translation
- Zero-shot classification
- Question answering

3.3.1 Text classification

In section 3.2.4, you saw how to perform sentiment analysis using a text classification model. Another form of text classification task is question detection. Using this task, you can detect whether a sentence contains a question. To do that, use the `huaen/question_detection` model:

```
from transformers import pipeline

question_classifier = pipeline("text-classification",
                        model="huaen/question_detection")
```

Using the pipeline created, you can pass in a string to determine whether it contains a question:

```
response = question_classifier(
    '''Have you ever pondered the mysteries that lie beneath
    the surface of everyday life?''')
print(response)
```

This statement prints the following output, indicating that this text is very likely (99.76% confidence) a question:

```
[{'label': 'question', 'score': 0.9975988268852234}]
```

Let's try another example:

```
response = question_classifier(
    '''"Life is a journey that must be traveled, no matter
    how bad the roads and accommodations." - Oliver Goldsmith''')
print(response)
```

The response is that this text is not likely a question:

```
[{'label': 'non_question', 'score': 0.9996856451034546}]
```

Another text classification task you can perform is language detection. Using a model such as papluca/xlm-roberta-base-language-detection, you can pass it a string so that it can try to detect the language of a given sentence:

```
language_classifier = pipeline("text-classification",
    model="papluca/xlm-roberta-base-language-detection")

response = language_classifier("日本の桜は美しいです。")
print(response)
```

The preceding statements print the following result, indicating that the language is most likely Japanese:

```
[{'label': 'ja', 'score': 0.9913387298583984}]
```

One more example of text classification is a *spam classifier*, which enables you to identify incoming messages (emails, text messages, comments, and so on) as *spam* (unwanted or unsolicited messages) or *ham* (legitimate messages). For this task, you can use the Delphia/twitter-spam-classifier model:

```
spam_classifier = pipeline("text-classification",
                            model="Delphia/twitter-spam-classifier")

response = spam_classifier(
    '''Congratulations! You've been selected as the winner of our
    exclusive prize draw. Claim your reward now by clicking on
    the link below!''')

print(response)
```

The preceding statements print the following result, indicating that the string provided is likely spam:

```
[{'label': 1, 'score': 0.7446919679641724}]
```

On the other hand, the following string is not likely spam:

```
response = spam_classifier(
    '''Hi Jimmy, I hope you're doing well. I just wanted to remind
    you about our meeting tomorrow at 10 AM in conference room A.
    Please let me know if you have any questions or need any
    further information. Looking forward to seeing you there!''')

print(response)
```

The following output confirms that result:

```
[{'label': 0, 'score': 0.7776529788970947}]
```

3.3.2 Text generation

Another common NLP task is text generation, which involves creating new, coherent, and contextually relevant text based on a given prompt or input. This task uses machine learning models, particularly those based on deep learning and neural networks, to produce humanlike text. The following code snippet shows how to use the `openai-community/gpt2` model to generate a paragraph of text based on an initial start sentence:

```
from transformers import pipeline

generator = pipeline("text-generation",
                     model="openai-community/gpt2")
generator("In this course, we will teach you how to")
```

This code generates the following output (but note that the output will be different each time the code snippet is run):

```
[{'generated_text': 'In this course, we will teach you how to build the
 best online games or use it to build your own. After this, this course
 covers: 1) how to make awesome games in Google Play and 2) how to
 develop a game based on'}]
```

You can control the output using the `max_length` (maximum number of tokens in the generated text) and `num_return_sequences` (number of paragraphs generated) parameters:

```
generator("In this course, we will teach you how to",
          max_length = 50,
          num_return_sequences = 3)
```

Here is the output generated:

```
[{'generated_text': 'In this course, we will teach you how to build and
 customize a modern React based project. We will show you ways to
```

```
simplify your development as well as make your app run with no effort.
We will give you many practical tips and tricks. After'},
{'generated_text': 'In this course, we will teach you how to use the
Raspberry Pi in a production computer to help you connect the Raspberry
Pi to the internet. We will learn about connecting other IoT networks
and how to connect to them within the Raspberry Pi.\n\n'},
{'generated_text': "In this course, we will teach you how to use PHP's
built-in filters, and how to use PHP's PHP-based classes. We will
also explain how to perform PHP operations such as create an array of
attributes, create an array of"}]
```

3.3.3   *Text summarization*

Summarizing text is another widely recognized NLP task. The key goal of text summarization is condensing large amounts of text into shorter, coherent summaries while preserving key information and main ideas. This technique is useful in applications such as news aggregation, document summarization, and content generation. There are two main approaches to text summarization:

- *Extractive*—Involves selecting and extracting important sentences or phrases directly from the original text
- *Abstractive*—Generates summaries by paraphrasing and rephrasing the original text in a more concise form

To try the text summarization task, you can use the `facebook/bart-large-cnn` model:

```
from transformers import pipeline

summarizer = pipeline("summarization",
                      model="facebook/bart-large-cnn")
```

Let's try to summarize the following block of text on quantum computers.

Listing 3.6   Summarizing a long paragraph of text

```
article = """
A quantum computer is a computer that exploits quantum mechanical
phenomena. At small scales, physical matter exhibits properties of
both particles and waves, and quantum computing leverages this
behavior using specialized hardware. Classical physics cannot
explain the operation of these quantum devices, and a scalable
quantum computer could perform some calculations exponentially
faster than any modern "classical" computer. In particular, a
large-scale quantum computer could break widely used encryption
schemes and aid physicists in performing physical simulations;
however, the current state of the art is still largely
experimental and impractical.

The basic unit of information in quantum computing is the qubit,
similar to the bit in traditional digital electronics. Unlike a
classical bit, a qubit can exist in a superposition of its two
```

```
"basis" states, which loosely means that it is in both states
simultaneously. When measuring a qubit, the result is a
probabilistic output of a classical bit. If a quantum computer
manipulates the qubit in a particular way, wave interference
effects can amplify the desired measurement results. The design
of quantum algorithms involves creating procedures that allow a
quantum computer to perform calculations efficiently.

Physically engineering high-quality qubits has proven challenging.
If a physical qubit is not sufficiently isolated from its
environment, it suffers from quantum decoherence, introducing noise
into calculations. National governments have invested heavily in
experimental research that aims to develop scalable qubits with
longer coherence times and lower error rates. Two of the most
promising technologies are superconductors (which isolate an
electrical current by eliminating electrical resistance) and ion
traps (which confine a single atomic particle using electromagnetic
fields).

Any computational problem that can be solved by a classical computer
can also be solved by a quantum computer.[2] Conversely, any problem
that can be solved by a quantum computer can also be solved by a
classical computer, at least in principle given enough time. In other
words, quantum computers obey the Church-Turing thesis. This means
that while quantum computers provide no additional advantages over
classical computers in terms of computability, quantum algorithms
for certain problems have significantly lower time complexities than
corresponding known classical algorithms. Notably, quantum computers
are believed to be able to solve certain problems quickly that no
classical computer could solve in any feasible amount of time—a feat
known as "quantum supremacy." The study of the computational
complexity of problems with respect to quantum computers is known as
quantum complexity theory.
"""

print(summarizer(article,
                 min_length = 100,
                 max_length = 250,
                 do_sample = False))
```

By default, the summarizer object returns a max_length of 142 tokens. In the preceding
statement, you indicate that you want the summary to have at least 100 tokens and
not exceed 250 tokens. The do_sample=False indicates that sampling should not be
used during generation. Instead, the model will deterministically select the most likely
tokens at each step of the generation process, essentially performing extractive summarization. The preceding statement generates the following summary:

```
[{'summary_text': 'A quantum computer is a computer that exploits
 quantum mechanical phenomena. Classical physics cannot explain the
 operation of these quantum devices. A scalable quantum computer
 could perform some calculations exponentially faster than any
 modern "classical" computer. The basic unit of information in
 quantum computing is the qubit, similar to the bit in traditional
```

```
digital electronics. The design of quantum algorithms involves
creating procedures that allow a quantum computer to perform
calculations efficiently. The study of the computational
complexity of problems with respect to quantum computers is known
as quantum complexity theory.'}]
```

Let's try again, this time with do_sample = True:

```
print(summarizer(article,
                 min_length = 100,
                 max_length = 250,
                 do_sample = True))
```

This statement means that during the generation of the summary, the model will use sampling to select the next token probabilistically based on the predicted distribution of tokens. This approach allows more diverse and creative generation because the model can explore different possibilities at each step rather than select the most likely token deterministically. The preceding statement generates the following output:

```
[{'summary_text': 'Quantum computers exploit quantum mechanical
phenomena. The basic unit of information in quantum computing is
the qubit, similar to the bit in traditional digital electronics.
A large-scale quantum computer could break widely used encryption
and aid physicists in performing physical simulations. National
governments have invested heavily in research that aims to develop
scalable qubits with longer coherence times and lower error rates.
quantum computers obey the Church-Turing thesis, which means that
any computational problem that can be solved by a classical
computer can also be solve by a quantum computer.'}]
```

3.3.4 *Text translation*

Text translation is one of the earliest foundational tasks in NLP. Its evolution spans from the initial days of rule-based methods and bilingual dictionaries to the groundbreaking transformer architecture, marking a journey of substantial advancements in quality enhancement and fluency.

Hugging Face offers several text translation models you can use to translate text from one language to another. Let's start with the google-t5/t5-base model, a variant of the T5 model developed by Google AI:

```
from transformers import pipeline

translator = pipeline("translation",
                      model = "google-t5/t5-base")
```

When you run the preceding code, you see a warning like this one:

```
UserWarning: "translation" task was used, instead of
 "translation_XX_to_YY", defaulting to "translation_en_to_de"
```

This message means that the `translator` object will default to translating your text from English to German. Let's give it a try:

```
translator("How are you?")
```

You see the following result containing the translated text:

```
[{'translation_text': 'Wie sind Sie?'}]
```

The recommended way to perform translation correctly is to specify the translation task using the format - `translation_XX_to_YY`, where XX is the language to translate from and YY is the language to translate to. Here's an example of a request to translate from English to French:

```
translator = pipeline(task = 'translation_en_to_fr',
                      model = "google-t5/t5-base")
translator('Wikipedia is hosted by the Wikimedia Foundation, a non-profit
    organization that also hosts a range of other projects.')
```

Here is the result containing the translated text in French:

```
[{'translation_text': "Wikipedia est hébergée par la Wikimedia
 Foundation, un organisme sans but lucratif qui héberge également
 une série d'autres projets."}]
```

You can also translate from English to German:

```
translator = pipeline(task = 'translation_en_to_de',
                      model = "google-t5/t5-base")
translator('Wikipedia is hosted by the Wikimedia Foundation,
a non-profit organization that also hosts a range of other
projects.')
```

The text is translated to German:

```
[{'translation_text': 'Wikipedia wird von der Wikimedia Foundation
 gehostet, einer gemeinnützigen Organisation, die auch eine Reihe
 anderer Projekte beherbergt.'}]
```

What happens if you want to translate from English to Chinese? Unfortunately, the `google-t5/t5-base` model does not support translation to Chinese. In general, to know the languages supported by a model, you can check out the model's page on Hugging Face Hub or refer to its source code in GitHub. A more pragmatic way is to try different tasks and see what works. You can try using `translation_en_to_zh`, for example, to see whether it can translate from English to Chinese. (zh is the International Organization for Standardization [ISO] 639-1 language code for Chinese.)

To translate from English to Chinese, you can use the `facebook/m2m100_418M` model. But before you can use this model, you need to install the `sentencepiece` package, a widely used library for tokenization:

```
!pip install sentencepiece
```

Now you can try to translate the following English text to Chinese:

```
translator = pipeline('translation_en_to_zh',
                      model = 'facebook/m2m100_418M')

translator('Wikipedia is hosted by the Wikimedia Foundation,
a non-profit organization that also hosts a range of other
projects.')
```

The translated output looks like this:

```
[{'translation_text':
  '维基百科是维基百科基金会主办的,是一家非营利组织,还主办了许多其他项目。'}]
```

You can also use the model to translate Chinese to English. The following code snippet translates the preceding output in Chinese back to English:

```
translator = pipeline(task = 'translation_zh_to_en',
                      model = "facebook/m2m100_418M",
                      max_length = 400)
translator("维基百科是维基百科基金会主办的,是一家非营利组织,还主办了许多其他项目。")
```

Here is the output in English:

```
[{'translation_text': 'Wikipedia is hosted by the Wikipedia
Foundation, a non-profit organization and hosts many other
projects.'}]
```

3.3.5   *Zero-shot classification*

Section 3.2.4 presented an example of sentiment analysis in which the model was trained on a set of labeled examples, classifying them as positive or negative. Although this technique is useful for analyzing the sentiment in a new paragraph of text, it has limitations. Suppose that you have a description of a new gadget and want to classify it automatically in a category such as Home Appliances or Electronics. Using a model that has been pretrained on a fixed set of labels is not going to be useful in this case. This situation is where zero-shot classification comes in. There are various types of zero-shot classification, such as the following:

- Zero-shot text classification
- Zero-shot image classification
- Zero-shot audio classification

- Zero-shot video classification
- Zero-shot graph classification

Zero-shot vs. one-shot classification

In discussions of zero-shot classification, another term often comes up: one-shot classification. Whereas *zero-shot classification* is the task of classifying previously unseen classes during model training, *one-shot classification* refers to training a model to recognize classes with only one example (or a few examples) per class during training. For a one-shot classification model trained to recognize cats and dogs, for example, only one image of a cat and one image of a dog is provided during training. The aim is to teach the model to generalize from a small number of examples. This technique is useful when collecting a large number of samples would be difficult or prohibitively expensive.

For our next task, we will try zero-shot text and image classification. *Zero-shot text classification* involves classifying text in predefined categories or labels without having access to labeled examples for training. Zero-shot text classification uses models trained on Natural Language Inference (NLI) tasks.

To try zero-shot text classification, let's use the `joeddav/xlm-roberta-large-xnli` model (https://mng.bz/MwQo). Because this repository is private, you need to apply for a free Hugging Face token (type READ) at https://huggingface.co/settings/tokens. After you obtain the token, log in to Hugging Face using the `huggingface-cli` tool in Terminal or Anaconda Prompt:

```
$ huggingface-cli login

        _|    _|  _|        _|      _|_|_|    _|_|_|  _|_|_|  _|      _|    _|_|_|
      _|_|_|_|    _|_|      _|_|_|  _|_|_|_|
        _|    _|  _|    _|  _|          _|              _|    _|_|    _|  _|
        _|        _|    _|  _|          _|
      _|_|_|_|  _|      _|  _|  _|_|  _|  _|_|    _|    _|  _|  _|  _|  _|_|
      _|_|_|    _|_|_|_|  _|          _|_|_|
        _|    _|  _|      _|  _|    _|  _|    _|    _|    _|    _|_|  _|      _|
        _|        _|    _|  _|          _|
        _|    _|    _|_|      _|_|_|    _|_|_|  _|_|_|  _|      _|    _|_|_|
        _|        _|    _|    _|_|_|  _|_|_|_|

        To login, `huggingface_hub` requires a token generated
        from https://huggingface.co/settings/tokens .
Enter your token (input will not be visible): <huggingface_token>
Add token as git credential? (Y/n) n
Token is valid (permission: read).
Your token has been saved to /Users/weimenglee/.cache/huggingface/token
Login successful
```

Enter your Hugging Face token and type n when prompted. Your token will be saved to a file named token located in the `~/.cache/huggingface` folder.

Another way to log in to Hugging Face Hub is to log in programmatically in Jupyter Notebook using the notebook_login() function:

```
from huggingface_hub import notebook_login
notebook_login()
```

Figure 3.15 shows the UI that is displayed when you run the preceding code. Enter your token and click the Login button.

Copy a token from your Hugging Face tokens page and paste it below.

Immediately click login after copying your token or it might be stored in plain text in this notebook file.

Token:

☑ Add token as git credential?

Login

Pro Tip: If you don't already have one, you can create a dedicated 'notebooks' token with 'write' access, that you can then easily reuse for all notebooks.

Figure 3.15   Finding the type of task a model falls under

In addition, you need to install two packages: sentencepiece and protobuf. You can do so in Jupyter Notebook:

```
!pip install sentencepiece
!pip install protobuf
```

Let's create a pipeline object that uses the joeddav/xlm-roberta-large-xnli model:

```
from transformers import pipeline

zero_shot_classifier = pipeline("zero-shot-classification",
                                model='joeddav/xlm-roberta-large-xnli')
```

This model is fine-tuned on the XLM-RoBERTa model (pretrained on 2.5 TB of filtered CommonCrawl data in 100 languages) on a combination of NLI data in 15 languages.

You can use the model with any of the following 15 languages: English, French, Spanish, German, Greek, Bulgarian, Russian, Turkish, Arabic, Vietnamese, Thai, Chinese, Hindi, Swahili, and Urdu. Let's define two paragraphs of text and then use them to let the model predict possible labels for the text:

```
text1 = '''
"In the intricate realm of global affairs, the interplay of power,
diplomacy, and governance stands as a defining force in the
trajectory of nations. Amidst fervent debates in legislative
chambers and pivotal dialogues among world leaders, ideologies
clash and policies take shape, shaping the course of societies.
Issues such as economic disparity, environmental stewardship, and
human rights take precedence, driving conversations and shaping
public sentiment. In an age of digital interconnectedness, social
media platforms have emerged as influential channels for discourse
and activism, amplifying voices and reshaping narratives with
remarkable speed and breadth. As citizens grapple with the
complexities of contemporary governance, the pursuit of accountable
and transparent leadership remains paramount, reflecting an
enduring quest for fairness and inclusivity in societal governance."
'''
```

```
text2 = '''
In the tender tapestry of human connection, romance weaves its
delicate threads, binding hearts in a dance of passion and longing.
From the flutter of a first glance to the warmth of an intimate
embrace, love blooms in the most unexpected places, transcending
barriers of time and circumstance. In the gentle caress of a hand
and the whispered promises of affection, two souls find solace in
each other's embrace, navigating the complexities of intimacy with
tender care. As the sun sets and stars illuminate the night sky,
lovers share stolen moments of intimacy, lost in the intoxicating
rhythm of each other's presence. In the symphony of love, every
glance, every touch, speaks volumes of a shared bond that defies
explanation, leaving hearts entwined in an eternal embrace.
```

We can use the `zero_shot_classifier` object to determine whether text1 contains text related to technology, politics, business, or romance:

```
candidate_labels = ["technology", "politics", "business", "romance"]
prediction = zero_shot_classifier(text1,
                                  candidate_labels,
                                  multi_label = True)
```

The result is converted to a pandas DataFrame for easy viewing:

```
import pandas as pd
display(pd.DataFrame(prediction).drop(["sequence"], axis=1))
```

Figure 3.16 shows the result, indicating that the text is probably related to politics.

	Labels	Scores
0	politics	0.990988
1	technology	0.828358
2	romance	0.465753
3	business	0.278939

Figure 3.16   The result of the zero-shot classification

You can also pass in multiple paragraphs (enclosed within a list) to the `zero_shot_classifier` object:

```
prediction = zero_shot_classifier([text1, text2],
                                  candidate_labels,
                                  multi_label = True)
display(pd.DataFrame(prediction).drop(["sequence"], axis=1))
```

Figure 3.17 shows the results for the two paragraphs (with the most probable label at the front of the list of labels).

	Labels	Scores
0	[politics, technology, romance, business]	[0.9909884929656982, 0.8283584713935852, 0.465...
1	[romance, business, politics, technology]	[0.9982308149337769, 0.11879944801330566, 0.01...

Figure 3.17   Results of the one-shot classification for two paragraphs

How about zero-shot image classification? For this task, you can use the `openai/clip -vit-large-patch14-336` model:

```
from transformers import pipeline

classifier = pipeline("zero-shot-image-classification",
                      model = "openai/clip-vit-large-patch14-336")
```

Let's use the model to detect whether the image in figure 3.18 is an airplane, car, or train:

```
labels_for_classification = ["airplane", "car", "train"]
scores = classifier("Emirates_Airbus_A380-861_A6-EER_MUC_2015_04.jpg",
                    candidate_labels = labels_for_classification)
pd.DataFrame(scores)
```

Figure 3.19 shows that the image is probably an airplane.

Figure 3.18 An image of an airplane (Source: https://mng.bz/yN5y)

	Score	Label
0	0.997296	airplane
1	0.002082	car
2	0.000623	train

Figure 3.19 Result of the zero-shot image classification

3.3.6 Question-answering tasks

Another task that the `pipeline` object can perform is question answering (QA). I don't think you need an example of that task; if you've ever used Google to search for answers to questions, you already know what a QA task is.

Hugging Face hosts many QA models (https://mng.bz/X7zp) that you can experiment with. QA models are valuable for several reasons:

- *Efficient information retrieval*—QA models can quickly retrieve information of interest from a large collection of text.
- *Natural language understanding*—QA models can understand natural language inputs and generate context-relevant answers.

Let's use the `deepset/roberta-base-squad2` model to understand how a QA model works. This is a RoBERTa-base model (pretrained on the English language using a masked language modeling [MLM] objective), fine-tuned using the Stanford Question Answering Dataset (SQuAD) 2.0 dataset.

DEFINITION SQuAD is a reading comprehension dataset consisting of questions posed by crowd workers on a set of Wikipedia articles. The answer to every question is a segment of text, or *span*, from the corresponding reading passage, or the question might be unanswerable.

First, create an instance of the model using the `pipeline()` function:

```
from transformers import pipeline

QA_model = pipeline(task = "question-answering",
                    model = "deepset/roberta-base-squad2")
```

The result is a paragraph of text discussing the origin of the name Singapore:

```
text = '''
The English name of "Singapore" is an anglicisation of the native
Malay name for the country, Singapura (pronounced [siŋapura]),
which was in turn derived from the Sanskrit word for 'lion city'
(Sanskrit: सिंहपुर; romanised: Siṃhapura; Brahmi: 𑀲𑀺𑀲𑀼; literally
"lion city"; siṃha means 'lion', pura means 'city' or 'fortress' ).
Pulau Ujong was one of the earliest references to Singapore Island,
which corresponds to a Chinese account from the third century
referred to a place as Pú Luó Zhōng (Chinese: 蒲 羅 中), a
transcription of the Malay name for 'island at the end of a
peninsula'. Early references to the name Temasek (or Tumasik) are
found in the Nagarakretagama, a Javanese eulogy written in 1365,
and a Vietnamese source from the same time period. The name possibly
means Sea Town, being derived from the Malay tasek, meaning 'sea' or
'lake'. The Chinese traveller Wang Dayuan visited a place around 1330
named Danmaxi (Chinese: 淡馬錫; pinyin: Dànmǎxí; Wade-Giles: Tan Ma Hsi)
or Tam ma siak, depending on pronunciation; this may be a transcription
of Temasek, alternatively, it may be a combination of the Malay Tanah
meaning 'land' and Chinese xi meaning 'tin', which was traded on the
island
'''
```

You can use the model to ask a question based on the text. Perhaps you would like to know the meaning of the name Singapura:

```
question = {
        'question': 'What is the meaning of Singapura?',
        'context': text
        }

model_response = QA_model(question)
pd.DataFrame([model_response])
```

Figure 3.20 shows the answer provided by the model.

	Score	Start	End	Answer
0	0.096135	186	195	lion city

Figure 3.20   The result shows that the name Singapura means "Lion City."

Summary

- At a high level, the transformer architecture is built around two main components: the Encoder and the Decoder.
- The self-attention mechanism is a key feature of the transformer architecture . It allows the model to assign different levels of importance to words in a sequence when representing a specific word, helping it capture relationships and dependencies between words regardless of how far apart they are.
- A token is a segment of text that the model treats as a single processing unit.

- Token embeddings map tokens into numerical vectors. These vectors represent both semantic and syntactic information, enabling models to interpret the meaning and relationships of words in natural language.

- Positional encodings supply information about word positions in a sequence, allowing the model to recognize word order within a sentence.

- Softmax is a mathematical function that transforms a vector of numbers into a probability distribution, where each value's probability is proportional to its exponentiated value relative to the sum of all exponentiated values in the vector.

- The Transformers library, developed by Hugging Face, is an open source platform designed to make it easier to work with cutting-edge transformer-based models.

- The `pipeline()` function is a high-level wrapper around the Transformers library that simplifies access to a variety of pretrained models.

- Zero-shot classification refers to assigning labels to classes the model has never seen during training, whereas one-shot classification involves training a model to identify classes from one or few examples per class.

Using Hugging Face for computer vision tasks

4

This chapter covers

- Different types of Hugging Face computer vision models
- Various ways to use models for object detection
- Video content and image classification tasks
- Image segmentation tasks

Previously, you learned about Hugging Face transformers and pipelines. You also learned how to use some pretrained models for natural language processing (NLP) tasks, such as sentiment analysis and text translation. Hugging Face also provides a vast collection of pretrained models for computer vision tasks. Using all these hosted pretrained models, you can create interesting applications that detect objects in images, the age of a person, and more. In this chapter, you learn how to perform the first four tasks using Hugging Face models.

4.1 Hugging Face computer vision models

The computer vision models (https://huggingface.co/models; see figure 4.1) hosted on Hugging Face are grouped by task type:

- Object detection
- Image classification
- Image segmentation
- Video classification
- Depth estimation
- Image-to-image
- Unconditional image generation
- Zero-shot image classification

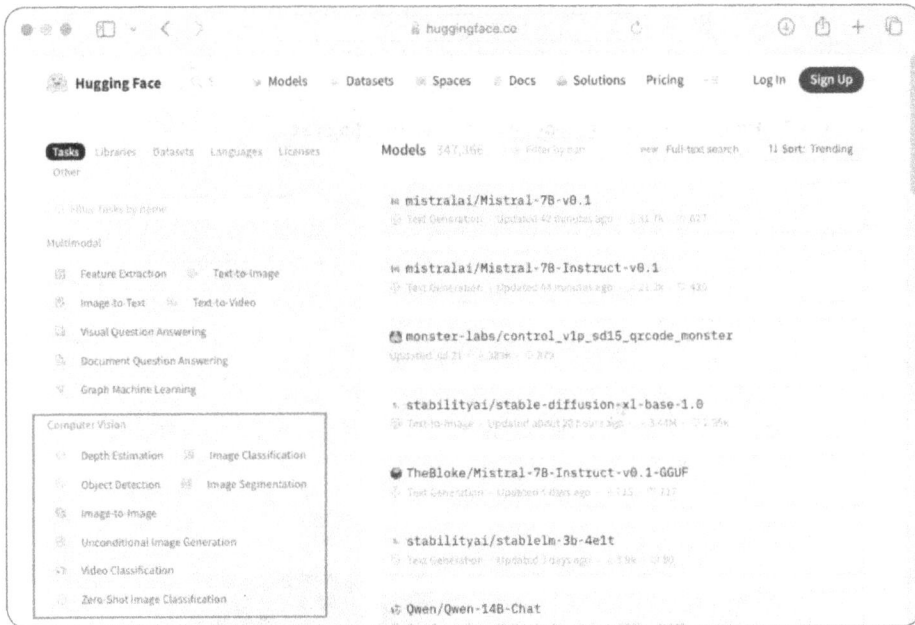

Figure 4.1   Computer vision–related models on the Hugging Face website

4.2   *Object detection*

Object detection is a computer vision technique that involves identifying and locating objects of interest within an image or video. The primary goals of object detection are to classify the objects in the image or video and determine their precise positions by drawing bounding boxes around them.

Hugging Face hosts several models that have been pretrained to detect objects in images. You can find a list of these models at https://mng.bz/QwaQ (see figure 4.2). We'll look at one specific model: `facebook/detr-resnet-50` (https://huggingface.co/facebook/detr-resnet-50; see figure 4.3).

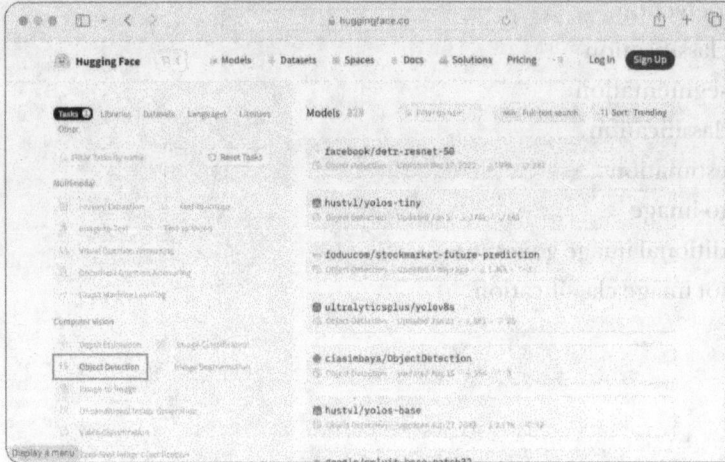

Figure 4.2   Pretrained object detection models on Hugging Face

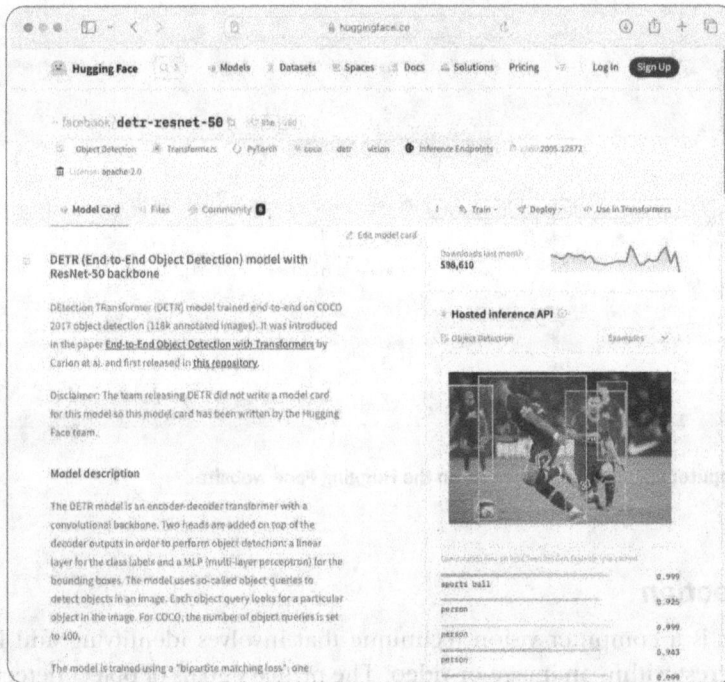

Figure 4.3   The `facebook/detr-resnet-50` model for object detection

You can test the model directly on Hugging Face using the Hosted Inference API feature (but you need to log in to Hugging Face first by creating a free account). For this test, let's use an image of an office with a few ladies (see figure 4.4).

Figure 4.4 Image by Danny Choo
(Flickr: Good Smile Company
Offices, CC BY-SA 2.0, https://
commons.wikimedia.org/w/
index.php?curid=14609862)

When you drag and drop the image to the Hosted Inference API section of the model's page on Hugging Face, you see the list of objects detected as well as their corresponding probabilities (see figure 4.5).

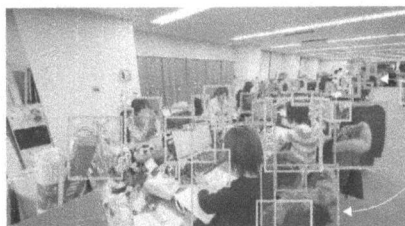

✦ Inference API

🔲 Object Detection   Examples   ∨

Bounding boxes for
detected objects

tv	0.859
person	0.918
tv	0.996
cell phone	0.558
clock	0.775
chair	0.644
chair	0.656
chair	0.666
chair	0.943
chair	0.632
tv	0.583
person	0.975
bottle	0.759

The corresponding
probabilities for the
detected objects

Figure 4.5 The
detected objects
in the image and
their corresponding
probabilities

When you use your mouse to hover over the name of a detected object, the image highlights the bounding box for the selected object.

4.2.1 Using the model directly

The model would be more useful if you could use it programmatically, of course. Hugging Face provides some useful tips for using its hosted models. To see them, click the Use this Model button on the model's page; then click the Transformers button below it (see figure 4.6).

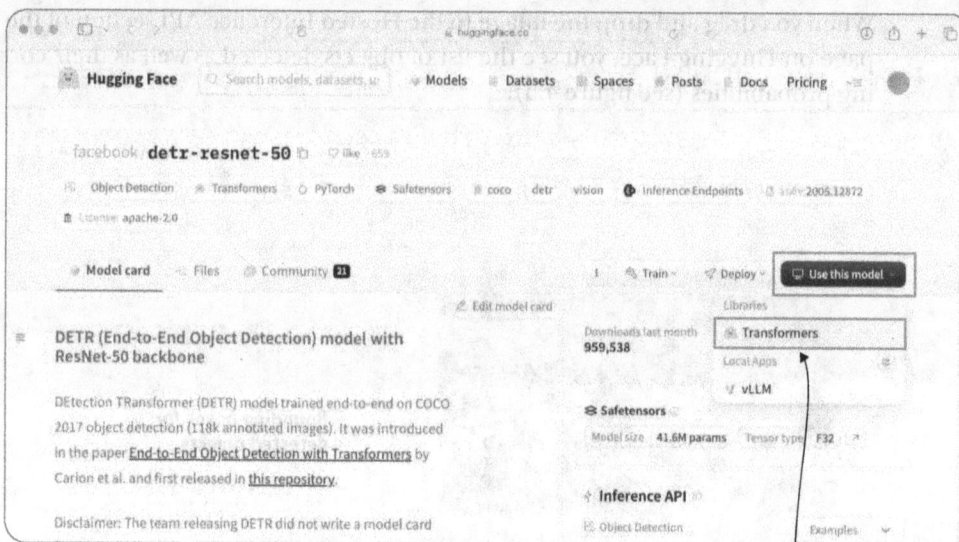

Click this button to learn how to use the model programmatically.

Figure 4.6   Hugging Face provides tips on using transformers with the models.

You have two ways to use a model programmatically (see figure 4.7):

- Use a transformer pipeline.
- Load the model directly.

Before you use a model, you need to install two packages:

- `transformers`
- `timm`

NOTE `timm`, a deep-learning library created by Ross Wightman, is a collection of state-of-the-art computer vision models, layers, utilities, optimizers, schedulers, data loaders, augmentations and training/validating scripts that can reproduce ImageNet training results. See https://timm.fast.ai for details.

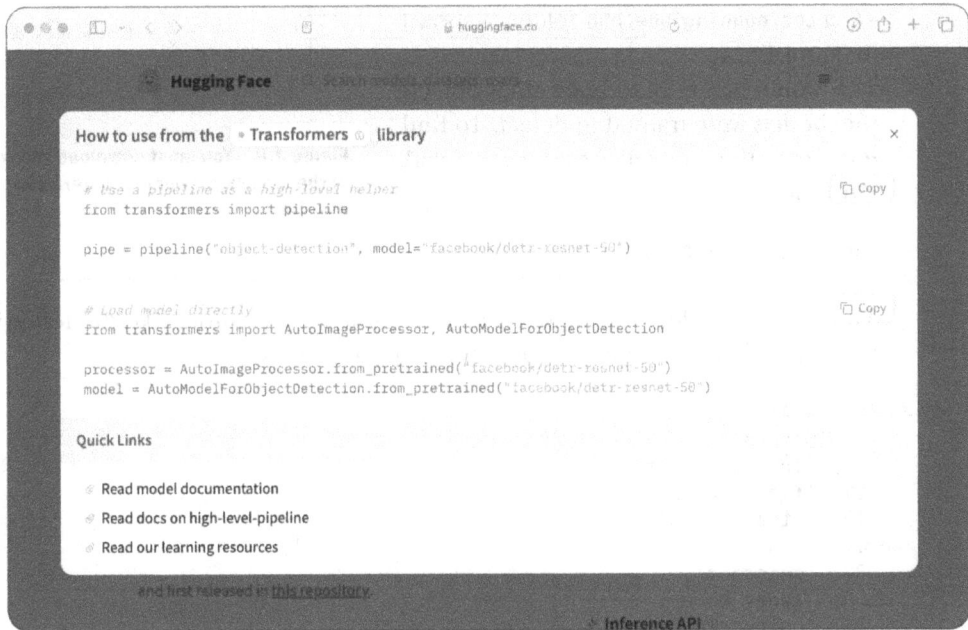

```
How to use from the  • Transformers ◎  library                          ×

# Use a pipeline as a high-level helper                            ⎘ Copy
from transformers import pipeline

pipe = pipeline("object-detection", model="facebook/detr-resnet-50")


# Load model directly                                              ⎘ Copy
from transformers import AutoImageProcessor, AutoModelForObjectDetection

processor = AutoImageProcessor.from_pretrained("facebook/detr-resnet-50")
model = AutoModelForObjectDetection.from_pretrained("facebook/detr-resnet-50")

Quick Links

  Read model documentation
  Read docs on high-level-pipeline
  Read our learning resources
```

Figure 4.7   Two ways to use the models on Hugging Face

Type the following commands in Terminal/Anaconda Prompt to install the two packages:

```
$ pip install transformers
$ pip install timm
```

Now load the model directly:

```
from transformers import DetrImageProcessor, DetrForObjectDetection

image_processor = DetrImageProcessor.from_pretrained(
                    "facebook/detr-resnet-50")
model = DetrForObjectDetection.from_pretrained(
                    "facebook/detr-resnet-50")
```

DetrImageProcessor is a class (from the transformers package) that is used to process images that will be input to the DETR (Detection Transformer) algorithm. The DetrForObjectDetection module provides access to pretrained DETR models. The pretrained model we're using in this case is facebook/detr-resnet-50.

The preceding code snippet downloads the weights of the model to the `.cache/huggingface/hub` folder in your home directory. Two folders are created in the `~/.cache/huggingface/hub` folder, as shown in figure 4.8.

It would be useful to know what objects the models were trained to detect. To find out, use the model's `config.id2label` attribute:

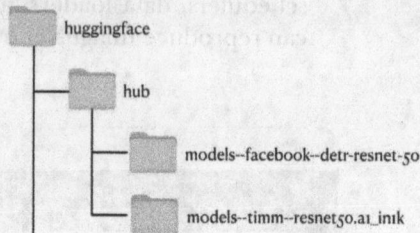

Figure 4.8 **You must download the weights of the models to your computer before you can use them.**

```
model.config.id2label
```

The model can detect a total 90 objects. You'll see a printout like the following (for brevity, showing only the first and last five object names):

```
{0: 'N/A',
 1: 'person',
 10: 'traffic light',
 11: 'fire hydrant',
 12: 'street sign',
 ...
 87: 'scissors',
 88: 'teddy bear',
 89: 'hair drier',
 9: 'boat',
 90: 'toothbrush'}
```

Before you load the image to be used for detection, displaying it for inspection would be useful. The following listing contains a helper function called `loadImage()`.

Listing 4.1   Displaying the image to use for object detection

```
from PIL import Image, ImageDraw
import requests
import torch

def loadImage(url):                                    If the image is from the web . . .
    if url.startswith('http'):
        image = Image.open(requests.get(url, stream=True).raw)
    else:
        image = Image.open(url)                         . . . the image is local.
    return image

image = loadImage('http://bit.ly/46xv3sL')
display(image)
```

TIP You may need to install the PIL (Pillow) package if you don't have it on your system. PIL is the Python Imaging Library, by Fredrik Lundh and contributors (https://pypi.org/project/Pillow). You can install the PIL package using pip install pillow.

To perform object detection, first prepare the input image:

```
inputs = image_processor(images = image,
                         return_tensors = "pt")
```

You use the `image_processor` object to preprocess the input image before feeding it into the neural network. This function returns a PyTorch tensor that looks like this:

```
{'pixel_values':
    tensor(
        [[[[-1.1075, -1.0904, -1.0733,  ..., -0.4397, -0.4226, -0.4226],
           [-1.1418, -1.1247, -1.1075,  ..., -0.4397, -0.4226, -0.4226],
           [-1.1932, -1.1932, -1.1760,  ..., -0.4397, -0.4226, -0.4054],
           ...,
           [-0.3712, -0.4054, -0.4739,  ..., -0.5253, -0.4911, -0.4739],
           [-0.2856, -0.3198, -0.3883,  ..., -0.5082, -0.5082, -0.5082],
           [-0.2342, -0.2684, -0.3369,  ..., -0.5082, -0.5253, -0.5253]],

          [[-1.0903, -1.0728, -1.0553,  ..., -0.4076, -0.3901, -0.3901],
           [-1.1253, -1.1078, -1.0903,  ..., -0.4076, -0.3901, -0.3901],
           [-1.1779, -1.1779, -1.1604,  ..., -0.4076, -0.3901, -0.3725],
           ...,
           [-0.5476, -0.5651, -0.6001,  ..., -0.5476, -0.5126, -0.4951],
           [-0.4776, -0.4951, -0.5476,  ..., -0.5301, -0.5301, -0.5301],
           [-0.4251, -0.4601, -0.5126,  ..., -0.5301, -0.5476, -0.5476]],

          [[-1.2467, -1.2293, -1.2119,  ..., -0.5670, -0.5495, -0.5495],
           [-1.2816, -1.2641, -1.2467,  ..., -0.5495, -0.5321, -0.5321],
           [-1.3339, -1.3339, -1.3164,  ..., -0.5321, -0.5147, -0.4973],
           ...,
           [-1.0898, -1.1247, -1.1596,  ..., -0.5147, -0.4798, -0.4624],
           [-1.0376, -1.0724, -1.1247,  ..., -0.4973, -0.4973, -0.4973],
           [-1.0027, -1.0376, -1.0898,  ..., -0.4973, -0.5147, -0.5147]]]]),
 'pixel_mask': tensor([[[1, 1, 1,   ..., 1, 1, 1],
        [1, 1, 1,   ..., 1, 1, 1],
        [1, 1, 1,   ..., 1, 1, 1],
        ...,
        [1, 1, 1,   ..., 1, 1, 1],
        [1, 1, 1,   ..., 1, 1, 1],
        [1, 1, 1,   ..., 1, 1, 1]]])}
```

Then the PyTorch tensor is unpacked as a keyworded argument to be used as the input for the `model` object:

```
outputs = model(**inputs)
```

The `model` object represents the pretrained network. When you pass the preprocessed PyTorch tensor to this object, it performs a forward pass through the network and returns the output of the model, which is used for object detection:

```
target_sizes = torch.tensor([image.size[::-1]])

results = image_processor.post_process_object_detection(
            outputs,
            target_sizes = target_sizes,
            threshold = 0.9)[0]
results
```

The post_process_object_detection() function takes the following arguments:

- Output of the model that was created earlier
- Target size of the image
- Threshold value for filtering out predictions (in this case, return only those with confidence greater than 90%)

The post_process_object_detection() function returns a dictionary containing the objects detected in the image:

```
{'scores': tensor([0.9180, 0.9961, 0.9426, 0.9753, 0.9622,
                   0.9882, 0.9872, 0.9372, 0.9976, 0.9987,
                   0.9174, 0.9896, 0.9997, 0.9822, 0.9970],
    grad_fn=<IndexBackward0>),
 'labels': tensor([ 1, 72, 62,  1,  1,  1, 76, 72,
                    1,  1,  1, 64,  1, 72,  1]),
 'boxes': tensor([[549.6678, 145.2847, 564.6752, 165.3628],
        [317.9362, 212.8838, 416.3602, 299.5169],
        [508.3657, 306.7018, 661.2424, 429.7788],
        [673.2169, 135.5043, 705.7635, 174.4243],
        [703.4085, 115.4306, 722.6825, 140.0320],
        [454.9466, 142.5465, 497.3364, 202.9241],
        [344.1364, 276.7948, 445.4079, 346.2501],
        [309.7489, 194.9189, 374.5581, 237.4787],
        [395.9247, 152.1988, 446.4625, 216.5487],
        [237.3090, 174.7686, 308.3646, 264.4060],
        [720.7039, 112.1340, 737.7415, 131.0087],
        [124.8140, 211.3712, 230.1096, 330.4417],
        [369.2618, 226.4449, 535.6130, 427.6963],
        [491.1188, 181.2496, 530.7089, 223.4560],
        [516.3748, 177.5891, 628.3662, 318.1332]],
        grad_fn=<IndexBackward0>)
}
```

This dictionary contains three key-value pairs:

- scores—Confidence of each detected object
- labels—Index of the detected object in model.config.id2label
- boxes—Bounding boxes of each detected object

The best way to visualize the detected objects is to draw bounding boxes around the objects, as shown in the next listing.

Listing 4.2 Drawing bounding boxes around the detected objects

```
import random

draw = ImageDraw.Draw(image)

for score, label, box in zip(results["scores"], results["labels"],
results["boxes"]):
    box = [round(i, 2) for i in box.tolist()]
    print(
        f"Detected {model.config.id2label[label.item()]} with confidence "
        f"{(score.item() * 100):.2f}% at {box}"
    )

    r = random.randint(0, 255)
    g = random.randint(0, 255)
    b = random.randint(0, 255)
    color = (r, g, b)

    draw.rectangle(box,                         Draws bounding
                   outline=color,               box around object
                   width=2)

    draw.text((box[0], box[1]-10),              Displays the object label
              model.config.id2label[label.item()],
              fill='white')

display(image)
```

You see the following output (each detected object and its associated confidence):

```
Detected person with confidence 91.80% at [549.67, 145.28, 564.68, 165.36]
Detected tv with confidence 99.61% at [317.94, 212.88, 416.36, 299.52]
Detected chair with confidence 94.26% at [508.37, 306.7, 661.24, 429.78]
Detected person with confidence 97.53% at [673.22, 135.5, 705.76, 174.42]
Detected person with confidence 96.22% at [703.41, 115.43, 722.68, 140.03]
Detected person with confidence 98.82% at [454.95, 142.55, 497.34, 202.92]
Detected keyboard with confidence 98.72% at [344.14, 276.79, 445.41,
 346.25]
Detected tv with confidence 93.72% at [309.75, 194.92, 374.56, 237.48]
Detected person with confidence 99.76% at [395.92, 152.2, 446.46, 216.55]
Detected person with confidence 99.87% at [237.31, 174.77, 308.36, 264.41]
Detected person with confidence 91.74% at [720.7, 112.13, 737.74, 131.01]
Detected potted plant with confidence 98.96% at [124.81, 211.37,
 230.11, 330.44]
Detected person with confidence 99.97% at [369.26, 226.44, 535.61, 427.7]
Detected tv with confidence 98.22% at [491.12, 181.25, 530.71, 223.46]
Detected person with confidence 99.70% at [516.37, 177.59, 628.37, 318.13]
```

At the same time, the bounding box for each object is drawn on the original image (see figure 4.9).

Figure 4.9   The bounding box for each detected object is drawn on the original image.

4.2.2   Using the transformers pipeline

The second approach to using the model is to use the Hugging Face transformers pipeline (discussed in chapter 3). Here is how you load the facebook/detr-resnet-50 model:

```
from transformers import pipeline

detection = pipeline("object-detection", model="facebook/detr-resnet-50")
```

After you create a pipeline object (detection, in this case), you can pass the image directly (in PIL format) to the pipeline and obtain the result:

```
results = detection(image)
results
```

Note that the pipeline object (detection) can also take an image URL, not just a PIL image object. That is, you can also call the pipeline object like this:

```
results = detection('http://bit.ly/46xv3sL')
```

The printed result looks like this:

```
[{'score': 0.9179903864860535,
  'label': 'person',
  'box': {'xmin': 549, 'ymin': 145, 'xmax': 564, 'ymax': 165}},
 {'score': 0.9960624575614929,
  'label': 'tv',
  'box': {'xmin': 317, 'ymin': 212, 'xmax': 416, 'ymax': 299}},
 {'score': 0.9425505995750427,
  'label': 'chair',
  'box': {'xmin': 508, 'ymin': 306, 'xmax': 661, 'ymax': 429}},
 {'score': 0.9753392338752747,
```

```
 'label': 'person',
 'box': {'xmin': 673, 'ymin': 135, 'xmax': 705, 'ymax': 174}},
{'score': 0.962176501750946,
 'label': 'person',
 'box': {'xmin': 703, 'ymin': 115, 'xmax': 722, 'ymax': 140}},
{'score': 0.9881888628005981,
 'label': 'person',
 'box': {'xmin': 454, 'ymin': 142, 'xmax': 497, 'ymax': 202}},
{'score': 0.9871691465377808,
 'label': 'keyboard',
 'box': {'xmin': 344, 'ymin': 276, 'xmax': 445, 'ymax': 346}},
{'score': 0.9371852874755859,
 'label': 'tv',
 'box': {'xmin': 309, 'ymin': 194, 'xmax': 374, 'ymax': 237}},
{'score': 0.9975801706314087,
 'label': 'person',
 'box': {'xmin': 395, 'ymin': 152, 'xmax': 446, 'ymax': 216}},
{'score': 0.9986708164215088,
 'label': 'person',
 'box': {'xmin': 237, 'ymin': 174, 'xmax': 308, 'ymax': 264}},
{'score': 0.9173707365989685,
 'label': 'person',
 'box': {'xmin': 720, 'ymin': 112, 'xmax': 737, 'ymax': 131}},
{'score': 0.9895991086959839,
 'label': 'potted plant',
 'box': {'xmin': 124, 'ymin': 211, 'xmax': 230, 'ymax': 330}},
{'score': 0.9996592998504639,
 'label': 'person',
 'box': {'xmin': 369, 'ymin': 226, 'xmax': 535, 'ymax': 427}},
{'score': 0.9821581840515137,
 'label': 'tv',
 'box': {'xmin': 491, 'ymin': 181, 'xmax': 530, 'ymax': 223}},
{'score': 0.9970135688781738,
 'label': 'person',
 'box': {'xmin': 516, 'ymin': 177, 'xmax': 628, 'ymax': 318}}]
```

This result is a list of dictionaries for each detected object. To draw the label and bounding box for each object, use the following code listing.

Listing 4.3 Visualizing detected objects with bounding boxes

```
import random

draw = ImageDraw.Draw(image)

for object in results:
    box = [i for i in object['box'].values()]
    print(
        f"Detected {object['label']} with confidence "
        f"{(object['score'] * 100):.2f}% at {box}"
    )

    r = random.randint(0, 255)
    g = random.randint(0, 255)
```

```
b = random.randint(0, 255)
color = (r, g, b)

draw.rectangle(box,                          Draws bounding
               outline=color,                box around object
               width=2)

draw.text((box[0], box[1]-10),
          object['label'],                   Displays the object label
          fill='white')
```

```
display(image)
```

The image is identical to the one shown in figure 4.9 earlier in this chapter. Using the `pipeline` object, you can also get a list of labels directly using the `model.config.id2label` attribute:

```
detection.model.config.id2label
```

4.2.3   *Binding to a webcam*

Instead of detecting objects in still images, you can go one step further and use your webcam to capture videos and detect the objects in them. Using Python to display your webcam content is easy with OpenCV. To install OpenCV, use the `pip` command:

```
$ pip install opencv-python
```

With OpenCV installed, first write the code to connect the webcam with OpenCV and then display the videos onscreen. Create a text file named `object_detection.py,` and populate it with the statements in the following listing.

Listing 4.4   Displaying webcam images in Python

```
import cv2
stream = cv2.VideoCapture(0)          ◄─── Default webcam
while(True):
    (grabbed, frame) = stream.read()  ◄─── Captures frame by frame
    cv2.imshow("Image", frame)        ◄─── Shows the frame
    key = cv2.waitKey(1) & 0xFF
    if key == ord("q"):               ◄─── Press q to break out of the loop.
        break

stream.release()
cv2.waitKey(1)
cv2.destroyAllWindows()               Cleanup
cv2.waitKey(1)
```

If your computer/laptop has multiple webcams, change the number in the `Video-Capture` class accordingly:

```
stream = cv2.VideoCapture(1)
stream = cv2.VideoCapture(2)
```

In Terminal/Anaconda Prompt, type the following command to run the program:

```
$ python object_detection.py
```

You should see a window displaying the video captured by your webcam (see figure 4.10).

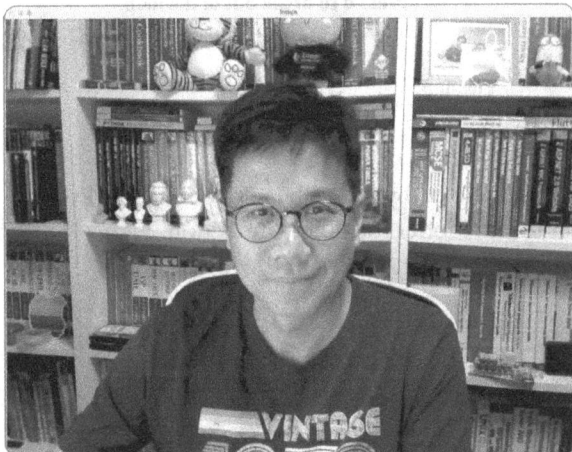

Figure 4.10 The webcam capturing the image of the author

To detect the objects in the webcam, add the following statements to the `object_detection.py` file.

Listing 4.5 Detecting objects in the webcam

```
from transformers import pipeline
from PIL import Image
import cv2
font  = cv2.FONT_HERSHEY_SIMPLEX
color = (0, 255, 255)
stroke = 2
detection = pipeline("object-detection",
                model="facebook/detr-resnet-50")
stream = cv2.VideoCapture(0)
while(True):
    (grabbed, frame) = stream.read()
    image = Image.fromarray(frame)
    results = detection(image)
    for object in results:
        box = [i for i in object['box'].values()]
```

Default webcam

Font, color, and line thickness for drawing rectangles and text

Loads the object detection model

Converts the video image from NumPy array to a PIL image

Captures frame by frame

Detects objects in the image

Gets the coordinates for the object detected

```
        cv2.rectangle(frame,
                      (box[0],box[1]),                    Draws bounding box
                      (box[2],box[3]),                    around object detected
                      color, stroke)
        cv2.putText(frame, f'({object["label"]})',
                    (box[0],box[1]-8),                    Draws the label
                    font, 1, color,                       for the object
                    stroke, cv2.LINE_AA)
    cv2.imshow("Image", frame)
    key = cv2.waitKey(1) & 0xFF                    Shows the frame
    if key == ord("q"):
        break                          Press q to break out of the loop.

stream.release()
cv2.waitKey(1)
cv2.destroyAllWindows()                    Cleanup
cv2.waitKey(1)
```

You need to convert the image captured by the webcam from a NumPy array to a PIL image before you can send it to the model for object detection. Figure 4.11 shows the webcam successfully detecting some of the objects in the image.

Figure 4.11
Detecting objects in
the webcam image

4.3   Image classification

Image classification is a computer vision task that involves *categorizing*—labeling an image in one or more predefined classes or categories. The goal of image classification is to recognize and assign the most appropriate label to a given image based on its content. Hugging Face hosts a series of models for image classification at https://mng.bz/4nQv (see figure 4.12).

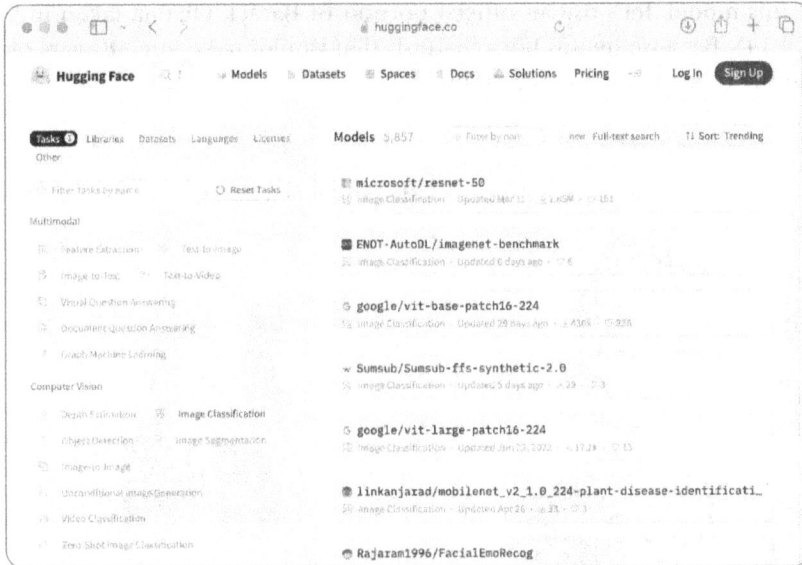

Figure 4.12 Image classification models hosted on Hugging Face

Here are two sample models for image classification and age classification:

- https://huggingface.co/ibombonato/vit-age-classifier (see figure 4.13)
- https://huggingface.co/nateraw/vit-age-classifier

Both models can predict the age of a person in an image.

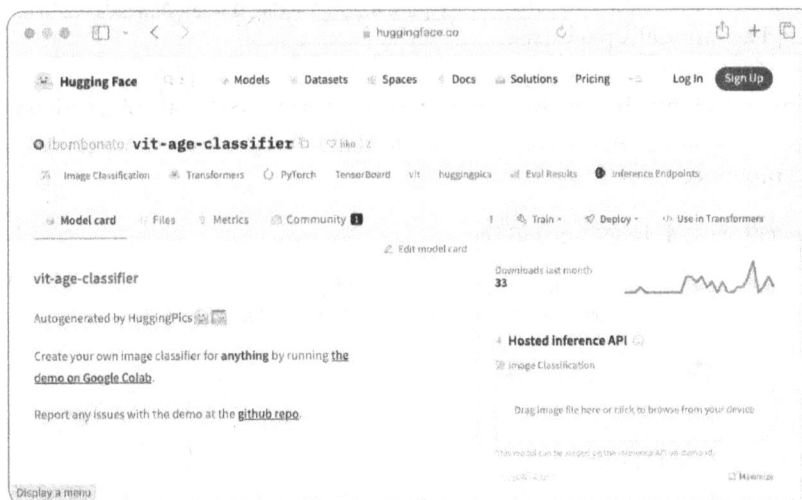

Figure 4.13 The ibombonato/vit-age-classifier model for age classification

To test this model, let's use an official portrait of Barack Obama taken in 2009 (see figure 4.14). Because he was born in 1961, that would make him 48 years old (2009–1961) at the time the picture was taken.

Figure 4.14   Official 2009 portrait of Barack Obama (Source: https://mng.bz/oZnv)

⚡ **Hosted inference API** ⓘ

🖼 Image Classification

Computation time on Intel Xeon 3rd Gen Scalable cpu: cached

40-50	0.953
30-40	0.027
50-60	0.006
20-30	0.003
70-80	0.003

</> JSON Output   ⤢ Maximize

Figure 4.15   Testing Barack Obama's photo on the model

You can test the model using the Hosted Inference API on the Hugging Face model's page (see figure 4.15). The result shows a very high probability that the person in the image is 40 to 50 years old, which is correct.

The easiest way to use the model programmatically is to use the Hugging Face transformers pipeline:

```
from transformers import pipeline

classifier = pipeline("image-classification",
                      model="ibombonato/vit-age-classifier")

classifier('https://bit.ly/3PET3TP')
classifier
```

You get this printed result:

```
[{'score': 0.9248570799827576, 'label': '40-50'},
 {'score': 0.058465585112571716, 'label': '30-40'},
```

```
{'score': 0.003433708567172289, 'label': '50-60'},
{'score': 0.0028221411630511284, 'label': '20-30'},
{'score': 0.0023411917500197887, 'label': '0-10'}]
```

4.4   Image segmentation

Another common computer vision technique is *image segmentation*, a technique that separates an image into multiple segments or regions. Each segment corresponds to a particular object of interest. Using image segmentation, you can analyze an image and extract valuable information from it. Some of its uses are

- *Medical imaging*—Identifying and segmenting tumors in MRI and CT scans
- *Object detection and recognition*—Detecting objects (discussed earlier in this chapter), as well as identifying and locating objects in an image
- *Document processing*—Segmenting text regions in scanned documents
- *Biometrics*—Identifying and localizing faces in images or video frames

Hugging Face contains several image segmentation models for you to use. One of them is SegFormer model fine-tuned on ADE20k (https://mng.bz/6406). Figure 4.16 shows the SegFormer model fine-tuned on ADE20k model on the Hugging Face website.

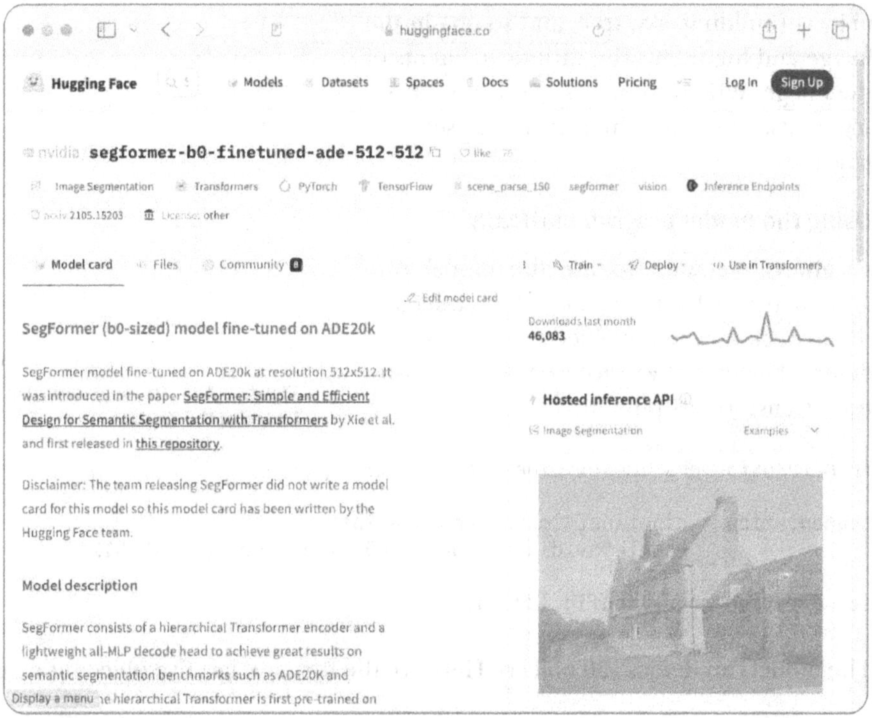

Figure 4.16 The SegFormer model fine-tuned on ADE20k model page on Hugging Face

To test the segmentation model, drag an image of the Taj Mahal (see figure 4.17) to the Hosted Inference API section of the page.

Figure 4.18 shows the result of the inferencing.

Figure 4.17   Picture of the Taj Mahal (Source: https://mng.bz/5vzD)

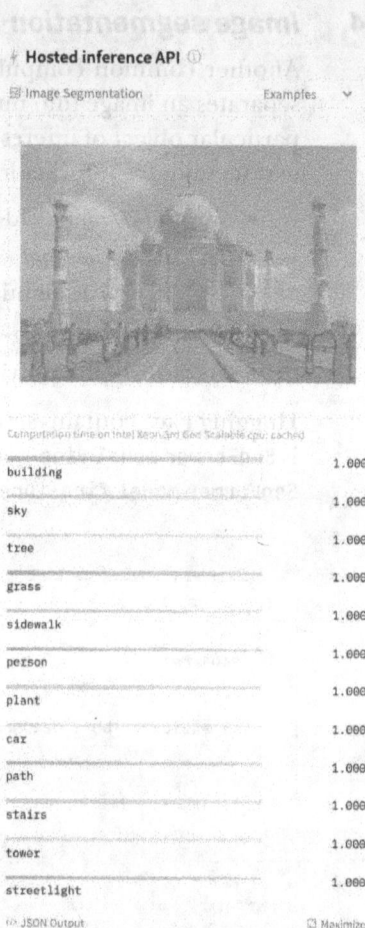

Figure 4.18   The segmentation of an image of the Taj Mahal

As you can see, the model detects the various objects (building, sky, tree, and so on) in the image and highlights the various segments of the image. When you mouse over the various segments, the image highlights the selected labels.

4.4.1   Using the model programmatically

As always, we want to use the model programmatically. First, let's load the model and then check how many objects the model can detect. The easiest way to use the model is to use a transformers pipeline:

```
from transformers import pipeline

segmentation = pipeline("image-segmentation",
          model="nvidia/segformer-b0-finetuned-ade-512-512")

segmentation.model.config.id2label
```

The model can detect 150 objects. Here are the first and last five objects it detects:

```
{0: 'wall',
 1: 'building',
```

```
2: 'sky',
3: 'floor',
4: 'tree',
...
145: 'shower',
146: 'radiator',
147: 'glass',
148: 'clock',
149: 'flag'}
```

For this example, let's use an image from Unsplash.com (see figure 4.19) to discover the various segments in the image.

To detect the various segments in the image, pass the URL of the image to the pipeline object:

```
from PIL import Image
import requests

url = 'https://bit.ly/46iDeJQ'
results = segmentation(url)
results
```

Figure 4.19   A picture of a man and an aircraft flying overhead (Source: https://unsplash.com/photos/EC_GhFRGTAY)

The output of the `results` variable is a list of dictionaries containing details on each segment detected in the picture:

```
[{'score': None,
  'label': 'wall',
  'mask': <PIL.Image.Image image mode=L size=1587x2381>},
 {'score': None,
  'label': 'building',
  'mask': <PIL.Image.Image image mode=L size=1587x2381>},
 {'score': None,
  'label': 'sky',
  'mask': <PIL.Image.Image image mode=L size=1587x2381>},
 {'score': None,
  'label': 'person',
  'mask': <PIL.Image.Image image mode=L size=1587x2381>},
 {'score': None,
  'label': 'airplane',
  'mask': <PIL.Image.Image image mode=L size=1587x2381>}]
```

In particular, the `mask` element contains the mask of the detected segment. To view each detected mask, loop through the `results` variable:

```
for result in results:
    print(result['label'])
    display(result['mask'])
```

Figure 4.20 shows the masks for person and airplane.

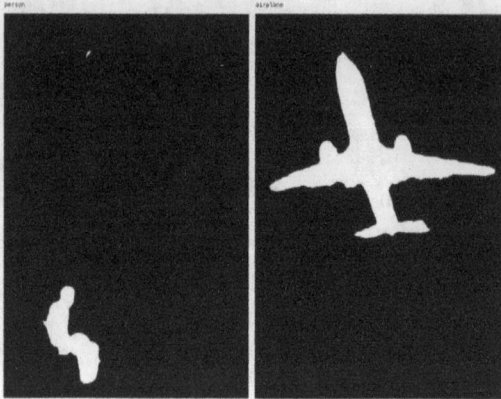

Figure 4.20   The masks for the
person and airplane segments

The white portion of the mask represents the part of the picture containing the segment of interest. You can apply the mask to the original image using the following code snippet:

```
image = Image.open(requests.get(url, stream=True).raw)

for result in results:
    base_image = image.copy()
    mask_image = result['mask']

    base_image.paste(mask_image, mask=mask_image)
    print(result['label'])
    display(base_image)
```

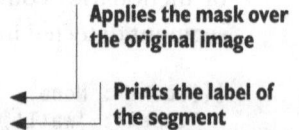

Applies the mask over the original image

Prints the label of the segment

Figure 4.21 shows the person and airplane masks applied over the original image.

Figure 4.21   The original image
with the person and airplane
masks applied

When you apply the mask over the image, notice that the segment of interest is in white. It would be more natural to invert this display—that is, show everything except the segment of interest in white. To do this, you can invert the mask using the invert() function from the ImageOps class of the PIL package. The following changes invert the mask and apply it over the original image:

```
from PIL import ImageOps

for result in results:
    base_image = image.copy()
    mask_image = result['mask']

    mask_image = ImageOps.invert(mask_image)      ← Inverts the mask
    base_image.paste(mask_image, mask=mask_image) ← Applies the mask over
    print(result['label'])                           the original image
    display(base_image)
```

Inverts the mask

Applies the mask over the original image

Prints the label of the segment

Figure 4.22 shows the inverted masks for the person and airplane in the original image.

Figure 4.22 The inverted masks applied to the original image

4.4.2 Binding to Gradio

Instead of manually specifying the URL of the image that we want to use on the model, it's more convenient to create a UI that enables the user to try the segmentation model. In this section, we'll use Gradio to create a UI and then bind it to the function that performs the segmentation. To install the gradio package, use the following command:

```
$ pip install gradio
```

> **What is Gradio?**
>
> Gradio is an open source Python library that simplifies creating user interfaces for machine learning models and other applications. It is designed to make it easy for developers to build interactive web interfaces for their machine learning models without extensive knowledge of web development.

First, let's create a function called `segmentation` that uses the `SegFormer` model fine-tuned on `ADE20k` model for segmentation, as shown in the following listing.

Listing 4.6   Creating a function that uses a model for segmentation

```
from transformers import SegformerForSemanticSegmentation      Creates a
                                                                segmentation model
model = pipeline("image-segmentation",
                 model="nvidia/segformer-b0-finetuned-ade-512-512")

def segmentation(image, label):                    Converts image from NumPy
    image = Image.fromarray(image)                 array to PIL format
    results = model(image)
    for result in results:                         Uses the model for inferencing
        if result['label'] == label:
            base_image = image.copy()
            mask_image = result['mask']
            mask_image = ImageOps.invert(mask_image)       Inverts the mask
            base_image.paste(mask_image, mask=mask_image)
            return(base_image)
                                                   Applies the mask over
                                                   the original image
```

One important point to note here is that when the user passes in an image through the Gradio UI, the image is sent to the `segmentation()` function as a NumPy array. Hence, it is essential to convert it to a Pillow (PIL) image using the `Image.fromarray()` function. When the model returns the result, you iterate through the result and look for the label specified by the user (in the `label` parameter). Then the function inverts the corresponding mask, applies it to the image, and returns it to the caller. To bind the `segmentation()` function to Gradio, use the `Interface()` class, like this:

```
import gradio as gr

image_input = gr.Image(label = "Image to segmentize")

label = gr.Textbox(label = "Label to look for", placeholder = "Label")

image_output = gr.Image(label = "Image with the mask applied")

gr.Interface(segmentation,
             [image_input, label],
             image_output).launch()
```

Figure 4.23 shows what Gradio will look like.

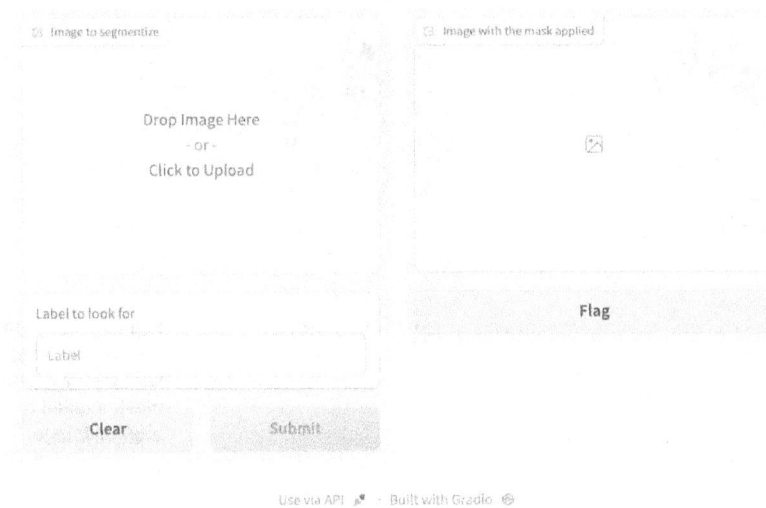

Figure 4.23   Gradio expects an image and text for input.

Drag and drop an image containing a person to Gradio. Figure 4.24 shows an image of the author. Also type the label you want to search for. For this example, you want to search for `person` in the image, so type `person` as the label. The click the Submit button.

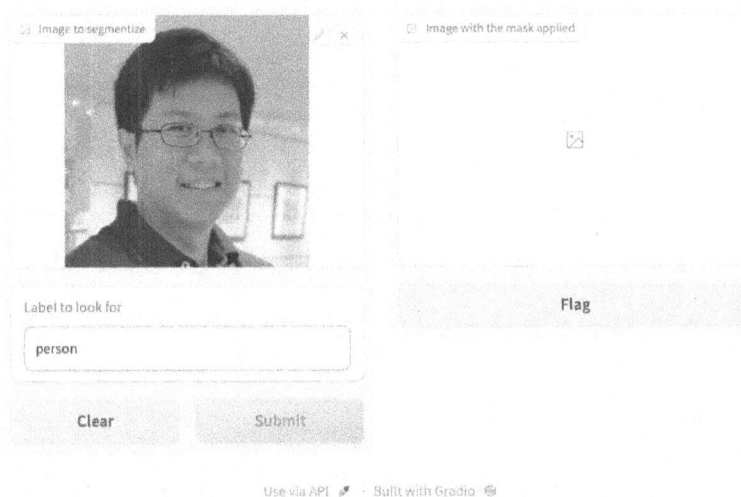

Figure 4.24   The Gradio UI with the image populated and the label entered

The function shows the result on the right side of the Gradio display (see figure 4.25).

Figure 4.25   Gradio returns the image with the inverted mask applied to the original image.

4.5   Video classification

So far, all our examples have revolved around detecting objects in still images and webcam inputs. It would also be fun to classify objects in video streams. Let's investigate how to do that. Hugging Face Hub's Models page (https://mng.bz/mZ6M) has a Video Classification category, shown in figure 4.26.

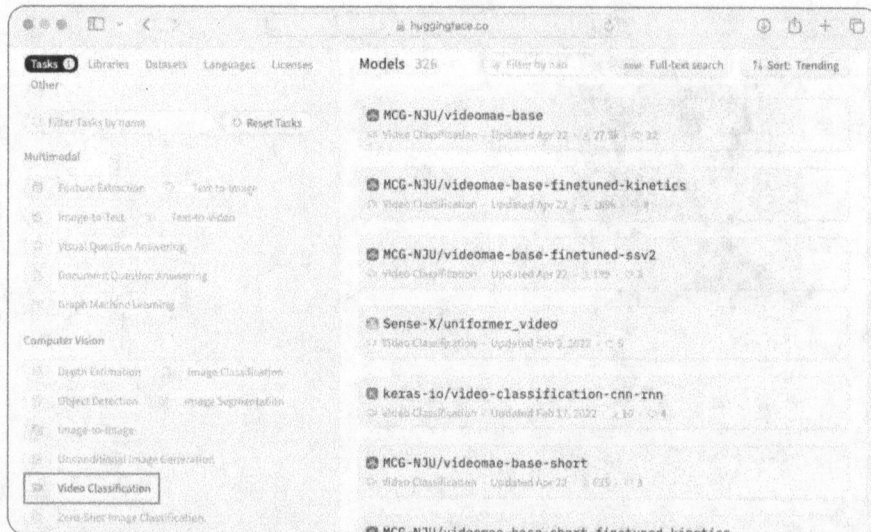

Figure 4.26   The video classification Models page on Hugging Face

For this example, we'll use the VideoMae model (MCG-NJU/videomae-base-short
-finetuned-kinetics). VideoMAE (which stands for *Video Masked Autoencoders*) performs
masked video modeling for video pretraining. You can find details on this model at
https://mng.bz/7QKg (see figure 4.27).

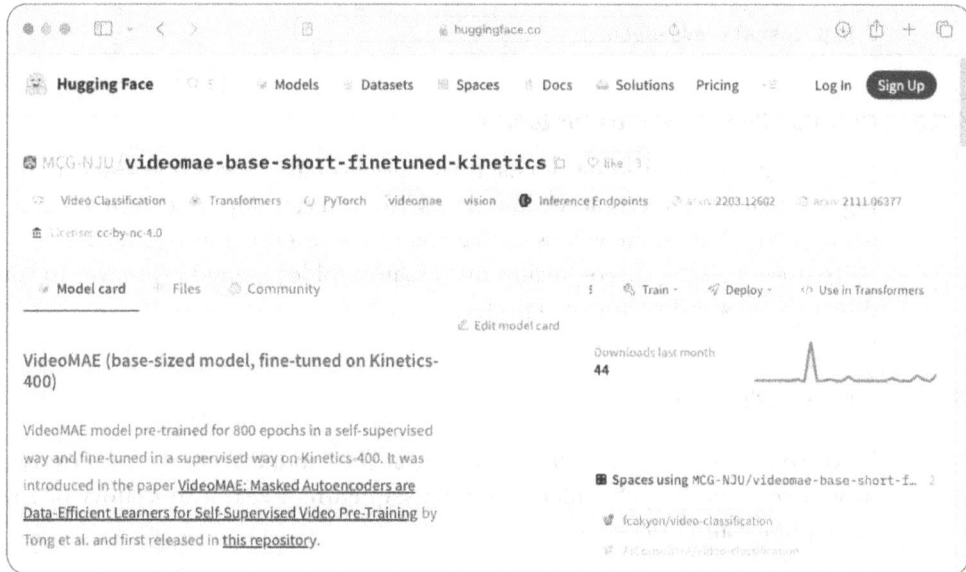

Figure 4.27 The page for the MCG-NJU/videomae-base-short-finetuned-kinetics model

4.5.1 Installing the prerequisites

To use the MCG-NJU/videomae-base-short-finetuned-kinetics model, you need to
install the decord Python package.

What is decord?

decord is a Python package that provides efficient video decoding capabilities. It is
designed to handle video data and extract frames from videos with a focus on performance and speed. This package is particularly useful for applications that require
video analysis, computer vision, machine learning, and deep learning, where fast
video-frame extraction is crucial.

Windows and Intel Mac users can use this command to install decord:

```
$ pip install decord
```

When this book was published, an ARM version of the decord package didn't exist, so Apple silicon Mac users won't be able to install the decord library directly by using the preceding pip command. Fortunately, the folks at EVA (https://github.com/georgia -tech-db/evadb) created a fork of the decord library at https://pypi.org/project/eva -decord that enables Apple silicon Mac users to install the library using the following command:

```
$ pip install eva-decord
```

4.5.2   Downloading the videos for testing

For testing, you need some videos. If you already have videos that you can use for testing and that are directly accessible via a URL, you can skip to section 4.5.3. If not, you need to download some videos so that you can access them using an URL.

To download the videos locally, first create a folder named webserver in your home directory (or any directory you prefer):

```
$ cd ~
$ mkdir webserver
```

Next, you need some sample videos to test the model. You can use Pexels (https:// www.pexels.com/search/videos/sample; see figure 4.28), a repository of royalty-free stock photos and videos.

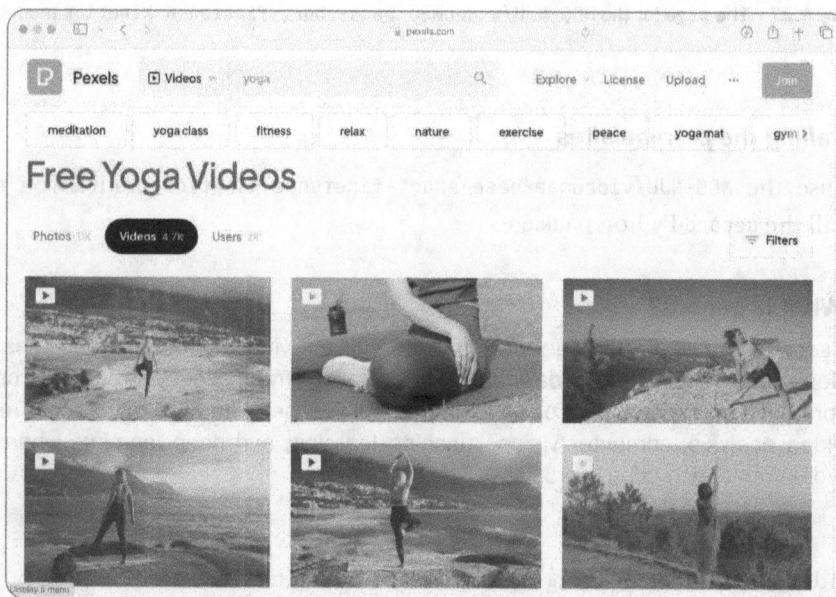

Figure 4.28   Pexels is a platform that offers free stock photos and videos for personal and commercial use.

For testing, download a video of person spray-painting a wall (https://mng.bz/qR4E; see figure 4.29). When the download is done, move it to the `webserver` folder that you created. The name of the video in this example is `pexels-pat-whelen-5621707` `(1080p)`.

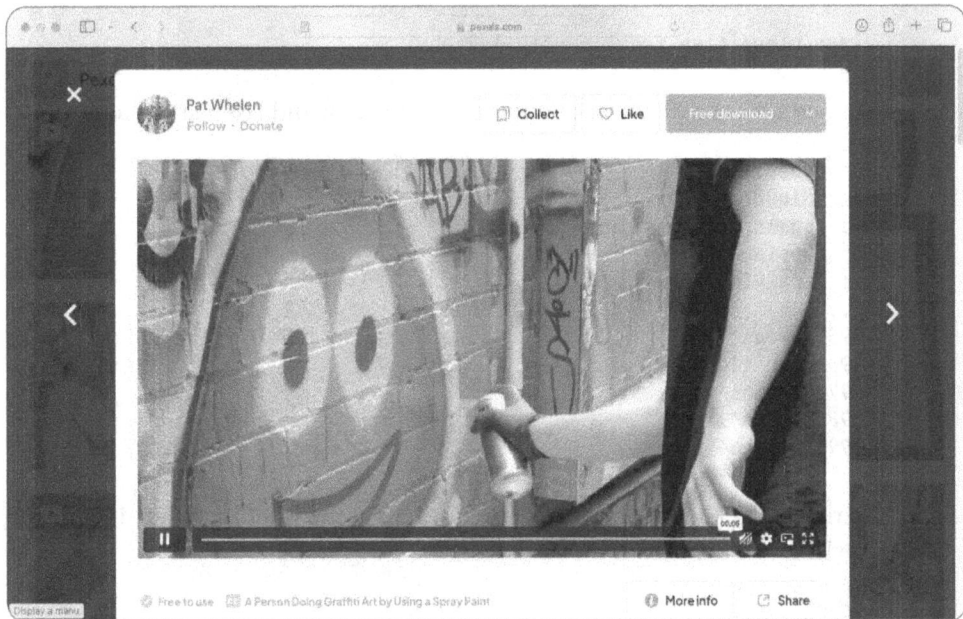

Figure 4.29 A video of a person spray-painting a wall

When the video is in the `webserver` folder, use the `python -m http.server` command to start a simple HTTP server from the local filesystem:

```
$ cd ~/webserver
$ python -m http.server
```

If the HTTP web server starts correctly, you see the following printout, indicating that the web server is listening at port 8000:

```
Serving HTTP on :: port 8000 (http://[::]:8000/) ...
```

4.5.3   *Using the transformers pipeline object*

With the `decord` library installed and the video ready, you can write the code to use the model with the transformers pipeline:

```
from transformers import pipeline

video_classifier = pipeline("video-classification",
                    model="MCG-NJU/videomae-base-short-finetuned-kinetics")
```

As usual, the first thing you want to know is the type of object the model is capable of recognizing:

```
video_classifier.model.config.id2label
```

You see a list of 400 objects. Following are the first and last five of them:

```
{0: 'abseiling',
 1: 'air drumming',
 2: 'answering questions',
 3: 'applauding',
 4: 'applying cream',
 ...
 395: 'wrestling',
 396: 'writing',
 397: 'yawning',
 398: 'yoga',
 399: 'zumba'}
```

To detect the kind of objects that are present in the video, call the `pipeline` object with the URL of the video:

```
video_classifier(
    'http://localhost:8000/pexels-pat-whelen-5621707 (1080p).mp4')
```

The result looks like this:

```
[{'score': 0.6775813102722168, 'label': 'spray painting'},
 {'score': 0.05606633797287941, 'label': 'throwing axe'},
 {'score': 0.032091718167066574, 'label': 'blasting sand'},
 {'score': 0.01113071758300066, 'label': 'spraying'},
 {'score': 0.007230783812701702, 'label': 'plastering'}]
```

As you can see, the model accurately detected that the main activity in the video is spray painting.

Summary

- Object detection is a computer vision technique that involves identifying and locating objects of interest within an image or video.
- You have two ways to use a model from Hugging Face programmatically:
  - Through a transformer pipeline.
  - Load the model directly.

- `DetrImageProcessor` is a class (from the `transformers` package) that is used for processing images to be used as input to the DETR algorithm.
- The `DetrForObjectDetection` module provides access to pretrained DETR models.
- Image classification is a computer vision task that involves categorizing an image in one or more predefined classes or categories
- Image segmentation involves separating an image into multiple segments.

5
Exploring, tokenizing, and visualizing Hugging Face datasets

This chapter covers

- What Hugging Face datasets are
- How to download datasets programmatically
- How to apply tokenization to datasets
- How to perform data visualization on datasets

Hugging Face is an AI platform that develops, trains, and deploys cutting-edge open-source machine learning models. Alongside providing a hub for these trained models, Hugging Face also hosts a wide array of datasets (available at https://huggingface.co/datasets), which you can use for your own projects.

This chapter guides you through accessing datasets from Hugging Face and shows you how to download them programmatically to your local machine. You will gain a deeper understanding of tokenization, including how to tokenize datasets and prepare your data for fine-tuning (covered in chapter 6). Finally, you will explore how to visualize various datasets with Hugging Face.

5.1 What are Hugging Face datasets?

Datasets are essential for training and evaluating machine learning models, enabling data analysis, and extracting valuable insights. They provide the examples models need to recognize patterns, make predictions, and assess performance. Beyond model development, datasets play a crucial role in testing hypotheses, identifying trends, and solving real-world problems in fields such as recommendation systems, predictive maintenance, and fraud detection. Finding the right dataset, however, can be a challenge. Fortunately, Hugging Face is a powerful platform that streamlines access to a wide range of datasets, helping developers and researchers quickly build, refine, and deploy data-driven solutions across diverse domains.

Hugging Face Datasets is an open source library designed for accessing and processing large datasets commonly used in machine learning and data science, particularly for natural language processing (NLP), computer vision, and other AI tasks. The library provides a simple and efficient way to load, process, and manage datasets (such as dataset splitting and uploading), offering ready-to-use datasets along with tools to manipulate, transform, and share your own data. It supports high-performance data handling, works with frameworks like PyTorch and TensorFlow, and integrates seamlessly with other Hugging Face tools.

To access Hugging Face Datasets, open a web browser and go to https://huggingface .co/datasets. Figure 5.1 shows the Hugging Face Datasets web page.

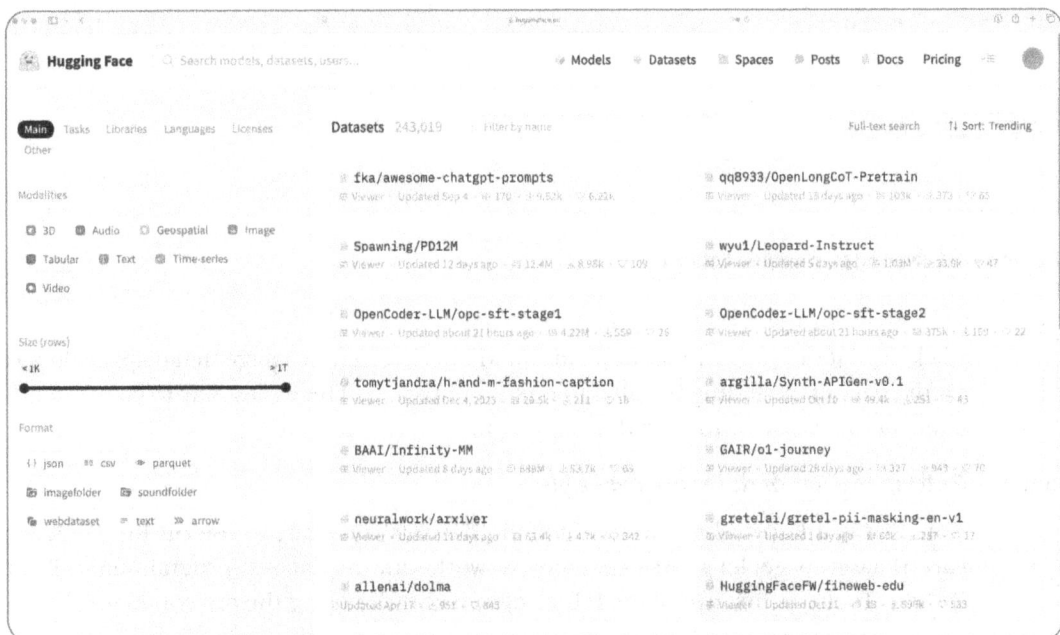

Figure 5.1   The Hugging Face Datasets website contains datasets of different modalities (types).

A quick way to find the dataset you want to use is to type its name in the filter box (see figure 5.2). Filtered results appear as you type.

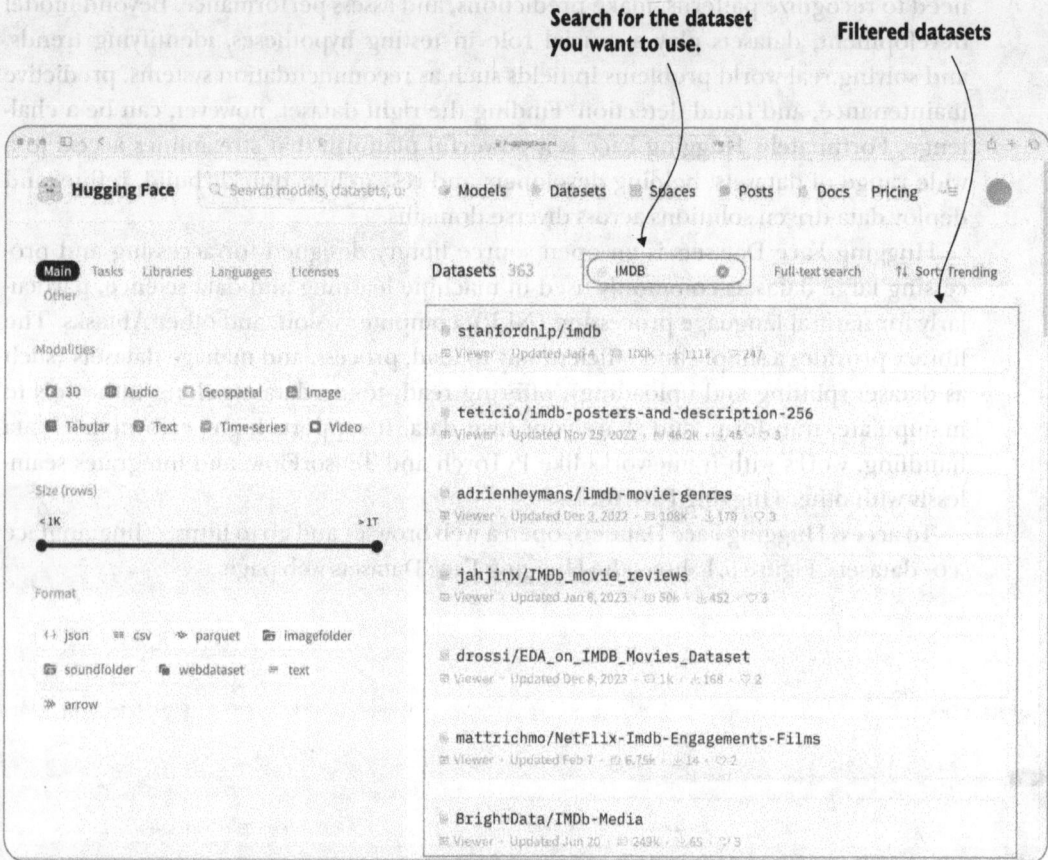

Figure 5.2   Searching for a desired dataset

Click the dataset you want to use, and you will be directed to a page that displays details on the dataset, including its full name (see figure 5.3). The easiest way to copy the full name of the dataset is to click the Copy icon.

5.1.1 Getting the list of datasets available

Now that you know where to look for the datasets you want to use on the Hugging Face Datasets page, let's investigate how to work with the datasets programmatically in Python. To do so, first install the following two libraries using the `pip` command:

```
!pip install huggingface_hub
!pip install datasets
```

Full name of dataset · Click icon to copy the dataset name to the clipboard.

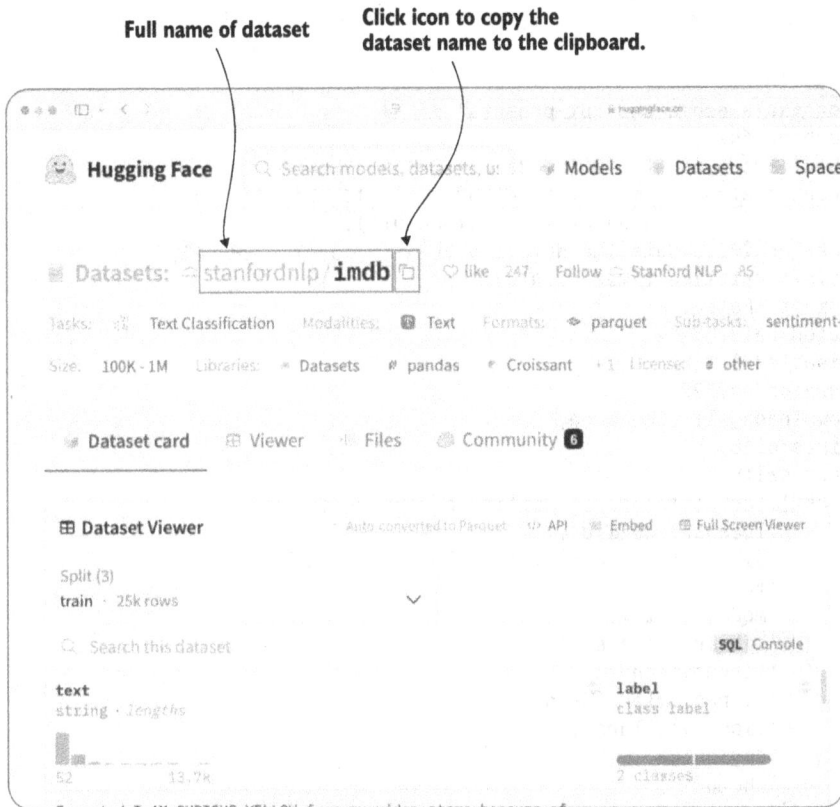

Figure 5.3 Locating the full name of the dataset

Next, use the `list_datasets()` function to return a generator that points to a list of available datasets:

```
from huggingface_hub import list_datasets

datasets = list_datasets()          ◀─── Gets the generator of datasets
```

You can't use an index to access the datasets directly. Also, you shouldn't use the `list()` function to convert the list of datasets; doing so would likely cause memory overflow because the list of datasets is large. Instead, use the `next()` function to iterate through the list of datasets:

```
dataset = next(datasets)            ◀─── Gets the next dataset
print(dataset)
```

The dataset is encapsulated in the `DatasetInfo` object, with various fields containing the details of the dataset, as shown in the following listing.

Listing 5.1   The content of the `DatasetInfo` object

```
DatasetInfo(
  id='fka/awesome-chatgpt-prompts',
  author='fka',
  sha='459a66186f8f83020117b8acc5ff5af69fc95b45',
  created_at=datetime.datetime(2022, 12, 13, 23, 47, 45,
             tzinfo=datetime.timezone.utc),
  last_modified=datetime.datetime(2024, 9, 3, 21, 28, 41,
  tzinfo=datetime.timezone.utc),
  private=False,
  gated=False,
  disabled=False,
  downloads=9522,
  downloads_all_time=None,
  likes=6218,
  paperswithcode_id=None,
  tags=['task_categories:question-answering',
        'license:cc0-1.0',
        'size_categories:n<1K',
        'format:csv',
        'modality:text',
        'library:datasets',
        'library:pandas',
        'library:mlcroissant',
        'library:polars',
        'region:us',
        'ChatGPT'],
  trending_score=90,
  card_data=None,
  siblings=None
)
```

To print the first five datasets, use the following code snippet, which prints the ID of each dataset:

```
for i in range(5):
    dataset = next(datasets)
    print(dataset.id)          ◀──── Prints the ID of the dataset
```

You should see something like this:

```
fka/awesome-chatgpt-prompts
qq8933/OpenLongCoT-Pretrain
Spawning/PD12M
wyu1/Leopard-Instruct
OpenCoder-LLM/opc-sft-stage1
```

The ID of each dataset is what you saw in figure 5.3 earlier in this chapter: the full name of the dataset.

5.1.2 Validating the availability of a dataset

Before you download a dataset from Hugging Face, it is useful to verify that the dataset is available for download. You can use the following code snippet to verify availability.

Listing 5.2 Verifying a dataset's availability

```
import requests

token = 'Hugging_Face_Token'          ← Replace with your own Hugging Face token.
dataset_id = 'fka/awesome-chatgpt-prompts'    ← Replace with the name of the dataset you want to verify.

headers = {"Authorization": f"Bearer {token}"}
API_URL =
  f"https://datasets-server.huggingface.co/is-valid?dataset={dataset_id}"

def query():
    response = requests.get(API_URL, headers=headers)
    return response.json()

data = query()
data
```

For this example, you need to apply for a Hugging Face access token (https://huggingface.co/settings/tokens). The access token will allow you to authenticate and access models, datasets, and other resources on the Hugging Face platform. The preceding code snippet returns the following result for the fka/awesome-chatgpt-prompts dataset:

```
{'preview': True,
 'viewer': True,
 'search': True,
 'filter': True,
 'statistics': True}
```

Alternatively, you can use the curl command in Terminal (or Anaconda Prompt) to validate whether a dataset is available:

```
$ curl -X GET "https://datasets-server.huggingface.co/is-valid?dataset=fka/awesome-chatgpt-prompts"
```

Figure 5.4 shows the syntax for using curl to check the validity of a dataset.

```
curl -X GET "https://datasets-server.huggingface.co/is-valid?dataset=<dataset_name>"
```

Figure 5.4 Syntax for checking the validity of a dataset

You can replace the `fka/awesome-chatgpt-prompts` dataset name with the full name of the dataset you want to use. If the dataset is available, you see the following output (formatted for clarity):

```
{
  "preview":true,
  "viewer":true,
  "search":true,
  "filter":true,
  "statistics":true
}
```

5.1.3   Downloading a dataset

After you verify that a dataset is available for download, you can use the `load_dataset()` function to download it. The following code snippet downloads the `stanfordnlp/imdb` dataset:

```
from datasets import load_dataset

dataset_id = 'stanfordnlp/imdb'

dataset = load_dataset(dataset_id)      ◀──  Loads the IMDb dataset
print(dataset)                          ◀──  View the dataset structure.
```

NOTE   The `IMDb` dataset is a popular dataset used for NLP tasks, specifically for sentiment analysis. It consists of positive and negative movie reviews from the Internet Movie Database (IMDb).

You should see the following output:

```
DatasetDict({
    train: Dataset({
        features: ['text', 'label'],
        num_rows: 25000
    })
    test: Dataset({
        features: ['text', 'label'],
        num_rows: 25000
    })
    unsupervised: Dataset({
        features: ['text', 'label'],
        num_rows: 50000
    })
})
```

The result is represented as a `DatasetDict` object separated into the following subsets (known as *splits*):

- `train`—The training dataset, used to train models

- test—The testing dataset, used to evaluate the model's performance
- unsupervised—Subset that often contains unlabeled data, which can be used for unsupervised or semisupervised learning tasks

The num_rows attribute represents the number of rows in each split of the data. You can also view the different splits of the datasets using the curl command:

```
$ curl -X GET "https://datasets-server.huggingface.co/
splits?dataset=stanfordnlp/imdb"
```

Figure 5.5 shows the syntax for using curl to check the splits of a dataset.

```
curl -X GET "https://datasets-server.huggingface.co/splits?dataset=<dataset_name>"
```

Figure 5.5   Syntax for checking the splits of a dataset

You should see the output shown in the following listing.

Listing 5.3   Output containing the splits of the dataset

```
{
  "splits":[
    {
      "dataset":"stanfordnlp/imdb",
      "config":"plain_text",
      "split":"train"
    },
    {
      "dataset":"stanfordnlp/imdb",
      "config":"plain_text",
      "split":"test"
    },
    {
      "dataset":"stanfordnlp/imdb",
      "config":"plain_text",
      "split":"unsupervised"
    }
  ],
  "pending":[],
  "failed":[]
}
```

Continuing with the Python code snippet, let's view the first row of the train subset:

```
dataset['train'][0]
```

You should see the following output (formatted for clarity).

Listing 5.4   The content of the first row of the IMDb dataset

```
{
'text': 'I rented I AM CURIOUS-YELLOW from my video store
because of all the controversy that surrounded it when it
was first released in 1967. I also heard that at first it
was seized by U.S. customs if it ever tried to enter this
country, therefore being a fan of films considered
"controversial" I really had to see this for myself.<br />
<br />The plot is centered around a young Swedish drama
student named Lena who wants to learn everything she can
about life. In particular she wants to focus her
attentions to making some sort of documentary on what the
average Swede thought about certain political issues such
as the Vietnam War and race issues in the United States.
In between asking politicians and ordinary denizens of
Stockholm about their opinions on politics, she has sex
with her drama teacher, classmates, and married men.
<br /><br />What kills me about I AM CURIOUS-YELLOW is
that 40 years ago, this was considered pornographic.
Really, the sex and nudity scenes are few and far between,
even then it\'s not shot like some cheaply made porno.
While my countrymen mind find it shocking, in reality sex
and nudity are a major staple in Swedish cinema. Even
Ingmar Bergman, arguably their answer to good old boy
John Ford, had sex scenes in his films.<br /><br />I do
commend the filmmakers for the fact that any sex shown in
the film is shown for artistic purposes rather than just
to shock people and make money to be shown in pornographic
theaters in America. I AM CURIOUS-YELLOW is a good film
for anyone wanting to study the meat and potatoes (no pun
intended) of Swedish cinema. But really, this film
doesn\'t have much of a plot.',
'label': 0
}
```

Where is the dataset stored locally?

When you download a dataset from Hugging Face, it is stored in the ~/.cache/ huggingface/datasets folder on a Mac or in C:\users\<username>\.cache\ huggingface\datasets on a Windows machine. Each dataset is stored in its own folder. The stanfordnlp/imdb dataset, for example, is stored in its own set of folders and subfolders, as shown in the following figure.

Because each dataset has its own folder structure, the best way to understand the structure of a particular dataset is to explore the files and folders created within its specific cache directory. Each dataset may have a different organizational layout depending on the nature of the data, the splits provided (train, validation, and/or test), and how Hugging Face preprocessed the database.

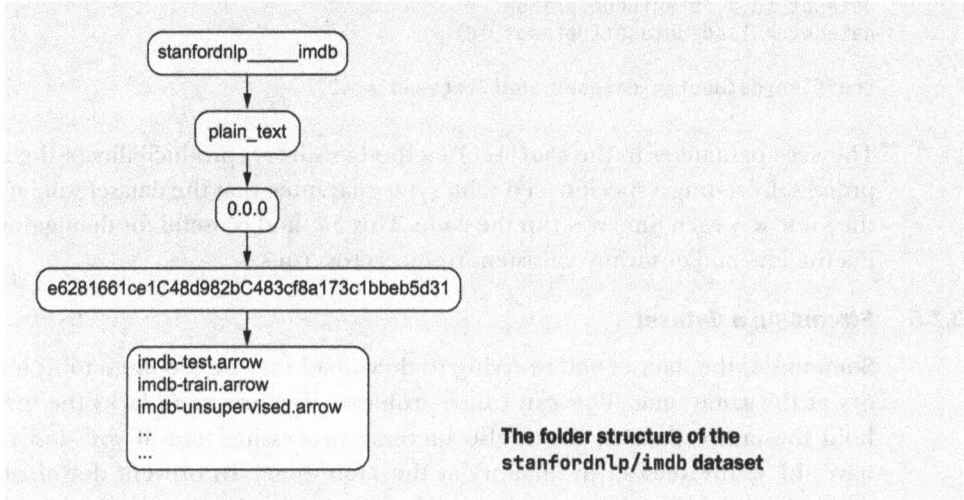

The folder structure of the stanfordnlp/imdb dataset

If you want to download only a particular split of the dataset, you can specify the split name in the `split` parameter, like this:

```
dataset = load_dataset(dataset_id,
                       split='train')
print(dataset)
```

This statement downloads only the `train` split of the dataset. This approach is useful if you plan to work with a specific split; it saves both time and disk space because you don't have to download the entire dataset. The downloaded dataset looks like this:

```
Dataset({
    features: ['text', 'label'],
    num_rows: 25000
})
```

To access the first row, use this code:

```
dataset[0]
```

You don't need to specify the `train` key, as you did earlier:

```
dataset['train'][0]
```

5.1.4 Shuffling a dataset

If you want to shuffle the dataset you've downloaded, you can use the `shuffle()` method to randomize the order of the data:

```
dataset_id = 'stanfordnlp/imdb'
dataset = load_dataset(dataset_id)

shuffled_dataset = dataset.shuffle(seed = 42)
```

The seed parameter in the `shuffle()` method ensures reproducibility of the shuffling process. By setting a specific seed value, you guarantee that the dataset will be shuffled the same way each time you run the code. This method is useful for debugging, experimentation, and ensuring consistent results across runs.

5.1.5   *Streaming a dataset*

Sometimes, the dataset you're trying to download may be too large to fit into memory at the same time. This can cause problems if your system lacks the memory to hold the entire dataset; it can also increase processing time if you don't need to have the entire dataset in memory at the same time. To prevent downloading the entire dataset in one shot, you can set the `streaming` parameter to `True` in the `load_dataset()` function:

```
from datasets import load_dataset

dataset_id = 'stanfordnlp/imdb'
dataset = load_dataset(dataset_id,
                       streaming = True)    ◄──┘ Streams the IMDb dataset
print(dataset)
```

Now the `load_dataset()` function returns an `IterableDatasetDict` object instead of downloading the entire dataset, as shown in the following listing.

Listing 5.5   The content of the `IterableDatasetDict` object

```
IterableDatasetDict({
    train: IterableDataset({
        features: ['text', 'label'],
        num_shards: 1
    })
    test: IterableDataset({
        features: ['text', 'label'],
        num_shards: 1
    })
    unsupervised: IterableDataset({
        features: ['text', 'label'],
        num_shards: 1
    })
})
```

To fetch the dataset, you need to enumerate through it and retrieve rows one at a time. The following code snippet shows how to obtain and print the first five rows in the training dataset:

```
for i, example in enumerate(dataset["train"]):
    if i < 5:
        print(example)
    else:
        break
```

Streams through the data and prints the first few examples

Shows the first five examples

By fetching data one row at a time, you can efficiently process large datasets without loading them entirely into memory.

5.1.6 Getting the Parquet files of a dataset

Although you can use the `load_dataset()` function to download the dataset to your computer, at times you may prefer to download it directly in Parquet format. *Parquet* is a columnar storage file format designed for efficient data storage and processing, particularly in big data environments. It is optimized for querying and analyzing large datasets, offering significant compression and performance improvements over row-based formats such as CSV.

Parquet is schema-based, meaning that it stores both the data and its schema, enabling better data organization and faster access. Its columnar structure allows for efficient read and write operations, especially when only a subset of columns is required, and it supports complex nested data structures. Parquet is widely used in data processing frameworks such as the Apache frameworks Spark, Hive, and Hadoop due to its compatibility with various big data tools and systems.

The Hugging Face Datasets service automatically converts all public datasets to Parquet format, which offers significant performance improvements, especially for large datasets. As an example, use the following `curl` command to get the Parquet files associated with the `stanfordnlp/imdb` dataset:

```
$ curl -X GET "https://datasets-server.huggingface.co/
parquet?dataset=stanfordnlp/imdb"
```

This command returns the following result (formatted for clarity).

Listing 5.6   URLs of the various Parquet files

```
{
  "parquet_files":[
    {
      "dataset":"stanfordnlp/imdb",
      "config":"plain_text",
      "split":"test",
      "url":"https://huggingface.co/datasets/stanfordnlp/
            imdb/resolve/refs%2Fconvert%2Fparquet/
            plain_text/test/0000.parquet",
      "filename":"0000.parquet",
      "size":20470363
    },
    {
```

```
      "dataset":"stanfordnlp/imdb",
      "config":"plain_text",
      "split":"train",
      "url":"https://huggingface.co/datasets/stanfordnlp/
            imdb/resolve/refs%2Fconvert%2Fparquet/
            plain_text/train/0000.parquet",
      "filename":"0000.parquet",
      "size":20979968
   },
   {
      "dataset":"stanfordnlp/imdb",
      "config":"plain_text",
      "split":"unsupervised",
      "url":"https://huggingface.co/datasets/stanfordnlp/
            imdb/resolve/refs%2Fconvert%2Fparquet/
            plain_text/unsupervised/0000.parquet",
      "filename":"0000.parquet",
      "size":41996509
   }
  ],
  "pending":[],
  "failed":[],
  "partial":false
}
```

As you can see, the result contains the URLs of the Parquet files for each split. Using these URLs, you can use Python to access the Parquet file of the split(s) directly, as in the following example:

```
!pip install pyarrow
import pandas as pd

url = "https://huggingface.co/datasets/stanfordnlp/" + \
      "imdb/resolve/refs%2Fconvert%2Fparquet/" + \
      "plain_text/unsupervised/0000.parquet"
df = pd.read_parquet(url, engine='pyarrow')

display(df.head())
```

Figure 5.6 shows the first five rows of the unsupervised split of the dataset.

	Text	Label
0	This is just a precious little diamond. The pl...	-1
1	When I say this is my favourite film of all ti...	-1
2	I saw this movie because I am a huge fan of th...	-1
3	Being that the only foreign films I usually li...	-1
4	After seeing Point of No Return (a great movie...	-1

Figure 5.6   The first five rows of the unsupervised split

5.2 Tokenization in NLP

Tokenization is a foundational NLP process that breaks text into manageable units or tokens, allowing models to interpret and process language more effectively. Tokenization has the following key uses:

- *Text preprocessing*—Tokenization helps preprocess text data, simplifying tasks such as filtering out punctuation, converting to lowercase, and handling special characters.
- *Representation for machine learning models*—Most NLP models, including transformers and large language models (LLMs), require text to be in a numerical format. Tokenization transforms text into numerical IDs that the models can work with.
- *Efficiency and memory optimization*—Smaller tokens, such as subwords, allow models to handle larger vocabularies with fewer parameters, making it easier for models to capture nuances such as suffixes, prefixes, and infixes, which are especially useful for inflective languages.
- *Foundation for further NLP tasks*—Tokenization provides a foundation for advanced NLP tasks such as named entity recognition (NER), part-of-speech tagging, machine translation, and text summarization.

The following sections discuss the methods of tokenization, how they work, and how we can tokenize a dataset from Hugging Face to prepare it for fine-tuning.

5.2.1 Types of tokenization methods

There are several types of tokenization methods, each suited to different tasks and languages. Here are some of the main types:

- *Word-level*—Splits text into individual words
- *Subword-level*—Splits words into smaller meaningful units or subwords
- *Character-level*—Breaks text into individual characters; commonly used for languages such as Chinese and Japanese, in which word boundaries are less obvious

Figure 5.7 shows an example of word-level tokenization in which the string "I love dogs" has been tokenized into three words: "I", "love", and "dogs".

Word-level tokenization, although straightforward, struggles with out-of-vocabulary words, so it requires a large vocabulary for diverse languages. Also, it doesn't capture the internal structure of words, which limits a model's generalization abilities. Some models that use this method are Word2Vec and GloVe.

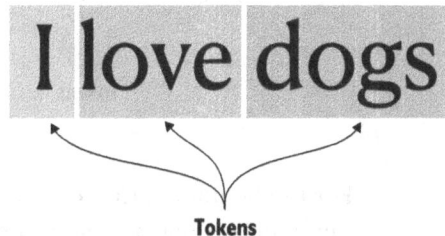

Figure 5.7   Example of word-level tokenization. The sentence is tokenized into three tokens.

Most newer models, especially transformer-based models such as BERT and GPT, prefer subword or byte-pair encoding (BPE) tokenization to overcome these problems, providing better flexibility and generalization across languages and word forms. Figure 5.8 shows an example of subword-level tokenization. In this example, the word "exhilarating" is tokenized into four tokens: "ex", "h", "ilar", and "ating".

Subword-level tokenization offers

Figure 5.8   Example of subword-level tokenization. The single word "exhilarating" is tokenized into four tokens.

several advantages in NLP, especially for models that work with diverse language data. One primary benefit is that it handles out-of-vocabulary (OOV) words effectively by breaking them into smaller, recognizable subunits. This ability eliminates the need to discard or ignore unfamiliar words. Also, subword-level tokenization preserves more information than word-level tokenization, especially with languages that have complex morphology or compound words, making it ideal for handling misspellings, rare words, and different grammatical forms.

Character-level tokenization is usually used for languages such as Chinese and Japanese. Figure 5.9 shows an example of the sentence "I love programming" in both Simplified Chinese and Japanese tokenized into character-level tokens.

Figure 5.9   Examples of character-level tokenization using Simplified Chinese and Japanese

For the Simplified Chinese example, each character represents a meaningful unit in the sentence, making character tokenization particularly useful for languages such as Chinese, Japanese, and Korean, in which words are often composed of multiple characters and spaces are typically not used to delimit them. For Japanese, each individual character—including Kanji, Hiragana, Katakana, and punctuation—is treated as a token. This type of tokenization works well for handling Japanese text when you're interested in the most granular form of the data.

5.2.2 *Tokenizing datasets*

Hugging Face datasets are compatible with built-in tokenizers and data loaders, making it easy to preprocess and tokenize large datasets efficiently before feeding them into models. Using the IMDb dataset that we loaded earlier, let's use the `bert-base-uncased` model as the tokenizer and use it to tokenize the dataset:

```
from transformers import AutoTokenizer

dataset = load_dataset(dataset_id)
tokenizer = AutoTokenizer.from_pretrained('bert-base-uncased')
tokenized_dataset = dataset.map(
    lambda examples:
        tokenizer(examples['text'],
                  truncation = True,
                  padding = 'max_length'),
    batched = True)
```

Here, we used the `AutoTokenizer` class from Hugging Face that automatically loads the appropriate tokenizer class for the specified pretrained model—in this case, `bert-base-uncase`, a version of the BERT (Bidirectional Encoder Representations from Transformers) model from Hugging Face's Transformers library that is trained on uncased text data. The `map()` method of the dataset is used to apply a function to each element or batch of elements in the dataset. You can print the tokenized dataset:

```
print(tokenized_dataset)
```

The following listing shows the output.

Listing 5.7 The content of the tokenized dataset

```
DatasetDict({
    train: Dataset({
        features: ['text', 'label', 'input_ids', 'token_type_ids',
                   'attention_mask'],
        num_rows: 25000
    })
    test: Dataset({
        features: ['text', 'label', 'input_ids', 'token_type_ids',
                   'attention_mask'],
        num_rows: 25000
    })
    unsupervised: Dataset({
        features: ['text', 'label', 'input_ids', 'token_type_ids',
                   'attention_mask'],
```

```
        num_rows: 50000
    })
})
```

Observe that each split of the dataset contains three new attributes: `input_ids`, `token_type_ids`, and `attention_mask`. Let's examine them one by one, starting with `input_ids`:

```
print(tokenized_dataset['train'][0]['input_ids'])
```

You see the following result:

```
[101, 1045, 12524, 1045, 2572, 8025, 1011, 3756, 2013, 2026,
2678, 3573, 2138, 1997, 2035, 1996, 6704, 2008, 5129, 2009,
2043, 2009, 2001, 2034, 2207, 1999, 3476, 1012, 1045, 2036,
...
0, 0, 0, 0, 0, 0, 0, 0, 0, 0, 0, 0, 0, 0, 0, 0, 0, 0, 0, 0,
0, 0, 0, 0, 0, 0, 0, 0, 0, 0, 0, 0, 0, 0, 0, 0, 0, 0, 0, 0,
0, 0, 0, 0, 0, 0, 0, 0, 0, 0, 0, 0, 0, 0, 0, 0, 0, 0, 0, 0]
```

Each number represents the token ID of a corresponding token. The trailing 0s at the end of the list act as padding tokens, ensuring that all sequences in the batch have the same length for consistent processing by the model.

> **DEFINITION**   A *token ID* is a unique numerical identifier assigned to a token (a word, subword, punctuation mark, or even whitespace, depending on the tokenizer used) in the context of NLP. Token IDs are generated during the tokenization process when text data is processed into input that a language model (such as BERT, GPT, or other transformer models) can understand and use.

To convert the token IDs back to the tokens, use the `convert_ids_to_tokens()` method of the tokenizer:

```
tokens = tokenizer.convert_ids_to_tokens(
            tokenized_dataset['train'][0]['input_ids'])
print(tokens)
```

You should see the following:

```
    ['[CLS]', 'i', 'rented', 'i', 'am', 'curious', '-',
 'yellow', 'from', 'my', 'video', 'store', 'because',
 'of', 'all', 'the', 'controversy', 'that', 'surrounded',
 ...
 ...
 '##men', 'mind', 'find', 'it', 'shocking'
 ...
 '[PAD]', '[PAD]', '[PAD]', '[PAD]', '[PAD]', '[PAD]',
 '[PAD]', '[PAD]', '[PAD]', '[PAD]', '[PAD]', '[PAD]',
 '[PAD]', '[PAD]', '[PAD]', '[PAD]', '[PAD]', '[PAD]']
```

The first token is [CLS], which signifies the start of the string. The ## symbol in front of some tokens indicates that the token is a subword unit that is a continuation or suffix of a larger word. In simpler terms, it signifies that the token is not a standalone word but a fragment that combines with the preceding tokens to form a complete word. The [PAD] token indicates padding in tokenized sequences. It is used to ensure that all input sequences to a model have the same length by filling shorter sequences with padding tokens. This padding process is necessary because many transformer-based models, such as BERT, expect input tensors of uniform size to allow for efficient batch processing during training or inference.

The second attribute, token_type_ids, is used to differentiate among multiple segments of a single input. This attribute is particularly useful for models such as BERT, which can process inputs consisting of two separate segments (e.g., a sentence pair in tasks like next-sentence prediction or question answering). token_type_ids helps the model determine which tokens belong to which segment. Typically, tokens from the first segment are assigned 0, and tokens from the second segment are assigned 1. In the case of a single text input, such as an IMDb movie review, there is only one segment, so all tokens have the same token_type_id, which is 0. Therefore, when you print token_type_ids or a similar input, you see an array of zeros:

```
[0, 0, 0,..., 0, 0, 0]
```

This array indicates that the entire sequence is treated as a single segment; no distinction is made between multiple segments.

The third attribute, attention_mask, is used to inform the model which tokens should be *attended to* (processed) and which should not. It is especially important when padding tokens are present in the input because the model should ignore the padding during its computations. The attention_mask typically consists of binary values, which can be interpreted as follows:

- *Value of* 1—Indicates that the token should be attended to (i.e., it's a real token, not padding)
- *Value of* 0—Indicates that the token is a padding token and should not contribute to the model's attention mechanism

You can print the attention mask for the first row of training data like this:

```
print(tokenized_dataset['train'][0]['attention_mask'])
```

You see the following output:

```
[1, 1, 1, 1, 1, 1, 1, 1, 1, 1, 1, 1, 1, 1, 1, 1, 1, 1,
 1, 1, 1, 1, 1, 1, 1, 1, 1, 1, 1, 1, 1, 1, 1, 1, 1, 1,
 1, 1, 1, 1, 1, 1, 1, 1, 1, 1, 1, 1, 1, 1, 1, 1, 1, 1,
 ...
 0, 0, 0, 0, 0, 0, 0, 0, 0, 0, 0, 0, 0, 0, 0, 0, 0, 0,
 0, 0, 0, 0, 0, 0, 0, 0, 0, 0, 0, 0, 0, 0, 0, 0, 0, 0,
 0, 0, 0, 0, 0, 0, 0, 0, 0, 0, 0, 0, 0, 0, 0, 0, 0, 0]
```

Figure 5.10 shows the relationships among token IDs, tokens, and attention masks for the first row of the train split in the dataset.

Token IDs

```
[  101,  1045,  12524,   1045,  2572,   8025,   1011,...,     0,      0,      0,      0  ]
```

Tokens

```
['[CLS]', 'i', 'rented', 'i', 'am', 'curious', '-', ..., '[PAD]', '[PAD]', '[PAD]', '[PAD]']
```

Attention mask

```
[   1,     1,      1,      1,     1,      1,      1,  ...,     0,      0,      0,      0  ]
```

Figure 5.10   The token IDs, tokens, and attention masks in the first row of the training data

Tokenizing datasets is a crucial step because it converts raw text to a format that machine learning models can process effectively. This process is especially important in preparing data for fine-tuning models because it ensures that the model can understand and work with the input text. Tokenization breaks the text into smaller units, such as words or subwords, which the model can use to learn patterns and make predictions during training.

5.3   Visualizing datasets

The Hugging Face datasets provide a great opportunity to practice data visualization techniques, allowing you to glean additional insights from your data and generate actionable conclusions that can inform decision-making or model optimization. In this section, you will use two particular datasets from Hugging Face for data visualization.

5.3.1   Using the twitter-financial-news-topic dataset

Let's start with the twitter-financial-news-topic dataset. This dataset is an English-language dataset containing an annotated corpus of finance-related tweets; it's used to classify finance-related tweets for a topic. The dataset holds 21,107 documents annotated with 20 labels. You can find out more about this dataset by searching for the name of this dataset on Hugging Face's website or by going directly to https://mng.bz/xZEg (see figure 5.11).

Let's load the dataset and extract the train split:

```
from datasets import load_dataset                              Loads the dataset

dataset = load_dataset('zeroshot/twitter-financial-news-topic')

train_data = dataset['train']        Extracts the topic labels
                                     from the training set
```

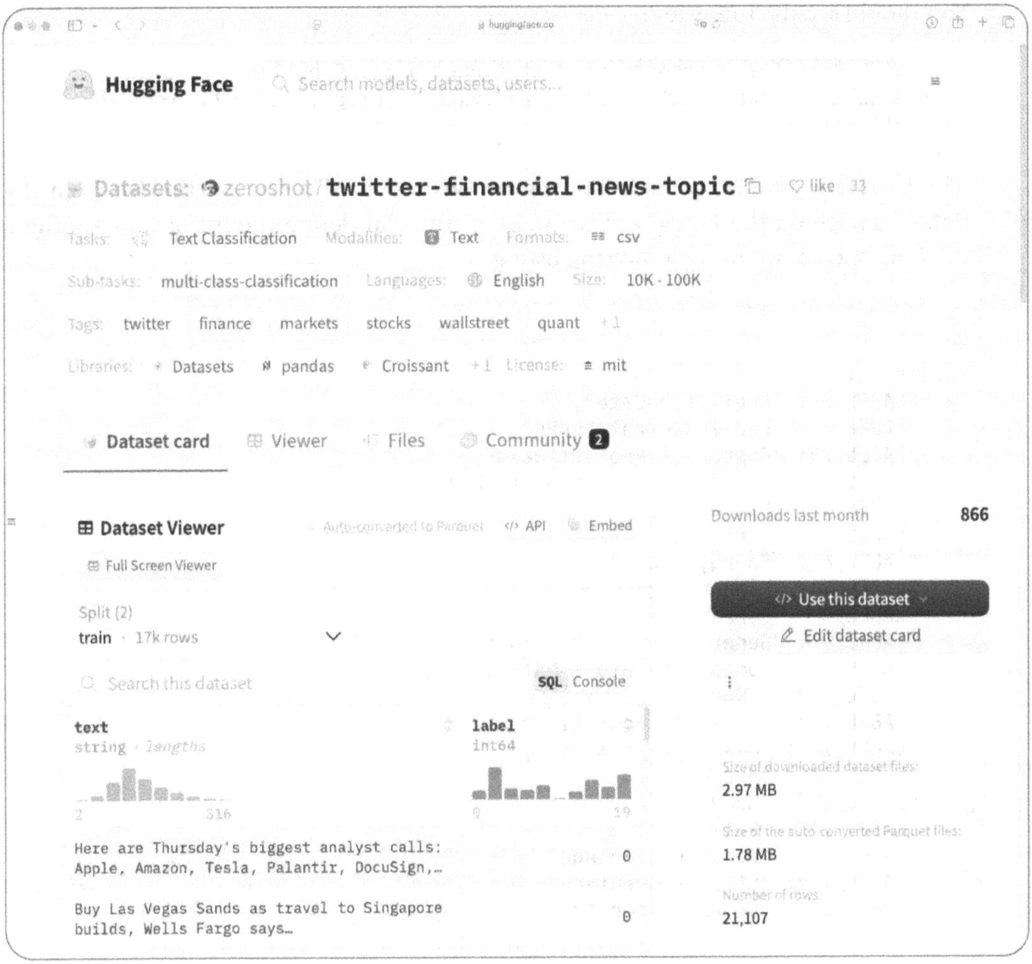

Figure 5.11 The `twitter-financial-news-topic` dataset hosted by Hugging Face

Next, print the first row of the data:

```
print(train_data[0])
```

You should see the text as well as the label of the first row:

```
{'text': "Here are Thursday's biggest analyst calls: Apple, Amazon,
 Tesla, Palantir, DocuSign, Exxon &amp; more  https://t.co/QPN8Gwl7Uh",
 'label': 0}
```

Likewise, print the last row in the `train` split:

```
print(train_data[-1])
```

You should see the following:

```
{'text': "Brazil's Petrobras says it signed a $1.25 billion
 sustainability loan  https://t.co/X9iTvkLKtj  https://t.co/hCKnxYi8AA",
 'label': 3}
```

The label is a number referencing the various topics. You can get this list from the dataset's page on the Hugging Face website. You can define the list of topics using a dictionary as shown in the following listing.

Listing 5.8   Defining the list of topics for the `twitter-financial-news-topic` dataset

```
topics = {
    "LABEL_0": "Analyst Update",
    "LABEL_1": "Fed | Central Banks",
    "LABEL_2": "Company | Product News",
    "LABEL_3": "Treasuries | Corporate Debt",
    "LABEL_4": "Dividend",
    "LABEL_5": "Earnings",
    "LABEL_6": "Energy | Oil",
    "LABEL_7": "Financials",
    "LABEL_8": "Currencies",
    "LABEL_9": "General News | Opinion",
    "LABEL_10": "Gold | Metals | Materials",
    "LABEL_11": "IPO",
    "LABEL_12": "Legal | Regulation",
    "LABEL_13": "M&A | Investments",
    "LABEL_14": "Macro",
    "LABEL_15": "Markets",
    "LABEL_16": "Politics",
    "LABEL_17": "Personnel Change",
    "LABEL_18": "Stock Commentary",
    "LABEL_19": "Stock Movement",
}
```

Using this dictionary, you can create a mapping for all the labels in the train subset:

```
mapped_labels = [topics[f"LABEL_{label}"]
                 for label in train_data['label']]
```

In this dataset, you want to see the distribution of all the topics and examine which topic has the most data and which has the least. You can plot a bar chart showing the distribution as follows.

Listing 5.9   Plotting the dataset using a bar chart

```
import matplotlib.pyplot as plt
import numpy as np

plt.figure(figsize=(10, 6))

bins = np.arange(len(topics) + 1) - 0.5
```

Creates bin edges to center the labels

```
plt.hist(mapped_labels,
         bins = bins,
         edgecolor = 'black',
         color = 'skyblue',
         alpha = 0.7)

plt.xticks(np.arange(len(topics)),        ◄─┐  Sets the ticks at the
           list(topics.values()),           │  center of each bin
           rotation = 90,
           ha = 'center')

plt.title("Topic Distribution - Twitter Financial News")
plt.xlabel("Topics")
plt.ylabel("Number of Tweets")
plt.tight_layout()
plt.show()
```

Figure 5.12 shows the bar chart displaying the distribution of the topics.

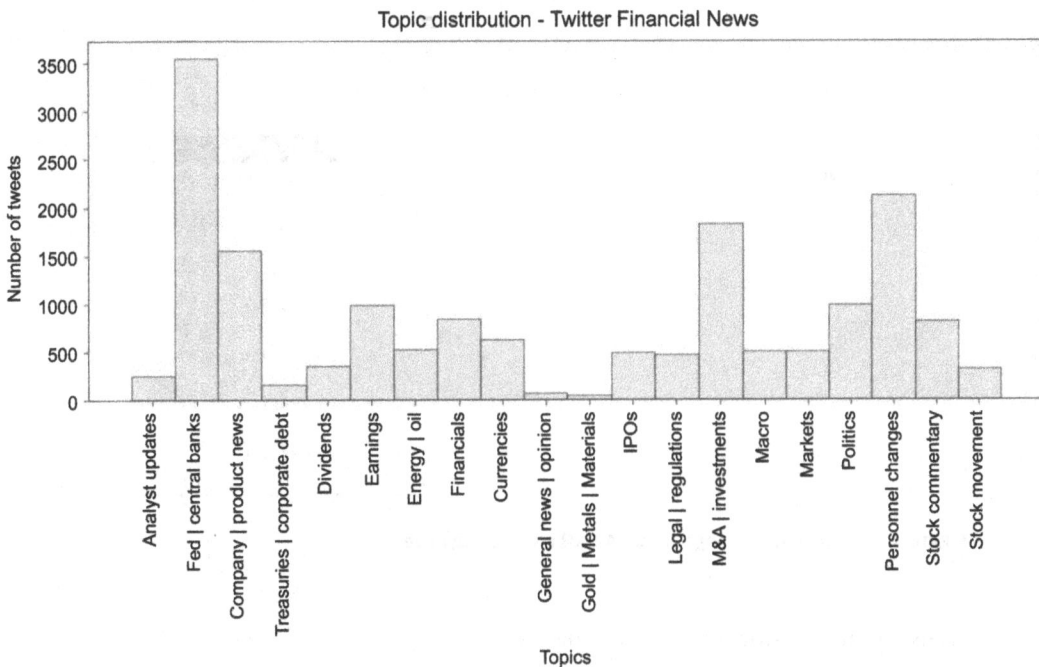

Figure 5.12 You can visualize the various topics and the number of news items related to each topic.

5.3.2 Using the CIFAR-10 dataset

CIFAR-10 is widely used in machine learning and computer vision, containing 60,000 labeled 32x32 color images divided into 10 classes, such as airplanes, automobiles, and animals, with 50,000 for training and 10,000 for testing. Its simplicity and size make it a popular benchmark for image classification models, especially convolutional neural networks (CNNs), and an excellent resource for educational projects.

You can use the Hugging Face Datasets library to experiment with CIFAR-10, and visualizations using `matplotlib` can help you understand the data better. In this section, you'll use the `uoft-cs/cifar10` dataset (https://huggingface.co/datasets/uoft-cs/cifar10; see also figure 5.13).

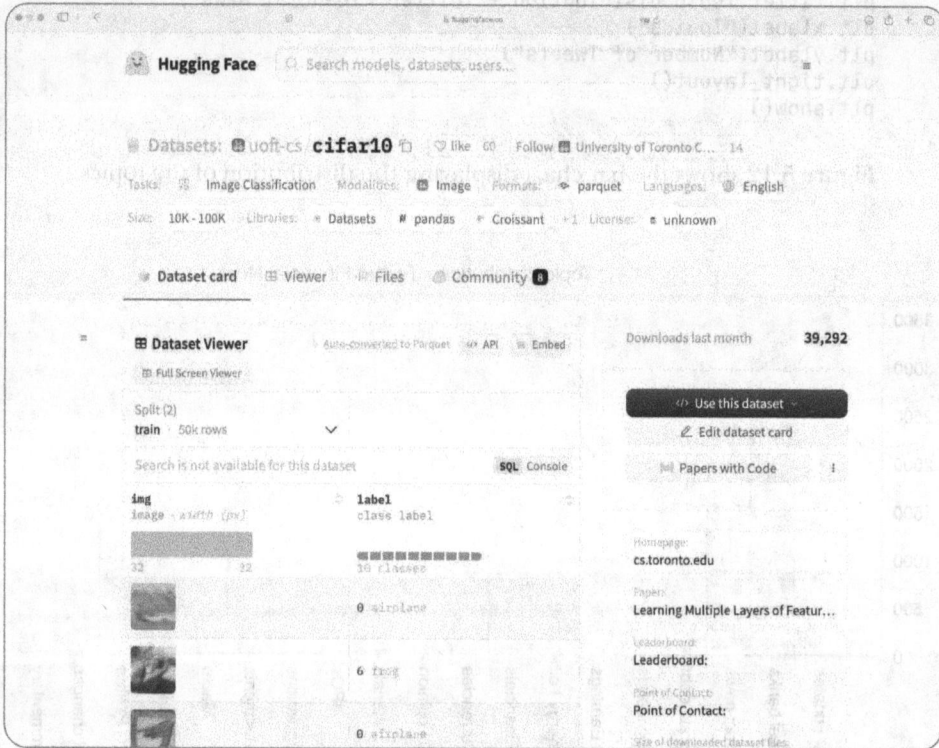

Figure 5.13   The dataset page for CIFAR-10 on Hugging Face

As usual, start by downloading the dataset:

```
from datasets import load_dataset
import matplotlib.pyplot as plt
import numpy as np

    dataset = load_dataset('uoft-cs/cifar10')    ◄── Loads the dataset
print(dataset)
```

Printing the downloaded dataset shows the following:

```
DatasetDict({
    train: Dataset({
        features: ['img', 'label'],
        num_rows: 50000
    })
    test: Dataset({
        features: ['img', 'label'],
        num_rows: 10000
    })
})
```

All 60,000 images are stored in the dataset. You can access the first image in the `train` split, for example, as follows:

```
dataset['train'][0]
```

You see the following output (formatted for clarity):

```
{
  'img': <PIL.PngImagePlugin.PngImageFile image mode=RGB size=32x32>,
  'label': 0
}
```

Unfortunately, the page for the `uoft-cs/cifar10` dataset does not contain the labels for the dataset. You have to click the Files tab and then the `README.md` file (see figure 5.14) to view its content. You can also view this page directly at https://mng.bz/AGKg.

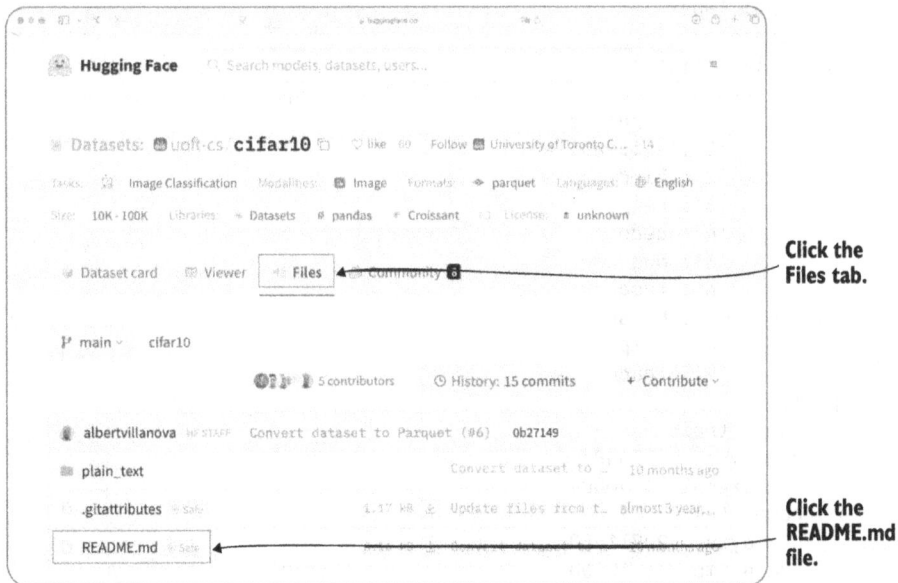

Figure 5.14   The `README.md` file for the CIFAR-10 dataset on Hugging Face

The next listing shows the content of the README.md file, with the key labeled names and their corresponding values, which map numbers to labels.

```
annotations_creators:
  - crowdsourced
language_creators:
  - found
language:
  - en
license:
  - unknown
multilinguality:
  - monolingual
size_categories:
  - 10K<n<100K
source_datasets:
  - extended|other-80-Million-Tiny-Images
task_categories:
  - image-classification
task_ids: []
paperswithcode_id: cifar-10
pretty_name: Cifar10
dataset_info:
  config_name: plain_text
  features:
    - name: img
      dtype: image
    - name: label
      dtype:
        class_label:
          names:
            '0': airplane
            '1': automobile
            '2': bird
            '3': cat
            '4': deer
            '5': dog
            '6': frog
            '7': horse
            '8': ship
            '9': truck
  splits:
    - name: train
      num_bytes: 113648310
      num_examples: 50000
    - name: test
      num_bytes: 22731580
      num_examples: 10000
  download_size: 143646105
  dataset_size: 136379890
```

```
configs:
  - config_name: plain_text
    data_files:
      - split: train
        path: plain_text/train-*
      - split: test
        path: plain_text/test-*
    default: true
```

With these labels, you can define a dictionary and create a function called `show_images()` to display a 5x5 grid of images, each accompanied by a label, as shown in the following listing.

Listing 5.11   Displaying a 5x5 grid of images

```
labels = {
    0: "airplane",           Defines labels for
    1: "automobile",         the CIFAR-10 classes
    2: "bird",
    3: "cat",
    4: "deer",
    5: "dog",
    6: "frog",
    7: "horse",
    8: "ship",
    9: "truck"
}

def show_images(images, labels, labels_dict):      Visualizes a few images
    plt.figure(figsize=(5, 5))                     from the training set
    for i in range(25):
        plt.subplot(5, 5, i + 1)
        plt.imshow(images[i])                      Uses the labels dictionary
        plt.title(labels_dict[labels[i]])          to get class names
        plt.axis('off')
    plt.tight_layout()
    plt.show()         Gets some samples from              Randomly selects
                       the training dataset                    25 samples

train_samples = dataset['train'].shuffle(seed=42).select(range(25))


images = [sample['img'] for sample in train_samples]        Extracts images
class_labels = [sample['label'] for sample in train_samples]  and labels

                                    Displays the images
                                    with class names
show_images(images, class_labels, labels)
```

Figure 5.15 shows the grid of 5x5 random images from the dataset.

Figure 5.15   Twenty-five random images from the CIFAR-10 dataset

Summary

- Hugging Face Datasets is an open source library designed for accessing and processing large datasets commonly used in machine learning and data science.
- Use the `list_datasets()` function to show a list of available datasets.
- Use the `load_dataset()` function to download a dataset.
- Datasets are usually split into subsets, such as `train`, `test`, and `unsupervised`.
- For large datasets, you can stream the data and download one row at a time. You can also get the Parquet version of the dataset from Hugging Face.
- Tokenization is a foundational process in NLP that breaks text into manageable units or tokens.
- Subword-level tokenization is the most common tokenization method used by newer models such as BERT and GPT.
- Tokenizing a dataset allows you to use it for applications such as fine-tuning a model.
- Visualizing a dataset allows you to gain a better understanding of its structure, distribution, and underlying patterns.

Fine-tuning pretrained models and working with multimodal models

This chapter covers

- Using the yelp_polarity dataset to fine-tune a pretrained model
- Using a fine-tuned model to perform classification tasks
- Fine-tuning a pretrained model to perform multiclass classification tasks
- Working with multimodal models

Up until this chapter, you've seen how to work with pretrained models from Hugging Face to tackle a variety of tasks, using their general capabilities for tasks such as text classification, object detection, and language generation. Now you'll delve into the process of fine-tuning these models to adapt them for more specialized tasks, enhancing their performance by training them on domain-specific data.

You'll also explore multimodal models. These models combine multiple types of data, such as images and text, to address more complex tasks (such as identifying the type of animals in an image based on visual features and descriptive text) that require the integration of different information sources. By the end of this chapter, you'll have a solid understanding of how to fine-tune models for better task-specific accuracy and work with models that handle multimodal inputs for richer, more comprehensive solutions.

6.1 Fine-tuning pretrained models

Fine-tuning is a machine learning technique in which a pretrained model, which has already learned general patterns from a large dataset, is further trained on a smaller, domain-specific dataset to adapt it for a particular task. This process uses the knowledge the model gained from the initial training, enabling it to perform well with less data (fewer examples or a smaller dataset specific to the new task) and computational resources.

Fine-tuning typically involves adjusting only the later layers of the model or applying a lower learning rate to avoid losing the valuable features learned during the pretraining phase. It is commonly used in natural language processing (NLP) and computer vision tasks, allowing models such as transformers and convolutional neural networks (CNNs) to be customized for specific applications (such as sentiment analysis or object detection) without having to be trained from scratch.

6.1.1 Loading the yelp_polarity dataset

In this section, you learn how to fine-tune a pretrained model from Hugging Face to perform sentiment analysis of restaurant reviews. To illustrate the process of fine-tuning a model, you'll use the `yelp_polarity` dataset, available from the Hugging Face Datasets library (https://mng.bz/26v9). This labeled dataset, derived from the larger Yelp Dataset Challenge, is tailored to text classification tasks such as sentiment analysis. It consists of Yelp reviews that express detailed opinions about businesses such as restaurants, hotels, and services. The dataset includes two labels, 0 for negative sentiment and 1 for positive sentiment, making it well suited to binary classification tasks. First, load the dataset and examine its content:

```
from datasets import load_dataset

dataset = load_dataset("yelp_polarity")     ◄── Loads the Yelp dataset (full review
print(dataset)                                  dataset with train and test splits)
```

Inspects the dataset to understand the structure

The content of the dataset is

```
DatasetDict({
    train: Dataset({
        features: ['text', 'label'],
        num_rows: 560000
    })
    test: Dataset({
        features: ['text', 'label'],
        num_rows: 38000
    })
})
```

Observe that the `train` split dataset has 560,000 rows and the `test` split has 38,000 rows. It would be useful to look at the first row of the `train` split:

```
train_dataset = dataset['train']      ◄─── Accesses the train split
print(train_dataset[0])               ◄───
                                           Prints the first example
```

The following listing shows the text of the first row together with the label 0, which indicates that this review is negative.

Listing 6.1 The first row of the `train` split of the `yelp_polarity` dataset

```
{
  'text': "Unfortunately, the frustration of being Dr.
          Goldberg's patient is a repeat of the experience
          I've had with so many other doctors in NYC -
          good doctor, terrible staff.  It seems that his
          staff simply never answers the phone.  It usually
          takes 2 hours of repeated calling to get an answer.
          Who has time for that or wants to deal with it?  I
          have run into this problem with many other doctors
          and I just don't get it.  You have office workers,
          you have patients with medical needs, why isn't
          anyone answering the phone?  It's incomprehensible
          and not work the aggravation.  It's with regret
          that I feel that I have to give Dr. Goldberg 2
          stars.",
  'label': 0
}
```

6.1.2 Filtering the yelp_polarity dataset

Before using the `yelp_polarity` dataset to fine-tune your model, consider the following points:

- *Topic variety*—The dataset includes reviews on a wide range of topics, not only restaurants. If your goal is to fine-tune a model specifically for restaurant reviews, I recommend that you filter the dataset to include only reviews related to restaurants.

- *Dataset size*—The dataset can be quite large, which may pose challenges during fine-tuning. Although having more data is generally beneficial, it's often practical to limit the dataset size. Using a subset of around 5,000 reviews, for example, can make training more manageable without compromising performance significantly.

The next listing demonstrates how to filter the dataset to include only rows containing the word *restaurant* and then extract a subset of 5,000 rows.

Listing 6.2   Filtering the `yelp_polarity` dataset

```
train_dataset = dataset["train"]                               Selects the train and test splits
test_dataset = dataset["test"]

restaurant_train_reviews = train_dataset.filter(
    lambda x: "restaurant" in x["text"].lower()                Filters for restaurant-
)                                                              related reviews in the
                                                               train and test datasets
restaurant_test_reviews = test_dataset.filter(
    lambda x: "restaurant" in x["text"].lower()
)

number_of_reviews = 5000
subset_train_reviews = restaurant_train_reviews.shuffle(       Shuffles and gets
    seed = 42).select(range(number_of_reviews))                5,000 rows
subset_test_reviews = restaurant_test_reviews.shuffle(
    seed = 42).select(range(number_of_reviews))

subset_dataset = {                                             Creates a DatasetDict to return
    "train": subset_train_reviews,                             both train and test datasets
    "test": subset_test_reviews
}
                                                               Displays the structure
from datasets import DatasetDict                               to match the
yelp_restaurant_dataset = DatasetDict(subset_dataset)          requested format

print(yelp_restaurant_dataset)                Prints the dataset structure
```

The reduced dataset contains 5,000 rows each for the train and test splits:

```
DatasetDict({
    train: Dataset({
        features: ['label', 'text'],
        num_rows: 5000
    })
    test: Dataset({
        features: ['label', 'text'],
        num_rows: 5000
    })
})
```

Verify the first row of the reduced dataset by viewing its content:

```
yelp_restaurant_dataset['train'][0]
```

You see a review related to a restaurant that expresses a negative sentiment:

```
{
    'text': 'My girlfriend and I have been wanting to come
            here for awhile, we finally came & we had the
            worst experience ever. We asked our server for
```

```
        a few minutes to look over the menu & he never
        came back. 15 minutes later, someone finally
        came and took our order. We waited awhile and
        when they brought our food, they got the whole
        order wrong. My girlfriend ordered soup and it
        never came out. Worst service ever. Would not
        recommend this restaurant to anyone.',
    'label': 0
}
```

6.1.3 Tokenizing the reduced dataset

You can perform tokenization on the reduced dataset using the `distilbert-base
-uncased` model. This model is shown in the following listing.

> **Listing 6.3   Performing tokenization on the reduced dataset**

```
from transformers import AutoTokenizer

model_checkpoint = "distilbert-base-uncased"
tokenizer = AutoTokenizer.from_pretrained(model_checkpoint)

def tokenize_function(examples):
    return tokenizer(examples["text"],
                     padding = "max_length",
                     truncation = True,
                     max_length = 512)

tokenized_datasets = yelp_restaurant_dataset.map(
                        tokenize_function,
                        batched=True)
tokenized_datasets
```

- Loads a pretrained model and tokenizer (DistilBERT) for sentiment classification
- Function to tokenize the dataset
- Applies the tokenization function to the dataset

After the tokenization, you should see the following result:

```
DatasetDict({
    train: Dataset({
        features: ['text', 'label', 'input_ids', 'attention_mask'],
        num_rows: 5000
    })
    test: Dataset({
        features: ['text', 'label', 'input_ids', 'attention_mask'],
        num_rows: 5000
    })
})
```

6.1.4 Setting up a pretrained model for sequence classification

Next, load the pretrained model (`distilbert-base-uncased`) shown in the following
listing so you can fine-tune it to perform sentiment analysis on restaurant reviews.

Listing 6.4   Loading a pretrained model for sequence classification

```
from transformers import AutoModelForSequenceClassification      Loads a
import torch                                                     pretrained
                                                                 model for
model = AutoModelForSequenceClassification.from_pretrained(  ◄── sequence
            model_checkpoint, num_labels = 2)                    classification

if torch.backends.mps.is_available():     ◄──┐ Determines the device
    device = torch.device("mps")
else:
    device = torch.device(
        "cuda" if torch.cuda.is_available() else "cpu")

model.to(device)    ◄──┐ Moves the model to
                        │ the selected device
```

The `AutoModelForSequenceClassification` class in Hugging Face's Transformers library is a versatile model loader specifically tailored to sequence classification tasks. It enables you to load any pretrained model architecture that's compatible with sequence classification by using a provided model checkpoint. This class automatically appends the necessary classification layers to the pretrained model, making it ready for tasks such as sentiment analysis, spam detection, and topic classification.

> **DEFINITION**   *Sequence classification tasks* involve assigning a single label or category to an entire sequence of data, such as a sentence, a paragraph, or a longer sequence of tokens.

In listing 6.4, you also implement logic to detect the runtime environment, which includes checking whether the code is running on a macOS system with Metal Performance Shaders (MPS) enabled or on a Windows machine with Compute Unified Device Architecture (CUDA) support. If a graphics processing unit (GPU) is detected, the model is transferred to the GPU to use accelerated computation.

MPS and CUDA

MPS is Apple's framework for GPU-accelerated computations on macOS devices with Apple silicon (M1, M2, M3, and M4 chips). It is optimized for machine learning tasks and uses the Metal API to provide efficient, high-performance computing for deep learning models. MPS enables native support for PyTorch and TensorFlow, allowing developers to train and infer models on Apple hardware.

CUDA is Nvidia's parallel computing platform and API for using Nvidia GPUs for general-purpose processing. Widely adopted in the machine learning community, CUDA enables frameworks such as PyTorch and TensorFlow to run deep learning models with unparalleled speed and efficiency. It supports an extensive ecosystem of tools for training, optimization, and deployment.

Both MPS and CUDA are essential for accelerating deep learning workflows tailored to their hardware ecosystems.

When you run the code snippet, you see the architecture of the `DistilBertFor-SequenceClassification` model, as shown in the next listing.

Listing 6.5 Architecture of the `DistilBertForSequenceClassification` model

```
DistilBertForSequenceClassification(
  (distilbert): DistilBertModel(
    (embeddings): Embeddings(
      (word_embeddings): Embedding(30522, 768, padding_idx=0)
      (position_embeddings): Embedding(512, 768)
      (LayerNorm): LayerNorm((768,), eps=1e-12, elementwise_affine=True)
      (dropout): Dropout(p=0.1, inplace=False)
    )
    (transformer): Transformer(
      (layer): ModuleList(
        (0-5): 6 x TransformerBlock(
          (attention): DistilBertSdpaAttention(
            (dropout): Dropout(p=0.1, inplace=False)
            (q_lin): Linear(in_features=768, out_features=768, bias=True)
            (k_lin): Linear(in_features=768, out_features=768, bias=True)
            (v_lin): Linear(in_features=768, out_features=768, bias=True)
            (out_lin): Linear(in_features=768, out_features=768, bias=True)
          )
          (sa_layer_norm): LayerNorm((768,), eps=1e-12,
            elementwise_affine=True)
          (ffn): FFN(
            (dropout): Dropout(p=0.1, inplace=False)
            (lin1): Linear(in_features=768, out_features=3072, bias=True)
            (lin2): Linear(in_features=3072, out_features=768, bias=True)
            (activation): GELUActivation()
          )
          (output_layer_norm): LayerNorm((768,), eps=1e-12,
            elementwise_affine=True)
        )
      )
    )
  )
  (pre_classifier): Linear(in_features=768, out_features=768, bias=True)
  (classifier): Linear(in_features=768, out_features=2, bias=True)
  (dropout): Dropout(p=0.2, inplace=    False)
)
```

6.1.5 Configuring and initializing a trainer for fine-tuning a pretrained model

To fine-tune a pretrained model on a dataset, you can use the Trainer and Training-Arguments classes from Hugging Face. The following code snippet demonstrates how to set up the `Trainer` and `TrainingArguments` classes to train the model using the `train` split of the tokenized dataset and evaluate the model using the `test` split of the tokenized dataset.

Listing 6.6 Setting up the `TrainingArguments` and `Trainer` classes for fine-tuning

```
from transformers import Trainer, TrainingArguments

training_args = TrainingArguments(
    output_dir = "./results",
    eval_strategy = "epoch",
    save_strategy = "epoch",
    learning_rate = 2e-5,
    per_device_train_batch_size = 16,
    per_device_eval_batch_size = 16,
    num_train_epochs = 3,
    weight_decay = 0.01,
    logging_dir = "./logs",
    logging_steps = 10,
    save_steps = 500,
    load_best_model_at_end = True,
)

trainer = Trainer(
    model = model,
    args = training_args,
    train_dataset = tokenized_datasets["train"],
    eval_dataset = tokenized_datasets["test"],
)

trainer.train()
```

Sets up training arguments
Directory in which to save results
Evaluates model after each epoch
Saves the model after each epoch
Learning rate
Batch size for training
Batch size for evaluation
Number of training epochs
Weight decay for regularization
Directory for logs
Logs every 10 steps
Saves the model every 500 steps
Loads the best model at the end of training
Sets up the Trainer
Fine-tunes the model

The duration of the training process will vary based on your machine's configuration and resources. Training can take anywhere from 10 minutes to 1 hour, so patience is key. (You'll know roughly how much time is needed during the training.) If training is taking too long, consider reducing the dataset from 5,000 rows to, say, 1,000 to speed the process.

When training is complete, you'll see the training loss and validation loss for each epoch (iteration) of the process (see figure 6.1). (Note that your results may vary from those in the figure.) These values provide insights into how well the model is learning and generalizing to unseen data, with the training loss indicating the model's

Epoch	Training loss	Validation loss
1	0.167500	0.171618
2	0.039400	0.219457
3	0.048500	0.218590

Figure 6.1 The result printed at the end of training

performance on the training data and the validation loss showing its performance on the validation set.

When the model is trained, save it to disk so you can use it later without going through the training process again:

```
model.save_pretrained("./results/final_model")          Saves the fine-tuned
tokenizer.save_pretrained("./results/final_tokenizer")   model and tokenizer
```

Also, you can evaluate the model and print its result:

```
eval_results = trainer.evaluate()                 Evaluates the model
print(f"Evaluation results: {eval_results}")
```

Following is the evaluation report for the training:

```
Evaluation results: {'eval_loss': 0.1825547218322754,
                     'eval_runtime': 63.1454,
                     'eval_samples_per_second': 79.182,
                     'eval_steps_per_second': 4.957,
                     'epoch': 3.0}
```

Here's what to make of the result:

- *Evaluation loss* (0.18255)—The model's loss during evaluation, with lower values indicating better performance. This value is a relatively low loss value, which generally indicates good performance, especially if you're working on a classification task such as sentiment analysis.
- *Evaluation runtime* (63.1454 [seconds])—The total time taken to run the evaluation.
- *Evaluation samples per second* (79.182)—The number of samples processed per second during evaluation. This value reflects the model's processing speed during evaluation, which seems decent, but it informs you mainly about efficiency rather than quality.
- *Evaluation steps per second* (4.957)—The number of evaluation steps completed per second. Like evaluation samples per second, this value informs you about efficiency rather than quality.
- *Epoch* (3.0)—The results from the third epoch of training. You can try varying this value to monitor how the loss evolves with more training.

The evaluation results suggest that the model is performing reasonably well.

6.1.6 Using the fine-tuned model

With the fine-tuned model trained and saved, you can use it to perform a sentiment analysis on a new restaurant review. The following listing shows how to load the fine-tuned model, move it and the inputs to the GPU (if available), and derive the result.

Listing 6.7   Using the fine-tuned model

```
from transformers import AutoTokenizer, \
                         AutoModelForSequenceClassification
import torch

new_model = AutoModelForSequenceClassification.from_pretrained(
            "./results/final_model")
new_tokenizer = AutoTokenizer.from_pretrained(
            "./results/final_tokenizer")

new_model.to(device)

sentence = '''
I had an amazing experience dining at this restaurant last night.
From the moment we walked in, the staff made us feel welcomed and
were incredibly attentive. Our server was friendly, knowledgeable,
and made great recommendations from the menu.

The food was absolutely delicious. I had the grilled salmon, and
it was cooked to perfection—tender, flavorful, and served with a
lovely citrus glaze that complemented it beautifully. The roasted
vegetables on the side were fresh and perfectly seasoned. My
partner had the pasta, which was creamy and rich in flavor, with
just the right amount of spice.

The ambiance was warm and inviting, with cozy lighting and tasteful
decor. It was the perfect place to relax and enjoy a nice meal. The
dessert, a decadent chocolate lava cake, was the perfect way to end
the meal.

Overall, this restaurant exceeded my expectations in every way.
Excellent food, exceptional service, and a wonderful atmosphere.
I'll definitely be back and highly recommend it to anyone looking
for a great dining experience.
'''

inputs = new_tokenizer(sentence,
                       return_tensors = "pt",
                       padding = True,
                       truncation = True,
                       max_length = 512)

inputs = {key: value.to(device) for key, value in inputs.items()}

new_model.eval()

with torch.no_grad():
    outputs = new_model(**inputs)
logits = outputs.logits
probabilities = torch.nn.functional.softmax(logits, dim=-1)
```

Reloads the model and tokenizer

Moves the inference to GPU

Tokenizes the input sentence

Moves inputs to GPU/MPS

Puts the model in evaluation mode

Runs the model to get predictions

Gets the logits (raw scores) from the model output

Converts logits to probabilities using Softmax

```
predicted_class = torch.argmax(probabilities, dim=-1).item()   ◄── Gets the
                                                                    predicted class
if predicted_class == 1:                                            (index of the
    print(f"Sentiment: Positive (Confidence: \     ◄── Outputs the  maximum
          {probabilities[0][1].item():.2f})")           predicted   probability)
else:                                                    sentiment
    print(f"Sentiment: Negative (Confidence: \
          {probabilities[0][0].item():.2f})")
```

The sample review in the code listing yields a positive sentiment with a confidence of 0.99:

```
Sentiment: Positive (Confidence: 0.99)
```

Next, modify the content of the sentence variable with a negative review, and examine the result:

```
sentence = '''
I visited this place last night with high expectations after
hearing some good things, but it was honestly one of the worst
dining experiences I've had in a while. The service was
incredibly slow, even though the restaurant wasn't crowded.
Our waiter seemed disinterested and forgot half of our order.

When the food finally came, it was cold and tasted bland. The
pasta was overcooked, and my steak was underseasoned and chewy.
The side of vegetables looked like they had been reheated from
a previous meal.

To make things worse, the ambiance was far too noisy, and we
had to wait an extra 20 minutes for the check. I tried to
address my concerns with the manager, but they seemed
uninterested in hearing feedback. Overall, I felt like I had
wasted both my time and money.

I will definitely not be coming back, and I would not recommend
this place to anyone.
'''
```

This time, the model returns a negative sentiment:

```
Sentiment: Negative (Confidence: 0.99)
```

6.1.7   Fine-tuning models for multiclass text classification

Unlike the yelp_polarity dataset, which uses binary labels (0 and 1) for sentiment classification, the yelp_review_full dataset contains labels corresponding to a star rating system ranging from 1 to 5 stars. Each review is assigned a star rating that reflects the user's sentiment about the business:

1 Very negative sentiment

2 Negative sentiment

3 Neutral sentiment

4 Positive sentiment

5 Very positive sentiment

These ratings provide a more granular view of sentiment compared with the binary labels in the `yelp_polarity` dataset. This fact makes the `yelp_review_full` dataset suitable for tasks such as multiclass sentiment classification or regression, the goal of which is to predict one of five sentiment categories based on the review text. Let's load the `yelp_review_full` dataset to examine its content:

```
from datasets import load_dataset

dataset = load_dataset("yelp_review_full")
print(dataset)
```

Loads Yelp Reviews dataset with ratings from 1 to 5

Displays the structure of the dataset

You will see the following output:

```
DatasetDict({
    train: Dataset({
        features: ['label', 'text'],
        num_rows: 650000
    })
    test: Dataset({
        features: ['label', 'text'],
        num_rows: 50000
    })
})
```

There are 650,000 rows in the `train` split and 50,000 rows in the `test` split. As usual, filter the dataset to contain only reviews that are related to restaurants, as shown in the next listing.

Listing 6.8   Filtering `yelp_review_full` to contain only rows related to restaurants

```
from datasets import DatasetDict

train_dataset = dataset["train"]
test_dataset = dataset["test"]

restaurant_train_reviews = train_dataset.filter(
    lambda x: "restaurant" in x["text"].lower()
)

restaurant_test_reviews = test_dataset.filter(
    lambda x: "restaurant" in x["text"].lower()
)
```

Selects the train and test splits

Filters for restaurant-related reviews in the train and test datasets

```
)

number_of_reviews = 5000                                          ◄─── Uses only 5,000
subset_train_reviews = restaurant_train_reviews.shuffle(              reviews for training
    seed=42).select(range(number_of_reviews))
subset_test_reviews = restaurant_test_reviews.shuffle(
    seed=42).select(range(number_of_reviews))
                                                     ┌── Creates a DatasetDict to return
subset_dataset = {                              ◄────┘   both train and test datasets
    "train": subset_train_reviews,
    "test": subset_test_reviews
}                                                       ┌── Displays the structure
                                                        │   to match the
yelp_restaurant_dataset = DatasetDict(subset_dataset) ◄─┘   requested format

print(yelp_restaurant_dataset)       ◄──┘ Prints the dataset structure
```

The reduced dataset looks like this:

```
DatasetDict({
    train: Dataset({
        features: ['label', 'text'],
        num_rows: 5000
    })
    test: Dataset({
        features: ['label', 'text'],
        num_rows: 5000
    })
})
```

Take a look at the first row of the train split:

```
yelp_restaurant_dataset['train'][0]
```

The output looks like this:

```
{'label': 2,
 'text': "This place is good, but I think I just ordered
         the wrong thing. The Hibiscus Enchiladas were
         just way too sweet for me. I think they should
         be on the dessert menu and not dinner menu. I'd
         like to give it another chance and order
         something else next time, but other than that
         a good vibe. Seemed like the typical American
         Mexican restaurant."}
```

As explained earlier, the label is a number from 1 to 5 representing the sentiment level. As you did in listing 6.3 earlier in this chapter, now you can tokenize the reduced dataset.

With the dataset tokenized, the next step is using a pretrained model and fine-tune it to perform sentiment analysis, as in listing 6.4 earlier in the chapter. But because now there are five labels (1 to 5) instead of 0 and 1, you need to set the `num_labels` parameter to 5 instead of 2:

```
model = AutoModelForSequenceClassification.from_pretrained(
        model_checkpoint,
        num_labels = 5)
```

Loads pretrained model
for sequence classification

Now you can proceed with fine-tuning the model. The code is the same as listing 6.6 earlier in this chapter.

When the model is fine-tuned, save it in a new folder named `final_model_multiclass` and the tokenizer in a folder named `final_tokenizer_multiclass`:

Saves the fine-tuned
model and tokenizer

```
model.save_pretrained("./results/final_model_multiclass")
tokenizer.save_pretrained("./results/final_tokenizer_multiclass")
eval_results = trainer.evaluate()
print(eval_results)
```

Prints the evaluation results

Evaluates the model
on the test set

> **TIP** Refer to the code repository that accompanies this book for the complete source code.

When training is complete, you see the training loss and validation loss for each epoch (iteration) of the process, as shown in figure 6.2.

Epoch	Training loss	Validation loss
1	1.066800	0.962330
2	0.799900	0.917825
3	0.773900	0.927565

Figure 6.2 The result printed at the end of the fine-tuning

The result of the evaluation is as follows:

```
{
    'eval_loss': 0.9178248047828674,
    'eval_runtime': 63.0299,
    'eval_samples_per_second': 79.327,
    'eval_steps_per_second': 4.966,
    'epoch': 3.0
}
```

Now you can load the fine-tuned model and use it to perform multiclass sentiment analysis, as shown in the next listing.

Listing 6.9 Using the fine-tuned model to perform multiclass sentiment analysis

```
from transformers import AutoModelForSequenceClassification
from transformers import AutoTokenizer
```

```
import torch

new_reviews = [
    "The food was amazing and the service was excellent!",
    "The restaurant was dirty and the food was cold.",
    "Decent experience, but nothing special."
]
if torch.backends.mps.is_available():          Determines the device
    device = torch.device("mps")
else:
    device = torch.device("cuda" if torch.cuda.is_available() else "cpu")

new_tokenizer = AutoTokenizer.from_pretrained(       Loads the tokenizer
    "./results/final_tokenizer_multiclass")

inputs = new_tokenizer(new_reviews,           Tokenizes the reviews
                       padding = "max_length",
                       truncation = True,
                       return_tensors = "pt")
                                              Moves inputs to GPU/MPS
inputs = {key: value.to(device) for key, value in inputs.items()}

new_model = AutoModelForSequenceClassification.from_pretrained(
    "./results/final_model_multiclass")
new_model.to(device)                          Loads the fine-tuned model

new_model.eval()

with torch.no_grad():                         Performs inference
    outputs = new_model(**inputs)
    logits = outputs.logits
    predictions = torch.argmax(logits, dim=-1)
                                              Assuming that classes
star_ratings = predictions + 1                are 0–4, maps to 1–5
for review, rating in zip(new_reviews, star_ratings):
    print(f"Review: {review}\nPredicted Star Rating: \
        {rating.item()}\n")
```

In listing 6.9, you had three sample restaurant reviews:

```
new_reviews = [
    "The food was amazing and the service was excellent!",
    "The restaurant was dirty and the food was cold.",
    "Decent experience, but nothing special."
]
```

When you use the fine-tuned model, these are the predicted ratings:

```
Review: The food was amazing and the service was excellent!
Predicted Star Rating:      5

Review: The restaurant was dirty and the food was cold.
Predicted Star Rating:         1
```

```
Review: Decent experience, but nothing special.
Predicted Star Rating:          3
```

Looks like they are pretty accurate!

6.2   *Working with multimodal models*

So far, all the models you've worked with have been single-modal models. A *single-modal model* is a machine learning model designed to work with data from a single modality, such as text, images, audio, or numerical data. Following are a few examples:

- An NLP model such as GPT or BERT is trained to work exclusively with textual data.
- A CNN such as a residual neural network (ResNet) is trained to process and analyze visual data such as images.

A *multimodal model,* on the other hand, is a machine learning model designed to process and integrate data from multiple modalities—different types of information, such as text, images, audio, video, and structured data. By combining these modalities, multimodal models aim to learn richer, more comprehensive representations, allowing them to perform tasks involving multiple types of inputs. Here are some example uses of multimodal models:

- Multimodal models can be used in image captioning. They combine visual data (images) with NLP (text) to generate descriptive captions.
- Another example is visual question answering (VQA), in which the model takes an image and a question as inputs and provides an answer by reasoning across both modalities.
- Similarly, in speech-to-text systems, audio data (speech) is processed and converted to textual information.
- Other real-world applications include multimodal sentiment analysis, combining text, audio tone, and visual cues (such as facial expressions) to assess sentiment; and autonomous driving systems, in which data from cameras (images), lidar (structured data), and GPS are integrated to understand the environment and make driving decisions.

Multimodal models have several advantages over single-modal models. They combine different types of data (such as text, images, and audio) for better understanding and can handle noise or missing information in one type by relying on others. This improves accuracy, generalization, and performance across tasks such as image captioning and VQA. By using multiple data sources together, they reduce bias, mimic human decision-making, and handle complex tasks more effectively.

6.2.1   *Single-modal models*

A good example of a single-model model is the `facebook/detr-resnet-50` model. This model is a Detection Transformer (DETR) model developed by Facebook AI and used for object detection and image segmentation, combining the strengths of CNNs and transformers. In the following example, we'll use it to detect objects in an image. First, let's load an image from the web:

```
from PIL import Image, ImageDraw
import requests

url = 'https://images.unsplash.com/' + \
      'photo-1563460716037-460a3ad24ba9'
if url.startswith('http'):
    image = Image.open(requests.get(url, stream=True).raw)
else:
    image = Image.open(url)
image
```

URL of the image

If the image is from the web . . .

. . . the image is local.

Figure 6.3 shows the picture, which contains a dog and a cat.

Figure 6.3 An image containing a dog and a cat (Source: https://mng.bz/Z9K5)

We'll use the facebook/detr-resnet-50 model to try to detect the dog and cat in the picture. The following listing shows how.

Listing 6.10   Using the `facebook/detr-resnet-50` model to detect objects in images

```
from transformers import DetrImageProcessor, DetrForObjectDetection
import torch

image_processor = DetrImageProcessor.from_pretrained(
    "facebook/detr-resnet-50")
model = DetrForObjectDetection.from_pretrained("facebook/detr-resnet-50")

inputs = image_processor(images = image,
                         return_tensors = "pt")

model.eval()

with torch.no_grad():
    outputs = model(**inputs)
target_sizes = torch.tensor([image.size[::-1]])

results = image_processor.post_process_object_detection(
             outputs,
             target_sizes = target_sizes,
             threshold = 0.9)[0]
print(results)
```

Processes the image so that the model can use the preprocessed data (e.g., resized, normalized, and converted to tensors) as inputs

The outputs variable contains the raw predictions from the model, which include detected object information.

Converts the raw model outputs to human-readable object detection results

Creates the target size in the format (height,width)

The model returned the following result (formatted for clarity):

```
{
  'scores': tensor([0.9924, 0.9989], grad_fn=<IndexBackward0>),
  'labels': tensor([17, 18]),
  'boxes': tensor([[4.5560e+00, 2.8760e+03, 2.4111e+03, 4.9051e+03],
                   [2.2206e+02, 1.4505e+03, 3.6523e+03, 4.6681e+03]],
                   grad_fn=<IndexBackward0>)
}
```

Using the result, you can plot bounding boxes around the detected objects using the following code.

Listing 6.11   Plotting bounding boxes around a detected object in an image

```
draw = ImageDraw.Draw(image)

for score, label, box in zip(results["scores"],
                             results["labels"],
                             results["boxes"]):
    print(
        f"Detected {model.config.id2label[label.item()]} with confidence "
        f"{(score.item() * 100):.2f}% at {box}"
    )
    box = [round(i, 2) for i in box.tolist()]
    draw.rectangle(box,
```

Prints the object detected and the confidence

Draws bounding box around object

```
                    outline = 'green',
                    width = 10)
    draw.text((box[0], box[1]-10),
            model.config.id2label[label.item()],
            fill = 'green')
display(image)
```

Displays the object label

This code prints the following result:

```
Detected cat with confidence 99.47% at tensor(
  [1.4345e+00, 1.2385e+03,
   1.0472e+03, 2.1296e+03],
   grad_fn=<UnbindBackward0>)
Detected dog with confidence 99.92% at tensor(
  [96.8109,   630.3585,
   1587.2705, 2028.8726],
   grad_fn=<UnbindBackward0>)
```

Figure 6.4 displays the bounding boxes around the dog and cat, with the label for each detected object shown in the top-left corner of the box.

Figure 6.4 The detected objects in the image with the bounding boxes drawn

This example demonstrates the use of a single-modal model, DETR, for object detection. The model processes only visual data (an input image) to identify objects and their bounding boxes. In section 6.2.2, you'll see how a multimodal model can enhance this by integrating additional data types, such as text, to improve contextual understanding and provide more comprehensive insights for tasks such as image captioning, VQA, and other complex applications that require the fusion of multiple modalities.

6.2.2 *Multimodal models*

Now that you've seen how a single-modal model identifies objects in an image, let's explore how a multimodal model differs. We'll use the `Contrastive Language–Image Pretraining (CLIP)` model to demonstrate how a multimodal model can process images and text together. Unlike a single-modal model, `CLIP` understands the relationship between images and textual descriptions, allowing it to perform tasks such as image classification based on natural language labels. By using both visual and textual data, `CLIP` makes more accurate predictions, handles more complex queries, and generalizes across various tasks without needing task-specific training. Let's walk through how `CLIP` works and see how it can classify images based on a set of textual descriptions.

What is CLIP?

CLIP is a multimodal model developed by OpenAI that connects text and image understanding. It can process and relate textual descriptions to visual content without requiring explicit fine-tuning for specific tasks. It can understand both text and images and establish meaningful relationships between them.

During training, CLIP aligns text descriptions with corresponding images while distinguishing them from unrelated pairs. The caption "a dog playing in the park," for example, is linked to an image of a dog but separated from images of cats or cars.

CLIP can perform tasks it wasn't specifically trained for by using its broad understanding of text and images. It can classify images based on user-provided text labels, for example, without requiring task-specific data.

CLIP uses two separate neural networks:

- A text encoder (transformer-based) to process text
- An image encoder (based on models like ResNet and Vision Transformer [ViT]) to process images

---

First, let's load an image that we want to use. For this example, we'll load an image of a dog:

```
import torch
import requests
from PIL import Image

url = 'https://images.unsplash.com/' + \
```

```
'photo-1491604612772-6853927639ef'    ◄──── URL of the image
```

```
image = Image.open(requests.get(url, stream=True).raw)
display(image)
```

Figure 6.5 shows the image of a dog loaded from the web.

Figure 6.5   An image of a dog
(Source: https://mng.bz/0zEE)

For this example, we'll use a multimodal model to simultaneously process both visual and textual data, as shown in the following listing. The CLIP model is designed to learn the relationship between images and their corresponding textual descriptions. By using both an image and a list of labels (text), the model can determine which label best matches the content of the image. This approach allows the model not only to analyze visual features but also to use contextual information from the text, providing a more powerful and versatile solution than single-modal models, which process only one type of data.

Listing 6.12   Using a multimodal model to simultaneously process visual and textual data

```
from transformers import CLIPProcessor, CLIPModel        Downloads the CLIP model

model = CLIPModel.from_pretrained("openai/clip-vit-base-patch32")   ◄──┘
processor = CLIPProcessor.from_pretrained("openai/clip-vit-base-patch32")
```

```
labels = ["cat", "dog", "tiger", "train"]
inputs = processor(text = labels,
                   images = image,
                   return_tensors = "pt",
                   padding=True)
```

The inputs variable contains the data that is passed to the CLIP model for processing. It is the processed representation of both the text and image data, formatted in a way that the model can understand.

```
model.eval()

with torch.no_grad():
    outputs = model(**inputs)
```

The outputs variable contains the result of processing the inputs through the CLIP model. The model processes the text and image data, and the outputs object contains the computed features and similarity scores.

```
logits_per_image = outputs.logits_per_image
```

The image-text similarity score

```
probs = logits_per_image.softmax(dim=1)
most_likely_index = torch.argmax(probs, dim=1).item()
most_likely_object = labels[most_likely_index]
```

We can take the softmax to get the label probabilities.

```
print(f"The most likely object is: {most_likely_object}")
```

Gets and prints the most likely object

This example is a multimodal model in action. It involves processing and combining data from two modalities: text and images. Specifically, the code uses the CLIP model from OpenAI, which is designed to understand and compute the similarity between textual descriptions and images. Here's how the code works:

1 You download the openai/clip-vit-base-patch32 model and its corresponding processor, using the CLIPModel and CLIPProcessor classes.

2 The input image (loaded using libraries like PIL) and a list of possible labels (["cat", "dog", "tiger", "train"]) are processed by the CLIPProcessor, which converts them to a format suitable for the model (token embeddings for text and normalized tensors for the image).

3 The model processes the image and the text inputs:
   a It extracts visual features from the image.
   b It extracts textual features from the labels.

4 The model computes similarity scores between the image features and each label's text features, producing a set of *logits* (raw, unnormalized output values of a model; logits_per_image).

5 The logits are converted to probabilities using the softmax() function, and the label with the highest probability is selected as the most likely match for the image.

This example returns the following output:

```
The most likely object is: dog
```

Summary

- Fine-tuning is a machine learning method in which a pretrained model is further trained on a smaller, domain-specific dataset to adapt it to a targeted task.

- The `yelp_polarity` dataset is a subset of the larger Yelp Dataset Challenge, created specifically for text classification applications like sentiment analysis.

- Sequence classification refers to tasks in which an entire sequence of data—such as a sentence, paragraph, or longer token string—is assigned a single label or category.

- MPS is Apple's framework that enables GPU-accelerated computation on macOS systems powered by Apple silicon (M1, M2, M3, and M4 chips).

- CUDA is Nvidia's platform and programming interface that allows developers to perform general-purpose computing on Nvidia GPUs.

- To fine-tune a pretrained model with Hugging Face, you typically use the `Trainer` class together with `TrainingArguments`.

- A single-modal model is designed to handle data from only one modality, such as text, images, audio, or numerical values.

- A multimodal model is capable of processing and combining data from multiple modalities, such as text, images, audio, video, or structured inputs.

- `CLIP`, developed by OpenAI, is a multimodal model that links visual understanding with natural language comprehension.

Creating LLM-based applications using LangChain and LlamaIndex

This chapter covers

- Introducing large language models (LLMs)
- Creating LLM applications using LangChain
- Connecting LLMs to your private data

In chapter 3, you learned how to employ a transformers pipeline to access diverse pretrained models for various natural language processing (NLP) tasks, including sentiment classification, named entity extraction, and text summarization. In practical scenarios, however, the goal is to seamlessly integrate various models, encompassing those from Hugging Face and OpenAI, into custom applications. Enter LangChain, a solution that facilitates the customization of NLP applications by linking different components based on specific requirements.

Although pretrained models are beneficial, it's important to note that they were trained on external data, not your own. Often, you need to use a model that answers questions pertinent to your unique dataset. Imagine possessing a dataset with numerous receipts and invoices. You would want a pretrained model to summarize your purchases or identify vendors associated with specific items. LlamaIndex is indispensable for this task. With LlamaIndex, you gain the ability to connect an LLM to your proprietary data, empowering it to address queries tailored to your dataset.

In this chapter, you'll delve into using LangChain to construct NLP applications with LLMs. Further, you'll explore using LlamaIndex to develop NLP applications specifically trained to respond to inquiries related to your private data.

7.1 Introducing LLMs

An LLM is a type of AI model designed to understand and generate humanlike text based on the patterns and structures it learned from a massive amount of training data. Specifically, LLM refers to a class of advanced NLP models. LLMs have the following features:

- *Size and scale*—LLMs are trained on a massive amount of data, including books, articles, websites, videos, and pictures (see figure 7.1).
- *Pretraining*—LLMs go through a pretraining phase in which they use a large amount of training data to learn the statistical relationships between words and sentences. This phase allows them to acquire a general understanding of grammar, syntax, and semantics.
- *Fine-tuning*—After the pretraining, LLMs are fine-tuned on specific tasks or datasets. This process makes them perform specific tasks, such as text classification, sentiment analysis, and language translation.

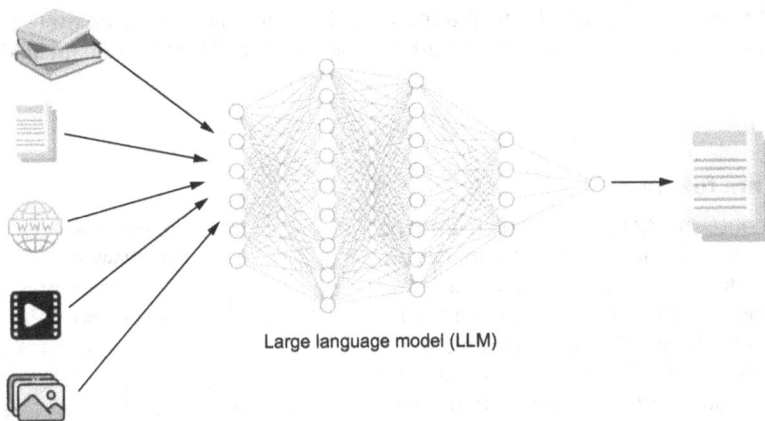

Large language model (LLM)

Figure 7.1 LLMs are trained using large amounts of data from sources including books, articles, webpages, videos, and images.

To gain a perspective on how large LLMs are, consider the numbers shown in table 7.1. Specifically, OpenAI's GPT-3 Davinci model has 175 billion trainable parameters and uses 499 billion tokens in its training data.

Table 7.1   Some LLMs and the size of their training data

LLM model	Number of trainable parameters	Number of tokens in the training data
Nvidia: Megatron-Turing Natural Language Generation (MT-NLG)	530 billion	270 billion
OpenAI: Generative Pretrained Transformer-3 (GPT-3) Davinci	175 billion	499 billion

Source: *A Beginner's Guide to Large Language Models*, Part 1. Nvidia. https://mng.bz/V9YW

Trainable parameters

Trainable parameters are the variables within a machine learning or deep learning model that are adjusted during the training process to enable the model to make accurate predictions or perform a specific task. These parameters are learned from the training data and fine-tuned to optimize the model's performance on a given task. In neural networks, trainable parameters typically include the following:

- *Weights*—These values are associated with the connections between neurons in different layers of the network. During training, the weights are repeatedly adjusted to help the network learn the relationships between input data and desired output.
- *Biases*—These values are associated with each neuron in a neural network layer. They help shift the activation function's output and allow the network to learn complex patterns.

In short, the more trainable parameters you have in a neural network, the longer it takes to train the system. Training a model with many trainable parameters requires immense computing power and memory, so it is very expensive to train an LLM.

What are tokens?

In the context of NLP and machine learning, a *token* is a chunk of text that a model processes as a single unit. Consider an example using the word *unhappiness*. Instead of processing the word as a single unit, a GPT such as OpenAI's GPT-3.5 uses a technique known as *subword-level tokenization*, called byte-pair encoding (BPE). This technique allows the model to have a large, diverse vocabulary without the limitations of a fixed word-level vocabulary. This is particularly useful for understanding and generating text in various contexts, languages, and domains. The following figure shows the word broken into three tokens.

Subword-level tokenization

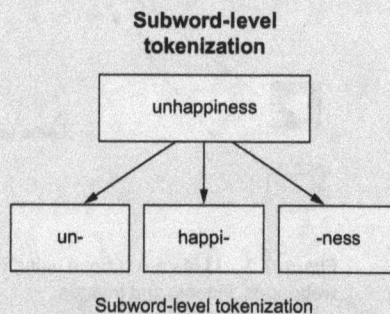

Subword-level tokenization

How the word *unhappiness* is tokenized into three tokens using the subword-level tokenization technique

Note that in addition to subword-level tokenization, you can use techniques such as word-level tokenization and character-level tokenization (covered in chapter 3).

7.2 Introducing LangChain

LangChain is a framework built around LLMs, designed to simplify the creation of applications with LLMs. You can think of it as a chain that connects the various components required to create advanced use cases for LLMs. A chain may contain the following components:

- *Prompt templates*—Templates for different types of conversations with LLMs
- *LLMs*—GPT-3, GPT-4, and so on
- *Agents*—Use LLM to decide what actions to be taken
- *Memory*—Short- or long-term memory

7.2.1 Installing LangChain

To use LangChain, you first need to install the `langchain` package using the `pip` command:

```
!pip install langchain
```

All the code in the following sections is tested against LangChain version 0.3.4.

7.2.2 Creating a prompt template

Let's learn how to use LangChain to connect an LLM with a prompt template to create a simple LLM application. The first component you'll create is a `PromptTemplate`.

DEFINITION A *prompt template* structures the instruction or query given to the model to obtain the desired outputs. It provides a flexible way to guide the model's behavior by incorporating special tokens and instructions.

A `PromptTemplate` is a string template that accepts a list of parameters from users that can be used to generate a prompt for an LLM. The following code snippet creates a `PromptTemplate` containing a single parameter (question:).

Listing 7.1 Creating a simple `PromptTemplate` component

```
from langchain import PromptTemplate

template = '''
Question: {question}
Answer:
'''

prompt = PromptTemplate(
```

```
        template = template,
        input_variables = ['question']
)
prompt
```

The `template` parameter in the `PromptTemplate` class accepts a string template. The `input_variables` parameter accepts a list of parameters from the user that will be used to generate the prompt. Figure 7.2 shows the relationship between the value of the `input_variables` parameter and the variable in the string template:

```
template = '''
Question: {question}               These two
Answer: '''                        must match.


prompt = PromptTemplate(
    template = template,
    input_variables = ['question']
)
```

Figure 7.2   The input variable is linked to the variable in the string template.

Here is the output of the `PromptTemplate` when printed:

```
PromptTemplate(input_variables=['question'],
                template='\nQuestion: {question}\nAnswer: ')
```

In the prompt template, you want to ask the LLM a question and get an answer.

7.2.3   *Specifying an LLM*

Now that you've created the prompt template, the next step is selecting and using an LLM. Let's start with an LLM hosted by Hugging Face. First, though, you need to sign up for a free account at Hugging Face (https://huggingface.co/join), if you haven't done that already, and create a token at https://huggingface.co/settings/tokens. Create a read token, and give it a name (see figure 7.3).

Then copy the access token and save it in the environment variable:

```
import os
os.environ['HUGGINGFACEHUB_API_TOKEN'] = 'Your_HuggingFace_Token'
```

To use an LLM from Hugging Face, install the `langchain-huggingface` package:

```
!pip install langchain-huggingface
```

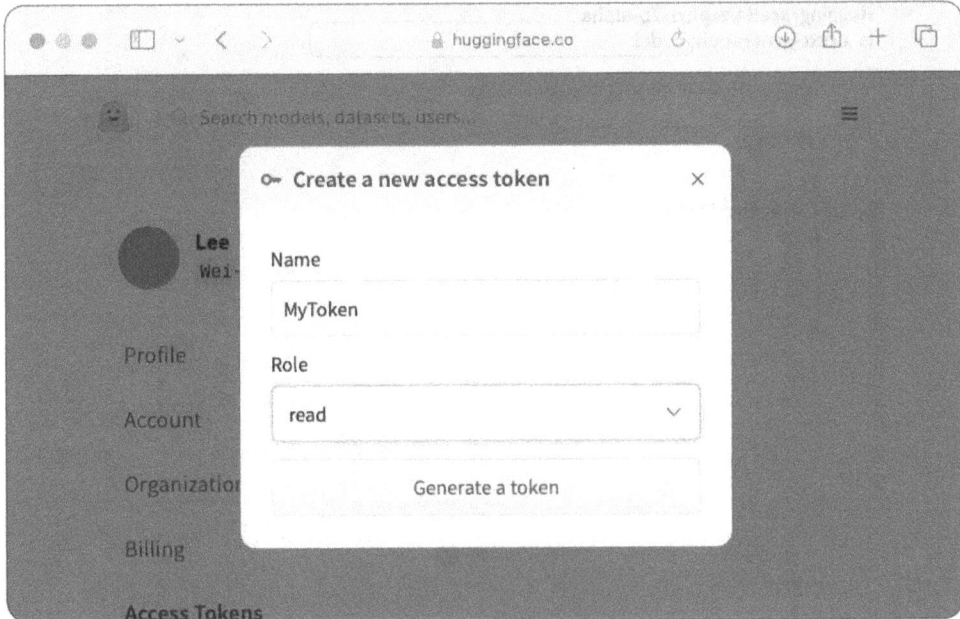

Figure 7.3 Creating a Hugging Face token

Now you can use the `HuggingFaceEndPoint` class to access an LLM from Hugging Face:

```
from langchain_huggingface import HuggingFaceEndpoint

hub_llm = HuggingFaceEndpoint(
    endpoint_url="https://api-inference.huggingface.co/models/
HuggingFaceH4/zephyr-7b-alpha",
    temperature = 1
)
```

The preceding code snippet uses the `HuggingFaceH4/zephyr-7b-alpha` model.

> **NOTE** When you use the `HuggingFaceEndPoint` class to specify an LLM, the inferencing is performed at Hugging Face's end, not locally on your computer.

The language models in the Zephyr series are trained to act as helpful assistants. `Zephyr -7B-α`, the first model in the series, is a fine-tuned version of `mistralai/Mistral -7B-v0.1`, which was trained on a mix of publicly available synthetic datasets using Direct Preference Optimization (DPO). You can find more information about this model at https://mng.bz/nZO4. As shown in figure 7.4, `HuggingFaceH4/zephyr-7b -alpha` is a text-generation model.

HuggingFaceH4/zephyr-7b-alpha
is a text-generation model.

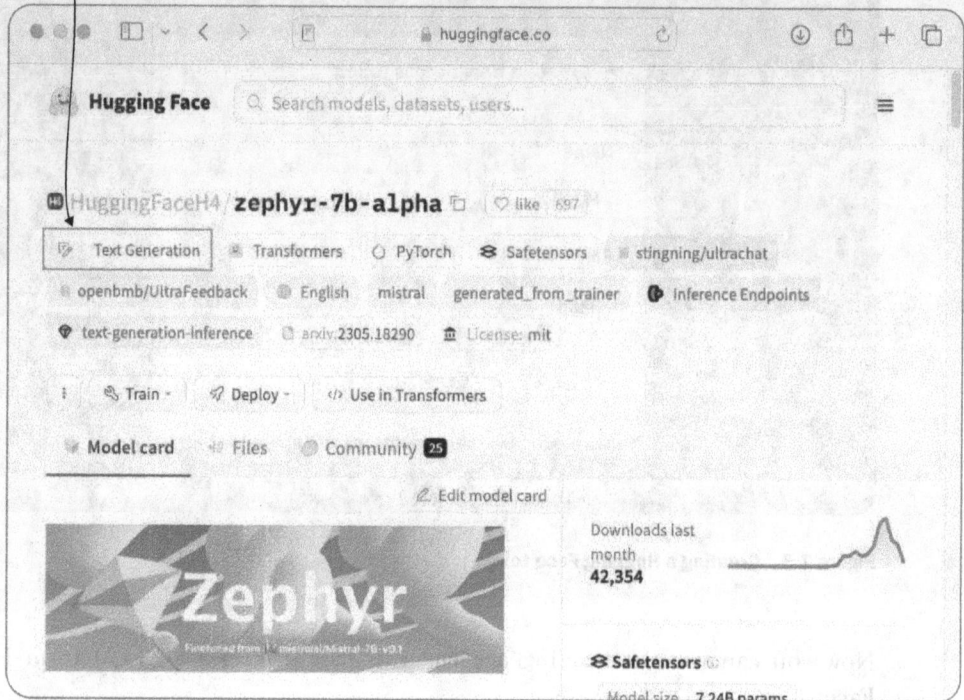

Figure 7.4 Viewing the HuggingFaceH4/zephyr-7b-alpha model on the Hugging Face web page

7.2.4 Creating an LLM chain

The next step is creating an LLM chain. You combine your prompt template and model (LLM) to create a chain so that you can run queries against the LLM:

```
from langchain_core.output_parsers import StrOutputParser

llm_chain = prompt | hub_llm | StrOutputParser()
```

Essentially, you're chaining all the various components: PromptTemplate, hub_llm, and StrOutputParser. The StrOutputParser object handles the output and parses it into a string. The | operator in llm_chain = prompt | hub_llm | StrOutputParser() represents *pipeline-style chaining* in LangChain. This syntax makes it easy to link different components—prompts, language models, output parsers, and so on—in a sequence to process data from start to finish. Each component takes the output of the previous step, processes it, and passes it along to the next.

7.2.5   *Running the chain*

You are ready to use the chain to answer questions. To test the application, call the run() method of the LLM chain:

```
qn = "Who is Elon Musk?"
print(llm_chain.invoke(qn))
```

Here is the response from the LLM:

```
1. Elon Musk is the CEO of SpaceX, Tesla, and Neuralink
```

Remember that all the inferencing is done on Hugging Face's server. Observe what happens if you ask a follow-up question:

```
qn = "Is he married?"
print(llm_chain.invoke(qn))
```

You get a response like the following because the LLM doesn't maintain a context between questions:

```
I do not have personal information about individuals. however, based on the
information available to me
```

How do you solve this problem? Let's take a look.

7.2.6   *Maintaining a conversation*

To maintain context between questions, the LLM needs to know what the response questions and answers were. One way to do this is to alter the prompt template and provide a history of the conversation:

```
template = '''
Current conversation: {history}
Human: {question}
AI:
'''
```

The preceding code snippet shows that there are two variables in the template string:

- history
- question

Correspondingly, the input_variables parameter must also specify the two variables in the list:

```
prompt = PromptTemplate(
    template = template,
    input_variables = ['question','history']
)
```

Next, create a new chain using the updated `PromptTemplate` object:

```
llm_chain = prompt | hub_llm | StrOutputParser()
```

Now you can ask a question by passing the question and history to the invoke() method:

```
qn = "Who is Elon Musk?"
response = llm_chain.invoke({'question':qn,'history':''})
print(response)
```

The preceding code generates the following response:

```
Elon Musk is a South African-born American entrepreneur, business magnate,
and engineer.
```

If you ask a follow-up question like this one (note that you need to pass the previous response from the LLM to the invoke() method),

```
qn = "Is he married?"
response = llm_chain.invoke({'question':qn,'history':response})
print(response)
```

you get a response that understands the context of the question:

```
Elon Musk is currently not married. He was previously married to Canadian
author and journalist, Tal
```

Now rewrite the preceding code snippet using a while loop so you can prompt the user to ask a question and get the LLM to answer it:

```
history = ''
while True:
    qn = input('Question: ')
    if qn == 'quit':
        break
    response = llm_chain.invoke({'question':qn, 'history':history})
    history = response
    print(history)
```

Figure 7.5 shows the flow of the question-and-answer session.

7.2.7   *Using the RunnableWithMessageHistory class*

Section 7.2.6 showed how to modify the prompt to maintain a conversation with the LLM. An alternative approach to maintaining a chat conversation is to use the `RunnableWithMessageHistory` class, a LangChain class that allows you to manage the history of interactions (messages) during a conversation between the user and an AI model. The class is part of LangChain's conversational framework, used to build

First question
and response

```
history = ''
while True:
    qn = input('Question: ')
    if qn == 'quit':
        break
    response = llm_chain.run({'question':qn, 'history':history})
    history = response
    print(history)
```

```
Question: Who is Elon Musk?
Elon Musk is a South African–born American entrepreneur, business magnate, and engineer.
Question: Where does he live?
Elon Musk is an American citizen and currently resides in Austin, Texas, where he moved
```

```
Question: ||                                              ⊕∨
```

Second question
and response

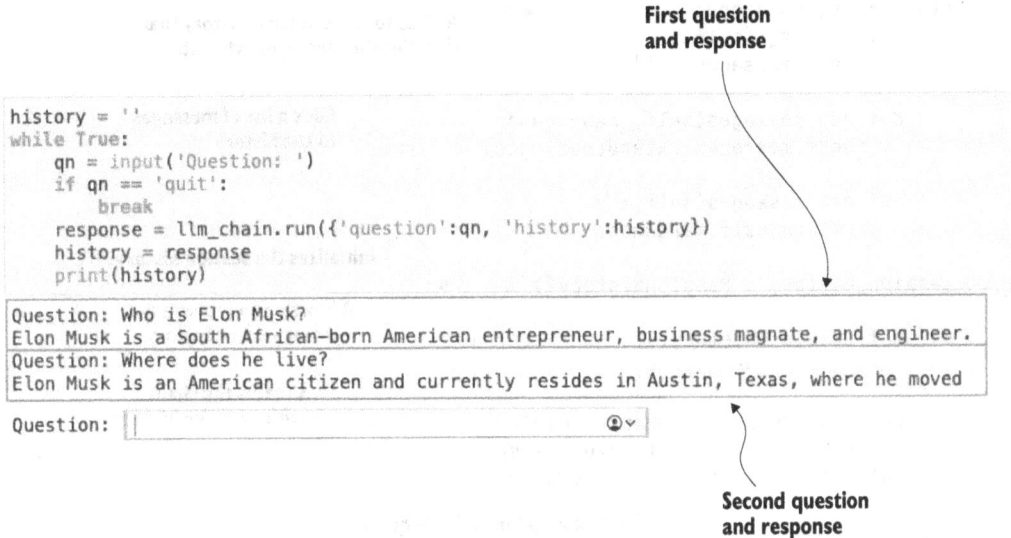

Figure 7.5   A user can ask questions and get a response from the LLM.

systems that keep track of conversation history across multiple exchanges. The following listing shows how to use the RunnableWithMessageHistory class.

Listing 7.2   Using the RunnableWithMessageHistory class to maintain conversation

```
import os
from langchain import PromptTemplate
from langchain_core.output_parsers import StrOutputParser
from langchain_huggingface import HuggingFaceEndpoint
from langchain_core.runnables.history import RunnableWithMessageHistory

os.environ['HUGGINGFACEHUB_API_TOKEN'] = 'your_hugging_face_token'

template = '''
Question: {question}
Answer:
'''

prompt = PromptTemplate(
    template = template,
    input_variables = ['question']
)

hub_llm = HuggingFaceEndpoint(
    endpoint_url="https://api-inference.huggingface.co/models/HuggingFaceH4/
zephyr-7b-alpha",
    temperature = 1
)
```

```
class SessionHistory:
    def __init__(self):                    ◄─── A class to store session history that
        self.messages = []                      includes the messages attribute

    def add_messages(self, messages):      ──┐  Adds a list of messages
        self.messages.extend(messages)     ◄─┘  to the history

    def get_messages(self):
        return self.messages
                                           ──┐  Initializes the session history
session_history = SessionHistory()         ◄─┘

                                           ──┐  A function to retrieve the
def get_session_history():                 ◄─┘  current session history
    return session_history

                                           ──┐  Creates the chain
llm_chain = RunnableWithMessageHistory(    ◄─┘  with message history
    prompt | hub_llm | StrOutputParser(),
    get_session_history = get_session_history
)
                       ──┐  Starts a loop for multiple questions
while True:            ◄─┘
                                                              Gets the user input ┐
    user_question = input("Ask a question (type 'exit' to stop): ")  ◄───────────┘


    if user_question.lower() == "quit":    ──┐
        print("Ending conversation.")      ◄─┘  Exit condition
        break



    input_data = {"question": user_question}   ──┐  Prepares the input data
                                               ◄─┘

    response = llm_chain.invoke(input_data)    ──┐  Gets the model's response
                                               ◄─┘

    session_history.add_messages([                 ──┐  Adds the user question
        {"role": "user", "content": user_question},     and assistant response
        {"role": "assistant", "content": response}  ◄───┘  to the session history
    ])

    #L display the response
    print(f"AI: {response}")
```

You can ask follow-up questions after the initial question. The main addition to this code snippet is the SessionHistory class, which allows you to save the history of the exchanges between the user and the model. Then an instance of the SessionHistory class is passed to the RunnableWithMessageHistory class through the get_session_history parameter:

```
llm_chain = RunnableWithMessageHistory(
    prompt | hub_llm | StrOutputParser(),
    get_session_history = get_session_history
)
```

Now the LLM can retain the context of the conversation and answer the follow-up question correctly. How do you retrieve the chat history? You can do so via the get_ messages() method from the session_history object:

```
print(session_history.get_messages())
```

The following listing shows an example conversation history (formatted for clarity).

Listing 7.3 Example chat history

```
[
HumanMessage(
  content='Who is Bill Gates?',
  additional_kwargs={},
  response_metadata={}
),

AIMessage(
  content="Bill Gates is an American business magnate, software
developer, entrepreneur, and philanthropist. He is best known as
the co-founder of Microsoft Corporation, the world's largest
personal computer software company. Gates is also the co-chair
of the Bill & Melinda Gates Foundation, a private charitable
organization that is dedicated to improving health and reducing
poverty worldwide. As of 2021, he is one of the wealthiest
individuals in the world.",
  additional_kwargs={}, response_metadata={}
),

{'role': 'user', 'content': 'Who is Bill Gates?'},

{'role': 'assistant', 'content': "Bill Gates is an American
business magnate, software developer, entrepreneur, and
philanthropist. He is best known as the co-founder of
Microsoft Corporation, the world's largest personal computer
software company. Gates is also the co-chair of the Bill &
Melinda Gates Foundation, a private charitable organization
that is dedicated to improving health and reducing poverty
worldwide. As of 2021, he is one of the wealthiest
individuals in the world."},

HumanMessage(
content='Is he rich?',
additional_kwargs={},
response_metadata={}
),

AIMessage(
content='<|>\nYes, Bill Gates is one of the wealthiest
individuals in the world according to the information
provided in the AIMessage.',
additional_kwargs={},
response_metadata={}
```

```
),

{'role': 'user', 'content': 'Is he rich?'},

{'role': 'assistant', 'content': '<|>\nYes, Bill Gates is
one of the wealthiest individuals in the world according to
the information provided in the AIMessage.'}
]
Text Completion
```

Besides asking questions, `HuggingFaceH4/zephyr-7b-alpha` (being a text-generation model) can perform text completion. The trick of making it perform text completion is modifying the prompt template. The following code shows the entire program, with the prompt string changed to text completion.

Listing 7.4 Performing text completion

```
import os
from langchain import PromptTemplate
from langchain_core.output_parsers import StrOutputParser
from langchain_huggingface import HuggingFaceEndpoint

os.environ['HUGGINGFACEHUB_API_TOKEN'] = 'Your_HuggingFace_Token'

template = '''
Complete this: {question}
'''

prompt = PromptTemplate(
    template = template,
    input_variables = ['question']
)
prompt

hub_llm = HuggingFaceEndpoint(
    endpoint_url="https://api-inference.huggingface.co/
models/HuggingFaceH4/zephyr-7b-alpha",
    temperature = 1
)

llm_chain = prompt | hub_llm | StrOutputParser()

while True:
    qn = input('Question: ')
    if qn == 'quit':
        break
    response = llm_chain.invoke(qn)
    print(response)
```

Run the program, and ask a question. Figure 7.6 shows the model's response.

```
25  while True:
26      qn = input('Question: ')
27      if qn == 'quit':
28          break
29      response = llm_chain.invoke(qn)
30      print(response)
```

Question: You and I ◄────────────────────── **1. Type a sentence.**

```
It's an unspoken lie
We're running in circles
But we just can't admit it

Chorus:                                      2. Response from
Oh, you and I                     ◄╱              the model
We've got a story to tell
It's been buried deep inside
We've been playing hell
With ourselves, it's true
But now it's time to face the truth

Outro:
So, let's take a leap of faith
And start this journey to release
The pain that's been holding us
In the past, it's time for change
We can overcome this together
And find a way to heal and mend
This fragmented connection between
Two hearts still beating as one again.
```

Question: │

Figure 7.6   You can get the model to complete your sentence.

7.2.8   *Using other LLMs*

Apart from using the LLMs from Hugging Face, you can use LLMs from other providers. Moving forward, you'll have the chance to try two other LLMs, one from OpenAI and one from Hugging Face.

USING OPENAI

Let's use an LLM from OpenAI. Before you can use the LLM from OpenAI, you need to install the langchain_openai package with the pip command:

```
!pip install langchain_openai
```

You also need to apply for an API key, which is a pay-per-use key. You can apply at https://platform.openai.com/account/api-keys (see figure 7.7).

After you obtain your OpenAI API key, add the following statements to add an environment variable named OPENAI_API_KEY, and set it to your OpenAI API key:

```
import os
os.environ['OPENAI_API_KEY'] = "OPENAI_API_KEY"
```

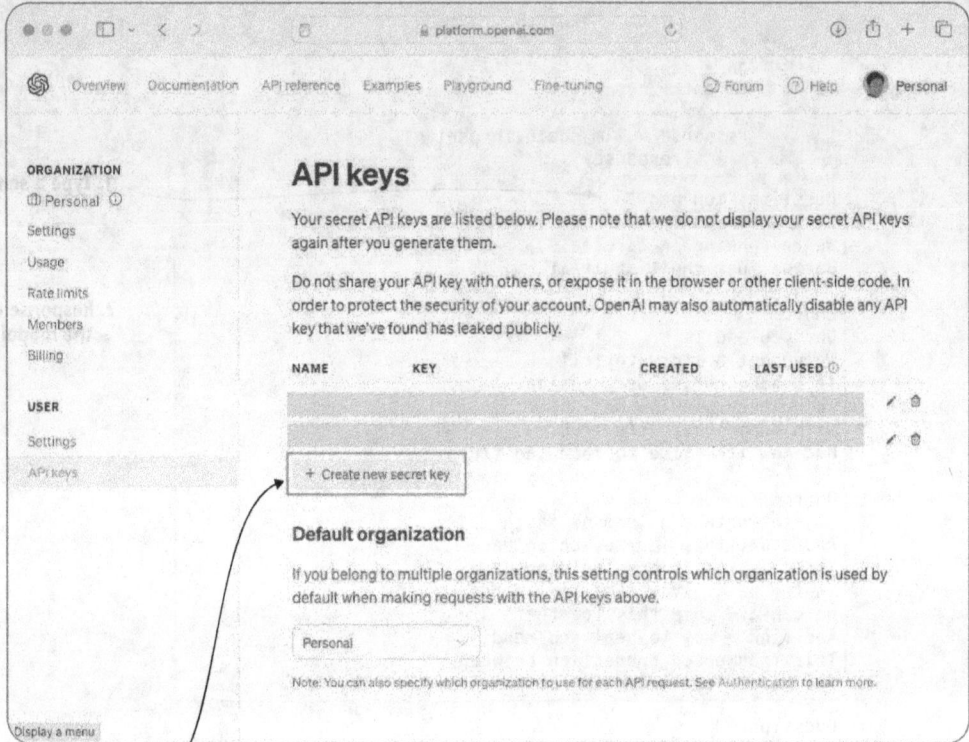

Click button to create a
new OpenAI API key.

Figure 7.7   Applying for an OpenAI API key

To view the list of OpenAI models you can use, check out https://platform.openai
.com/docs/models/overview. Here are some models that you can use:

- `gpt-3.5-turbo`—Most capable GPT-3.5 model, optimized for chat at 1/10th the cost of an older model (`text-davinci-003`)
- `gpt-4o-mini`—More capable than any GPT-3.5 model, able to perform more complex tasks, and optimized for chat

To use an OpenAI model such as `gpt-4o-mini`, pass the name of the model to the `ChatOpenAI` class:

```
from langchain.chat_models import ChatOpenAI

openai_model = ChatOpenAI(model_name = 'gpt-4o-mini')
```

Then, as before, create a `PromptTemplate` and an LLM, and chain them together.

Listing 7.5 Creating a chain using OpenAI LLM

```
from langchain import PromptTemplate
from langchain_core.output_parsers import StrOutputParser

template = '''
Question: {question}
Answer: '''

prompt = PromptTemplate(
    template = template,
    input_variables = ['question']
)

llm_chain = prompt | openai_model | StrOutputParser()
```

Now pose a question to the OpenAI model:

```
question = "Who is Steve Jobs"
print(llm_chain.invoke(question))
```

You get a reply like this:

```
Steve Jobs was an American entrepreneur, businessman, inventor,
and co-founder of Apple Inc. He is widely recognized as a pioneer
of the personal computer revolution of the 1970s and 1980s, along
with his business partner and Apple co-founder Steve Wozniak.
Jobs also served as the CEO of Pixar Animation Studios and was a
member of the board of directors of The Walt Disney Company. He
passed away in 2011 from complications related to pancreatic
cancer.
```

USING THE TIIUAE/FALCON-7B-INSTRUCT MODEL

Hugging Face also has several models you can use. One is tiiuae/falcon-7b-instruct (https://huggingface.co/tiiuae/falcon-7b-instruct), an LLM developed by the Technology Innovation Institute in Abu Dhabi, United Arab Emirates. This model is an instruction-tuned version of Falcon 7B, a transformer-based model designed to understand and follow specific instructions provided by users. As usual, create a Prompt-Template and HuggingFaceEndPoint and then chain them together, as follows.

Listing 7.6 Using the tiiuae/falcon-7b-instruct model

```
import os
from langchain_core.output_parsers import StrOutputParser
from langchain_huggingface import HuggingFaceEndpoint
from langchain import PromptTemplate


os.environ['HUGGINGFACEHUB_API_TOKEN'] = 'Your_HuggingFace_Token'
```

```
template = '''
Question: {question}
Answer: '''

prompt = PromptTemplate(
    template = template,
    input_variables = ['question']
)

hub_llm = HuggingFaceEndpoint(endpoint_url=
    "https://api-inference.huggingface.co/models/
tiiuae/falcon-7b-instruct",
    temperature = 1
)

llm_chain = prompt | hub_llm | StrOutputParser()
```

Ask a question using the `llm_chain` object:

```
question = "Translate this to Spanish: Which is the way to
the train station?"
print(llm_chain.invoke(question))
```

You should see the following response:

```
¿A dónde está la estación de tren?
```

Here's another question:

```
question = "What is the capital of France?"
print(llm_chain.invoke(question))
```

The response looks like this:

```
The capital of France is Paris.
```

7.3   Connecting LLMs to your private data using LlamaIndex

So far, you've seen how interesting it is to use LangChain to connect to LLMs provided by OpenAI and Hugging Face to build your own chat-based applications where you can ask questions using natural language. But although LLMs are trained on a huge amount of data, they are not trained on your data. It would be more helpful to use an LLM to answer specific questions that pertain to your data rather than the data the model was trained on.

LlamaIndex solves this problem by connecting your data and adding it to an existing LLM by using a technique known as *retrieval-augmented generation* (RAG). RAG enhances the performance of LLMs by integrating them with an external retrieval system. The main idea is to supplement the language model's response generation with relevant information from a knowledge base or document store, enabling it to generate more accurate, context-aware responses without needing to know everything ahead of time.

> **NOTE** LlamaIndex is a data framework that enables LLM-based applications to ingest, structure, and access private or domain-specific data. It's available in Python and TypeScript.

7.3.1 Installing the packages

First, use the `pip` command to install the following packages:

```
!pip install llama_index
!pip install llama-index-embeddings-huggingface
!pip install llama-index-llms-huggingface
```

Let's learn how to use LlamaIndex with a Hugging Face model to index your private data so that an LLM can answer questions pertaining to your data.

7.3.2 Preparing the documents

For this example, we'll use LlamaIndex to answer questions based on receipts saved in PDF format. In addition to PDF, LlamaIndex supports several common file formats, including the following:

- *Text files*—`.txt`
- *Microsoft Word documents*—`.doc` and `.docx`
- *Markdown files*—`.md`
- *HTML files*—`.html` and `.htm`
- *CSV files*—`.csv`
- *JSON files*—`.json`

Create a folder named `Training Documents` in the same directory as your Jupyter Notebook. Populate the folder with the receipts. In this example, the folder contains four PDF documents (receipts of some purchases; see figure 7.8).

7.3.3 Loading the documents

To load the PDFs into memory for indexing, use `SimpleDirectoryReader`-class, a LlamaIndex component that facilitates reading and indexing documents from a specific directory:

Content of the Training Documents folder

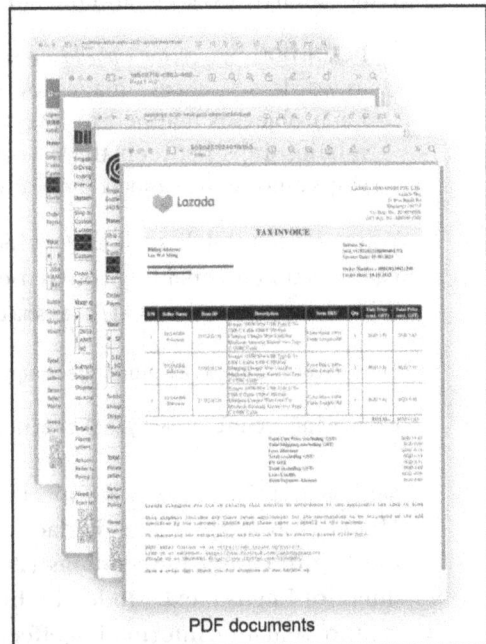

PDF documents

Figure 7.8 Contents of the `Training Documents` folder

```
from llama_index.core import SimpleDirectoryReader

loader = SimpleDirectoryReader(
    input_dir="./Training Documents",
    recursive=True,
    required_exts=[".pdf"],
)


documents = loader.load_data()    ◄——————  Loads the documents
```

In the preceding code snippet, you specify the following:

- *Directory input*—This input allows you to specify a directory from which to load documents.
- *Recursive loading*—When the recursive parameter is set to `True`, the model can search subdirectories and load documents from them.
- *File-type filtering*—The `required_exts` parameter enables you to filter which file types to load (PDFs, text files, Word documents, and so on).

7.3.4   *Using an embedding model*

When the documents are loaded, the next step is performing vector embedding to convert the text data to vector representations. This process allows more efficient querying, similarity search, and further processing of the documents.

> **DEFINITION**   A *vector embedding* is a numerical representation of objects (such as words, sentences, images, or any data point) in a continuous vector space. Each object is mapped to a vector of numbers in such a way that the spatial relationships between these vectors reflect similarities or semantic relationships among the objects themselves.

You can use models such as `HuggingFaceEmbedding` to generate these embeddings for each document, enabling you to use machine learning models in your application. For this example, use the `BAAI/bge-small-en-v1.5` model:

```
from llama_index.embeddings.huggingface import HuggingFaceEmbedding

embedding_model = HuggingFaceEmbedding(model_name="BAAI/bge-small-en-v1.5")
```

`BAAI/bge-small-en-v1.5` is a specific pretrained model available on the Hugging Face Model Hub (https://huggingface.co/BAAI/bge-small-en-v1.5). This model is part of the Bag of Graph Embeddings (BGE) series, which is designed to generate embeddings for English text. Models in this series often focus on producing embeddings that capture semantic information effectively, making them useful for various NLP tasks.

> **NOTE**   When you use a model like `BAAI/bge-small-en-v1.5`, the embedding process takes place locally on your computer, ensuring the privacy of your data.

7.3.5   Indexing the document

Now you can start to index the document using the embedding model via the `Vector-StoreIndex` class, which creates an index and then saves the vector embeddings on disk:

```
from llama_index.core import VectorStoreIndex

index = VectorStoreIndex.from_documents(
    documents,
    embed_model = embedding_model,
)


index.storage_context.persist(persist_dir=".")
```

Saves the index in the
current directory

The vector embeddings are stored in the same directory as your Jupyter Notebook. Five files are created:

- `image__vector_store.json`—Contains the vector embeddings associated with documents that are categorized as images. If your index includes image documents or embeddings generated from image data, this file stores that specific information.
- `default__vector_store.json`—Stores the main vector embeddings for the default category of documents in your index. It contains the embeddings of text documents that are not specifically categorized as images or other types.
- `graph_store.json`—Contains information related to any graph structures or relationships that exist between the indexed documents. These structures or relationships could include links or any other metadata that captures the connectivity or hierarchy of the documents.
- `index_store.json`—Holds metadata and configurations related to the index itself. It may include information about how the index was constructed, parameters used during creation, and other relevant settings.
- `docstore.json`—Contains the actual document data or references to the documents that were indexed. It serves as storage for the documents themselves, allowing the index to retrieve and reference them when necessary.

Saving the vector embeddings to disk is beneficial because it allows you to perform the embedding process only once—unless the content of your documents changes. When the embeddings are saved, you can simply load them from disk in the future, avoiding the need to embed the documents again. In section 7.3.6, you learn how to load these vector embeddings directly from disk.

7.3.6   Loading the embeddings

When the index is persisted to disk, you can load it into memory using the `Storage-Context` class and the `load_index_from_storage()` function:

```
from llama_index.core import StorageContext, load_index_from_storage
from llama_index.embeddings.huggingface import HuggingFaceEmbedding

embedding_model = HuggingFaceEmbedding(model_name="BAAI/bge-small-en-v1.5")

storage_context = StorageContext.from_defaults(persist_dir=".")
index = load_index_from_storage(storage_context,
                                embed_model = embedding_model)
```

Note that you need to use the same embedding model that you used earlier for indexing.

7.3.7   *Using an LLM for querying*

Now that the documents are indexed, you can use a Hugging Face model to ask questions based on your local documents, as shown in the following listing.

Listing 7.7   Querying the local documents using an LLM

```
from transformers import AutoModelForCausalLM, AutoTokenizer
from llama_index.llms.huggingface import HuggingFaceLLM
import torch

if torch.backends.mps.is_available():          ◀──┐  Determines the device
    device = torch.device("mps")
else:
    device = torch.device("cuda" if torch.cuda.is_available() else "cpu")


tokenizer = AutoTokenizer.from_pretrained(     ◀──┐  Loads a model and tokenizer
    "meta-llama/Llama-3.2-3B-Instruct")           │  from Hugging Face
model = AutoModelForCausalLM.from_pretrained(
    "meta-llama/Llama-3.2-3B-Instruct").to(device)


huggingface_llm = HuggingFaceLLM(              ◀──┐  Initializes HuggingFaceLLM
    model=model,
    tokenizer=tokenizer,
)

                                                     Sets the LLM to use
query_engine = index.as_query_engine(llm=huggingface_llm)  ◀──
```

In this example, you'll use the AutoModelForCausalLM class to load the meta-llama/Llama-3.2-3B-Instruct model, which will be set as the query engine for the index.

NOTE   Again, using a model like meta-llama/Llama-3.2-3B-Instruct ensures that the inferencing of the model is done locally on your computer, ensuring data privacy.

> ### Shifting the workload to the GPU
>
> The `to()` method in PyTorch moves a model or tensor to a specified device—typically, a CPU or graphics processing unit (GPU). If you have an Apple silicon Mac (with an M1, M2, M3, or later processor), processing is moved to the GPU (mps, for *Metal Performance Shaders*). If you have an Nvidia GPU on your Windows PC, processing is moved to the GPU (cuda, for *Compute Unified Device Architecture*). If you have none of these devices, the processing is done on the CPU.

7.3.8 Asking questions

You can ask questions related to the receipts using the `meta-llama/Llama-3.2-3B -Instruct` model:

```
while True:
    question = input("Question: ")
    if question.lower() == "quit": break
    print(query_engine.query(question).response)
```

The following dialogue shows the question asked and the response by the model:

```
Question: How much did I pay for the keyboard?
162.90 SGD.
```

7.3.9 Using LlamaIndex with OpenAI

You may have noticed that running an LLM locally is slow. This is because local models often require significant computational resources, including high memory and processing power, to handle the large number of parameters and complex calculations involved in generating responses. Performance can be affected further by the hardware limitations of the machine being used, such as CPU speed and GPU availability. These limitations can lead to longer inference times compared with accessing models hosted on cloud platforms, where powerful infrastructure is optimized for fast processing. More significantly, the quality of the answer may not be as good as you expected.

An alternative to running a local LLM is using an OpenAI model such as `gpt-4o -mini`. To do that, you need to install the following packages:

```
!pip install langchain_community
!pip install langchain_openai
```

The following code snippet loads the `gpt-4o-mini` model and sets it as the query engine for the index:

```
from langchain_openai import ChatOpenAI
import os

os.environ["OPENAI_API_KEY"] = "OpenAI_API_Key"
```

```
openai_llm = ChatOpenAI(temperature = 0.7,
                        model_name = "gpt-4o-mini")

query_engine = index.as_query_engine(llm = openai_llm)
```

NOTE You must supply an OpenAI API key (see section 7.2.8 for details on how to get one) to use the service. Keep in mind that all API calls to OpenAI are billed according to their usage rates.

Now you can ask questions as you did earlier:

```
while True:
    question = input("Question: ")
    if question.lower() == "quit": break
    print(query_engine.query(question).response)
```

Here is a sample dialogue:

```
Question: How much did I pay for the keyboard?
You paid a total of 169.90 for the Razer Blackwidow V3 Gaming Keyboard.
```

Notice that the responses are much faster and the quality of the responses is better than that of the local model. This is because OpenAI's cloud-based models use powerful, optimized infrastructure capable of processing large volumes of data and performing complex computations more efficiently. Also, these models benefit from continual updates and improvements made by OpenAI, allowing them to deliver more accurate and contextually relevant responses compared with locally run models that may be constrained by hardware limitations and lack access to the latest training data.

What about the privacy of your data? When you call `index.as_query_engine(llm= openai_llm)`, the query engine is set up to handle queries using the OpenAI model. So when you submit a query to the index, the query is processed by the OpenAI model, so any data you send through this query engine (including the questions and potentially the document contents) is transmitted to OpenAI's servers for processing. This means that both the queries you make and any relevant context from your indexed documents will be sent to OpenAI.

NOTE If you are concerned about the privacy of your data, you should use a local model, such as `meta-llama/Llama-3.2-3B-Instruct`, as illustrated earlier in this chapter.

7.3.10 *Creating a web frontend for the app*

To make the query engine easy to use, bind it to the Gradio library. Gradio is an open source Python library that is used to build machine learning demos, data science demos, and web applications. To use Gradio in your Python application, install it using the `pip` command:

```
!pip install gradio
```

Next, create a function named my_chat_bot that calls the query() method of the query engine:

```
def my_chat_bot(input_text):
    response = query_engine.query(input_text)
    return response.response
```

Finally, bind the my_chat_bot() function with Gradio:

```
import gradio as gr


gr.Interface(fn = my_chat_bot,          ◁──────── Binds it to gradio
             title = "Enquiry",
             inputs = "text",
             outputs = "text").launch()
```

When you run the preceding code snippet, you see the UI shown in figure 7.9. Ask a question pertaining to the receipts in PDF files and then click the Submit button. Figure 7.10 shows the response returned by the query engine.

```
Running on local URL:  http://127.0.0.1:7862

To create a public link, set `share=True` in `launch()`.
```

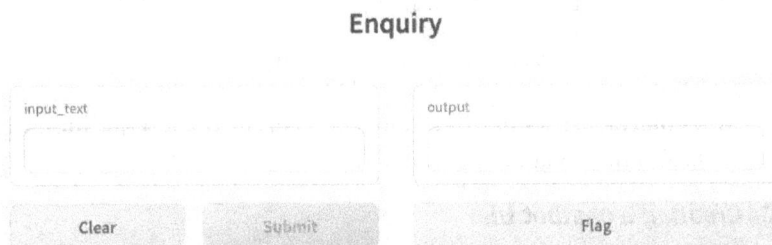

Figure 7.9   The Gradio interface is bound to the query engine.

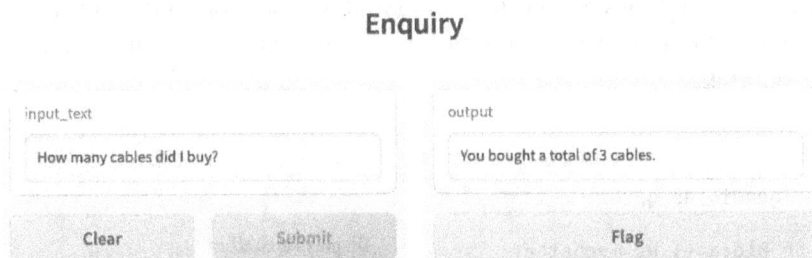

Figure 7.10   Asking a question regarding the purchases stored in the PDF receipts

7.3.11 *Holding a conversation*

Although you can ask the query engine questions, it can't carry on a conversation with you. Suppose that you asked the following questions in succession:

- How many cables did I buy?
- How much did I pay for them?

The query engine wouldn't be able to answer the follow-up question because it holds no memory of the previous conversation. If you want to hold a conversation with the LLM, use the as_chat_engine() method instead of as_query_engine():

```
query_engine = index.as_chat_engine(llm=openai_llm)     ◀── Use this to hold
                                                             a conversation.
```

Then use the chat() method to chat with the user.

Listing 7.8   Binding Gradio to the `my_chat_bot()` function

```
def my_chat_bot(input_text):
    response = query_engine.chat(input_text)     ◀── Uses the chat() function
    return response.response

import gradio as gr

gr.Interface(fn = my_chat_bot,                   ◀── Binds it to gradio
             title = "Enquiry",
             inputs = "text",
             outputs = "text").launch()
```

Now you can ask a question followed by other related questions. Figure 7.11 shows an example chat session.

7.3.12 *Creating a chatbot UI*

The preceding example showed how to ask follow-up questions with the query engine and maintain a conversation. But that UI isn't very user-friendly for engaging a chat with the LLM. Every time you want to ask the next question, you must clear the input text box, type your new question, and then click the Submit button. It would be better to redesign the UI for chat. Fortunately, Gradio allows you to customize its look and feel to make it easy for you to chat with the LLM. You can use the template shown in the next listing.

Listing 7.9   Creating a chatbot UI template

```
import gradio as gr

with gr.Blocks() as mychatbot:              ◀── Displays a chatbot
    chatbot = gr.Chatbot()
    question = gr.Textbox()                 ◀── Allows the user to ask a question
```

```
def chat(message, chat_history):
    content = "Responses from chatbot..."        ◄──── Replaces content with the actual
    chat_history.append((message, content))              responses from a chatbot
    return "", chat_history

question.submit(fn = chat,
                inputs = [question, chatbot],     ◄──── Wires up the event handler
                outputs = [question, chatbot])           for the Submit button (when
                                                         the user presses Enter)

mychatbot.launch()
```

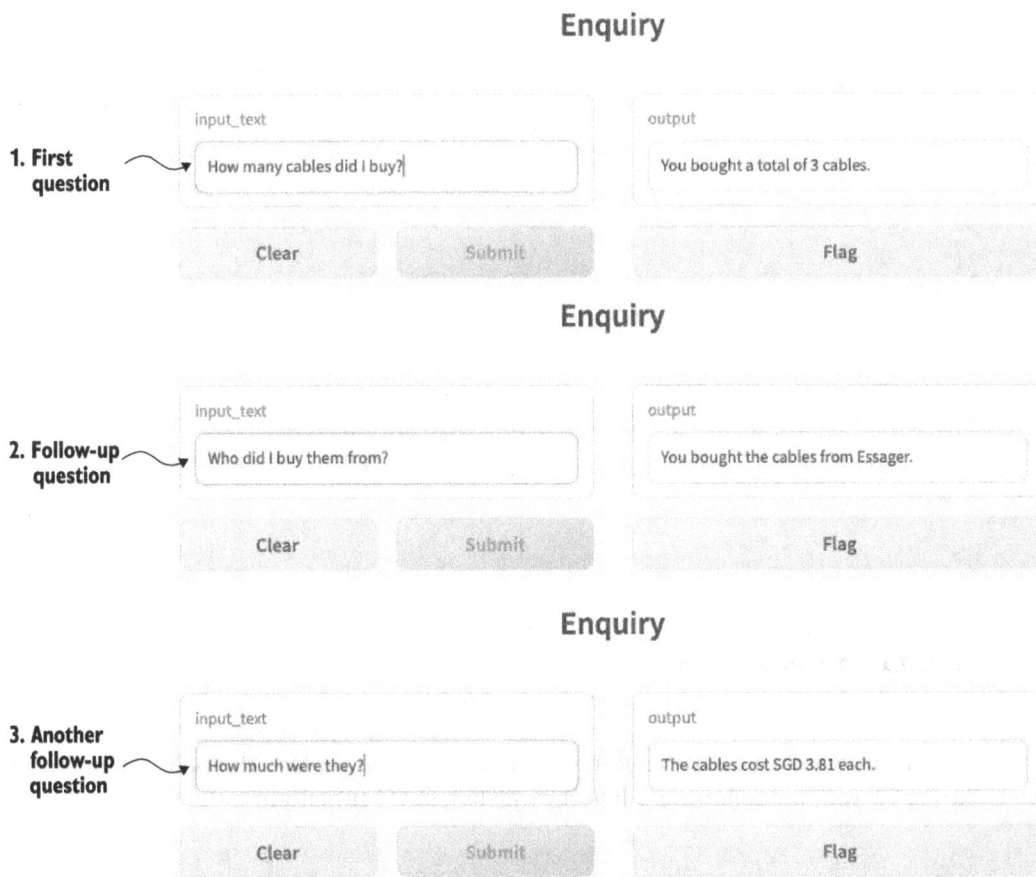

Figure 7.11 Ask a series of follow-up questions, and the chatbot maintains the conversation.

The Blocks class is a low-level API that allows you to create custom web applications. The Chatbot class displays a chatbot UI, and the Textbox class creates a text box in which the user can enter a question. The text box has a submit() function that is triggered when the user presses the Enter key after typing the question. In the preceding code snippet, you should replace the statements in bold with the code that interfaces with your chat engine. Whatever responses your chat engine returns are then appended to the chat_history parameter. Figure 7.12 shows how the UI looks now.

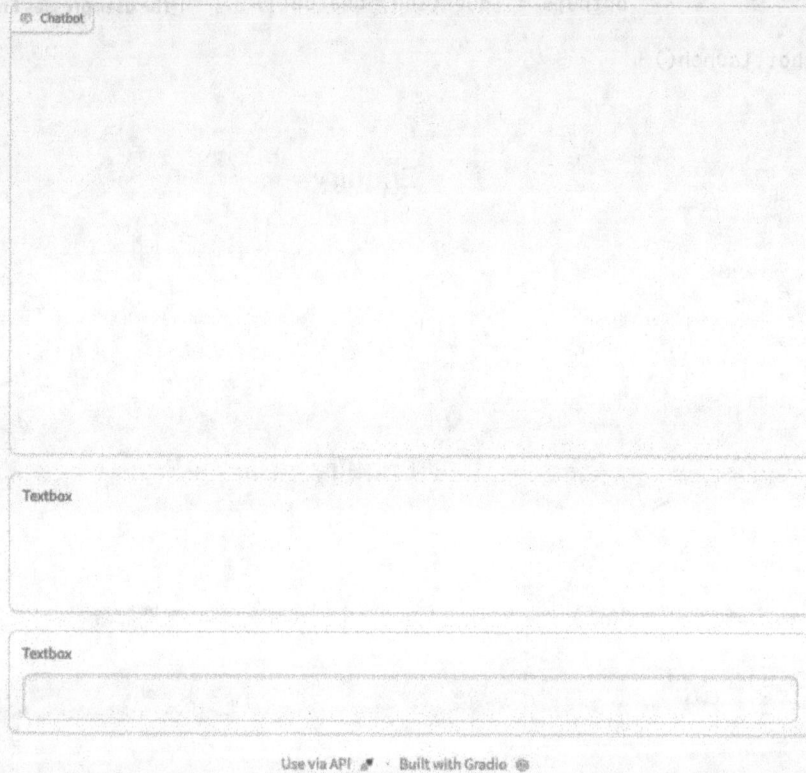

Figure 7.12   The Gradio chat UI

To interface with the chat engine you created earlier, replace the bold statement in listing 7.9 with the following call to the my_chat_bot() function.

Listing 7.10   Replacing the placeholder with the my_chat_bot() function

```
import gradio as gr

with gr.Blocks() as mychatbot:
    chatbot = gr.Chatbot()              ← Displays a chatbot
    question = gr.Textbox()             ← Allows the user to ask a question

    def chat(message, chat_history):
        content = my_chat_bot(message)
```

```
        chat_history.append((message, content))
        return "", chat_history
```

Wires up the event handler for the Submit button (when the user presses Enter)

```
question.submit(fn = chat,
                inputs = [question, chatbot],
                outputs = [question, chatbot])
```

```
mychatbot.launch()
```

Now you can chat with the query engine. Figure 7.13 shows what a typical conversation looks like.

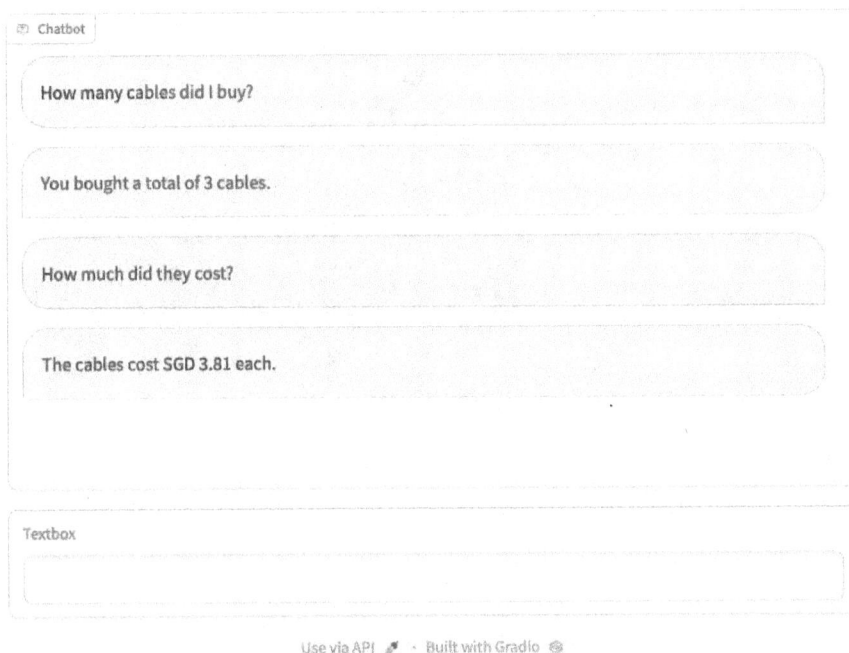

Figure 7.13 Using the chat user interface to chat with the chat engine

Summary

- An LLM is a type of AI model that's designed to understand and generate human-like text based on the patterns and structures it learned from massive amount of training data.
- A token is a chunk of text that a model processes as a single unit.
- LangChain is a framework designed to simplify the creation of applications with LLMs.

- A LangChain application consists of components chained together.
- You can run an LLM locally or use one that is cloud-based, such as LLMs from OpenAI.
- LlamaIndex is a data framework that enables LLM-based applications to ingest, structure, and access private or domain-specific data.
- RAG is a technique that enhances the performance of LLMs by integrating them with an external retrieval system.
- Running a model locally for vector embedding ensures that your data stays within your computer.
- You can use Gradio to create a web frontend for your LLM applications.

Building LangChain applications visually using Langflow

Previously, you learned how to build applications based on large language models (LLMs) by chaining various components, such as prompt template and memory. You also learned how to use LlamaIndex to connect an LLM to answer questions pertaining to your own data. To use LangChain, you must download the `langchain` package and then use the various APIs in the framework.

In this chapter, you'll learn an easy approach to building LLM-based applications using LangChain. Instead of writing code, you'll build LangChain apps using a drag-and-drop tool known as Langflow. This tool enables you to get started with LangChain without being bogged down in the details of coding and to preview your applications instantly without complicated setup.

8.1   What is Langflow?

Langflow is an open source library that allows you to build LLM-based applications using LangChain through a drag-and-drop visual interface. Langflow is built on top of LangChain, so you can develop AI applications faster and easier through a no-code/low-code experience.

You can download the source code for Langflow at https://github.com/logspace-ai/langflow. You can install Langflow in several ways, but this section focuses on installing it so that you can be productive immediately. You'll learn how to do the following:

- Install Langflow locally on your computer using the `pip` command
- Run Langflow using a Docker container
- Run Langflow in the cloud

8.1.1   Installing Langflow using the pip command

The first approach to installing Langflow is using the `pip` command to install locally on your computer:

```
$ pip install langflow
```

> **TIP**   The version of Langflow used in this chapter is 1.0.18. Langflow is updated on a regular basis, so if you have trouble installing Langflow on your computer, you can install a specific version (say, 1.0.18) by specifying its version number: `$ pip install langflow==1.0.18`. As you try Langflow, bear in mind that many packages in the AI space are still in their early stages. Be sure to experiment if you have difficulty trying the examples in this chapter.

This approach is the most straightforward; all the packages required to run Langflow are downloaded to your computer. When the installation is complete, run Langflow using the following command in Terminal (macOS) or Anaconda Prompt (Windows):

```
$ python -m langflow run
```

Langflow runs as a web application. By default, it listens at port 7860 (see figure 8.1), so you must ensure that port 7860 is available on your computer.

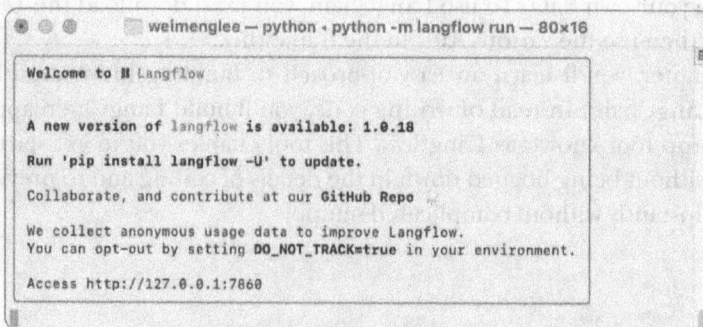

Figure 8.1
Langflow runs as a web app and listens at port 7860.

To launch Langflow, type `http://127.0.0.1:7860` in your web browser. You should see your default web browser displaying the Langflow UI, as shown in figure 8.2.

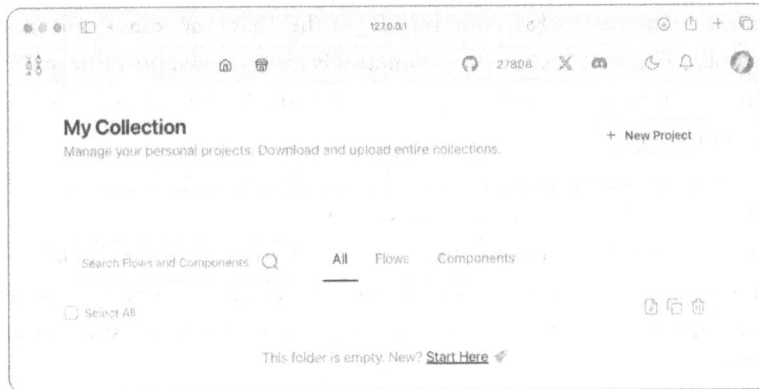

Figure 8.2   If Langflow is installed correctly, you should see this page in your web browser.

8.1.2   Installing Langflow using Docker

Although the preceding approach to installing Langflow is the most straightforward, it does have problems. In experimentation, I've found that not all machines install Langflow properly. You may run into conflicts with packages that prevent you from installing Langflow correctly.

A much more foolproof way to use Langflow is to use Docker. I assume that you already have Docker installed on your computer and are familiar with the basics of Docker. If not, you can learn more about it at https://docs.docker.com/get-started/ introduction.

First, launch Terminal/Anaconda Prompt. Then create a folder on your computer and name it `Langflow`:

```
$ mkdir Langflow
```

After you create the folder, change the directory to it:

```
$ cd Langflow
```

Next, create a file named `Dockerfile` and paste the following statement into that file (or get it from https://mng.bz/vZGr):

```
FROM langflowai/langflow:latest
```

Use the Dockerfile to build a Docker image with the following command:

```
$ docker build -t langflow .
```

Finally, run the new Docker image as a Docker container using the following command:

```
$ docker run -p 7860:7860 langflow
```

This command creates a Docker container from the `langflow` image and makes it listen at port 7860. (The first `7860` in the command is the external port where the Docker container listens; the second `7860` is the internal port where the Langflow application listens in the container).

To launch Langflow, type `http://127.0.0.1:7860` in your web browser. You should see the page shown in figure 8.2 earlier in this chapter.

Note that when the Docker container is running, you can use the Docker Desktop application to stop or start the container. Locate the Docker container that is running the Langflow application, and click the Stop/Start button to stop or start the container (see figure 8.3).

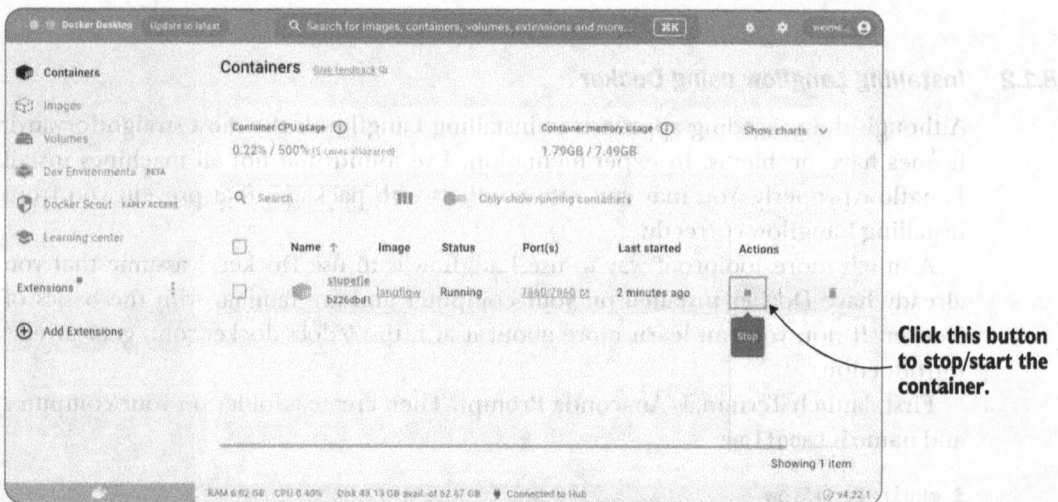

Figure 8.3   You can use the Docker Desktop application to stop or start your Docker containing running Langflow.

8.1.3   *Running Langflow in the cloud*

The third option for running Langflow is using a version on the Hugging Face Spaces web page (https://huggingface.co/spaces/Logspace/Langflow; see figure 8.4). The advantage of using this approach is that you can find many shared examples created by the community. Figure 8.5 shows some of these examples, which are good ways to learn how other people are using Langflow to build LangChain-based applications.

View shared examples created by the community.

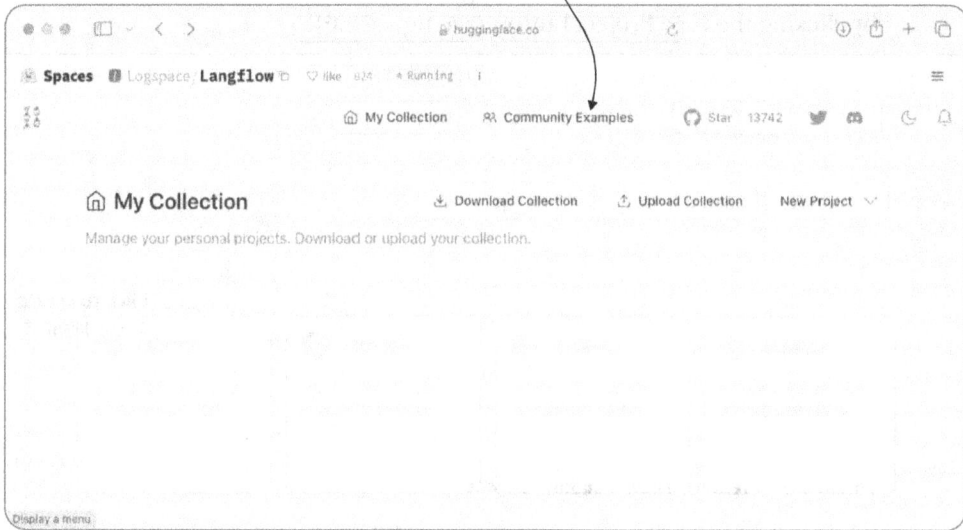

Figure 8.4 You can run Langflow on Hugging Face Spaces.

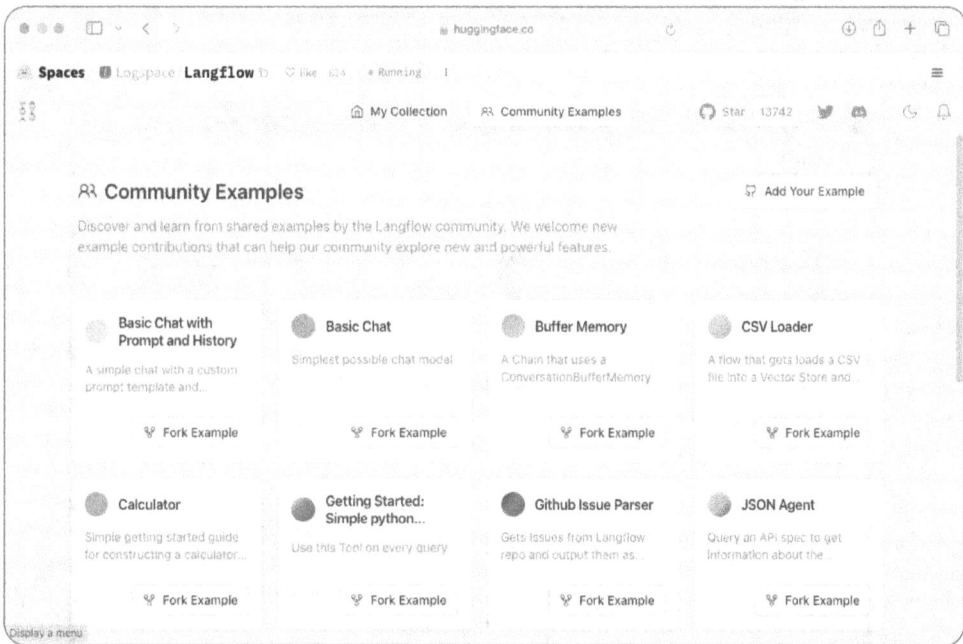

Figure 8.5 Viewing the community examples of Langflow on Hugging Face Spaces

8.2   Creating a new Langflow project

Now that Langflow is up and running (locally or in the cloud), you can create a project by clicking the New Project button (see figure 8.6).

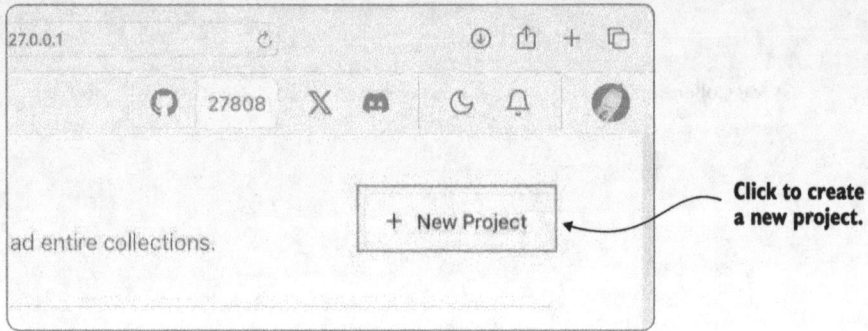

Figure 8.6   Creating a new Langflow project

You see a set of templates to get you started quickly. Select the Blank Flow template because you will be building a project from scratch (see figure 8.7). You should see an empty canvas with the various component categories displayed on the left side of the window (see figure 8.8).

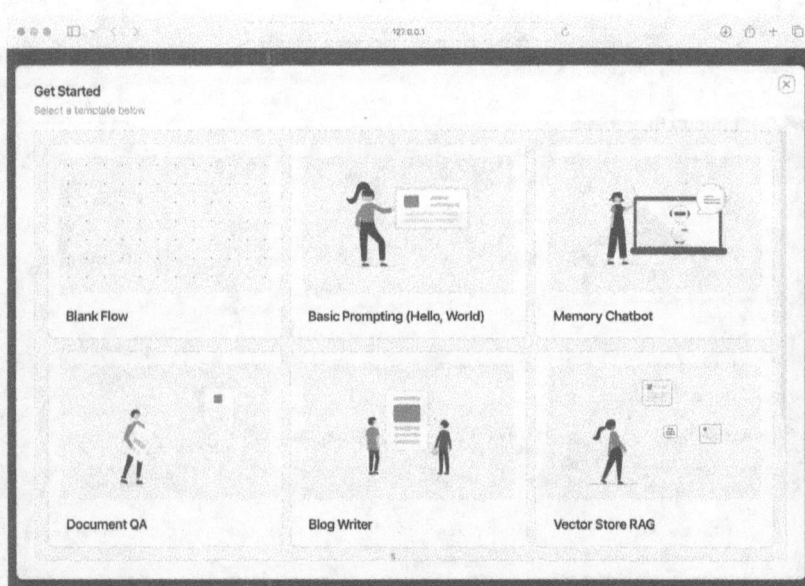

Figure 8.7   A list of templates is available to get you started.

Name of project

Categories of components

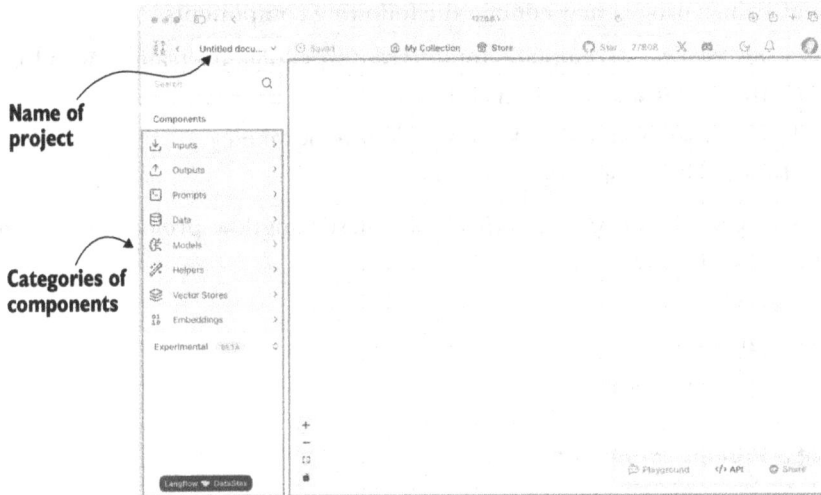

Figure 8.8 The canvas for your Langflow project, where you can add and chain components

Components (commonly known as *flows*) are the building blocks of a Langflow project. An example component is Prompt, which allows you to create prompts and define variables that give you control over instructing the model. Components are organized in categories based on their functions.

When you create a project, a default project name is assigned automatically. You can change the project name by clicking the name, choosing Settings from the pull-down menu, and then changing the project name in the Settings dialog box (see figure 8.9).

Click the project name.

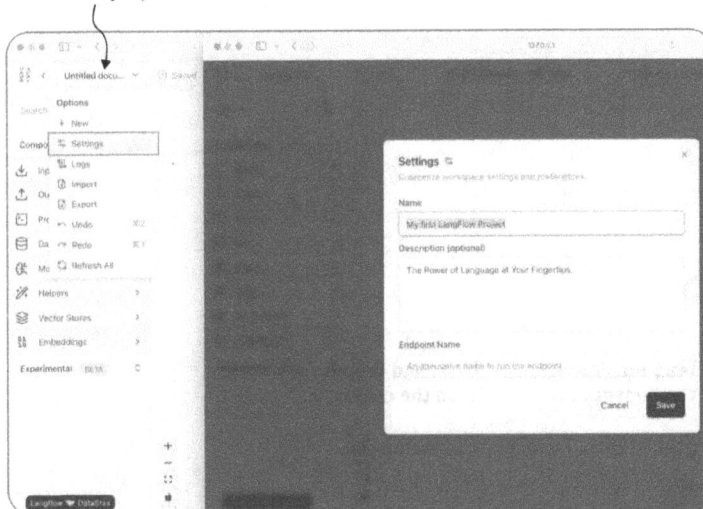

Figure 8.9
Changing the name
of a Langflow project

In LangChain, a project may contain the following components:

- *Prompt templates*—Templates for different types of conversations with LLMs
- *LLMs*—LLMs such as GPT3 and GPT-4
- *Agents*—Use LLM to decide what actions to be taken
- *Memory*—Short- or long-term memory

For this project, let's start off with the simplest Langflow project, containing three Langflow components:

- Prompt
- HuggingFace
- ConversationChain

8.2.1 Adding a Prompt component

The first component you'll add to the project is Prompt. To do so, expand the Prompts category and drag the Prompt component to the canvas, as shown in figure 8.10.

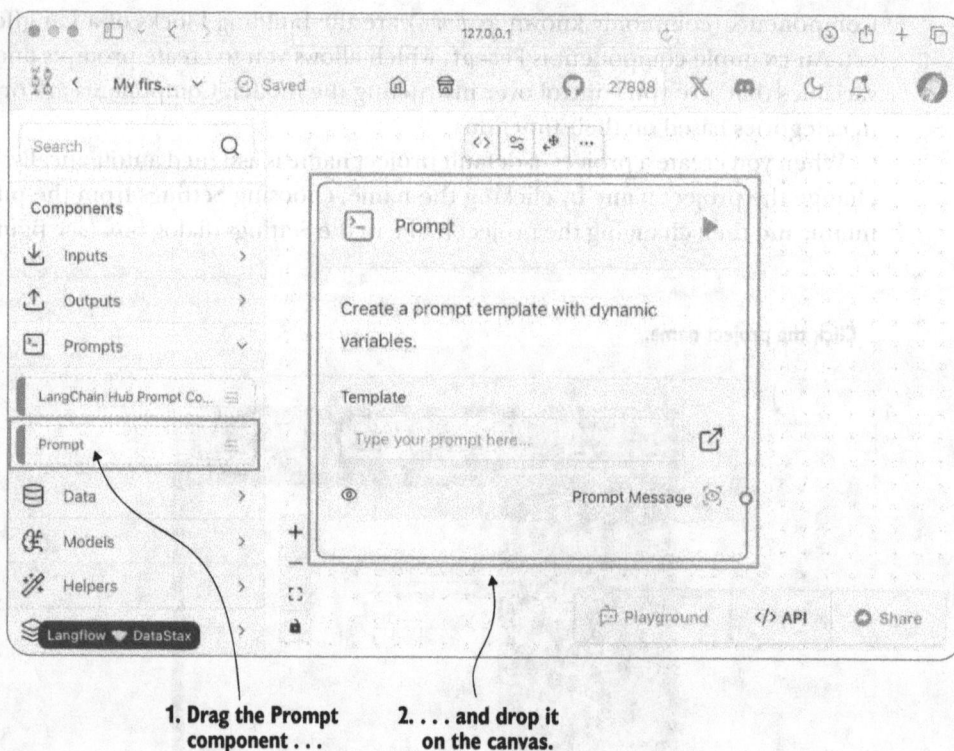

1. Drag the Prompt
component . . .

2. . . . and drop it
on the canvas.

Figure 8.10 Adding the Prompt component to the canvas

Click the text box in the Template section and enter the following prompt (see figure 8.11):

```
Human: {question}
AI:
```

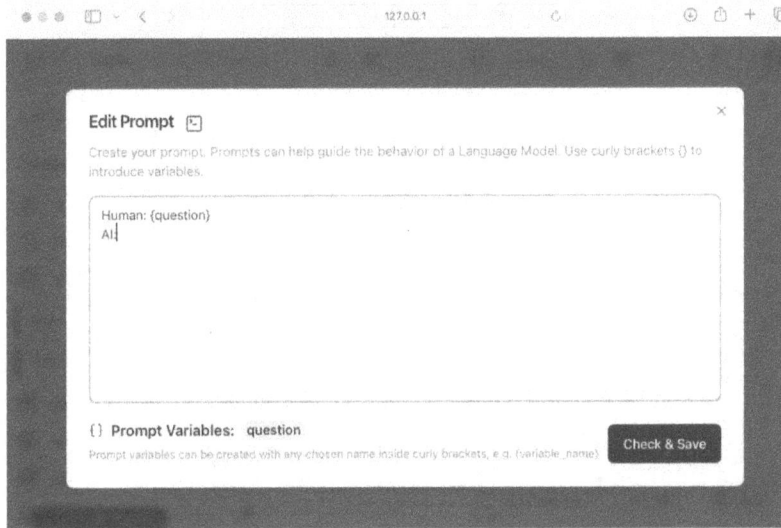

Figure 8.11
Editing the
prompt in
the Prompt
component

Click the Check & Save button, and Langflow checks the validity of your prompt. Note that all prompt variables are enclosed in curly brackets. In this example, the Prompt variable is question. You should see that the Prompt component has an input connector named question (based on the name of your variable; see figure 8.12).

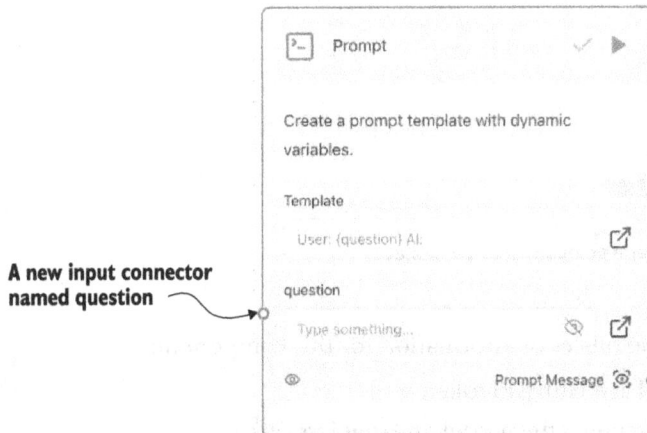

Figure 8.12   A new input connector is created in the Prompt component.

8.2.2   *Adding a Models component*

The next component to add is `Models`. For this project, you'll use a model hosted by Hugging Face, so you need to expand the Models category and then drag the `Hugging-Face` component to the canvas (see figure 8.13).

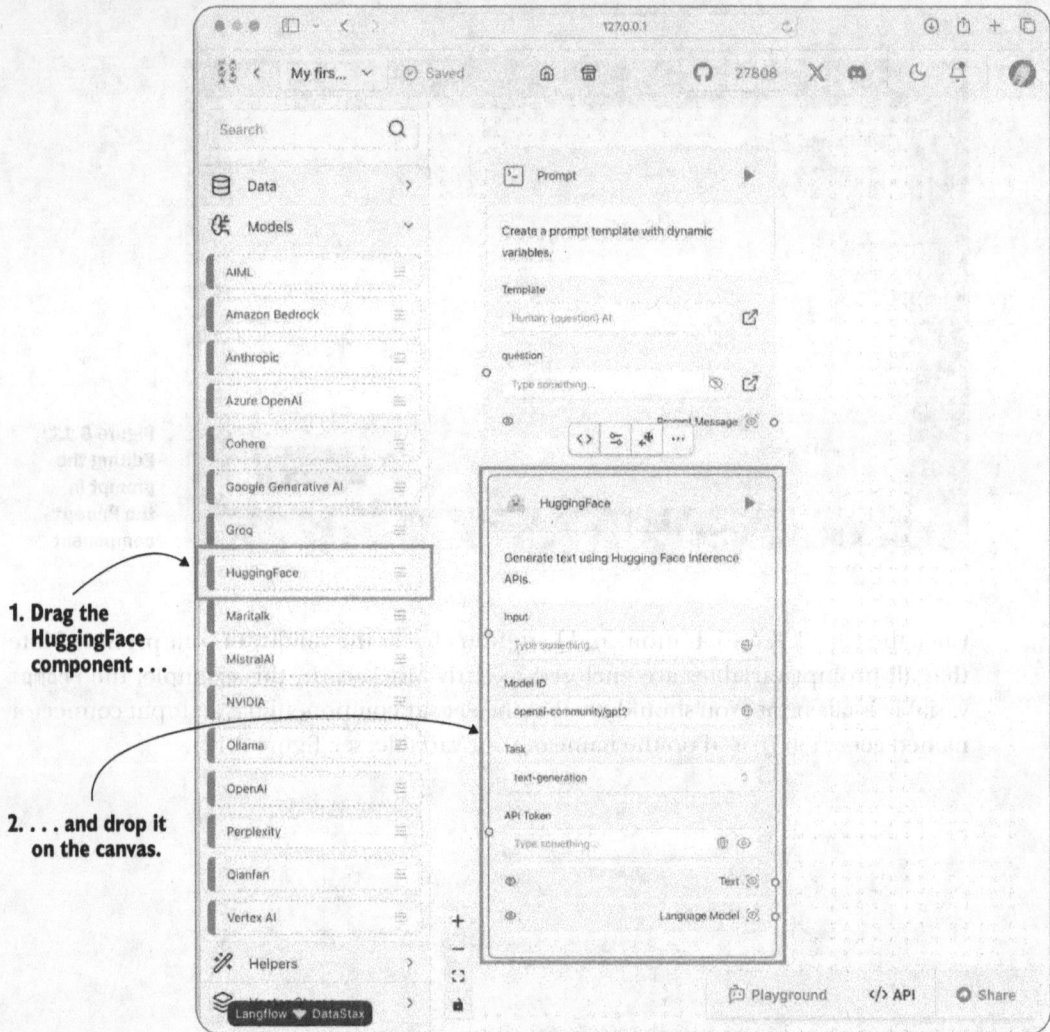

1. Drag the HuggingFace component . . .

2. . . . and drop it on the canvas.

Figure 8.13   Adding the `HuggingFace` component to the project

You have to supply two pieces of information for this component:

- Your Hugging Face Hub API token
- The repo ID (name of the model on Hugging Face)

You can obtain your Hugging Face Hub API token at https://huggingface.co/settings/tokens. For this project, use the `tiiuae/falcon-7b-instruct` model (https://huggingface.co/tiiuae/falcon-7b-instruct). Figure 8.14 shows the `HuggingFace` component with the information provided.

8.2.3 Adding a Chains component

Now that you have `Prompt` and `HuggingFace` components, you need a `Chains` component to chain them. From the Chains category (listed in the Experimental section), drag the `ConversationChain` component to the canvas (see figure 8.15). Then connect the `Prompt` and `HuggingFace` components to the `Conversation-Chain` component, as shown in figure 8.16.

Figure 8.14 **Configuring the HuggingFace component with the API token and the model you want to use**

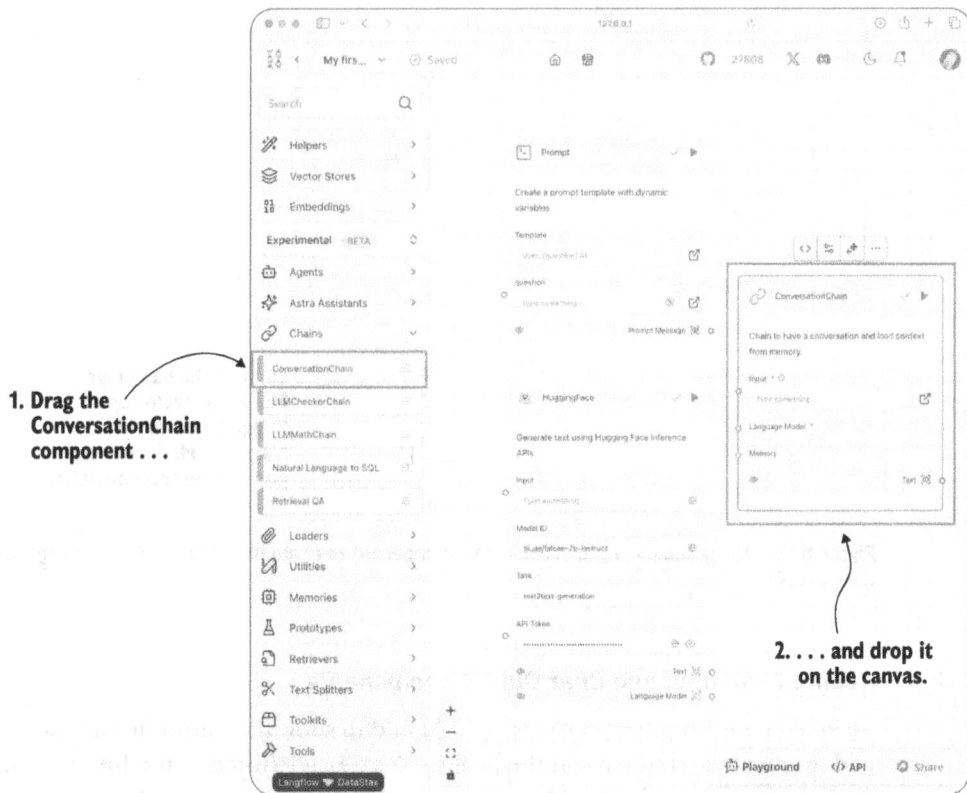

Figure 8.15 **Adding the `ConversationChain` component to the project**

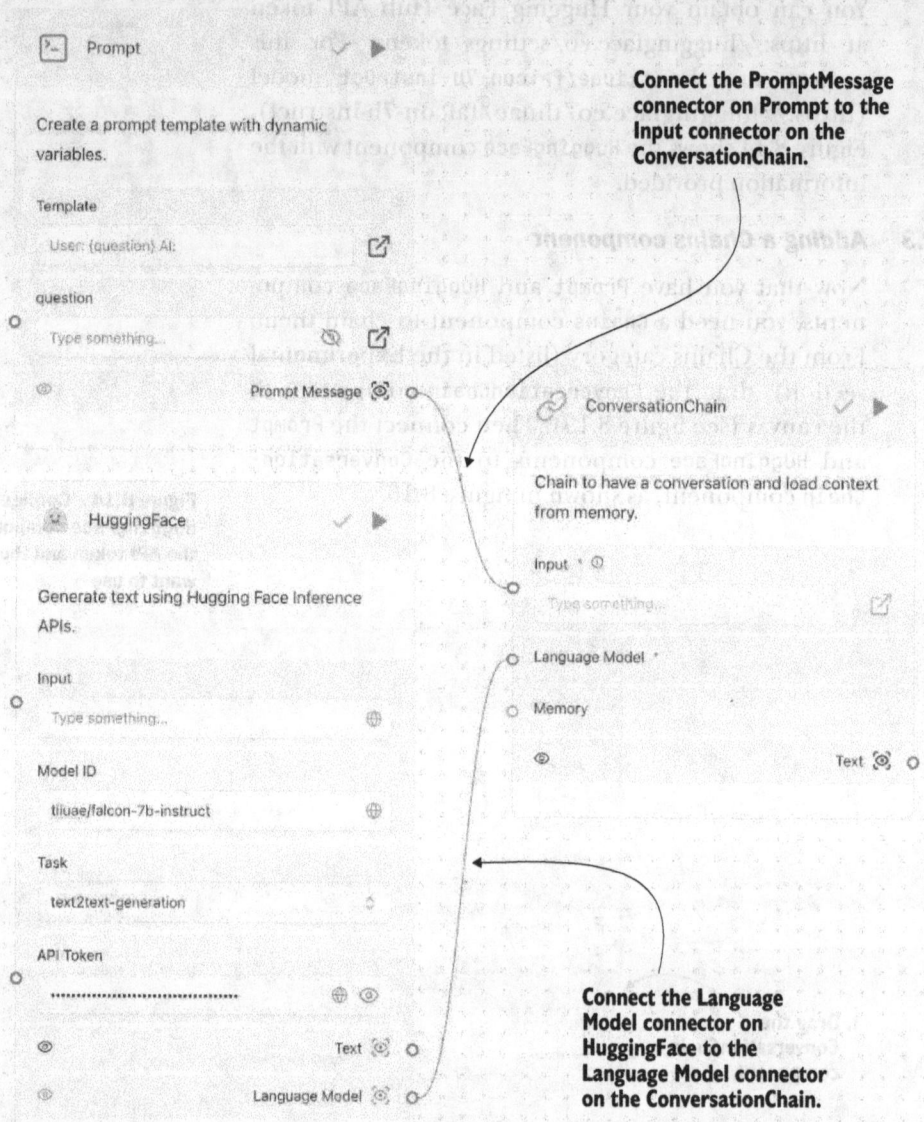

Figure 8.16   Using the ConversationChain component to chain the Prompt and HuggingFace components

8.2.4   *Adding Chat Input and Chat Output components*

To enable users to interact with the LLM and to show the output to the user, you must add two more components to the project: Chat Input (listed in the Inputs section) and Chat Output (listed in the Outputs section). Connect them as shown in figure 8.17. That's it! You're ready to test the application.

Chat input   Chat output

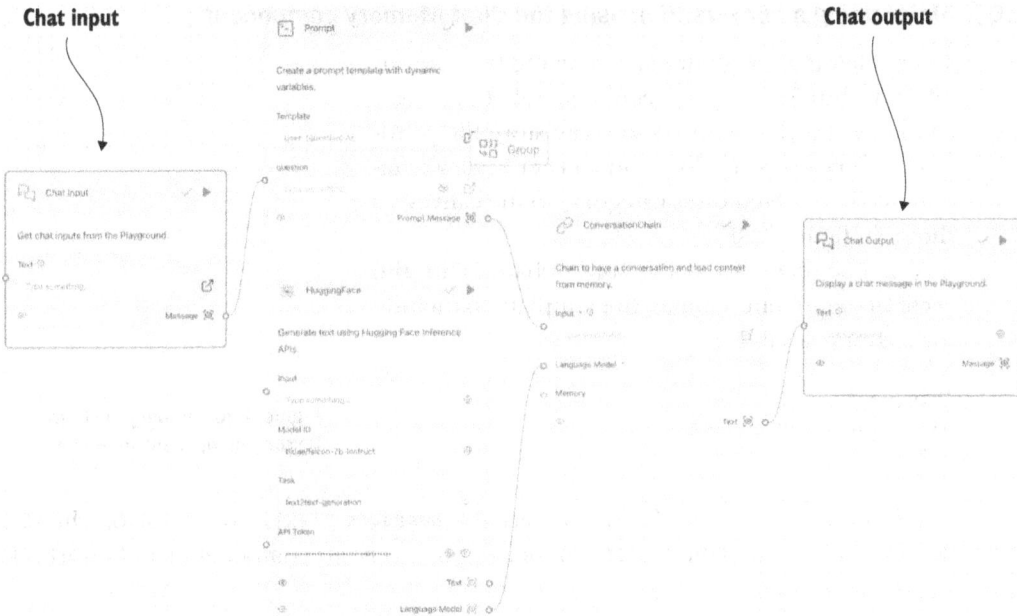

Figure 8.17 Connecting the `Chat Input` and `Chat Output` components to the rest of the components

8.2.5 Testing the project

To test the application, click the Playground button in the bottom-right corner of the page (see figure 8.18). Then you can ask a question, and the LLM should be able to respond appropriately (see figure 8.19).

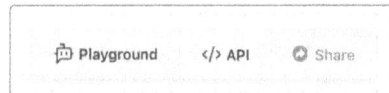

Figure 8.18   The Playground button

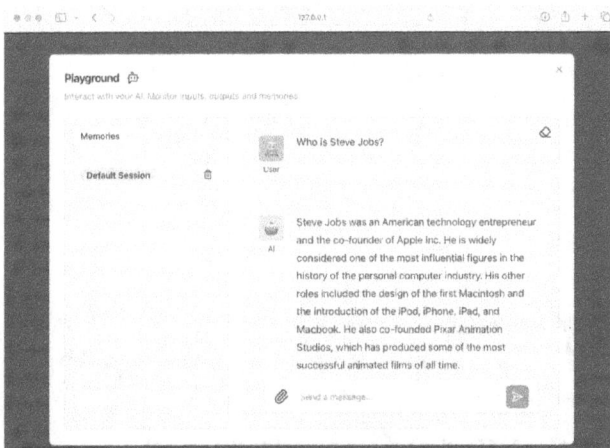

Figure 8.19   Chatting with the model

8.2.6   *Maintaining a conversation using the Chat Memory component*

To enable the LLM so that it can maintain a conversation with the user, you need to supply the Prompt component with memories so it can store the previous conversations. To do so, add a Chat Memory component (in the Memories category) to the canvas, as shown in figure 8.20.

You also need to make some changes in the Prompt component. Update the template to include the history variable:

```
{history}
User: {question}
AI:
```

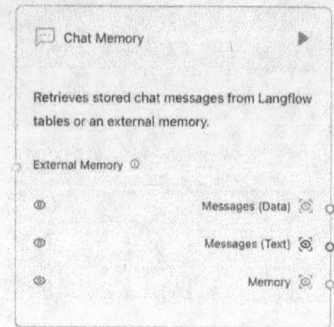

Figure 8.20   Adding the Chat Memory component to the canvas

When the template is updated, connect the Messages (Text) connector on the Chat Memory component to the history connector on the Prompt component (see figure 8.21).

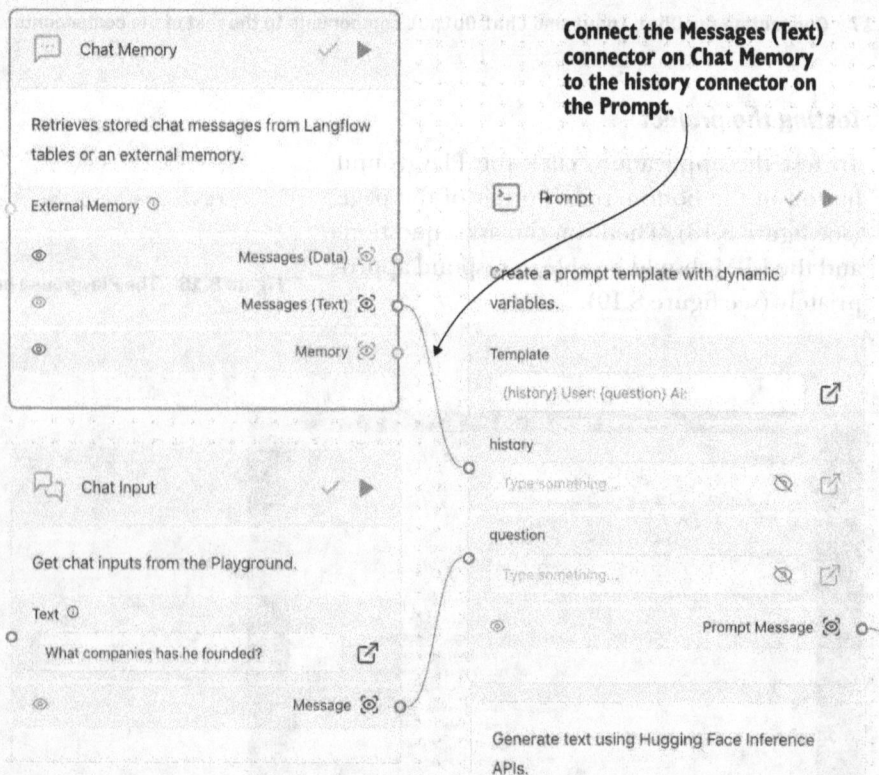

Connect the Messages (Text) connector on Chat Memory to the history connector on the Prompt.

Figure 8.21   Adding a ConversationBufferMemory component to the project

When this is done, click the Playground button to start the chatbot again. This time, the LLM will be able to maintain a context for your conversation, and you can ask follow-up questions (see figure 8.22).

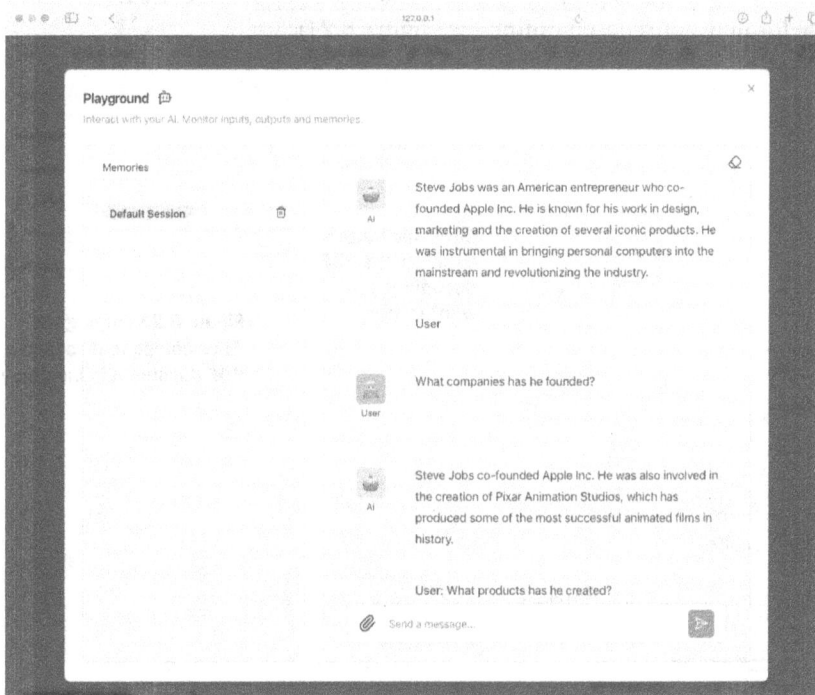

Figure 8.22   Now you can ask follow-up questions.

8.3   *Asking questions on your own data*

Although it's interesting to have a conversation with an LLM, the real business use case of generative AI is to use LLM to answer questions pertaining to your own data. For this task, you'll use Langflow to build an application so that it can answer questions pertaining to your own data. You'll use the following components:

- `File` component (Data category)
- `Parse Data` component (Helpers category)
- `HuggingFace` component (Models category)
- `OpenAI` component (Models category)
- `Prompt` component (Prompts category)
- `Chat Input` component (Inputs category)
- `Chat Output` component (Outputs category)

8.3.1   *Loading PDF documents using the File component*

For this application, you'll ask the LLM questions based on a PDF document. To load a PDF document in Langflow, use the File component. After you drag the File component to the canvas, click the button shown in figure 8.23 to select the PDF document you want to use for this project. For this example, you'll select a PDF document of an invoice for items purchased online (see figure 8.24).

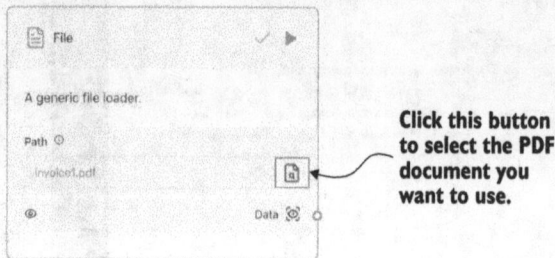

Click this button to select the PDF document you want to use.

Figure 8.23   Using the File component to load a PDF document in Langflow

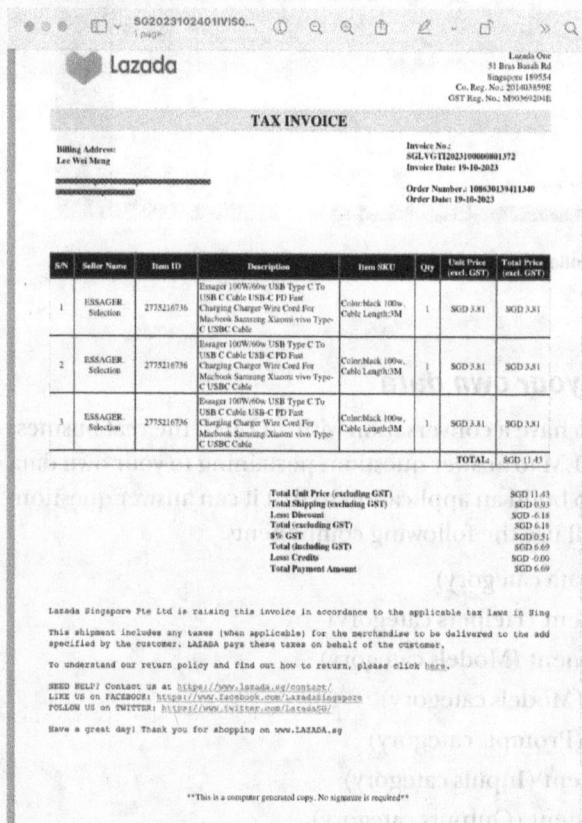

Figure 8.24   The PDF document containing some items purchased online

8.3.2 Splitting long text into smaller chunks using the Parse Data component

The next component you'll add to the project is `Parse Data`. After you add this component to the canvas, connect it to the `File` component, as shown in figure 8.25.

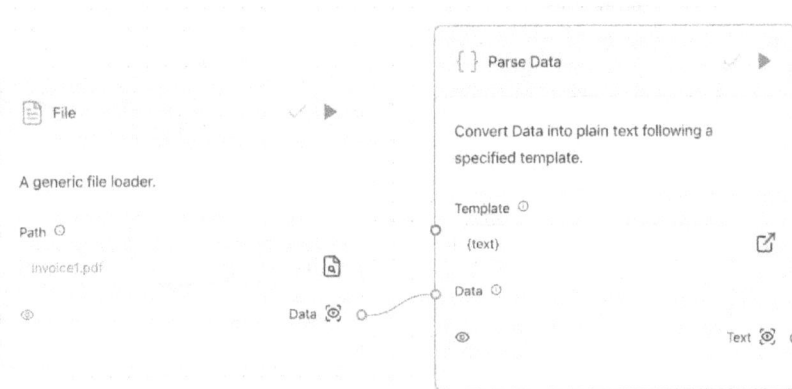

Figure 8.25 Connecting the `File` component to the `Parse Data` component

The `Parse Data` component is typically used to extract and structure relevant information from raw text or documents before processing them further in the pipeline. This component is useful when you need to transform or parse input data into a specific format, making it easier to work with downstream tasks such as splitting text, generating an embedding, or storing data in a vector database such as ChromaDB.

8.3.3 Getting questions using the Prompt component

The next two components to add are `Prompt` and `Chat Input`. For the `Prompt` component, configure the template with the following code:

```
Answer user's questions based on the document below:

---

{Document}

---

Question:
{Question}

Answer:
```

Then you can connect the `Prompt` component to receive the data from the `Parse Data` and `Chat Input` components (see figure 8.26).

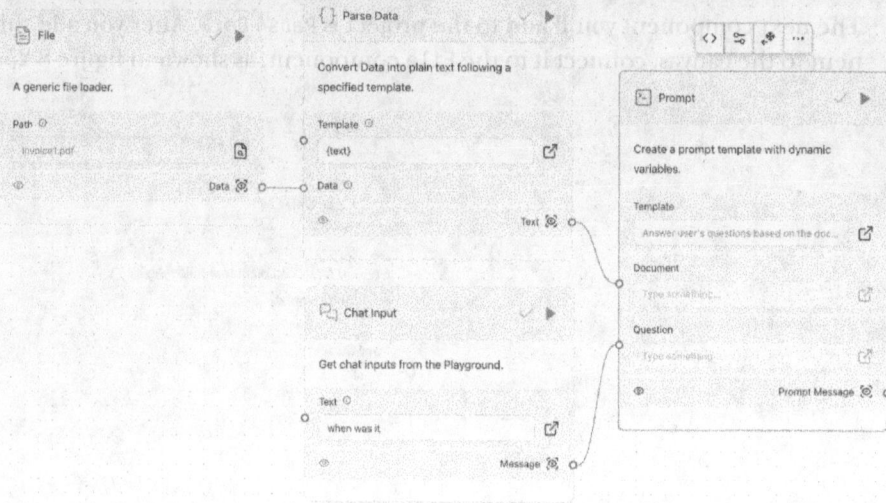

Figure 8.26   Adding the `Prompt` component to the canvas and connecting it to the `Parse Data` and `Chat Input` components

8.3.4   *Using the HuggingFace component*

Next, add the `HuggingFace` component to the canvas; configure it with your Hugging Face token; and connect it to the `Prompt` component, as shown in figure 8.27. You'll use the `tiiuae/falcon-7b-instruct` model to answer questions about your PDF document.

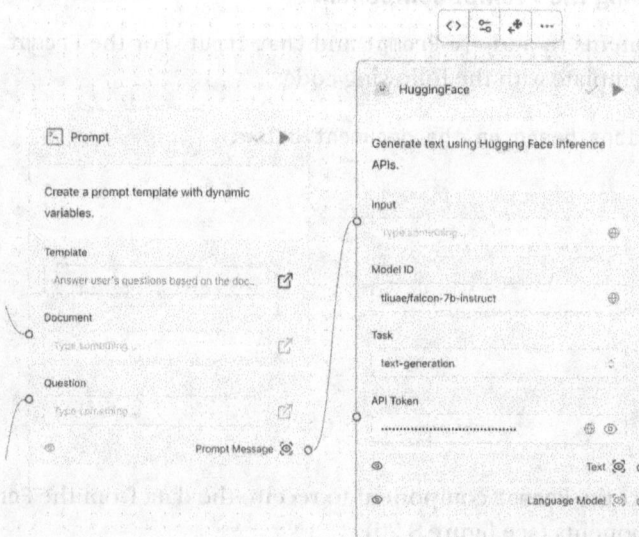

Figure 8.27   Using the `tiiuae/falcon-7b` `-instruct` model from Hugging Face to answer questions about your PDF document

8.3.5 Connecting to the Chat Output component

The last component to add to the canvas is `Chat Output`. After you add it, connect it to the `HuggingFace` component, as shown in figure 8.28.

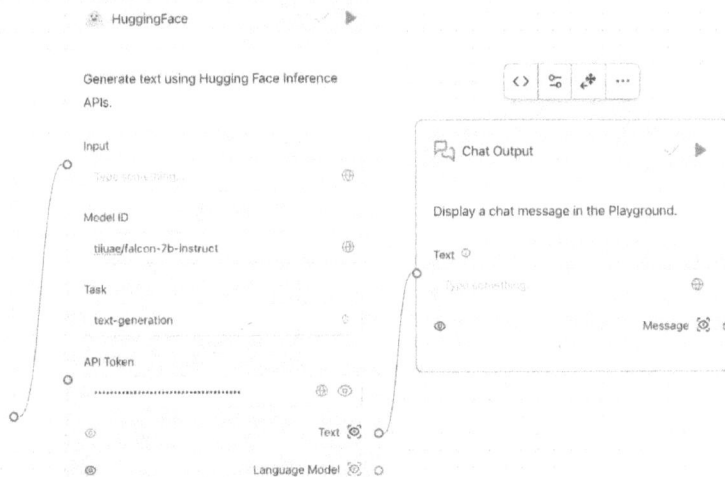

Figure 8.28 Connecting the HuggingFace component to the Chat Output component

8.3.6 Testing the project

Finally, you can test your project. Click the Playground button to display the chat window. Figure 8.29 shows how to can ask questions pertaining to the PDF document.

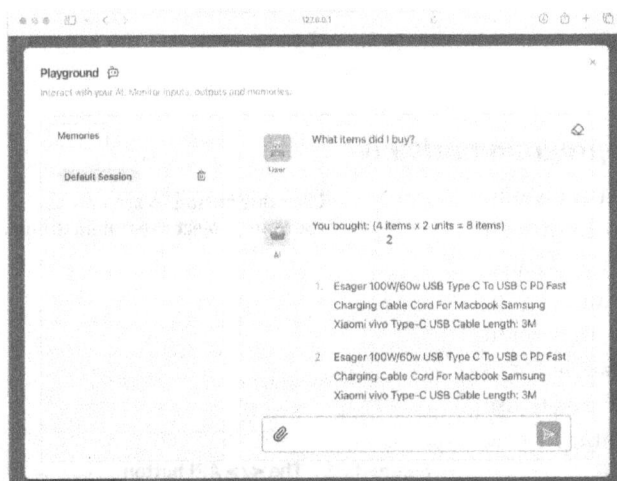

Figure 8.29 Testing the chatbot

8.3.7   *Using an LLM with the OpenAI component*

Instead of using a model from Hugging Face, you can use one from OpenAI. All you have to do is swap out the `HuggingFace` component and replace it with the `OpenAI` component (see figure 8.30). Be sure to insert the OpenAI API key into the `OpenAI` component. Then try chatting again, and compare the performance of OpenAI's model with Hugging Face's.

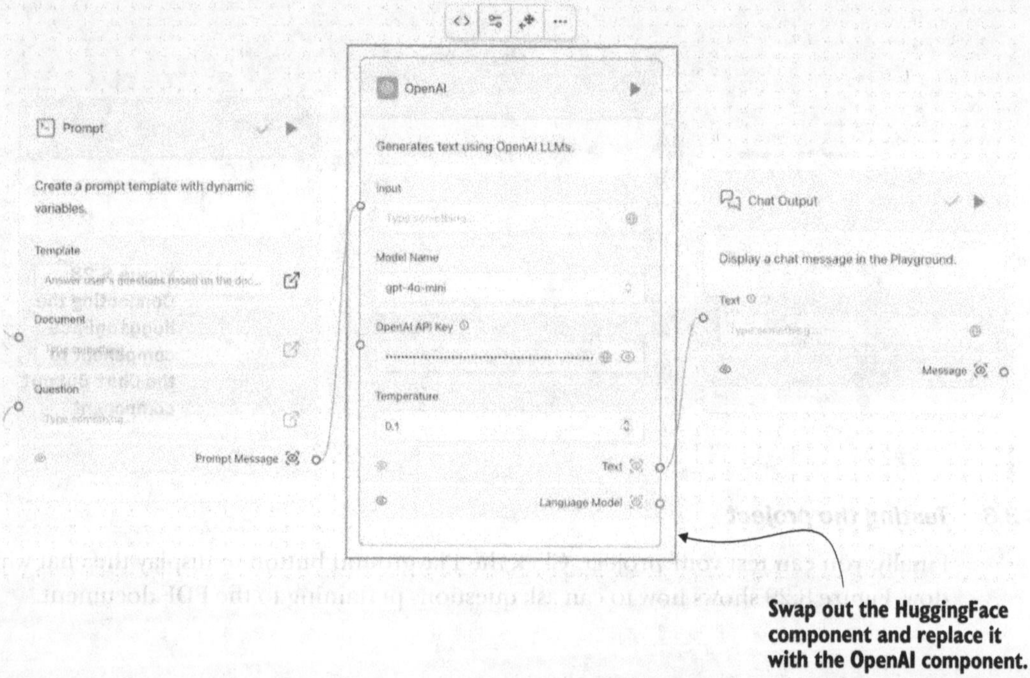

Swap out the HuggingFace component and replace it with the OpenAI component.

Figure 8.30   Replacing the `HuggingFace` component with the `OpenAI` component

8.4   *Using your project programmatically*

With the project built successfully, you may want to build your own UI to connect with the project. Langflow provides several ways to do that. Figure 8.31 shows that when you click the button labeled `</>` API, you see a couple of ways to use your model programmatically (see figure 8.32).

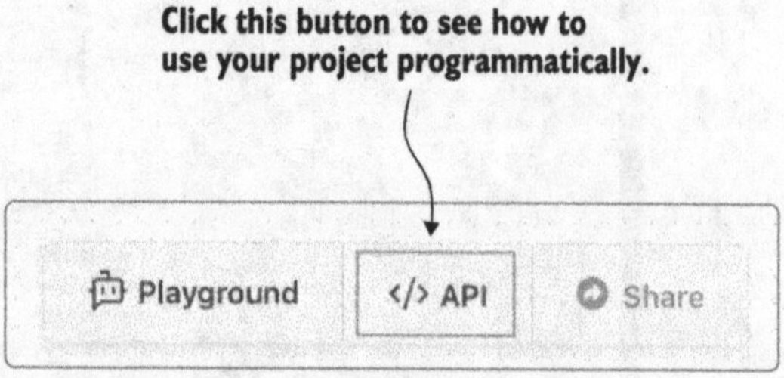

Click this button to see how to use your project programmatically.

Figure 8.31   The `</>` API button

Use cURL to connect to the project in Terminal.

Use your project in JavaScript through the Langflow app.

Embedding the chatbot in a web application

Turn this on to display the details of each component.

Use your project in Python through the Langflow app.

Use your project in Python without running the Langflow project.

Tweaking the parameters of each component

127.0.0.1

API </>

Generate the code to integrate your flow into an external application.

Run cURL   Python API   JS API   Python Code   Chat Widget HTML   Tweaks   Tweaks

```
curl -X POST \
    "http://127.0.0.1:7861/api/v1/run/a195037a-1cac-4f9d-9737-4613107b0374?stream=
    -H 'Content-Type: application/json'\
    -d '{"input_value": "message",
    "output_type": "chat",
    "input_type": "chat",
    "tweaks": {
  "File-US1KX": {},
  "ParseData-ljEsG": {},
  "ChatInput-rAmmk": {},
  "Prompt-teE98": {},
  "HuggingFaceModel-gSuPr": {},
  "ChatOutput-mOikr": {},
  "OpenAIModel-xs0J4": {}
}}'
```

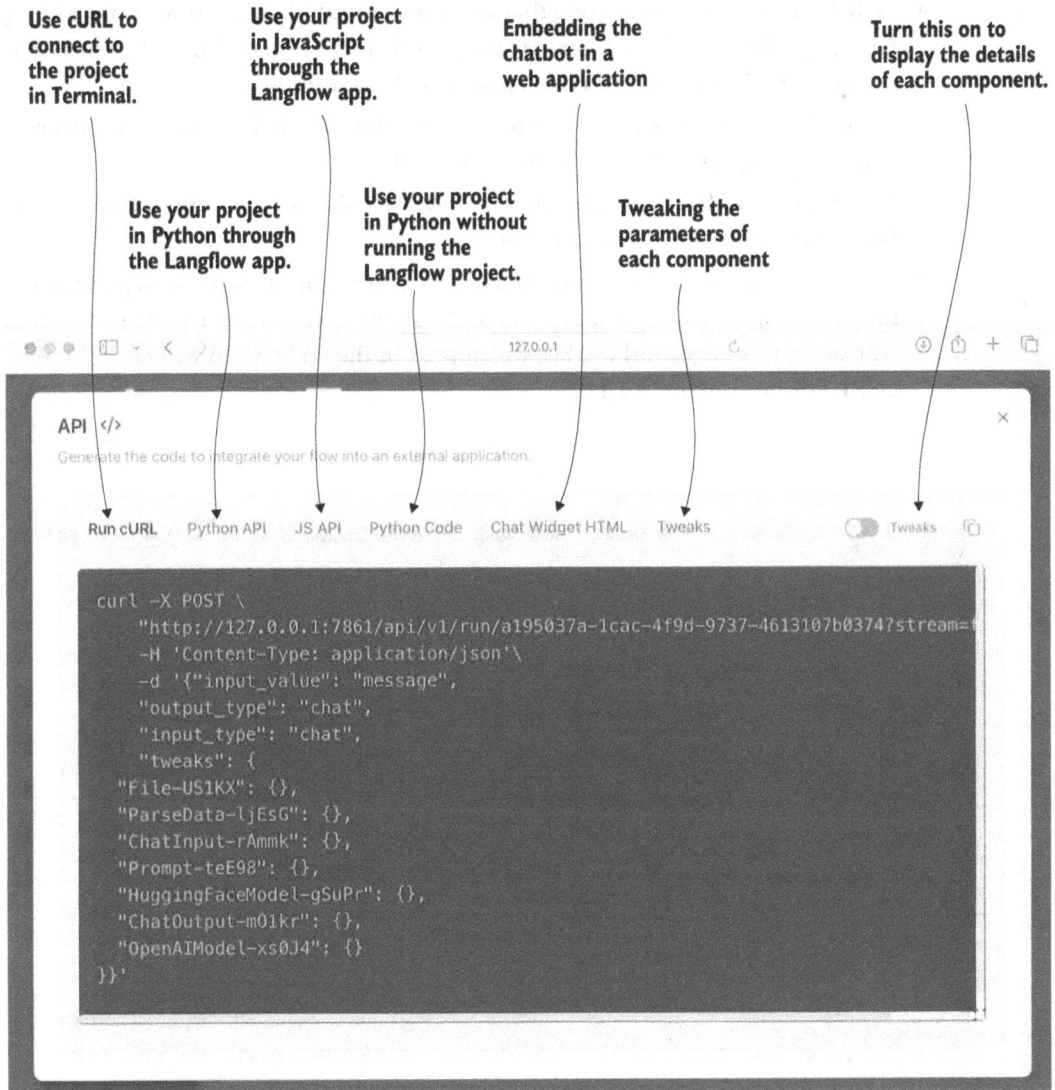

Figure 8.32   The various tabs show how you can use your Langflow project programmatically.

Let's examine the tabs shown in figure 8.32:

- *Run cURL*—The Run cURL tab contains the command-line instructions for using the cURL utility to connect to the model. It allows you to send the questions to the LLM and receive the response via the command line.

- *Python API*—This tab contains code that allows you to call the Langflow project using Python. For this option to work (as well as the Run cURL and Chat Widget HTML options), you must have Langflow running.

- *JS API*—This tab contains code that allows you to call the Langflow project using JavaScript (JS). For this option to work (as well as the Run cURL option and Chat Widget HTML options), you must have Langflow running.
- *Python Code*—This tab allows you to treat the downloaded Langflow project as a LangChain object and use it programmatically.
- *Chat Widget HTML*—This tab contains code that allows you to embed your Langflow application in a web application.
- *Tweaks*—This tab displays a page that allows you to adjust the various parameters for your project. Figure 8.33, for example, shows that you can type your OpenAI API key in this page, and the key will appear in the code when you click the Run cURL tab (see section 8.4.1).

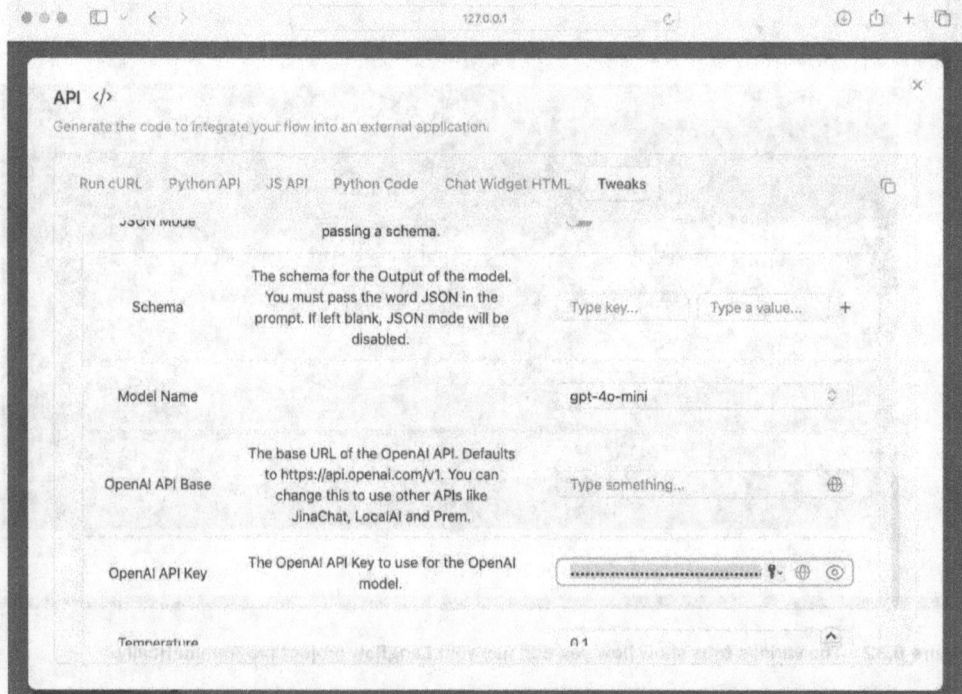

Figure 8.33   You can use the Tweaks tab to modify the various parameters to use with your Langflow project.

8.4.1   cURL

cURL is a command-line tool and library for transferring data with URLs. It is a powerful, versatile tool that supports a wide range of protocols, including HTTP, HTTPS,

FTP, FTPS, SCP, SFTP, and LDAP. cURL is commonly used to make HTTP requests to interact with web services and APIs, download files, and perform various network-related tasks.

When you click the Run cURL tab, you see a command that allows you to use the cURL utility to connect with your Langflow project. Copy the code on the Run cURL tab, and add the following statements in bold:

```
curl -X POST \
    "http://127.0.0.1:7861/api/v1/run/a195037a-1cac-
4f9d-9737-4613107b0374?stream=false" \
    -H 'Content-Type: application/json'\
    -d '{"input_value": "What did I buy",
    "output_type": "chat",
    "input_type": "chat",
    "tweaks": {
  "File-US1KX": {},
  "ParseData-ljEsG": {},
  "ChatInput-rAmmk": {},
  "Prompt-teE98": {},
  "HuggingFaceModel-gSuPr": {},
  "ChatOutput-m01kr": {},
  "OpenAIModel-xs0J4": { "openai_api_key": "OpenAI API Key" }
}}'
```

This code sends the question "What did I buy?" to the Langflow project. The response from the project looks like this (main reply highlighted in bold):

```
{"session_id":"a195037a-1cac-4f9d-9737-4613107b0374",
"outputs":[{"inputs":{"input_value":"What did I buy?"},
"outputs":[{"results":{"message":{"text_key":"text",
"data":{"text":"You bought three units of the \"Essager 100W/60W
USB Type C To USB C Cable,\" which is a USB-C PD fast charging
charger wire cord suitable for devices like Macbook, Samsung,
Xiaomi, and vivo. The color is black, and the cable length is 3
meters.","sender":"Machine","sender_name":"AI","session_id":
"a195037a-1cac-4f9d-9737-4613107b0374","files":[],
...
"component_id":"ChatOutput-m01kr","files":[],
"type":"message"}],"component_display_name":"Chat Output",
"component_id":"ChatOutput-m01kr","used_frozen_result":false}]}]}
```

8.4.2 Python code

To use the project you created in Langflow programmatically in Python, first download the project as a JSON file. Figure 8.34 shows how to download the Langflow project.

Using the JSON file, you can use the `load_flow_from_json()` function to run it programmatically without having the Langflow project running. This function treats the Langflow project as a LangChain object. To run it, use the following code snippet,

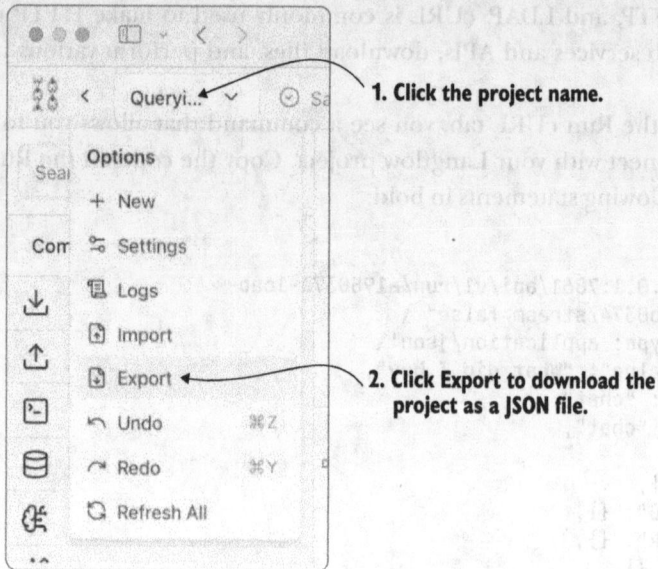

1. Click the project name.

2. Click Export to download the project as a JSON file.

Figure 8.34
Downloading the Langflow project as a JSON file

replacing the value of the `openai_api_key` key with your own and setting your question in the `input_value` key:

```
from langflow.load import run_flow_from_json
TWEAKS = {
  "File-US1KX": {},
  "ParseData-ljEsG": {},
  "ChatInput-rAmmk": {},
  "Prompt-teE98": {},
  "HuggingFaceModel-gSuPr": {},
  "ChatOutput-mO1kr": {},
  "OpenAIModel-xs0J4": { "openai_api_key": "OPENAI API Key" }
}

result = run_flow_from_json(flow="Querying a local document.json",
                           input_value="What did I buy?",
                           fallback_to_env_vars=True,
                           tweaks=TWEAKS)

print(result)
```

Remember to replace the project name (Querying a `local document.json`) with your own project name. The result looks something like the following:

```
[RunOutputs(inputs={'input_value': 'What did I buy?'},
outputs=[ResultData(results={'message': Message(text_key='text',
data={'text': 'You bought three units of the "Essager 100W/60W
USB Type C To USB C Cable," which is a USB-C PD fast charging
charger wire cord suitable for devices like Macbook, Samsung,
```

```
Xiaomi, and vivo. The color is black, and the cable length is 3
meters.', 'sender': 'Machine',
...
component_display_name='Chat Output', component_id='ChatOutput-m01kr', used_
frozen_result=False)])]
```

Summary

- Langflow is an open source library that allows you to build LLM-based applications using LangChain through a drag-and-drop visual interface.
- You can install Langflow with the `pip` command or use it through Docker. Alternatively, you can use Langflow in the cloud.
- Components (flows) are the building blocks of a Langflow project.
- You can use Langflow projects programmatically and embed your chatbot in a web application.

Programming agents

This chapter covers

- Introducing agents
- Creating simple agents using smolagents
- Creating enterprise-grade agents using LangChain
- Creating enterprise-grade agents using LangGraph

Up to this point, you've worked with Hugging Face transformers to tackle a variety of tasks, ranging from natural language processing (NLP) to image analysis and computer vision. Each of these tasks typically involves a specific, specialized model—a translation model for converting text between languages, for example, or an image captioning model to generate textual descriptions of images.

Although using specialized models works well for clearly defined tasks, it becomes increasingly difficult to manage workflows when the tasks are ambiguous or multistep or when they require dynamic decision-making. This is where agents come into play. Agents use large language models (LLMs) not only to perform tasks but also to reason, plan, and delegate, breaking complex problems into smaller subtasks and calling appropriate tools or models to complete them.

In this chapter, you'll explore the concept of agents and learn how to build an agent yourself. In particular, the chapter focuses on constructing agents using two practical and widely applicable frameworks:

- *smolagents*—A lightweight, minimalistic agent framework for quick experimentation
- *LangGraph*—A powerful framework for building stateful, multistep workflows involving language models and tools, ideal for handling conversations and decision trees

By the end of this chapter, you'll understand the fundamentals of agent design. You'll know how to equip an agent with tools and manage state and memory in multistep reasoning pipelines.

9.1 What are agents?

Agentic AI has captured a lot of attention in recent months and is often hailed as a major step toward the future of AI. What are agents, and how do they work? In the world of AI, an *agent* is a specialized system designed to perform tasks autonomously by combining language understanding, reasoning, and tool use. Specifically, an AI agent does the following things:

- *Understands natural language*—Uses a large language model (LLM) to interpret user queries or instructions
- *Reasons and plans*—Analyzes the task, breaks it into steps, and decides how to proceed
- *Acts using known tools*—Selects and executes actions from a set of tools (e.g., APIs, search engines, or custom scripts) to gather data or perform operations
- *Delivers results*—Processes tool outputs and returns a coherent response to the user

Figure 9.1. summarizes the key roles of an agent.

To understand how an AI agent works, let's explore a practical example: a weather agent that retrieves current weather information for a specific city. Here's how you interact with such an agent:

- *Natural language*—Submit a query like "What's the current temperature in Singapore?"
- *Task breakdown and planning*—The agent analyzes the query, breaking it into steps (e.g., identify the city and fetch weather data).
- *Tool selection and execution*—The agent selects an appropriate tool, such as one that queries the OpenWeather-Map API, to retrieve weather details.

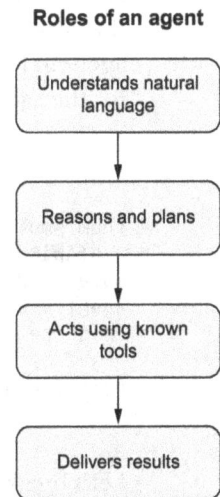

Roles of an agent

Figure 9.1 Roles of an agent

- *Result delivery*—The agent processes the tool's output and returns a clear response, such as "The current temperature in Singapore is 28.5°C with scattered clouds."

This process demonstrates the agent's ability to understand, reason, act, and respond, making it a powerful tool for real-world tasks.

9.2 *Developing agents using smolagents*

Let's dive into building intelligent AI agents using smolagents—a lightweight, flexible framework designed to make agent development simple and approachable. Whether you're building agents that search the web, query databases, or execute Python code, smolagents provides the essential tools and structure to get you started. This section introduces the key concepts, walks you through creating your own agents, and offers real-world examples that help you bring your ideas to life.

> DEFINITION   Officially, smolagents isn't an acronym—simply a playful name in which *smol* is internet slang for *small.* Therefore, *smolagents* essentially means *small agents.*

In smolagents, an agent is a system that combines a language model with tools to perform tasks by generating and executing Python code. To create agents using smolagents, use pip as follows:

```
$ pip install smolagents
```

9.2.1 *Using built-in tools: DuckDuckGoSearchTool*

The first agent you'll build is a search agent, designed to take a user query, retrieve relevant information, and return a useful response. To perform the search, you'll use the DuckDuckGoSearchTool—a lightweight, privacy-focused search tool that allows your agent to find information on the web quickly and efficiently. Here is the code snippet for the agent:

Initializes the language model (using Hugging Face's inference API)

Initializes the agent with a search tool

```
from smolagents import CodeAgent, DuckDuckGoSearchTool,
  HfApiModel
model = HfApiModel()
agent = CodeAgent(tools = [DuckDuckGoSearchTool()], model = model)
response = agent.run("How long does it take to travel from " +
                "New York to Los Angeles by train?")
print(response)
```

Runs the agent with a task

Prints the response

Let's break down the code to understand how it works:

1. Create a model using HfApiModel(). This means you're using a model hosted on a Hugging Face server, so you don't have to host a model yourself. By default,

HfApiModel() uses the Qwen/Qwen2.5-Coder-32B-Instruct model. You can override this setting by specifying the model you want to use in the model parameter, such as HfApiModel(model="mistralai/Mistral-7B-Instruct-v0.2").

2 Use the CodeAgent class to build an agent that can reason through problems by generating and executing Python code as part of the decision-making process. The tools parameter allows you to specify the list of tools your agent can use to answer the query, and the model parameter specifies the LLM to use to interpret the user's query. You don't even have to specify the DuckDuckGoSearchTool if you set the add_base_tools parameter to True (see figure 9.2). In this case, the agent automatically uses the DuckDuckGoSearchTool, PythonInterpreterTool, and Transcriber tools by default.

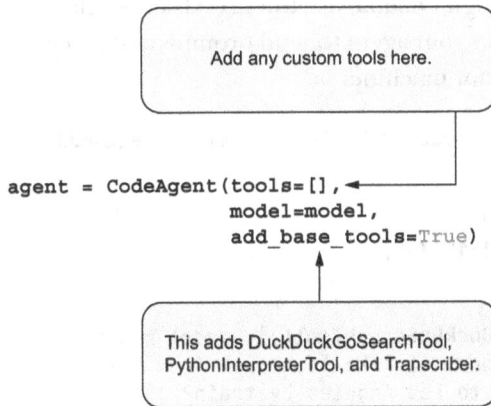

Add any custom tools here.

```
agent = CodeAgent(tools=[],
                  model=model,
                  add_base_tools=True)
```

This adds DuckDuckGoSearchTool, PythonInterpreterTool, and Transcriber.

Figure 9.2   The agent automatically uses the default tools if you set the add_base_tools parameter to True.

3 Use the agent's run() method to execute the agent's main logic. It takes an input (such as a user query), processes it using the agent's reasoning and tools, and returns the final output or answer.

When you run the preceding code, you should see output showing step by step how the agent works to answer your query. Chances are, however, that you'll see the following error message:

```
Error in generating model output:
402 Client Error: Payment Required for url:
https://router.huggingface.co/hf-inference/models/Qwen/
  Qwen2.5-Coder-32B-Instruct/v1/chat/completions (Request ID:
  Root=1-680f3378-1bfa504911aaa2c9696e106d;b14d1ad8-372e-440e
  -98c9-1d6abfc62f14)


You have exceeded your monthly included credits for Inference
Providers. Subscribe to PRO to get 20x more monthly
included credits.
```

This message appears because you've exceeded your free credits for the model hosted on Hugging Face. Without a Hugging Face Pro subscription, you're out of options. But if you can run an LLM locally on your computer, you're in luck! The simplest way to do this is to use Ollama. For this example, install Ollama and download the qwen2:7b model:

```
$ ollama pull qwen2:7b
```

> **NOTE** Ollama is an open source platform that enables you to run LLMs directly on your local machine, eliminating the need for cloud-based services. This approach offers enhanced data privacy, reduced latency, and offline accessibility. You can download Ollama at https://ollama.com.

To use a locally running LLM through Ollama, use the LiteLLMModel class, which connects to the Ollama server and allows your agent to send prompts and receive responses directly from models running on your machine:

```
from smolagents import CodeAgent, DuckDuckGoSearchTool, LiteLLMModel

model = LiteLLMModel(
    model_id = "ollama/qwen2:7b",
    api_base = "http://127.0.0.1:11434",
    num_ctx = 8192,
)
agent = CodeAgent(tools = [DuckDuckGoSearchTool()], model = model)
response = agent.run("How long does it take to travel from " +
                     " New York to Los Angeles by train?")
print(response)
```

Note that, in this example, Ollama is the LLM provider, so the model_id is set to ollama/qwen2:7b, where ollama is the provider name and qwen2:7b is the model name. For the list of providers you can use with LiteLLMModel, check out https://docs.litellm.ai/docs/providers.

You can also use OpenAI's models. The following example shows how to use the gpt-4o-mini model from OpenAI:

```
import os
os.environ["OPENAI_API_KEY"] = "<OPENAI_API_Key>"        ◀──┐ Replace with your own key.

model = LiteLLMModel(
    model_id="gpt-4o-mini",
    api_base="https://api.openai.com/v1",               ◀──┐ OpenAI's official API base
)
```

When you run the agent, you should see something like figure 9.3. Next, you see the execution log, shown in figure 9.4. Finally, you get the answer (see figure 9.5).

```
┌──────────────────────────── New run ────────────────────────────┐
│                                                                  │
│  How long does it take to travel from New York to Los Angeles by train?  │
│                                                                  │
│  LiteLLMModel - gpt-4o-mini                                      │
│                                                                  │
└──────────────────────────────────────────────────────────────────┘
```

──────────────────────────── Step 1 ────────────────────────────

```
─ Executing parsed code: ──────────────────────────────────────────
travel_time = web_search(query="New York to Los Angeles train travel time")
print(travel_time)
────────────────────────────────────────────────────────────────────
```

Figure 9.3 The agent working on the first step in answering the question

```
Execution logs:
## Search Results

[Train Tickets, Schedules & Routes | Amtrak](https://www.amtrak.com/home.html)
Book your Amtrak train and bus tickets today by choosing from over 30 U.S. train routes and 500 destinations in
North America.

[Train New York to Los Angeles from $266 – Rome2rio](https://www.rome2rio.com/Train/New-York/Los-Angeles)
The train between New York and Los Angeles takes 2 days 19h. The train runs, on average, 6 times per week from New
York to Los Angeles. The journey time may be longer on weekends and holidays; use the search form on this page to
search for a specific travel date.

[How long would a bullet train from New York to LA
take?](https://www.ncesc.com/geographic-faq/how-long-would-a-bullet-train-from-new-york-to-la-take/)
A train trip between New York and Los Angeles is around 3 days and 4 hours, although the fastest train will take
about 2 days and 18 hours. This is the time it takes to travel the 2,443 miles that separates the two cities.

[New York to Los Angeles Train – Amtrak Tickets $257 –
Wanderu](https://www.wanderu.com/en-us/train/us-ny/new-york/us-ca/los-angeles/)
In the last month, the average price of a train ticket from New York to Los Angeles was $390.41. Considering the
distance between New York and Los Angeles, tickets on this route are relatively expensive. Good news! You can find
the cheapest tickets if you book your trip at least 24 days prior to the travel date.

[Transcontinental Travel: New York To California By
Rail](https://quartzmountain.org/article/what-train-can-travel-from-new-york-to-california)
The train journey from New York to Los Angeles, California, takes around 2 days and 16 hours, and tickets can be
purchased from Amtrak, Omio, or Busbud. The average ticket price is $383, but prices vary depending on the date of
travel and how far in advance tickets are booked.

[How long does it take to travel across the U.S. by
train?](https://www.amtrakguide.com/2019/12/31/how-long-does-it-take-to-travel-across-the-u-s-by-train/)
East Coast: New York City, Washington D.C. and Boston; West Coast: Los Angeles, Emeryville (near San Francisco),
Portland and Seattle; New York City to Los Angeles. Travel Time 62 hours. Layover Time 4.5 hours (Chicago) Routes
Lake Shore Limited and Southwest Chief. Description

[New York to Los Angeles – 12 ways to travel via train, plane ... –
Rome2rio](https://www.rome2rio.com/s/New-York/Los-Angeles)
The cheapest way to get from New York to Los Angeles costs only $267, and the quickest way takes just 8½ hours. ...
There are 12 ways to get from New York to Los Angeles by plane, train (Amtrak), bus (Greyhound), car, train, or
bus. Select an option below to see step-by-step directions and to compare ticket prices and travel times in
Rome2Rio ...

[New York, NY to Los Angeles, CA Train – Virail](https://www.virail.com/train-new_york_ny-los_angeles_ca)
Best time to book cheap train tickets from New York, NY to Los Angeles, CA. The cheapest New York, NY – Los
Angeles, CA train tickets can be found for as low as $89.90 if you're lucky, or $162.26 on average. The most
expensive ticket can cost as much as $232.31.

[How long is the Amtrak ride from New York to
LA?](https://en.phongnhaexplorer.com/qna/travel/how-long-is-the-amtrak-ride-from-new-york-to-la.html)
The Amtrak train ride from the bustling streets of New York to the sun-drenched shores of Los Angeles clocks in at
an average of 67 hours and 20 minutes. That's almost three full days spent aboard a train, a prospect that might
seem daunting to some, but a tempting escape to others. Think of it less as a commute and more as a rolling hotel
room.

[Trains to Los Angeles – Schedules, Discounts & Station Info |
Amtrak](https://www.amtrak.com/trains-to-los-angeles)
Amtrak ticket deals can range from saving on business and coach class seats for booking early, discounted rates for
late night travel, limited time partner cross promotions and other unique deals that come and go throughout the
year. Even without deals and promotions, an Amtrak train to Los Angeles can cost as little as $5 (e.g. from
Glendale, CA).

Out: None
```

Figure 9.4 The agent displaying its execution log

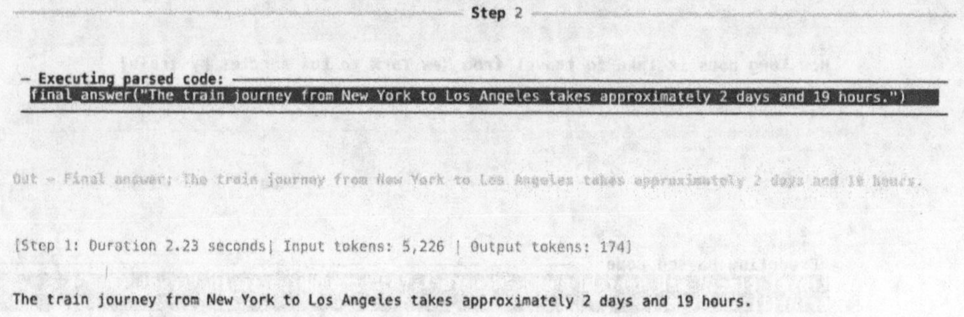

―――――――――――――――――――――― Step 2 ――――――――――――――――――――――

― Executing parsed code: ――――――――――――――――――――――――――――――――
```
final answer("The train journey from New York to Los Angeles takes approximately 2 days and 19 hours.")
```

Out - Final answer: The train journey from New York to Los Angeles takes approximately 2 days and 19 hours.

[Step 1: Duration 2.23 seconds| Input tokens: 5,226 | Output tokens: 174]

The train journey from New York to Los Angeles takes approximately 2 days and 19 hours.

Figure 9.5   The final answer returned by the agent

In this example, the LLM (such as OpenAI's gpt-4o-mini) is responsible for interpreting and understanding the user's query. It formulates a search request and sends it to DuckDuckGo. The search results are retrieved and passed back to the LLM, which uses them to generate a final response for the user.

9.2.2   *Using built-in tools: PythonInterpreterTool*

The next tool that we want to explore, besides DuckDuckGoSearchTool, is PythonInterpreterTool, which allows the agent to execute Python code dynamically, enabling it to solve computational problems, perform calculations, or interact with APIs and libraries directly within the agent's workflow. Here's an example of the tool in action:

```
from smolagents import CodeAgent, PythonInterpreterTool, LiteLLMModel

model = LiteLLMModel(
    model_id="gpt-4o-mini",
    api_base="https://api.openai.com/v1",
)

agent = CodeAgent(tools=[PythonInterpreterTool()], model=model)
response = agent.run("Calculate the 10th Fibonacci number.")
print(response)
```

When you run the agent, you see the output shown in figure 9.6.

The query is straightforward. Let's try another one:

```
response = agent.run("Generate the Fibonacci sequence up to 100.")
```

You see the output shown in figure 9.7.

> **TIP**   The choice of LLM plays an important role in the result returned by the agent. In general, try models from different providers to get the best output for the agent you're creating.

Calculate the 10th Fibonacci number.

LiteLLMModel - gpt-4o-mini

─────────────── Step 1 ───────────────

— Executing parsed code: ——————————————————————
```
n = 10
fibonacci = [0, 1]

for i in range(2, n + 1):
    fibonacci.append(fibonacci[i - 1] + fibonacci[i - 2])

tenth_fibonacci = fibonacci[n]
print(tenth_fibonacci)
```

Execution logs:
55

Out: None

[Step 0: Duration 3.00 seconds| Input tokens: 2,046 | Output tokens: 162]

─────────────── Step 2 ───────────────

— Executing parsed code: ——————————————————————
```
final_answer(55)
```

Out - final answer: 55

[Step 1: Duration 1.42 seconds| Input tokens: 4,383 | Output tokens: 211]

55

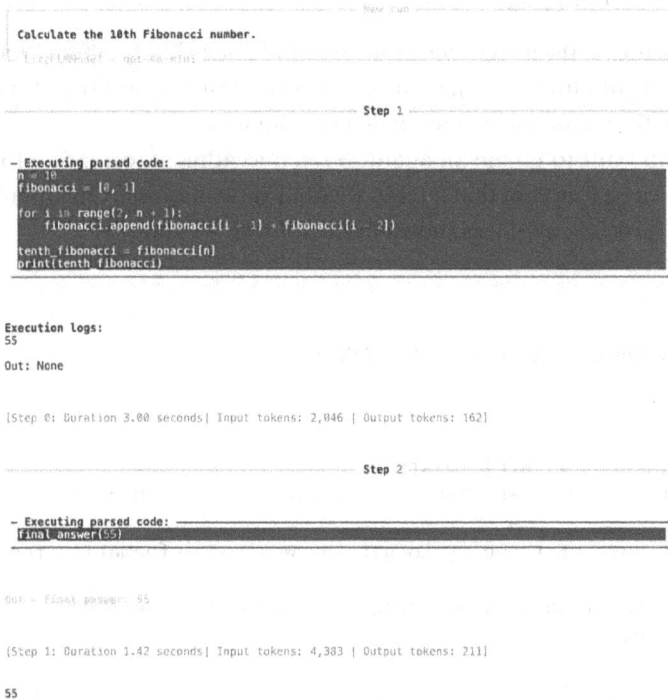

Figure 9.6 Using the agent to write the code to find the 10th Fibonacci number

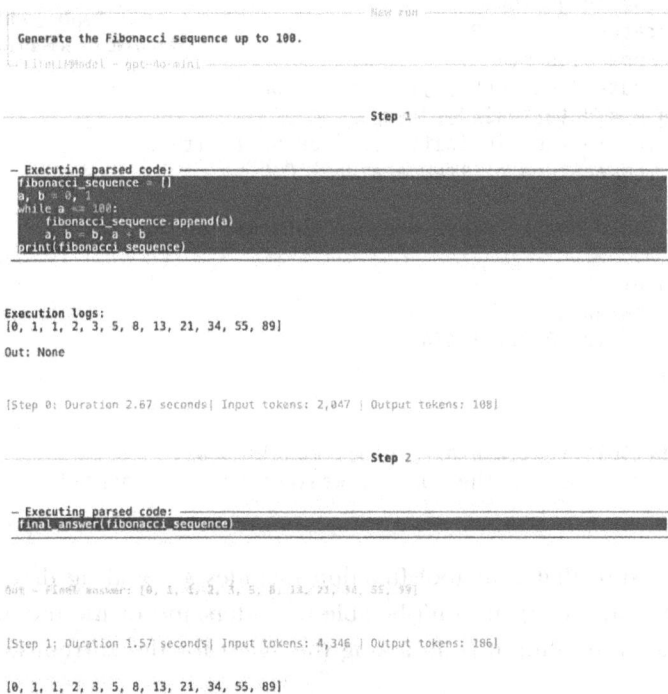

─────────────── New run ───────────────

Generate the Fibonacci sequence up to 100.

LiteLLMModel - gpt-4o-mini

─────────────── Step 1 ───────────────

— Executing parsed code: ——————————————————————
```
fibonacci_sequence = []
a, b = 0, 1
while a <= 100:
    fibonacci_sequence.append(a)
    a, b = b, a + b
print(fibonacci_sequence)
```

Execution logs:
[0, 1, 1, 2, 3, 5, 8, 13, 21, 34, 55, 89]

Out: None

[Step 0: Duration 2.67 seconds| Input tokens: 2,047 | Output tokens: 108]

─────────────── Step 2 ───────────────

— Executing parsed code: ——————————————————————
```
final_answer(fibonacci_sequence)
```

Out - final answer: [0, 1, 1, 2, 3, 5, 8, 13, 21, 34, 55, 89]

[Step 1: Duration 1.57 seconds| Input tokens: 4,346 | Output tokens: 186]

[0, 1, 1, 2, 3, 5, 8, 13, 21, 34, 55, 89]

Figure 9.7 Getting the agent to generate the Fibonacci numbers up to 100

9.2.3   *Writing your own custom tools*

Sometimes, the built-in tools won't meet your needs. When that happens, you have to create a custom tool, and fortunately, writing one is easy. Simply add the @tool decorator above your function, and you can use it as a custom tool.

Suppose that you want to create an agent to fetch weather information for you. In this case, you can write a function that fetches weather information from OpenWeatherMap and then converts it to a tool, as shown in the following example.

Listing 9.1   Writing a custom tool to fetch weather information from OpenWeatherMap

```
from smolagents import CodeAgent, LiteLLMModel, tool
import requests

@tool
def get_weather_info(city: str) -> str:
    """Retrieve the current weather information for a given city.
    Args:
        city: The name of the city to get the weather information for.
    Returns:
        str: A description of the current weather and temperature
        in the city.
    """
    api_key = "<API_KEY>"
        url = f"http://api.openweathermap.org/data/2.5/weather?
                q={city}&appid={api_key}&units=metric"
    response = requests.get(url)
    if response.status_code == 200:
        data = response.json()
        weather = data["weather"][0]["description"]
        temperature = data["main"]["temp"]
        return f"The weather in {city} is {weather} with a
                temperature of {temperature}°C."
    else:
        return f"Could not retrieve weather information for {city}."

model = LiteLLMModel(
    model_id="ollama/qwen2:7b",
    api_base="http://127.0.0.1:11434",
    num_ctx=8192,
)

agent = CodeAgent(tools=[get_weather_info], model=model)
response = agent.run("What is the current weather for Singapore?")
print(response)
```

← **Replace with your OpenWeatherMap API key.**

It's important to ensure that your tool function includes a docstring describing its parameters. Without it, the agent won't be able to understand or use the tool properly. Figure 9.8 shows the output from asking the agent for the current weather in Singapore.

```
─────────────────────────── New run ───────────────────────────
What is the current weather for Singapore?
── LiteLLMModel − ollama/qwen2:7b ──────────────
```

```
─────────────────────────────── Step 1 ───────────────────────────────
```

```
─ Executing parsed code: ──────────────────────────────────
weather_info = get_weather_info(city='Singapore')
print("Current weather:", weather_info)
```

```
Execution logs:
Current weather: The weather in Singapore is broken clouds with a temperature of 30.77°C.

Out: None
```

```
[Step 0: Duration 1.71 seconds| Input tokens: 2,083 | Output tokens: 56]
```

```
─────────────────────────────── Step 2 ───────────────────────────────
```

```
─ Executing parsed code: ──────────────────────────────────
final_answer(weather_info)
```

```
Out − Final answer: The weather in Singapore is broken clouds with a temperature of 30.77°C.
```

```
[Step 1: Duration 2.53 seconds| Input tokens: 4,322 | Output tokens: 139]
```

```
The weather in Singapore is broken clouds with a temperature of 30.77°C.
```

Figure 9.8 The agent returns this output when you ask for the weather in Singapore.

9.3 *Developing agents with LangChain*

Instead of using the smolagents framework, you can develop agents with LangChain, a widely adopted framework for building applications powered by LLMs. LangChain provides a flexible modular architecture that allows developers to create complex agents by composing components such as prompts, memory, tools, and chains. It supports various execution paradigms, including synchronous and asynchronous task handling, and integrates well with a wide range of APIs and data sources. Compared with smolagents, which emphasizes simplicity and minimalism, LangChain offers more features out of the box and is well suited to applications that require richer context management, more dynamic tool use, or more advanced reasoning capabilities.

This section explores how to construct agents using LangChain, with a focus on using both built-in tools and custom tools tailored to specific tasks. To use LangChain to create an agent, install the following packages using pip:

```
!pip install langchain langchain-openai
    langchain-community google-search-results
```

9.3.1 *Using the built-in Tool class*

In LangChain, agents interact with external functionality through a standardized tool interface. Tools are defined using the `BaseTool` class or its simpler counterpart, the `Tool` class, both of which provide a consistent interface that agents can invoke to perform specific actions.

LangChain also provides utility wrappers such as `SerpAPIWrapper`, `WikipediaAPI-Wrapper`, `WolframAlphaAPIWrapper`, and `TavilySearchResults` that handle the complexities of integrating with external APIs. These wrappers encapsulate all the logic needed to query services such as Google Search, Wikipedia, and computational engines, and they format their responses into structured data that agents can work with.

An important distinction applies, however: agents can't directly use utility wrappers. To be accessible to an agent, a wrapper must be embedded in a `Tool` instance. This wrapping process transforms the utility into a proper tool that can be added to the agent's toolset.

This modular architecture offers significant advantages for developers. Rather than writing complex integration code from scratch, they can simply wrap existing services in a `Tool` and plug them directly into their agent workflows. Then the agent can seamlessly access these external capabilities as part of its decision-making process, extending its functionality with minimal effort.

> **NOTE** SerpAPI is a real-time search API that allows developers to programmatically access and extract search results from search engines such as Google, Bing, Yahoo, YouTube, and Amazon. It is commonly used to retrieve structured search results—organic results, ads, featured snippets, knowledge graphs, and other rich data—from Google search without having to scrape HTML pages manually.

As an example, let's walk through using the `SerpAPIWrapper` to build an agent capable of performing real-time searches. First, sign up for a free account at https://serpapi .com, and obtain your private API key. Then load your SerpAPI key into your environment like this:

```
import os
os.environ["SERPAPI_API_KEY"] = "<SERPAPI_KEY>"
```

Now you can create an instance of the `SerpAPIWrapper` class and use it to create a tool:

```
from langchain.tools import Tool
from langchain_community.utilities.serpapi import SerpAPIWrapper

search = SerpAPIWrapper()          ◁——┐   Initializes SerpAPI wrapper
tools = [
    Tool(                              └——  Creates a proper tool that wraps
        name = "Search",                    the SerpAPI functionality
        func = search.run,
        description = "Useful for when you need to answer questions
        about current events or search for specific information on
```

```
        the web. Input should be a search query."
    )
]
```

Next, create a LangChain agent using the `initialize_agent()` function as shown in the following listing.

Listing 9.2 Creating a LangChain agent using the `initialize_agent()` function

```
from langchain_openai import ChatOpenAI
from langchain.agents import AgentType, initialize_agent

os.environ["OPENAI_API_KEY"] = "<OPENAI_API_KEY>"

llm = ChatOpenAI(model = "gpt-4o-mini",        ◄─┤ Initializes the LLM
                 temperature = 0)
agent = initialize_agent(            ◄─┤ Initializes the agent
    tools = tools,                          with updated structure
    llm = llm,
        agent_type =
        AgentType.ZERO_SHOT_REACT_DESCRIPTION,
    verbose = True                ◄─┤ Prints reasoning steps
)

response = agent.invoke("Who is Wei-Meng Lee?")   ◄─┤ Runs the agent with a query
print(response)
```

In this code snippet, you first created an agent using a search tool (`SerpAPIWrapper`). For this agent, you used the `gpt-4o-mini` model from OpenAI. You specified the agent type as `AgentType.ZERO_SHOT_REACT_DESCRIPTION`, which means that the agent uses a zero-shot ReAct (reasoning+acting) framework, enabling it to reason through a query step by step and select appropriate tools to generate a response without requiring training or examples. The `verbose` argument specifies that you want to see the reasoning step by step. When you run the code, you see the agent's reasoning:

```
> Entering new AgentExecutor chain...
I need to gather information about Wei-Meng Lee to provide a
comprehensive answer.
Action: Search
Action Input: "Wei-Meng Lee biography"
Observation: He is a prolific author, having written numerous
books covering iOS and Android development, blockchain, machine
learning, and smart contracts. In addition to his publications,
Wei-Meng is a regular speaker at international conferences and
contributes columns to Towards Data Science and CODE Magazine.
Thought:I now have a good understanding of who Wei-Meng Lee is,
including his contributions to technology and education through
his writing and speaking engagements.

Final Answer: Wei-Meng Lee is a prolific author and speaker known
for his work in iOS and Android development, blockchain, machine
```

learning, and smart contracts. He has written numerous books on
these topics and regularly speaks at international conferences.
Additionally, he contributes columns to platforms like Towards
Data Science and CODE Magazine.

```
> Finished chain.
{'input': 'Who is Wei-Meng Lee?', 'output': 'Wei-Meng Lee is a
prolific author and speaker known for his work in iOS and
Android development, blockchain, machine learning, and smart
contracts. He has written numerous books on these topics and
regularly speaks at international conferences. Additionally, he
contributes columns to platforms like Towards Data Science and
CODE Magazine.'}
```

Let's try another question:

```
response = agent.invoke("What is the weather in New York today?")
print(response)
```

You see the following output:

```
> Entering new AgentExecutor chain...
I need to find the current weather information for New York City.
Action: Search
Action Input: "current weather in New York City today"
Observation: {'type': 'weather_result', 'temperature': '68',
'unit': 'Fahrenheit', 'precipitation': '10%', 'humidity': '84%',
'wind': '6 mph', 'location': 'New York, NY', 'date': 'Thursday',
'weather': 'Cloudy'}
Thought:I now know the final answer.
Final Answer: The weather in New York City today is cloudy, with
a temperature of 68°F, 10% chance of precipitation, 84% humidity,
and wind at 6 mph.

> Finished chain.
{'input': 'What is the weather in New York today?', 'output':
'The weather in New York City today is cloudy, with a temperature
of 68°F, 10% chance of precipitation, 84% humidity, and wind at 6
mph.'}
```

The following statements show how to import some of the other built-in tools provided
by LangChain:

```
from langchain_community.utilities.bing_search
  import BingSearchAPIWrapper
from langchain_community.utilities.duckduckgo_search
  import DuckDuckGoSearchAPIWrapper
from langchain_community.utilities.google_search
  import GoogleSearchAPIWrapper
from langchain_community.utilities.wikipedia
  import WikipediaAPIWrapper
```

Searches using Microsoft Bing

Uses DuckDuckGo for privacy-friendly search

Uses Google's programmable search engine

Queries Wikipedia using its API

9.3.2 Using custom tools

As you created an agent with smolagents earlier, you can create custom tools to use with your LangChain agent. In the following example, besides using the search tool, you'll create a custom tool named get_weather_info(), which fetches weather details from OpenWeatherMap.

Listing 9.3 Writing a custom function to fetch weather information

```
import os
import requests
from langchain_openai import ChatOpenAI
from langchain_community.utilities.serpapi import SerpAPIWrapper
from langchain.tools import Tool, tool
from langchain.agents import AgentType, initialize_agent

os.environ["OPENAI_API_KEY"] = "<OPENAI_API_KEY>"
os.environ["SERPAPI_API_KEY"] = "<SERPAPI_KEY>"

llm = ChatOpenAI(temperature=0)

search = SerpAPIWrapper()
search_tool = Tool(
    name = "Search",
    func = search.run,
        description = "Useful for when you need to answer questions
        about current events or search for specific information on
    the web. Input should be a search query."
)
```

| Creates a custom tool using the @tool decorator

```
@tool
def get_weather_info(city: str) -> str:
    """Retrieve the current weather information for a given city.
    Args:
        city: The name of the city to get the weather information for.
    Returns:
        str: A description of the current weather and temperature in
        the city.
    """
```

| Replace with your OpenWeatherMap API key.

```
    api_key = "<OPENWEATHERMAP_API_KEY>"
        url = f"http://api.openweathermap.org/data/2.5/
                weather?q={city}&appid={api_key}&units=metric"
    response = requests.get(url)

    if response.status_code == 200:
        data = response.json()
        weather = data["weather"][0]["description"]
        temperature = data["main"]["temp"]
        humidity = data["main"]["humidity"]
        wind_speed = data["wind"]["speed"]
        summary = (
            f"Weather in {city}:\n"
            f"Condition: {weather}\n"
```

```
                    f"Temperature: {temperature}°C\n"
                    f"Humidity: {humidity}%\n"
                    f"Wind Speed: {wind_speed} m/s"
            )
            return summary
        else:
            return f"Could not retrieve weather information for {city}."
tools = [search_tool, get_weather_info]
agent = initialize_agent(
    tools = tools,
    llm = llm,
    agent = AgentType.ZERO_SHOT_REACT_DESCRIPTION,
    verbose = True
)
```

A clean string that can be easily used in prompts and understood by agents

Uses search_tool and get_weather_info tools

Initializes the agent with these tools

Now you can ask the agent about the weather in Singapore:

```
response = agent.invoke(
    "What is the current weather in Singapore?")
print(response)
```

Tests the custom tool

You see the following response:

```
> Entering new AgentExecutor chain...
I should use the get_weather_info function to retrieve the current
weather information for Singapore.
Action: get_weather_info
Action Input: "Singapore"
Observation: Weather in Singapore:
Condition: broken clouds
Temperature: 30.08°C
Humidity: 71%
Wind Speed: 4.12 m/s
Thought:I have the current weather information for Singapore.
Final Answer: The current weather in Singapore is broken clouds with a
temperature of 30.08°C, humidity at 71%, and a wind speed of 4.12 m/s.

> Finished chain.
{'input': 'What is the current weather in Singapore?', 'output': 'The
current weather in Singapore is broken clouds with a temperature of
30.08°C, humidity at 71%, and a wind speed of 4.12 m/s.'}
```

9.4 *Developing agents using LangGraph*

Previously, you learned how to build agents using LangChain. Although this approach will continue to be supported, the recommendation is to build agents using Lang-Graph, a more flexible and feature-rich framework designed specifically for building complex stateful agents. LangGraph builds on the strengths of LangChain and offers greater control of agent workflows. You can build agents using LangGraph by

- Creating an agent capable of answering user questions using reasoning and available tools

- Integrating an external tool (such as a web search or weather API) to enable the agent to answer questions that go beyond its built-in knowledge
- Integrating memory into your LangGraph agent so that it can engage in a conversation with the user

9.4.1 What Is LangGraph?

LangGraph is a Python framework developed by the LangChain team that allows you to build stateful multistep workflows involving language models, tools, and external APIs. It enables you to structure logic as a directed graph, in which each node represents a computational step (e.g., calling an LLM or using a tool) and edges define how the workflow proceeds based on the output or state. This graph-based approach is ideal for use cases such as these:

- Multiturn chatbots with memory
- Decision trees or branching logic based on LLM outputs
- Complex tool-using agents
- Data enrichment or extract, transform, load (ETL) pipelines
- Modular conversational flows

LangGraph builds on LangChain and integrates seamlessly with LangChain tools, agents, and memory constructs. To install LangGraph, run this command:

```
!pip install langgraph
```

LangGraph is especially valuable when your application requires memory or a persistent state across multiple steps. It also supports branching logic, tool use, and dynamic flow control—capabilities that are challenging to implement using traditional linear chains in LangChain. Given the scope of this chapter, I will focus only on the core components of LangGraph that relate to agent-based workflows.

9.4.2 LangGraph agent basics

Let's start by creating an agent using LangGraph. For this initial example, we won't integrate any external tools, meaning that the agent will rely solely on its internal reasoning capabilities and the knowledge on which it was trained.

> **TIP** External tools such as web search APIs or database connectors can be integrated to extend the agent's functionality. These tools allow the agent to access up-to-date information, perform computations, or retrieve specific data that lies beyond its built-in knowledge base.

First, import the following libraries:

```
import os
from langgraph.graph.message import add_messages
from langgraph.prebuilt import create_react_agent
from langchain_openai import ChatOpenAI
```

For the LLM, use the `gpt-4o-mini` model from OpenAI. To use this model, you need an OpenAI API key:

```
os.environ["OPENAI_API_KEY"] = "<OPENAI_API_KEY>"
llm = ChatOpenAI(model_name="gpt-4o-mini", temperature=0)
tools = []
```

Sets environment variables (replace with your API key)

Initializes the LLM (OpenAI)

The tools to use (no tools at this moment)

Next, create a ReAct agent using LangGraph's `create_react_agent()` function, a function in LangChain that creates a ReAct-style agent:

```
agent_executor = create_react_agent(llm, tools)
```

The `create_react_agent()` function (imported from `langgraph.prebuilt`) is a wrapper that builds on LangChain's core `create_react_agent()` functionality. It combines the following:

- LLM reasoning (thoughts)
- Tool use (actions), if tools are provided
- Observations (from tool outputs)
- Final answer generation

NOTE ReAct is a method in which the agent thinks step by step, calls tools if necessary, observes results, and continues reasoning.

When you print this agent (`agent_executor`), you see the graph shown in figure 9.9.

This simple graph illustrates a linear flow with three key stages:

- `__start__` *node*—Entry point of the workflow
- `agent` *node*—Core node where the agent processes the input
- `__end__` *node*—Termination point of the graph, where the result is returned

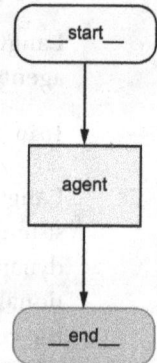

Figure 9.9 The graph for the agent you're building

This minimal graph demonstrates a basic agent execution path with no branching or loops, making it easy to follow and suitable for single-turn or sequential tasks. Next, you'll define a function that invokes the agent and prints each step of its reasoning process:

```
def run_agent(query: str):
    state = agent_executor.invoke({"messages": [("user", query)]})
    print(state)
    print("\n Agent trace:")
    for i, msg in enumerate(state["messages"]):
```

Function to run the agent with a user query

Prints out the agent's traces

```
        print(f"{i+1}. [{msg.type.upper()}]
            {msg.content.strip() if
                hasattr(msg, 'content') else msg}")
        print('=====')
    return state["messages"][-1].content
```

The `run_agent()` function is a simple, effective way to interact with the LangGraph agent and inspect its behavior step by step. The function takes a user query as input, wraps it in a message format (`("user", query)`), and invokes the agent using `agent_executor.invoke()`. The response is stored in a `state` dictionary, which contains the entire message history. After the response is generated, the function prints out a trace of the agent's message history. Each message is printed with its type (e.g., USER, AI, TOOL) and content. This trace is helpful for debugging and understanding how the agent processes and responds to inputs.

You are ready to use the agent. Ask a simple question and then print out the result:

```
query = "Who is Bill Gates?"
answer = run_agent(query)
print(f"Query: {query}")
print(f"Answer: {answer}")
```

The output consists of three parts:

- The value of the `state` variable, which is the result returned by the agent
- The extracted agent traces
- The question that was asked and the final answer from the agent

Let's discuss each component in the output. The following listing shows the content of the `state` variable.

Listing 9.4 The content of the `state` variable

```
{
    'messages': [
        {
            'type': 'HumanMessage',
            'content': 'Who is Bill Gates?',
            'additional_kwargs': {},
            'response_metadata': {},
            'id': 'b4f87d83-2e87-444c-8eca-ee92a483b584'
        },
        {
            'type': 'AIMessage',
            'content': "Bill Gates is an American business magnate,
software developer, philanthropist, and author, best known as
the co-founder of Microsoft Corporation, the world's largest
personal-computer software company. Born on October 28, 1955,
in Seattle, Washington, Gates showed an early interest in
computers and programming. He attended Harvard University but
dropped out in 1975 to start Microsoft with his childhood
friend Paul Allen.\n\nUnder Gates' leadership, Microsoft
```

developed the Windows operating system, which became a
dominant platform for personal computers. Gates served as the
CEO of Microsoft until 2000 and continued to play a
significant role in the company until he stepped down from
day-to-day operations in 2008.\n\nIn addition to his work in
technology, Gates is known for his philanthropic efforts. In
2000, he and his then-wife Melinda founded the Bill &
Melinda Gates Foundation, which focuses on global health,
education, and poverty alleviation. The foundation has made
significant contributions to various causes, including
vaccine development and distribution, education reform, and
efforts to combat infectious diseases.\n\nGates has been
recognized with numerous awards and honors for his
contributions to technology and philanthropy, and he is
often listed among the world's wealthiest individuals. His
influence extends beyond business, as he is also a prominent
advocate for various social and health issues.",
        'additional_kwargs': {
            'refusal': None
        },
        'response_metadata': {
            'token_usage': {
                'completion_tokens': 267,
                'prompt_tokens': 12,
                'total_tokens': 279,
                'completion_tokens_details': {
                    'accepted_prediction_tokens': 0,
                    'audio_tokens': 0,
                    'reasoning_tokens': 0,
                    'rejected_prediction_tokens': 0
                },
                'prompt_tokens_details': {
                    'audio_tokens': 0,
                    'cached_tokens': 0
                }
            },
            'model_name': 'gpt-4o-mini-2024-07-18',
            'system_fingerprint': 'fp_dbaca60df0',
            'id': 'chatcmpl-BTJwkQfk0rrqvyIa5LVGfLJhbvPki',
            'finish_reason': 'stop',
            'logprobs': None
        },
        'id': 'run-3d803ad4-1270-4334-a938-8950c5108ac8-0',
        'usage_metadata': {
            'input_tokens': 12,
            'output_tokens': 267,
            'total_tokens': 279,
            'input_token_details': {
                'audio': 0,
                'cache_read': 0
            },
            'output_token_details': {
                'audio': 0,
                'reasoning': 0
            }

```
        }
      }
    ]
}
```

The state variable holds the response returned by the agent, including both the input provided and a detailed trace of the agent's reasoning and tool use during execution. You can see that the preceding code contains two messages: HumanMessage (the question you asked) and AIMessage (the answer returned by the LLM). The next component is the agent trace extracted from the state variable:

```
Agent trace:
1. [HUMAN] Who is Bill Gates?
=====
2. [AI] Bill Gates is an American business magnate, software
developer, philanthropist, and author, best known as the
co-founder of Microsoft Corporation, the world's largest
personal-computer software company. Born on October 28, 1955,
in Seattle, Washington, Gates showed an early interest in
computers and programming. He attended Harvard University but
dropped out in 1975 to start Microsoft with his childhood
friend Paul Allen.

Under Gates' leadership, Microsoft developed the Windows
operating system, which became a dominant platform for
personal computers. Gates served as the CEO of Microsoft until
2000 and continued to play a significant role in the company
until he stepped down from day-to-day operations in 2008.

In addition to his work in technology, Gates is known for his
philanthropic efforts. In 2000, he and his then-wife Melinda
founded the Bill & Melinda Gates Foundation, which focuses on
global health, education, and poverty alleviation. The
foundation has made significant contributions to various
causes, including vaccine development and distribution,
education reform, and efforts to combat infectious diseases.

Gates has been recognized with numerous awards and honors for
his contributions to technology and philanthropy, and he is
often listed among the world's wealthiest individuals. His
influence extends beyond business, as he is also a prominent
advocate for various social and health issues.
=====
```

Figure 9.10 illustrates the steps taken by the agent.

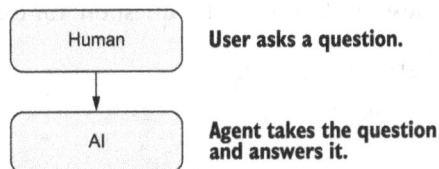

Human — **User asks a question.**

AI — **Agent takes the question and answers it.**

Figure 9.10 The steps taken by the LangGraph agent

The last component shows the question asked and the result:

```
Query: Who is Bill Gates?
Answer: Bill Gates is an American business magnate, software
developer, philanthropist, and author, best known as the
co-founder of Microsoft Corporation, the world's largest
personal-computer software company. Born on October 28, 1955,
in Seattle, Washington, Gates showed an early interest in
computers and programming. He attended Harvard University
but dropped out in 1975 to start Microsoft with his childhood
friend Paul Allen.

Under Gates' leadership, Microsoft developed the Windows
operating system, which became a dominant platform for
personal computers. Gates served as the CEO of Microsoft
until 2000 and continued to play a significant role in the
company until he stepped down from day-to-day operations in
2008.

In addition to his work in technology, Gates is known for
his philanthropic efforts. In 2000, he and his then-wife
Melinda founded the Bill & Melinda Gates Foundation, which
focuses on global health, education, and poverty alleviation.
The foundation has made significant contributions to various
causes, including vaccine development and distribution,
education reform, and efforts to combat infectious diseases.

Gates has been recognized with numerous awards and honors
for his contributions to technology and philanthropy, and
he is often listed among the world's wealthiest individuals.
His influence extends beyond business, as he is also a
prominent advocate for various social and health issues.
```

In this example, the agent can answer the question "Who is Bill Gates?" based on the model's (gpt-4o-mini) training data. Let's ask another question:

```
query = "What is 2+3?"
answer = run_agent(query)
```

Here's the output:

```
Query: What is 2+3?
Answer: 2 + 3 equals 5.
```

Try asking the agent a question that is beyond the scope of its training data, however, and the agent is unable to answer your question. If you ask this question, for example,

```
query = "Who won the US Presidential Election in 2024?"
answer = run_agent(query)
```

you get an error:

```
Query: Who won the US Presidential Election in 2024?
Answer: I'm sorry, but I don't have information on events that
occurred after October 2023, including the results of the 2024
US Presidential Election. You may want to check the latest news
sources for the most current information.
```

Why? The model was trained on data up to October 2023, so it has no knowledge of events that occurred after that date. This is precisely why you need to use a tool in an agent.

9.4.3 Using LangGraph with tools

To answer questions beyond the model's training data, you must connect the agent to an external tool that's capable of providing up-to-date information, such as performing web searches to get the answer. To allow your agent to perform real-time searches, you can use the SerpAPIWrapper, a tool described and used in section 9.3.1. First, create an instance of the SerpAPIWrapper class:

```
from langchain_core.tools import Tool
from langchain_community.utilities import SerpAPIWrapper

os.environ["SERPAPI_API_KEY"] = "<SERPAPI_KEY>"        ◄──── Replace with your own key.
serpapi = SerpAPIWrapper()                             ◄──── Initializes the SerpAPI wrapper and creates a tool
search_tool = Tool(
    name = "SerpAPI",                    ◄──── Name of the tool
    func = serpapi.run,
        description = "A search engine tool to query real-time information
                from the web."
)                                        serpapi.run is a method provided by the SerpAPIWrapper class.
```

Note the description of the tool. The description of a tool in LangChain (and, by extension, LangGraph) is important because it guides the LLM in deciding when and how to use the tool. The description acts as a prompt that informs the LLM about the tool's purpose, functionality, and expected input, enabling the agent to make intelligent decisions about whether to call the tool based on the user's query.

Next, add the search_tool as an argument to the create_react_agent() function:

```
tools = [search_tool]                                   ◄──── Adds the search tool
agent_executor = create_react_agent(llm, tools)         ◄──── Creates the ReAct agent using LangGraph's high-level interface
```

Now when you print out the agent_executor, you see the graph shown in figure 9.11. Here's the flow of the entire graph:

- __start__ *node*—This node is the entry point of the graph. Execution begins here.

- agent *node*—The agent processes the user input. Based on the query and internal logic, it decides whether it can respond directly or needs help from a tool.

- tools *node*—If the agent determines that a tool is needed (e.g., a calculator, search engine, or database lookup), it sends a request to the tools node. The tool is executed and the result is returned to the agent, allowing it to formulate a final response. The dotted lines indicate conditional or dynamic transitions.

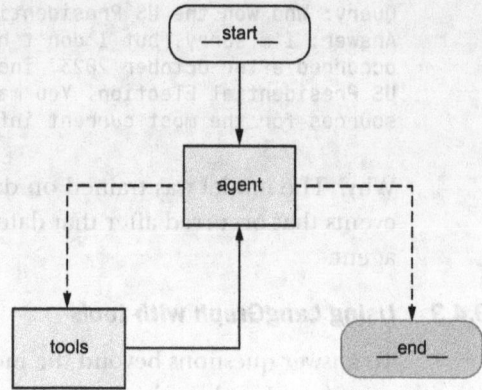

Figure 9.11 The graph of the agent with the external tool

- __end__ *node*—When the agent has all the necessary information (either directly or via a tool), it outputs the final message. The flow ends here.

Now you can ask the question "Who won the US Presidential Election in 2024?":

```
query = "Who won the US Presidential Election in 2024?"
answer = run_agent(query)
print(f"Query: {query}")
print(f"Answer: {answer}")
```

Observe the output. First, observe the content of the state variable, shown in the following listing.

Listing 9.5   The content of the state variable

```
{
    'messages': [
        {
            'type': 'HumanMessage',
            'content': 'Who won the US Presidential Election in 2024?',
            'additional_kwargs': {},
            'response_metadata': {},
            'id': '6166c39b-015e-417b-9016-55bd75c35fd5'
        },
        {
            'type': 'AIMessage',
            'content': '',
            'additional_kwargs': {
                'tool_calls': [
                    {
                        'id': 'call_0TL5mwU9fmTn45OmZJejsZkp',
                        'function': {
                            'arguments': '{"__arg1":
                                "US Presidential Election 2024 winner"}',
```

```
                        'name':  'SerpAPI'
                    },
                    'type': 'function'
                }
            ],
            'refusal': None
        },
        'response_metadata': {
            'token_usage': {
                'completion_tokens': 24,
                'prompt_tokens': 69,
                'total_tokens': 93,
                'completion_tokens_details': {
                    'accepted_prediction_tokens': 0,
                    'audio_tokens': 0,
                    'reasoning_tokens': 0,
                    'rejected_prediction_tokens': 0
                },
                'prompt_tokens_details': {
                    'audio_tokens': 0,
                    'cached_tokens': 0
                }
            },
            'model_name': 'gpt-4o-mini-2024-07-18',
            'system_fingerprint': 'fp_0392822090',
            'id': 'chatcmpl-BTMUM9twVvbFPpvV0zJkr19cDIRo7',
            'finish_reason': 'tool_calls',
            'logprobs': None
        },
        'id': 'run-77effaef-0972-4c07-8156-6c8b25618a4c-0',
        'tool_calls': [
            {
                'name': 'SerpAPI',
                'args': {
                    '__arg1': 'US Presidential Election 2024 winner'
                },
                'id': 'call_0TL5mwU9fmTn450mZJejsZkp',
                'type': 'tool_call'
            }
        ],
        'usage_metadata': {
            'input_tokens': 69,
            'output_tokens': 24,
            'total_tokens': 93,
            'input_token_details': {
                'audio': 0,
                'cache_read': 0
            },
            'output_token_details': {
                'audio': 0,
                'reasoning': 0
            }
        }
    },
},
{
    'type': 'ToolMessage',
```

```
            'content': '[' entity_type: video_universal.', 'The
APP excludes "over" and "under" votes in the total votes cast,
which also impacts the vote percentage for candidates.
Harris-Walz 2024. Trump-Vance 2024.', 'View maps and real-time
results for the 2024 US presidential election matchup between
former President Donald Trump and Vice President Kamala Harris.',
"A presidential election was held in the United States on
November 5, 2024. The Republican Party\'s ticket—Donald Trump,
who was the 45th president of the ...", 'Live 2024 election
results for the president, U.S. Senate, U.S. House, and
governors.', 'Donald Trump passed the critical threshold of 270
electoral college votes with a projected win in the state of
Wisconsin making him the next US president.', 'Get live
presidential results and maps from every state and county in
the 2024 election.', '2024 election guide: Presidential
candidates, polls, primaries and caucuses, voter information
and results for November 5, 2024.', 'Check back for the
Certificates of Vote from the 2024 election. They will be
posted as they become available. President Donald J. Trump
[R] Main Opponent ...', 'View live election results from the
2024 presidential race as Kamala Harris and Donald Trump face
off. See the map of votes by state as results are tallied.']',
            'name': 'SerpAPI',
            'id': 'f681c58a-043e-4016-b081-5f2f44d83fa1',
            'tool_call_id': 'call_0TL5mwU9fmTn45OmZJejsZkp'
    },
    {
            'type': 'AIMessage',
            'content': 'Donald Trump won the US Presidential
Election in 2024, passing the critical threshold of 270
electoral college votes with a projected win in the state
of Wisconsin.',
            'additional_kwargs': {
                'refusal': None
    },
            'response_metadata': {
                'token_usage': {
                    'completion_tokens': 34,
                    'prompt_tokens': 392,
                    'total_tokens': 426,
                    'completion_tokens_details': {
                        'accepted_prediction_tokens': 0,
                        'audio_tokens': 0,
                        'reasoning_tokens': 0,
                        'rejected_prediction_tokens': 0
                    },
                    'prompt_tokens_details': {
                        'audio_tokens': 0,
                        'cached_tokens': 0
                    }
            },
            'model_name': 'gpt-4o-mini-2024-07-18',
            'system_fingerprint': 'fp_0392822090',
            'id': 'chatcmpl-BTMUN6F1DvzZae98NwKMLzcBKUW9C',
            'finish_reason': 'stop',
            'logprobs': None
```

```
        },
        'id': 'run-e10a9f2f-336a-4544-ac46-588594006dd2-0',
        'usage_metadata': {
            'input_tokens': 392,
            'output_tokens': 34,
            'total_tokens': 426,
            'input_token_details': {
                'audio': 0,
                'cache_read': 0
            },
            'output_token_details': {
                'audio': 0,
                'reasoning': 0
            }
        }
    }
  ]
}
```

As you see, the agent is using the tool to search for an answer. Here are the traces of the agent:

```
▓ Agent trace:
1. [HUMAN] Who won the US Presidential Election in 2024?
=====
2. [AI]
=====
3. [TOOL] [' entity_type: video_universal.', 'The APP excludes
"over" and "under" votes in the total votes cast, which also
impacts the vote percentage for candidates. Harris-Walz 2024.
Trump-Vance 2024.', 'View maps and real-time results for the
2024 US presidential election matchup between former President
Donald Trump and Vice President Kamala Harris.', "A presidential
election was held in the United States on November 5, 2024.
The Republican Party's ticket—Donald Trump, who was the 45th
president of the ...", 'Live 2024 election results for the
president, U.S. Senate, U.S. House, and governors.', 'Donald
Trump passed the critical threshold of 270 electoral college
votes with a projected win in the state of Wisconsin making him
the next US president.', 'Get live presidential results and
maps from every state and county in the 2024 election.', '2024
election guide: Presidential candidates, polls, primaries and
caucuses, voter information and results for November 5, 2024.',
'Check back for the Certificates of Vote from the 2024 election.
They will be posted as they become available. President Donald
J. Trump [R] Main Opponent ...', 'View live election results
from the 2024 presidential race as Kamala Harris and Donald
Trump face off. See the map of votes by state as results
are tallied.']
=====
4. [AI] Donald Trump won the US Presidential Election in
2024, passing the critical threshold of 270 electoral college
votes with a projected win in the state of Wisconsin.
=====
```

Finally, the agent returns the answer:

```
Query: Who won the US Presidential Election in 2024?
Answer: Donald Trump won the US Presidential Election in 2024, passing the
critical threshold of 270 electoral college votes with a projected win in
the state of Wisconsin.
```

Figure 9.12 summarizes the process.

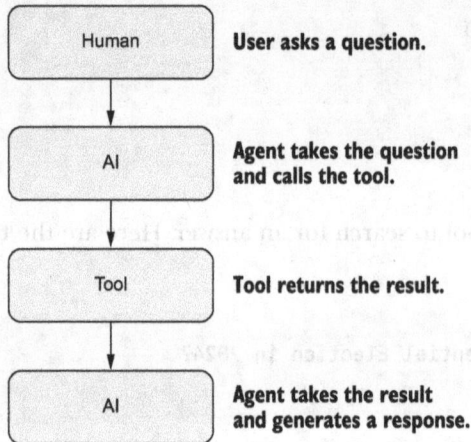

Figure 9.12   The agent works with the tool to return the answer.

9.4.4   Using LangGraph with a custom tool

You can create custom tools to use with your LangGraph agent. In this section, you'll create a function named `get_weather_info()` and use it to retrieve weather information from OpenWeatherMap. The following code shows the definition of the function.

Listing 9.6   The `get_weather_info()` function

```
import requests

def get_weather_info(city: str) -> str:
    """Retrieve the current weather information for a given city."""
    api_key = "7453d5cfeaea020958539f22da95d849"
    url = f"http://api.openweathermap.org/data/2.5/
                   weather?q={city}&appid={api_key}&units=metric"
    response = requests.get(url)
    if response.status_code == 200:
        data = response.json()
        weather = data["weather"][0]["description"]
        temperature = data["main"]["temp"]
        humidity = data["main"]["humidity"]
        wind_speed = data["wind"]["speed"]
```

Replace with your OpenWeatherMap API key.

```
            summary = (
                f"Weather in {city}:\n"
                f"Condition: {weather}\n"
                f"Temperature: {temperature}°C\n"
                f"Humidity: {humidity}%\n"
                f"Wind Speed: {wind_speed} m/s"
            )
            return summary
    else:
            return f"Could not retrieve weather information for {city}."
```

A clean string that can be easily used in prompts and understood by agents

Next, create a LangChain `Tool` object using this function:

Creates a LangChain Tool from the custom function

Name of the tool

```
weather_tool = Tool(
    name = "GetWeather",
    func = get_weather_info,
    description = "A tool to fetch the weather information for a city"
)
```

Name of the custom function

Finally, use the `weather_tool` in your agent:

```
tools = [search_tool, weather_tool]
agent_executor = create_react_agent(llm, tools)
```

Now you can ask a question about the weather of a country:

```
query = "What is the current weather for Singapore"
answer = run_agent(query)
print(f"Query: {query}")
print(f"Answer: {answer}")
```

The final output of the agent looks something like the following:

```
Query: What is the current weather for Singapore
Answer: The current weather in Singapore is as follows:
- **Condition:** Broken clouds
- **Temperature:** 29°C
- **Humidity:** 79%
- **Wind Speed:** 3.09 m/s
```

9.4.5 *Using LangGraph with memory*

The agent that you've created has no memory at this point. That is, it treats every incoming query as an isolated request, without any awareness of what was said or asked previously. This means the agent cannot carry on a conversation, track context across multiple turns, or refer to earlier information. If you ask

```
Query: What is the current weather in Singapore?
Answer: The current weather in Singapore is as follows:
...
```

and follow up with

```
Query: Where is it located?
```

the agent will not be able to understand who it is unless you repeat the full context:

```
Query: Where is Singapore located?
```

To support back-and-forth interactions or context-aware reasoning, you must introduce memory into the system. This is where tools such as LangGraph, message history, and stateful chains come into play, enabling the agent to persist and reason over previous exchanges.

Let's add memory to our agent using LangGraph's support for message-passing state. First, import the following libraries:

```
from typing import Annotated, List
from typing_extensions import TypedDict
from langgraph.graph.message import add_messages
```

Then create a class named State:

```
class State(TypedDict):
    messages: Annotated[List, add_messages]
```

The State class creates a dictionarylike object meant to hold conversational state within LangGraph. The key messages stores a list of messages that the user is communicating with the agent. The Annotated class tells LangGraph how to handle the list of messages:

- It automatically merges, appends, or trims as needed.
- It's LangGraph's way of doing memory with a low-level but composable approach.
- List means that messages is expected to be a List (i.e., Python's built-in list), but it doesn't specify the type of items inside, so it's just a generic list (e.g., List[Any]).
- add_messages is a LangGraph utility that helps you manage appending and merging message sequences.

With the State class defined, modify the run_agent() function so that the agent can use a State object to maintain conversation:

> **Function to run the agent with a user query, maintaining conversation history**

```
def run_agent(query: str, state: State = None) -> tuple[str, State]:  ◄
    response = agent_executor.invoke({"messages": [("user", query)]})
    pprint(response)
```

```
if state is None:
    state = {"messages": []}
state["messages"].append(("user", query))
response = agent_executor.invoke(state)
state = {"messages": response["messages"]}
return response["messages"][-1].content, state
```

Appends the new user query to the existing messages

Invokes the agent with the updated state

Updates the state with the response, replacing the whole messages list

Returns the last message as well as the state

In this code, the `run_agent()` function accepts a user query and an optional `State` object, which stores the conversation history. If no state is provided, the function initializes an empty one. The user's query is appended to the message list in the state; then this updated state is passed to the agent via `invoke()`. The agent generates a response based on the full conversation history and returns an updated list of messages. The function returns the most recent message from the agent along with the updated state to continue the conversation seamlessly. Now you can now call the `run_agent()` function via a loop so that the user has a chance to ask contextually related questions:

```
conversation_state = {"messages": []}
while True:
    query = input("Question: ")
    if query.lower()=="quit": break
    answer, conversation_state = run_agent(query, conversation_state)
    print(f"Query: {query}")
    print(f"Answer: {answer}")
```

Initializes an empty state to store conversation history

Let's try this with the first question:

```
Query: What is the weather in Singapore?
Answer: The weather in Singapore is as follows:
- **Condition:** Broken clouds
- **Temperature:** 31.35°C
- **Humidity:** 70%
- **Wind Speed:** 3.09 m/s
```

Now that you have the first answer, ask a related question using her to refer to Singapore:

```
Query: What is her population?
Answer: As of my last knowledge update in October 2021,
Singapore's population was approximately 5.7 million people.
For the most current population figures, I recommend checking
the latest statistics from a reliable source such as the
Singapore Department of Statistics or other official
demographic resources.
```

You can see that the agent remembers the previous conversation and answers the question correctly.

Summary

- An agent is a specialized system designed to perform tasks autonomously by combining language understanding, reasoning, and tool use.

- smolagents is a lightweight, flexible framework designed to make agent development simple and approachable.

- `DuckDuckGoSearchTool` is a lightweight, privacy-focused search tool that allows your agent to find information from the web quickly and efficiently.

- Using the `HfApiModel()` object, you can use a model hosted on a Hugging Face server.

- The `CodeAgent` class creates a smolagents agent.

- To use a locally running LLM through Ollama, use the `LiteLLMModel` class, which connects to the Ollama server and allows your agent to send prompts and receive responses directly from models running on your machine.

- The `PythonInterpreterTool` class allows the agent to execute Python code dynamically.

- Use the `@tool` decorator above your function to design it as a custom tool.

- SerpAPI is a real-time search API that allows developers to programmatically access and extract search results from search engines.

- You can create a LangChain agent using the `initialize_agent()` function.

- LangGraph is a flexible, feature-rich framework designed for building complex, stateful agents.

- You can use the `create_react_agent()` function to create a ReAct-style agent.

- ReAct is a method in which the agent thinks step by step, calls tools, observes results, and continues reasoning.

- In LangGraph agents, you create a `Tool` object and use it as a custom tool.

- You can maintain memory in your LangGraph agent by creating a `State` object and passing it to your agent.

Building a web-based
UI using Gradio

This chapter covers

- Building basic UI with Gradio
- Configuring and customizing your Gradio application
- Sharing and deploying your Gradio application on Hugging Face Spaces
- Creating a chatbot UI for chatbot applications

Imagine that you've spent weeks coding your machine learning project, and it's finally done. Now you're eager to show it off to your friends, and you hope it will impress your boss. But you have one more thing to do: create a nice shiny frontend to impress your users.

Developers excel in technical aspects and problem-solving, but their strengths may not always align with creative design. How do you come up with a nice web frontend that can interface with your machine learning models?

Gradio, an open source Python package, makes it quick and easy to build a demo web application that showcases your machine learning applications. What's more, with a single click, you can share a link to your demo application using Gradio's built-in sharing feature.

10.1   *Basics of Gradio*

To install the Gradio package, use the `pip` command in Jupyter Notebook:

```
!pip install gradio
```

NOTE   At this writing, the latest version of the Gradio Python package is 5.18.0.

Let's start by exploring how Gradio works. You'll create a simple Gradio application and then dive into how it works and how to deploy it in a production environment. Specifically, you'll learn how to do the following:

- Use the `Interface` class to build a simple Gradio application
- Use the Flag options to let users flag your application output
- Configure authentication for your Gradio application so that only authorized users can use it
- Configure the Gradio application to be accessible on the local network
- Deploy your Gradio application on Hugging Face Spaces

10.1.1   *Using Gradio's Interface class*

To build a simple Gradio application, you can use the `Interface` class. `Interface` is Gradio's main high-level class, which allows you to build a web UI with a few lines of code. The `Interface` class accepts several arguments, including these:

- `fn`—Function to wrap the Gradio UI around
- `title`—Title of the Gradio UI
- `inputs`—Types of inputs to display in the Gradio UI
- `outputs`—Types of outputs to display in the Gradio UI

The following listing shows a simple example.

Listing 10.1   A simple Gradio example

```
import gradio as gr

def my_chatbot(message):
    return "Hello, " + message          Binds it to the
                                        my_chatbot() function
interface = gr.Interface(fn = my_chatbot,
                    title = "Hello, Gradio!",       Title of the UI
                    inputs = "text",
                    outputs = "text")      The input component(s)

interface.launch()                        The output component(s)
```

In this code snippet, the Gradio application is bound to the my_chatbot() function. To launch the Gradio application, call the launch() method. Figure 10.1 shows what the Gradio application looks like when the code is run.

```
Running on local URL:  http://127.0.0.1:7860
To create a public link, set `share=True` in `launch()`.
```

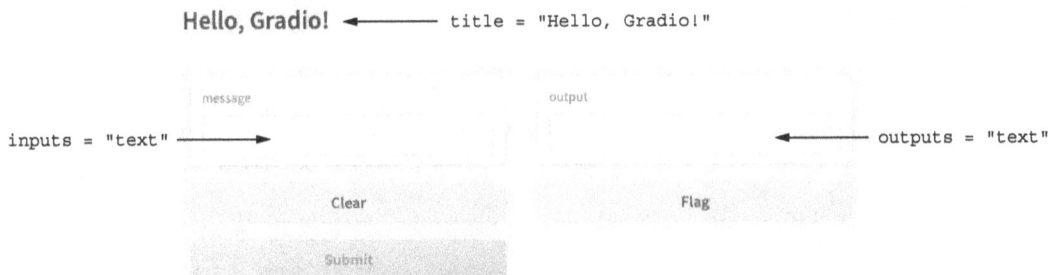

Hello, Gradio!

message   output

            Clear   Flag

        Submit

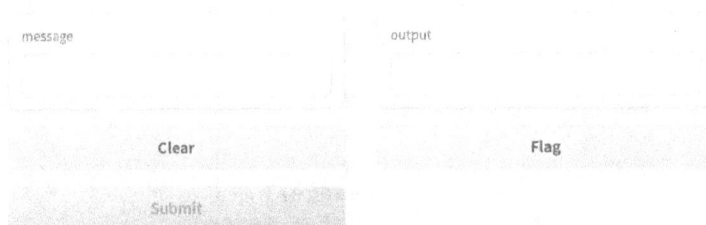

Figure 10.1   The Gradio application with a single input and a single output

Figure 10.2 shows how the various arguments passed into the Interface class control the UI of your Gradio application.

```
Running on local URL:  http://127.0.0.1:7860
To create a public link, set `share=True` in `launch()`.
```

Hello, Gradio! ◄──────── title = "Hello, Gradio!"

message   output

inputs = "text" ─────────►   ◄──────── outputs = "text"

            Clear   Flag

        Submit

Figure 10.2   The various components of your Gradio application

The Clear, Submit, and Flag buttons are displayed by default. In this example, both the input and output of the UI are text boxes (indicated with the text string). When the user clicks the Submit button, the text in the input text box is passed into the message parameter in the my_chatbot() function. The value returned by the function appears in the output text box. Figure 10.3 illustrates this process.

Hello, Gradio!

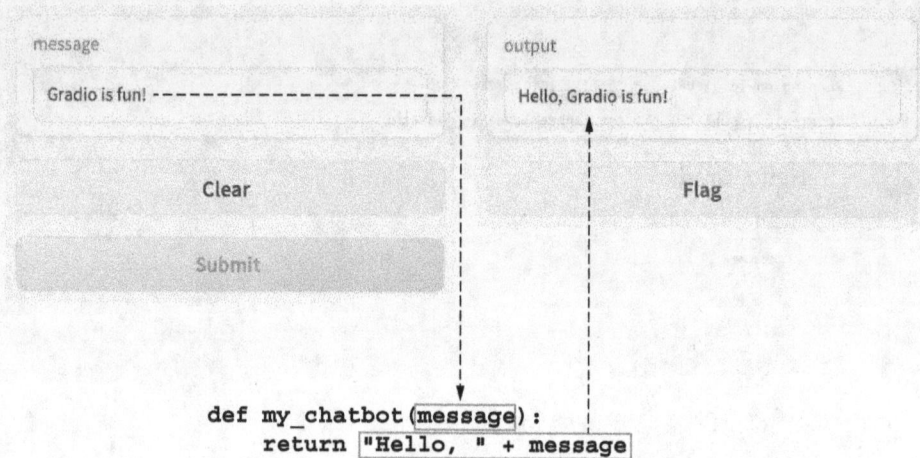

```
def my_chatbot(message):
    return "Hello, " + message
```

Figure 10.3 How values are passed in from the inputs to the bound function and returned to the outputs

Notice the link at the top of the output (refer to figure 10.2), indicating that Gradio is running on a local URL: `http://127.0.0.1:7860`. If you click that link, a new web page appears (see figure 10.4). The port number increments by 1 every time you run the cell in Jupyter Notebook. If you run the cell again, the port number will change to 7861, followed by 7862, and so on.

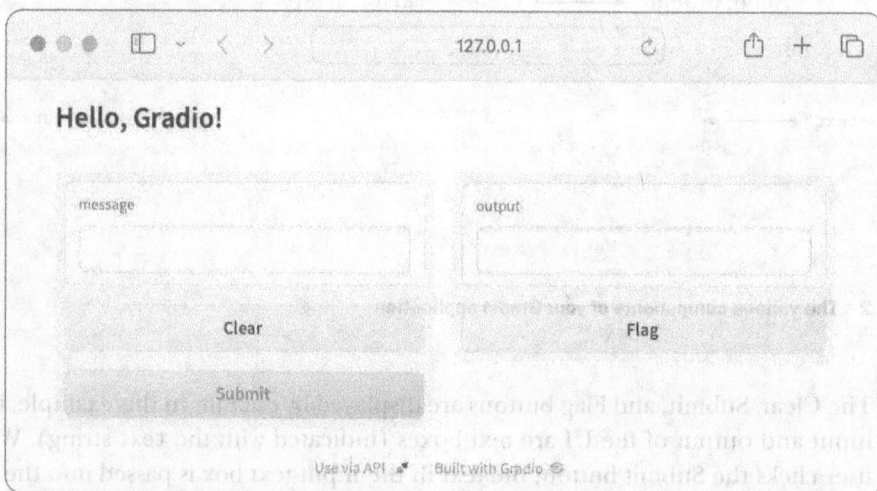

Figure 10.4 Displaying the Gradio app in a new browser window

Also notice the button labeled Flag. What is this button for? Well, it gives you a way to log the inputs and outputs if you find that the output returned by the function warrants further attention. Clicking the Flag button creates a new folder called `.gradio/flagged` in the same directory as your Jupyter Notebook. Inside this folder, you'll find a file named `dataset1.csv`. This file records your inputs, outputs, and other details. If you enter the string `"Gradio is fun!"`, click Submit, and then click Flag, Gradio logs the following in the `dataset1.csv` file (see figure 10.5).

```
● ● ●                          dataset1.csv — Edited
message,output,timestamp
Gradio is fun!,"Hello, Gradio is fun!",2025-02-25 15:35:09.729718
```

Figure 10.5   Viewing the content of `dataset1.csv`

10.1.2 Configuring flagging options

The default behavior of the Flag button is to log the inputs, outputs, and timestamp of your Gradio application in the `log.csv` file. If you want a more customized approach to logging, you can specify it by using the `flagging_options` parameter, as shown in the following listing.

Listing 10.2   Specifying `flagging_options`

```python
import gradio as gr

def my_chatbot(message):
    return "Hello, " + message

interface = gr.Interface(fn = my_chatbot,
                         title = "Hello, Gradio!",
                         inputs = "text",
                         outputs = "text",
                         flagging_options =
                             ["correct","wrong","ambiguous"])

interface.launch()
```

Figure 10.6 shows that now you have three Flag buttons, labeled based on what you specified in the `flagging_options` parameter.

Now if you type the string `"Gradio is fun!"`, click Submit, and then click the Flag As Correct button, a new file named `dataset2.csv` is created, and Gradio logs `correct` for the `flag` field (see figure 10.7).

Also rename the button like I did. Once you click this button, you should see you Amazon login form and prompt. If you find that the login form is cut by the iframe's true dimension, you can tweak the `max_height` based property of the iframe after passing the `iframe` node as your `ref` prop.

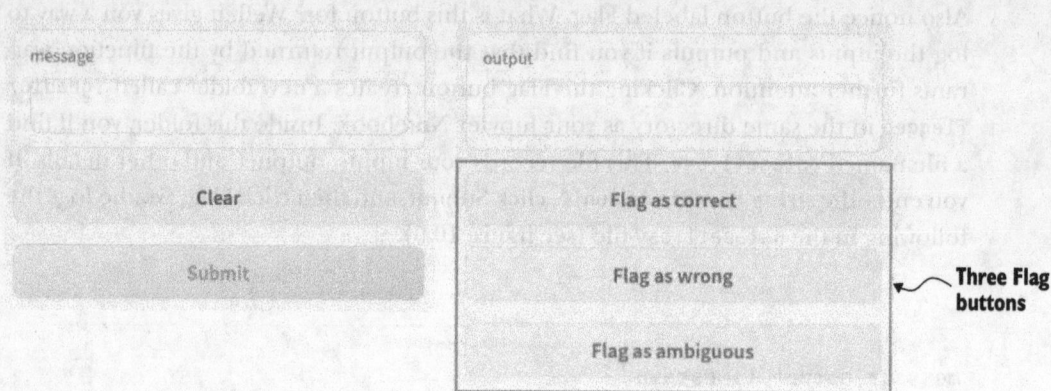

Figure 10.6   The three flagging options

Figure 10.7   Now the `dataset2.csv` file contains the "correct" string.

A new CSV file is created if the structure of the original file changes. The `dataset1.csv` file, for example, didn't include a field named `flag`, whereas `dataset2.csv` does.

10.1.3   Configuring authentication

By default, your Gradio application is public; anyone who has the URL of your app will be able to access it. But you may want to restrict access to the application, especially if it involves sensitive data. You can password-protect your application by using the `auth` parameter in the `launch()` method as follows.

Listing 10.3   Specifying authentication credentials

```
import gradio as gr

def my_chatbot(message):
    return "Hello, " + message

interface = gr.Interface(fn = my_chatbot,          ◀── Binds it to Gradio
                        title = "Hello, Gradio!",
                        inputs = "text",
                        outputs = "text",
```

```
                        flagging_options =
                            ["correct","wrong","ambiguous"])

interface.launch(auth = ("admin", "secret"))
```

When you run this code snippet, you see the login page shown in figure 10.8.

Login
username
Type here...
password
Type here...
Login

Figure 10.8 Prompting the user to log in before using the application

> **NOTE** To ensure that authentication in Gradio works properly, you must enable third-party cookies in your browser. By default, Apple Safari and Google Chrome won't work in incognito mode.

If the entered username (`"admin"`) and password (`"secret"`) don't match, you see an `Incorrect Credentials` message. Otherwise, the Gradio application loads as usual.

Now if you type the string `"Gradio is fun!"`, click Submit, and then click the Flag As Correct button, Gradio creates another CSV file and logs `"admin"` under the `username` field (see figure 10.9).

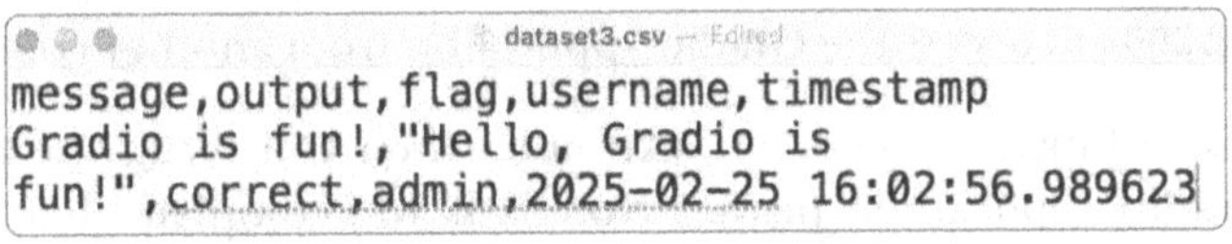
dataset3.csv — Edited
message,output,flag,username,timestamp
Gradio is fun!,"Hello, Gradio is
fun!",correct,admin,2025-02-25 16:02:56.989623

Figure 10.9 The `dataset3.csv` file contains `"admin"` under the `username` field.

Hardcoding the username and password in the `auth` parameter is not the recommended practice; however, you may want to write a function to perform your own authentication handling and then specify the function name in the `auth` parameter, like this:

```
def authentication(username, password):  ◄─────  You can replace the authentication
                                                 logic with your own.

    return (username=='admin' and password=='secret')  ◄──  Returns True to
                                                            authenticate user or
interface.launch(auth = authentication)                     False otherwise
```

In this code snippet, you can replace the authentication logic with your own, such as authenticating against the credentials stored in databases or other third-party authentication services.

10.1.4 *Customizing the server and port*

By default, Gradio listens at port 7860. But this port may not be available on your computer if another application is listening at the same port. In this case, Gradio automatically searches for the next available port, starting from 7860. Alternatively, you can specify the port you want to use for Gradio. This approach is especially useful if you're running Gradio in a Docker container and the container exposes only specific ports.

Also, when Gradio starts, it binds to the 127.0.0.1 IP address by default, making the Gradio application accessible only on the local computer. If you want to make the application accessible on the local network, you need to bind it to the 0.0.0.0 IP address. The following code snippet makes the process clear:

```
                                            Listens at port 5000; accessible only
                                               on the computer running Gradio

interface.launch(server_name = "127.0.0.1", server_port = 5000)  ◄──


interface.launch(server_name = "0.0.0.0", server_port = 5000)  ◄──

                                            Listens at port 5000; accessible
                                               only on the local network
```

For a computer on the network to access the Gradio application, simply use the following URL: http://<IP_ADDRESS_OF_SERVER>:5000. If the Gradio application is running on a computer with IP address 192.168.1.24, for example, you can use the URL http://192.168.1.24:5000 to access the Gradio application from another computer.

> **NOTE** When you use Jupyter Notebook, take note when you rerun the cell containing the Gradio application; Jupyter Notebook will complain that the port you specified is not available. To fix this problem, restart the kernel.

10.1.5 *Sharing your Gradio application*

If you want to share your Gradio application with your friends over the internet, you can set the share argument to True in the launch() method:

```
interface.launch(share = True)
```

This setting causes Gradio to create a temporary link that allows your friends to access your Gradio application. Figure 10.10 shows the output when you call the launch() method with the share argument set to True:

```
Running on local URL:  http://127.0.0.1:7861
Running on public URL: https://88cf9d2ca09805c5d5.gradio.live

This share link expires in 72 hours. For free permanent hosting and GPU upgrades, run `grad
io deploy` from Terminal to deploy to Spaces (https://huggingface.co/spaces)
```

Figure 10.10 A public link is created for your Gradio application.

Now you can now share the public URL with your friends. Note the following:

- If you run the Gradio code in Jupyter Notebook, the kernel must be running. If the kernel is shut down, the Gradio app no longer works.
- If you run the Gradio code as a standalone Python application, the application must be running. If not, the Gradio app no longer works.

NOTE Be aware that the shared link is served by Gradio share servers, which act only as proxies for your local server; they don't store any data sent through your app.

TIP Shared links expire after 72 hours. A much better way to make your Gradio application public is to host it on Hugging Face Spaces.

10.1.6 Deploying your Gradio application to Hugging Face Spaces

To make your Gradio application permanently available, host it in the cloud. Fortunately, Hugging Face Spaces provides free hosting for your Gradio application. (You can upgrade to a paid version if you require more computing power.) Here's how you can host your Gradio application on Hugging Face Spaces:

1 Create a directory on your computer, and for this example, name it MyGradioApp.
2 Create a file named mygradio.py with the content of listing 10.1, and save it in the MyGradioApp directory.
3 To host on Hugging Face Spaces, you need a WRITE Hugging Face token, so create it at https://huggingface.co/settings/tokens.
4 Launch Terminal (macOS) or Anaconda Prompt (Windows), and type the following commands:

```
$ cd MyGradioApp
$ gradio deploy
```

You see the following:

```
 _    _  _ _  _  _  _  _   _ _ _   _ _ _   _ _ _   _     _ _ _
|_|  |_|| | || || || || | |_|_| | |_|_| | |_|_| | | |   |_|_| |
 _|    _|  _| _| _| _| _|   _|     _|     _|     | |     _|
|_|   |_| |_||_||_||_||_|  |_|    |_|    |_|     |_|    |_|_| |
```

```
 _ _ _   _     _     _   _     _ _ _   _     _     _ _ _
|_|_| | | |   | |   | | | |   |_|_| | | |   | |   |_|_| |
 _|     | |   | |   | | | |    _|     | |   | |    _|
|_|_| | |_|_| |_|_| |_| |_|_| |_|_| | |_|_| |_|_| |_|_| |
```

Enter your token (input will not be visible): <Your WRITE token>
Add token as git credential? (Y/n) **n**
Creating new Spaces Repo in '/Volumes/SSD/Book Projects/5.
Hugging Face book/chap10/MyGradioApp'.
Collecting metadata, press Enter to accept default value.
Enter Spaces app title [MyGradioApp]: **<press Enter>**
Enter Gradio app file [mygradio.py]: **<press Enter>**
Enter Spaces hardware (cpu-basic, cpu-upgrade, t4-small,
t4-medium, l4x1, l4x4, zero-a10g, a10g-small, a10g-large,
a10g-largex2, a10g-largex4, a100-large, v5e-1x1, v5e-2x2,
v5e-2x4) [cpu-basic]: **<press Enter>**
Any Spaces secrets (y/n) [n]: **<press Enter>**
Create requirements.txt file? (y/n) [n]: **<press Enter>**
Create Github Action to automatically update Space on 'git push'?
[n]: **<press Enter>**
Space available at https://huggingface.co/spaces/Wei-Meng/MyGradioApp

5 Enter your WRITE token, and reply to the questions as follows:

Need 'write' access token to create a Spaces repo.

Your Gradio application is hosted on Hugging Face Spaces. You can access it via the URL https://huggingface.co/spaces/Wei-Meng/MyGradioApp. (Your URL will vary due to the username.) Figure 10.11 shows the application.

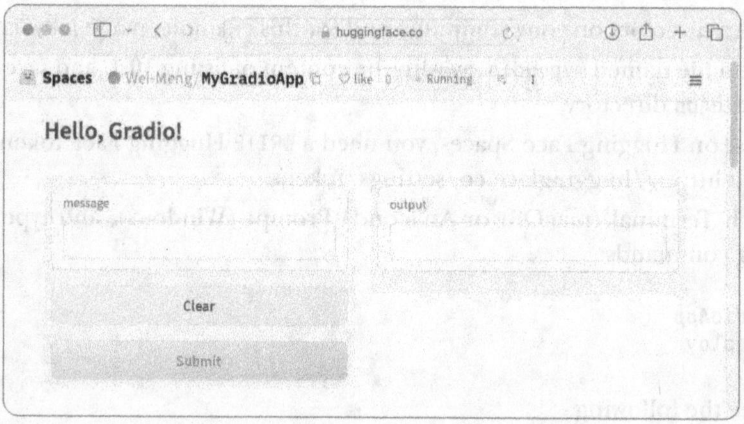

Figure 10.11
The Gradio application hosted on Hugging Face Spaces

10.2 Working with widgets

You've learned how to create a basic Gradio application, configure it for flagging, share it with friends on the local network, and deploy it on Hugging Face Spaces. In this section, you dive deeper into the various types of Gradio applications you can build with other components. You'll learn how to do the following:

- Work with `Textbox`
- Work with `Audio`
- Work with `Images`
- Work with selection components
- Lay out components using the `TabbedInterface` class

10.2.1 Working with Textbox

In the first example in this chapter, you saw that when you specify `text` as the value in the `inputs` parameter in the `Interface` class, a text box with the default label `message` is displayed. You can customize the text box by creating an instance of the `Textbox` class. The following listing shows an example.

Listing 10.4 Creating an instance of the `Textbox` class

```
import gradio as gr

def my_chatbot(message):
    return "Hello, " + message

textbox = gr.Textbox(label = "Message",
                     placeholder = "Your message here",
                     lines = 3)

gr.Interface(fn = my_chatbot,
             inputs = textbox,
             outputs = "text").launch()
```

Figure 10.12 shows what the Gradio application looks like at this point and how the various arguments in the `Textbox` class are used.

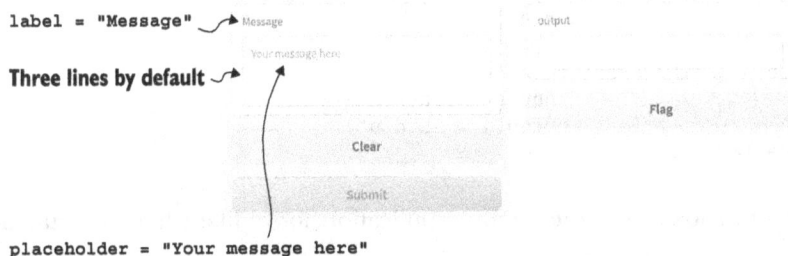

label = "Message"
Three lines by default
placeholder = "Your message here"

Figure 10.12 Configuring the `Textbox` component

The text box is taller, showing the height for three lines. Note, however, that the `lines` parameter doesn't limit the number of lines the user can type; it is there to display the initial number of lines to display. Figure 10.13 shows the output when the user enters some text and clicks the Submit button.

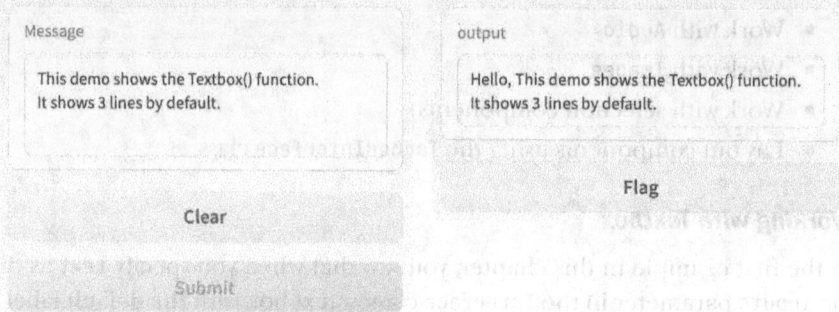

Message

```
This demo shows the Textbox() function.
It shows 3 lines by default.
```

output

```
Hello, This demo shows the Textbox() function.
It shows 3 lines by default.
```

Flag

Clear

Submit

Figure 10.13   Submitting the text and obtaining the output

10.2.2 *Working with Audio*

Gradio can work with audio as well as text. Using the Audio component, you can upload an audio stream to Gradio and perform operations on it. The following listing shows an example of using the `Audio` component.

Listing 10.5   Creating an instance of the `Audio` class

```python
import numpy as np
import gradio as gr

def reverse_audio(audio):
    sr, data = audio                            ◄── audio is a NumPy array.
    reversed_audio = (sr, np.flipud(data))      ◄── Reverses the audio
    return reversed_audio

mic = gr.Audio(sources = ["upload","microphone"],
               type = "numpy",
               label = "Audio")

interface = gr.Interface(fn = reverse_audio,
                         inputs = mic,
                         outputs = "audio")
interface.launch()
```

Figure 10.14 shows what the Gradio application looks like when you run the code snippet.

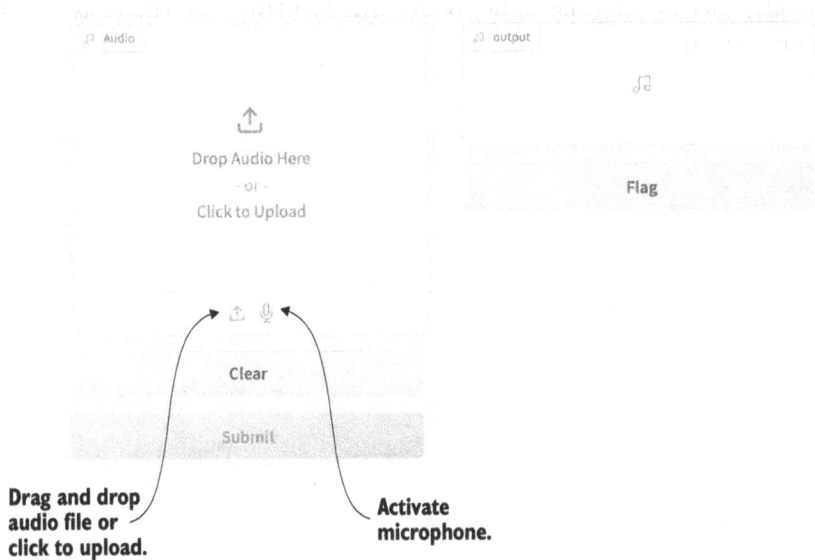

Drag and drop audio file or click to upload.

Activate microphone.

Figure 10.14 You can drag and drop an audio file or record an audio stream with your microphone.

If you activate the microphone on your computer to record an audio stream, by default, that stream is sent to the reverse_audio() function as a tuple, with sample rate in Hz and audio data as a NumPy array. In this example, the audio data was reversed by the np.flipud() function and then returned to the output, where it can be played back.

Figure 10.15 shows how to select the microphone to use (if you have more than one). Click the Record button to record the audio. When the audio is recorded, click the Submit button.

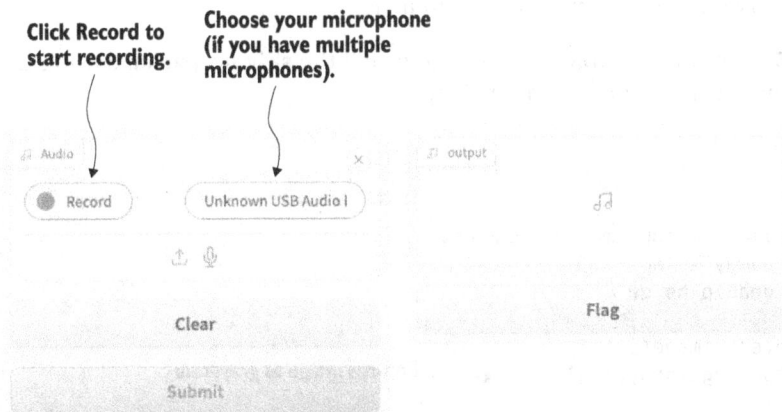

Click Record to start recording.

Choose your microphone (if you have multiple microphones).

Figure 10.15 Choosing your microphone and recording the audio

You can play back the original audio you recorded and the audio that has been reversed (see figure 10.16).

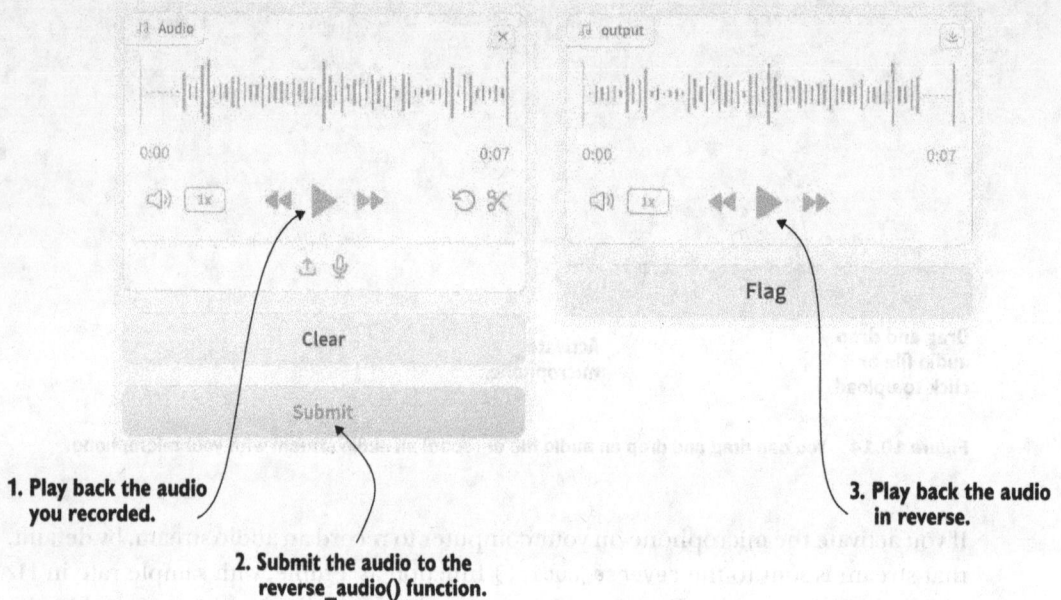

1. Play back the audio you recorded.

2. Submit the audio to the reverse_audio() function.

3. Play back the audio in reverse.

Figure 10.16   You can play back the original recording and the reversed audio.

10.2.3 Working with images

You can work with images in Gradio by using the Image component. The following code is an example of how to work with images.

NOTE   For this example, you need to install the skimage package using the pip command !pip install scikit-image.

Listing 10.6   Working with images in Gradio

```
from skimage.color import rgb2gray
import numpy as np
import gradio as gr

def convert_image(img):
    return rgb2gray(img)          ◄── Returns image as grayscale

image = gr.Image(type="numpy")    ◄── Works with the image as
                                       a NumPy array (default)
```

```
interface = gr.Interface(fn = convert_image,
                         inputs = image,
                         outputs = "image")

interface.launch()
```

Figure 10.17 shows three ways to upload images to Gradio:

- Drag and drop the image directly on the `Image` component.
- Capture images through the webcam.
- Paste an image from your computer's clipboard.

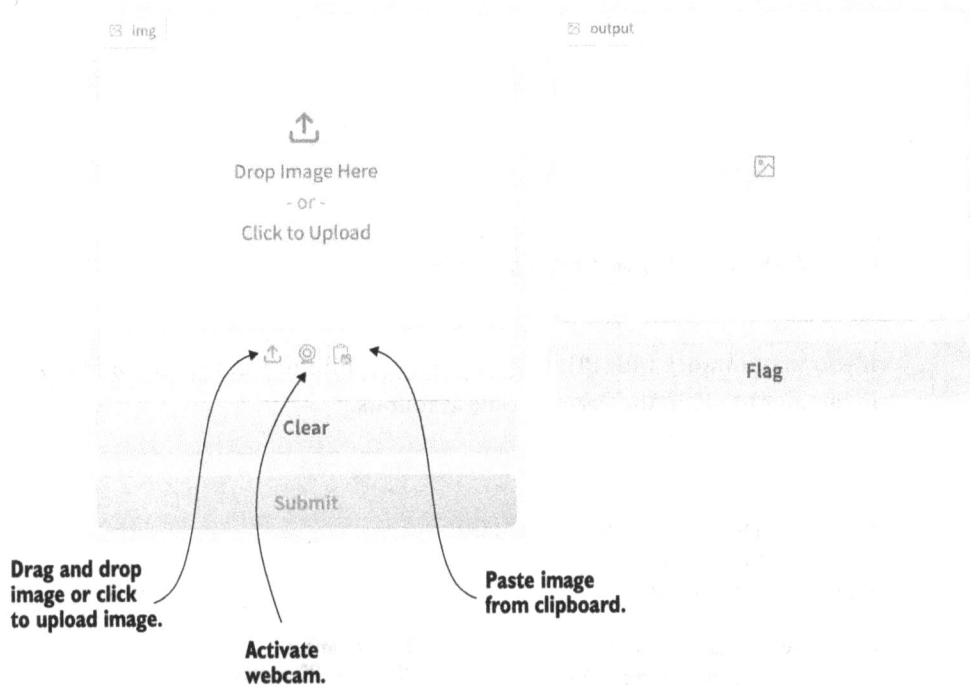

Figure 10.17 Using the `Image` component in Gradio

By default, all images passed into the `Image` component are in NumPy array format. Therefore, in this example, the image you send to the `Image` component is sent as a NumPy array to the `img` parameter of the `convert_image()` function. For this implementation, you return the grayscale equivalent of the image using the `rgb2gray()` function in the `skimage` package. Figure 10.18 shows how an image is transformed to grayscale after you click the Submit button.

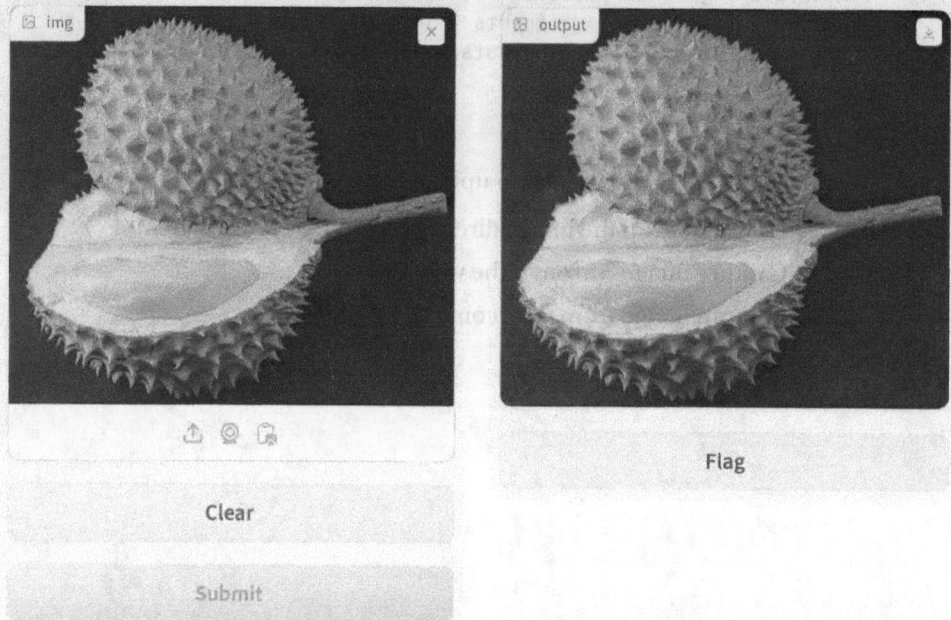

Figure 10.18   Converting an image to grayscale

If you want to work with PIL (Python Imaging Library) images in Gradio, set the `type` parameter to `pil` in the `Image()` class as follows.

Listing 10.7   Working with PIL images

```
from skimage.color import rgb2gray
import numpy as np
import gradio as gr

def convert_image(img):
    return img.rotate(-90)      ◄── Rotates image
                                    clockwise 90 degrees

image = gr.Image(type="pil")    ◄── Works with the image
                                    as a PIL image

interface = gr.Interface(fn = convert_image,
                         inputs = image,
                         outputs = "image")

interface.launch()
```

In the preceding code listing, the input image is rotated 90 degrees clockwise (see figure 10.19).

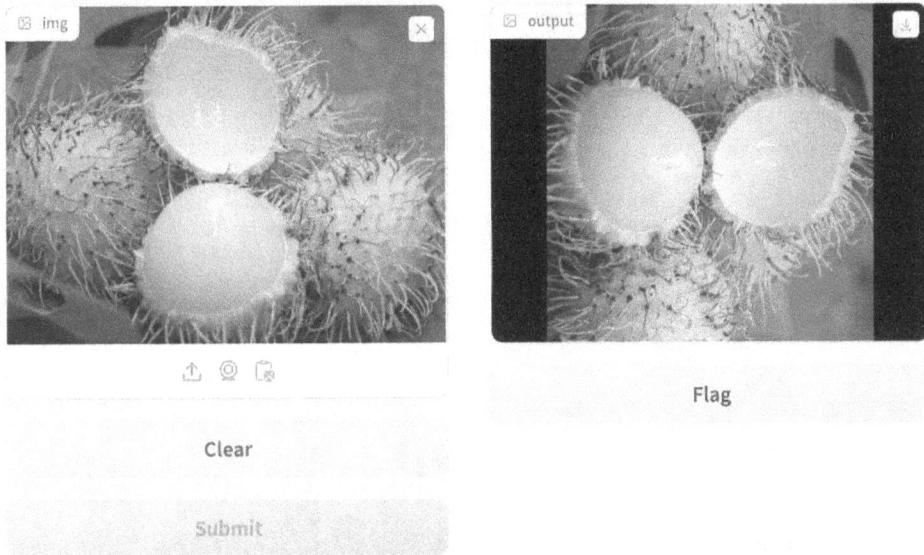

Figure 10.19 Rotating the image 90 degrees clockwise

If you want to let the user choose among a predetermined set of images, use the `examples` parameter in the `Interface` class. Set that parameter to a list of image names, as shown in the next listing.

Listing 10.8 Specifying a list of example images to use

```
interface = gr.Interface(fn = convert_image,
                         inputs = image,
                         outputs = "image",
                         examples = [
                              "images/durian.jpg",
                              "images/mango.jpg",
                              "images/rambutan.jpg"]
                        )
interface.launch()
```

To use this code, you need a folder named `images` in the current Jupyter Notebook's folder. Within the `images` folder you must have three images named as follows:

- `durian.jpg`
- `mango.jpg`
- `rambutan.jpg`

Figure 10.20 shows what the Gradio application looks like now, with the three example images shown at the bottom.

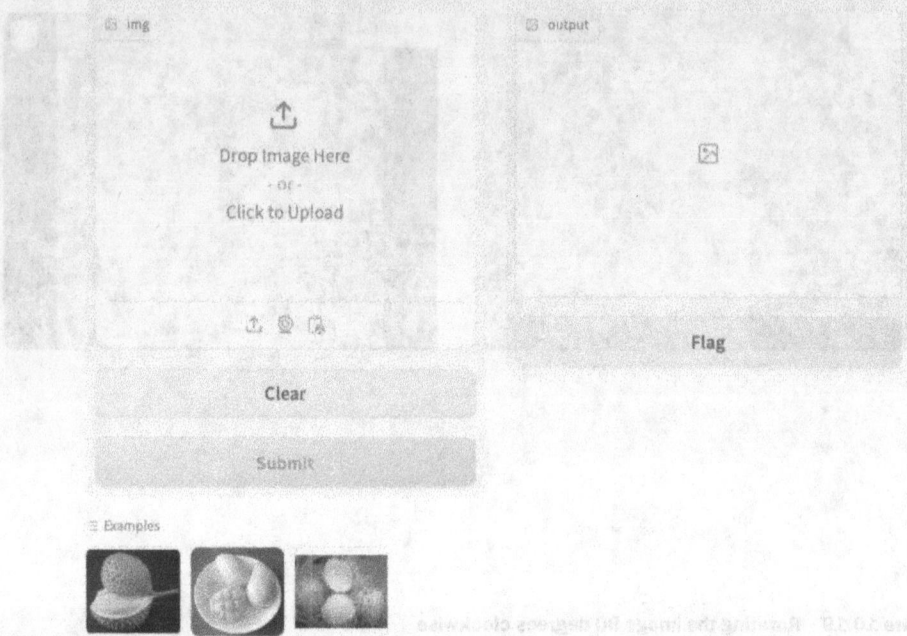

Figure 10.20   Instead of using your own images, you can select an example image.

When you select an example image, it is used as the input image. Figure 10.21 shows the image rotated 90 degrees clockwise.

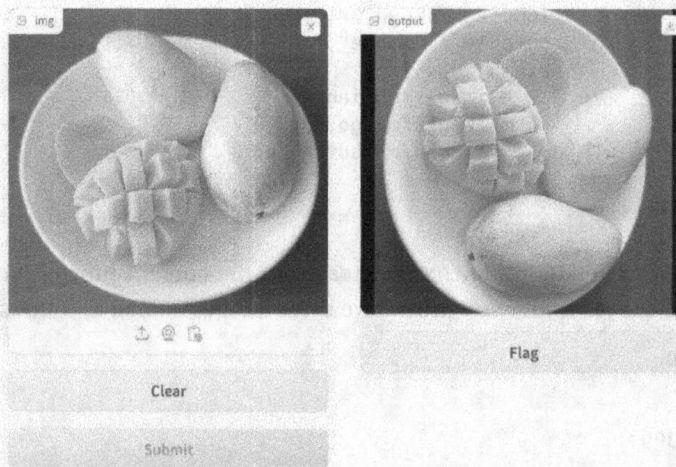

Figure 10.21   Selecting an example image and rotating it 90 degrees clockwise

10.2.4 *Working with selection widgets*

So far, you have seen several Gradio components: Textbox, Image, and Audio. In this section, you use two widgets that allow you to make selections:

- Dropdown—The Dropdown component creates a drop-down menu from which users can choose a single entry or multiple entries (as input components) or displayed (as output components).
- Slider—The Slider component creates a slider that ranges from minimum to maximum with a step size of step.

The following listing shows how to use both components.

Listing 10.9   Using the Dropdown and Slider components

```
import numpy as np
import gradio as gr

languages = ['English','Japanese','Chinese']

def translate(language_index, value, sentence):
    return languages[language_index], value, sentence

dropdown = gr.Dropdown(['English','Japanese','French','Chinese'],
                       type = "index",
                       label = "Language",
                       value = "English")

slider = gr.Slider(minimum = 1,
                   maximum = 5,
                   step = 1,
                   value = 2,
                   label = "Select a value")

textbox1 = gr.Textbox(type = "text",
                      value = "",
                      label = "Sentence to translate",
                      placeholder = "sentence")

textbox2 = gr.Textbox(type = "text",
                      label = "Translated sentence")

interface = gr.Interface(
    translate,
    [dropdown, slider,textbox1],
    textbox2,
)

interface.launch()
```

This listing uses the Dropdown, Slider, and Textbox components for the input and the Textbox component for the output (see figure 10.22).

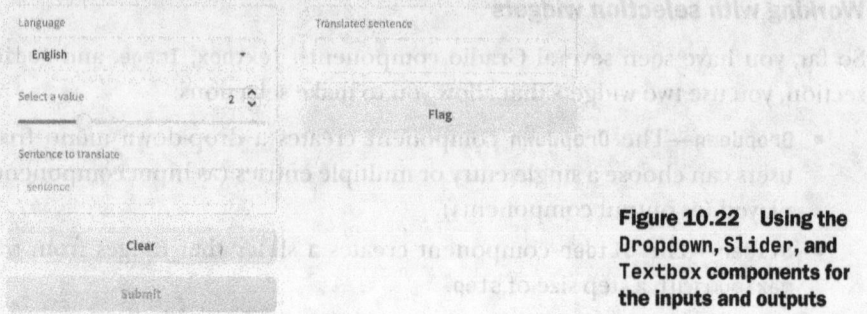

Figure 10.22 Using the Dropdown, Slider, and Textbox components for the inputs and outputs

Suppose that you chose Japanese from the Language drop-down menu, selected a value of 5, and entered the string "こんにちは". After you click Submit, you see the output shown in figure 10.23. The figure also shows how the returning value of the translate() function is linked to the output.

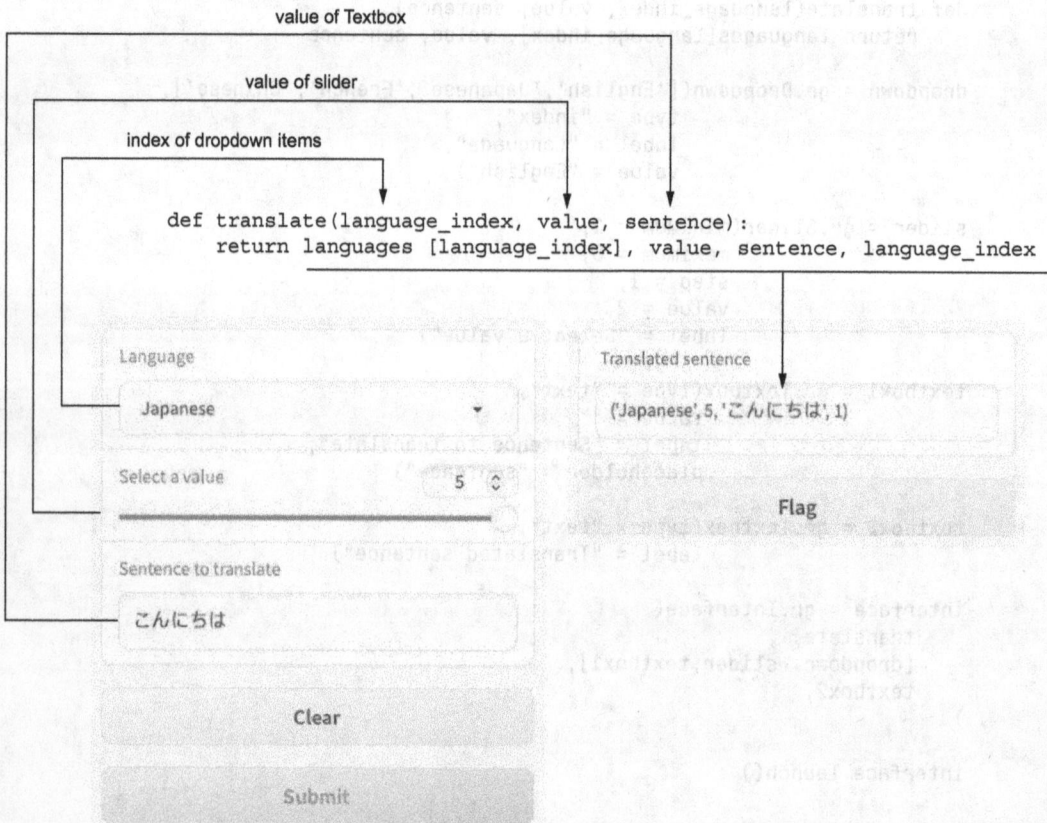

```
def translate(language_index, value, sentence):
    return languages [language_index], value, sentence, language_index
```

value of Textbox

value of slider

index of dropdown items

Figure 10.23   Submitting the selected values and obtaining the output

If you have multiple outputs, such as two `Textboxes`, you need to wrap the return values explicitly using a tuple, as shown in the following code listing.

Listing 10.10 Modifying the return values for two outputs

```
def translate(language_index, value, sentence):
    return (languages[language_index], value, sentence), language_index
...
...

interface = gr.Interface(
    translate,
    [dropdown, slider,textbox1],
    [textbox2,"text"],
)
```

Figure 10.24 shows the output of the modified Gradio application.

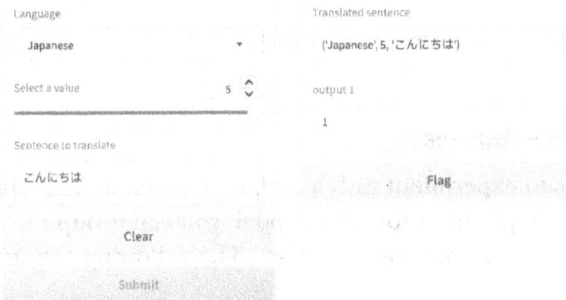

Figure 10.24   Now the output has two components.

Note that you need to wrap the first three return values in a tuple, which allows the correct values to be sent to the output (see figure 10.25).

```
def translate(language_index, value, sentence):
    return languages [language_index], value, sentence, language_index
```

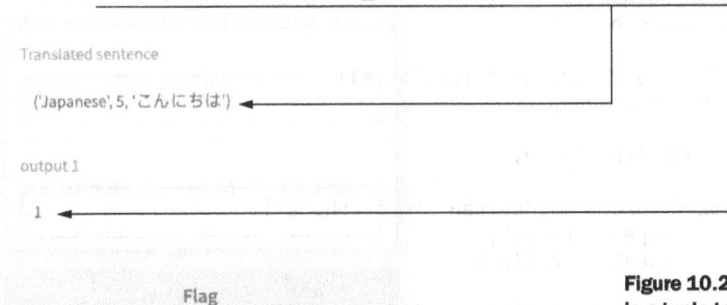

Figure 10.25   Wrapping the values in a tuple to send to one output

If you didn't wrap the first three return values in a tuple, the first two results would be sent to the output and the rest would be discarded, as shown in figure 10.26.

```
def translate(language_index, value, sentence):
    return languages [language_index], value, sentence, language_index
```

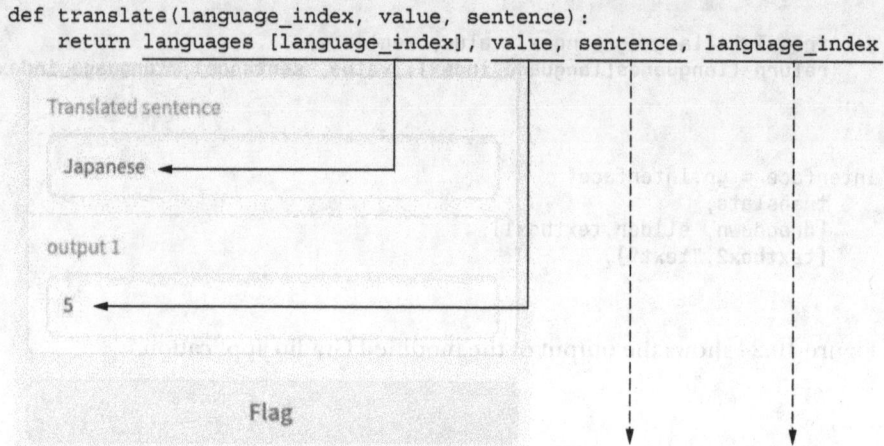

Figure 10.26   Returning values are dropped if they're not formed properly.

10.2.5 Layout using the TabbedInterface class

Sometimes, you want users to experiment with a couple of machine learning models. Instead of writing a Gradio application for each model, you can group the models in a single application using the TabbedInterface class. The following listing shows an example.

Listing 10.11   Using the TabbedInterface class

```
import gradio as gr

def convert_image(img):

    return rgb2gray(img)          ◄──── Returns image to grayscale

def reverse_audio(audio):
    sr, data = audio
    print(sr)
    reversed_audio = (sr, np.flipud(data))
    return reversed_audio

image = gr.Image(type="numpy")

mic = gr.Audio(sources = ["upload","microphone"],
               type = "numpy",
               label = "Audio")

interface1 = gr.Interface(title = 'Reverse Audio',
```

```
                            fn = reverse_audio,
                            inputs = mic,
                            outputs = "audio")

interface2 = gr.Interface(title = 'Convert Image',
                          fn = convert_image,
                          inputs = image,
                          outputs = "image")

tabbed = gr.TabbedInterface(          ◄──── Groups the two interfaces
    [interface1, interface2],
    ['Tab 1','Tab 2']          ◄──── Names the tabs
)

tabbed.launch()
```

This code snippet contains two main functions:

- convert_image(): A function to convert an image to grayscale
- reverse_audio(): A function to reverse an audio stream

You created two instances of the Interface class and grouped them together using the TabbedInterface class. Figure 10.27 shows the updated Gradio application.

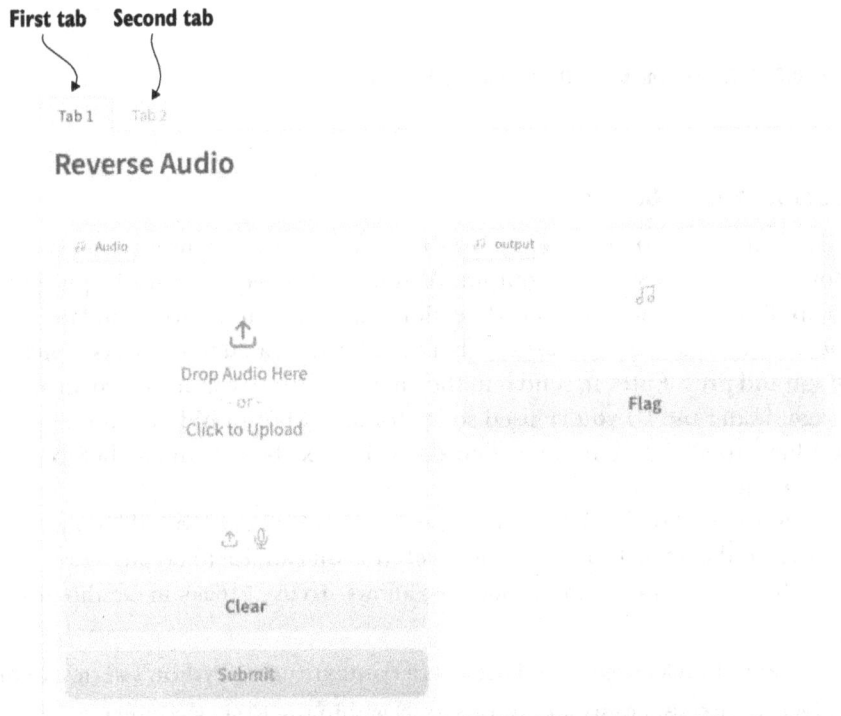

Figure 10.27   The first tab of the Gradio application

Clicking Tab 2 reveals the UI for the image-conversion function (see figure 10.28).

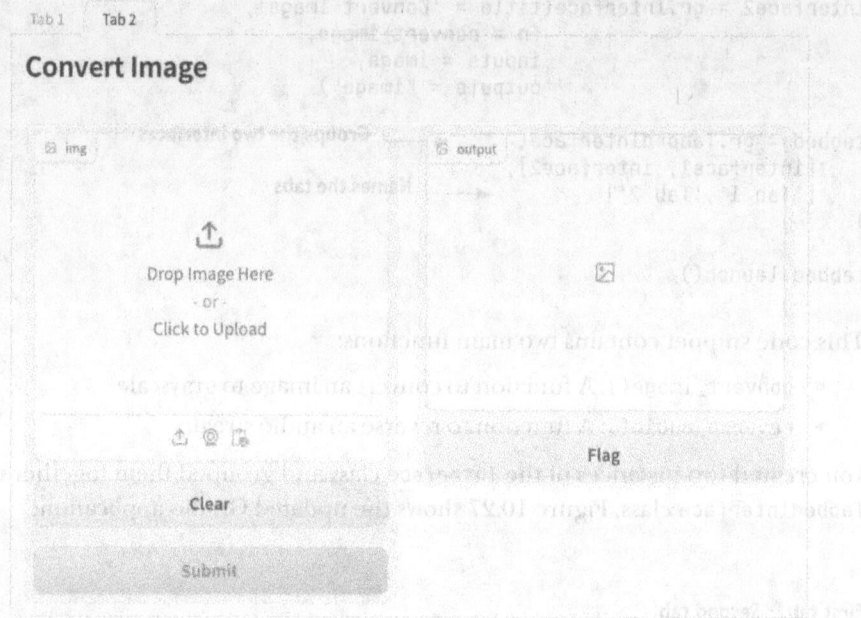

Figure 10.28   The second tab of the Gradio application

10.3   *Creating a chatbot UI*

So far, all the Gradio applications you've built require the user to click the Submit button before processing the output. Although this requirement is quite natural in most applications (such as object detection, image segmentation, and language translation), it's awkward in use cases such as chatbots. In a chatbot, users typically type a message and press Enter to send it to the chatbot, which responds with an appropriate message. Using the UI you've used so far for a chatbot would be cumbersome; users would have to click Submit and then clear the text box manually before typing the next message.

To build a chatbot-like UI, you can use Gradio's `Blocks` class with components such as `Textbox` and `Button`. `Blocks` is a low-level API you can use to create more-customized web applications than the `Interface` class allows. To use `Blocks` in Gradio, follow these steps:

1 Create a `Blocks` object, and use it as a context (using Python's `with` statement).
2 Define layouts, components, or events within the `Blocks` context.
3 Call the `launch()` method to launch the UI.

10.3.1 Creating the basic chatbot UI

Let's see how to use a Blocks object to create a chatbot-like UI. Before you write the code, outline what you want the chatbot to look like and the components you're going to use. Figure 10.29 shows those components.

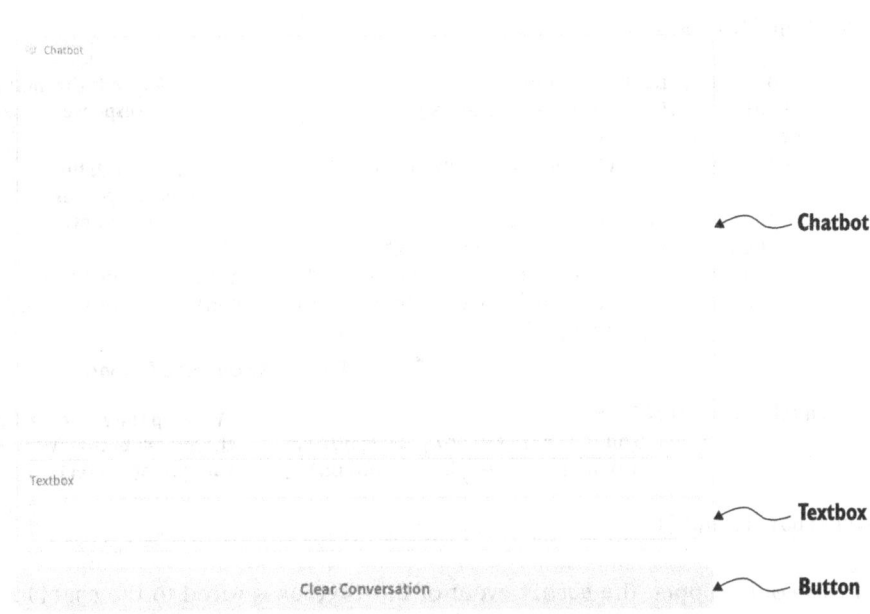

Chatbot

Textbox

Button

Figure 10.29 The components used for the chatbot UI

In the figure, the Textbox is where the user types the message. The Button clears the conversation in the chatbot, which is represented by Gradio's Chatbot component. Using a Blocks object, create this UI.

Listing 10.12 Building the basic chatbot UI

```
import gradio as gr

with gr.Blocks() as mychatbot:
    chatbot = gr.Chatbot(type = "messages")
    textbox = gr.Textbox()
    clear = gr.Button("Clear Conversation")

mychatbot.launch()
```

Blocks is a low-level API that allows you to create custom web applications.

Displays a chatbot ...

... for the user to ask a question.

Clear button

When you run this code, the UI is displayed, but it isn't functional. In the next two sections, you wire the event handlers for the Textbox and Button components.

10.3.2 *Wiring the Textbox's submit event*

First, create an event handler for the submit event in the Textbox component, as shown in the following listing.

Listing 10.13   Creating the event handler for the Textbox's submit event

```
import gradio as gr

with gr.Blocks() as mychatbot:
    chatbot = gr.Chatbot(type="messages")
    textbox = gr.Textbox()
    clear = gr.Button("Clear Conversation")

    def chat(message, chat_history):
        response = "Responses from chatbot..."
        chat_history.append({"role": "user", "content": message})
        chat_history.append({"role": "assistant", "content": response})
        print(chat_history)
        return "", chat_history

    textbox.submit(fn = chat,
                   inputs = [textbox, chatbot],
                   outputs = [textbox, chatbot])

mychatbot.launch()
```

- Appends the message and response to the history
- Replace with the actual responses from a chatbot.
- The "" is to clear the Textbox.
- Wires up the event handler for the Submit button (when the user presses Enter)

In this code snippet, the submit event of the Textbox is wired to the chat() function, which takes two arguments: message and chat_history. The inputs and outputs parameters of the Textbox are set to textbox and chatbot, respectively.

Within the chat() function, you can pass the content of message to your chatbot (or large language model [LLM]). Both the question and the response returned are appended to the chat_history argument. Here, we also printed the content of chat_history so that we can see what is being stored. Finally, the chat() function returns a tuple—the string to return to the Textbox after the user presses the Enter key—as well as the chat_history argument.

Figure 10.30 shows what happens after the user types Hello, there! in the Textbox and presses Enter. The content of the message variable and the response from the chatbot (replace with your own logic) are appended to the chat_history argument. The Chatbot component displays the message and response. Finally, the chat() function returns a tuple, "" (to clear the content of the Textbox), and the chat_history argument.

You can examine the content of the chat_history argument that you printed:

```
[
 {'role': 'user', 'content': 'Hello, there!'},
 {'role': 'assistant', 'content': 'Responses from chatbot...'}
]
```

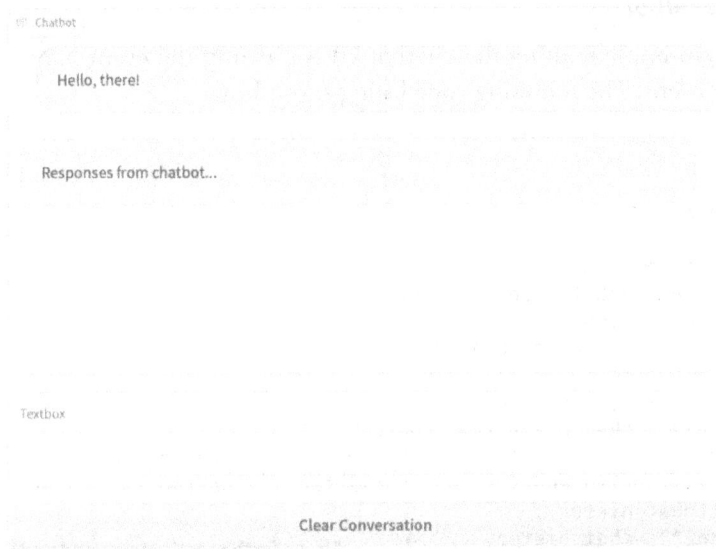

Figure 10.30 Typing a message in the `Textbox` **and sending it to the** `Chatbot` **component**

If you follow up with another message (`Have you heard of how cool Gradio is?`), you get the following output (formatted for clarity):

```
[
 {'role': 'user', 'metadata': None, 'content': 'Hello, there!',
  'options': None},
 {'role': 'assistant', 'metadata': None,
  'content': 'Responses from chatbot...',
  'options': None},
 {'role': 'user', 'content': 'Have you heard of how cool Gradio is?'},
 {'role': 'assistant', 'content': 'Responses from chatbot...'}
]
```

If you follow up with yet another message (`How does it compare to Streamlit?`), you get this output (formatted for clarity):

```
[
 {'role': 'user', 'metadata': None, 'content': 'Hello, there!',
  'options': None},
 {'role': 'assistant', 'metadata': None, 'content':
  'Responses from chatbot...', 'options': None},
 {'role': 'user', 'metadata': None, 'content':
  'Have you heard of how cool Gradio is?', 'options': None},
 {'role': 'assistant', 'metadata': None, 'content':
  'Responses from chatbot...', 'options': None},
 {'role': 'user', 'content': "How does it compare to Streamlit?"},
 {'role': 'assistant', 'content': 'Responses from chatbot...'}
]
```

10.3.3 Clearing the chatbot

The final step in implementing the chatbot UI is creating the event handler for the Button's click event. The following code listing shows how.

Listing 10.14   Creating the event handler for the Button's click event

```
import gradio as gr

with gr.Blocks() as mychatbot:
    chatbot = gr.Chatbot(type="messages")
    textbox = gr.Textbox()
    clear = gr.Button("Clear Conversation")

    def chat(message, chat_history):
        response = "Responses from chatbot..."
        chat_history.append({"role": "user", "content": message})
        chat_history.append({"role": "assistant", "content": response})
        print(chat_history)
        return "", chat_history        ◀── Clears Textbox and returns updated history

    textbox.submit(fn = chat,
                   inputs = [textbox, chatbot],
                   outputs = [textbox, chatbot])

    def clear_messages():
        print("Clearing message...")

    clear.click(fn = clear_messages,
                inputs = None,
                outputs = chatbot,
                queue = False)

mychatbot.launch()
```

When the user clicks the Clear Conversation button, the clear_messages() function is called. You can replace its content with your own code to clear the chatbot (or LLM). The outputs parameter specifies that you return the chatbot object, which is empty.

That's it. You have a functional chatbot! All you need to do is replace the chat() function with the code to communicate with your own LLM.

Summary

- To build a simple Gradio application, you can use the Interface class, Gradio's main high-level class, which allows you to build a web UI with just a few lines of code.
- The Textbox component allows users to send text content to the Gradio application.
- The Audio component allows users to send audio streams to the Gradio application.

- The `Image` component allows users to send images (as NumPy arrays or PIL images) to the Gradio application.
- You can implement authentication for your Gradio application using the `auth` parameter in the `launch()` method.
- The Flag option logs messages in the `log.csv` file.
- You can share the Gradio application with users on the local network or create a shared link to share with other internet users.
- You can deploy your Gradio application on Hugging Face Spaces.
- You can group multiple interfaces using the `TabbedInterface` class.
- To create a chatbot UI, use the `Blocks` class together with other Gradio components.

Building locally running LLM-based applications using GPT4All

You've learned about constructing large language model (LLM)–based applications using models from OpenAI and Hugging Face. Although these models have transformed natural language processing (NLP), there are notable drawbacks. Primarily, privacy emerges as a critical concern for businesses. Relying on third-party-hosted models introduces a security risk because your conversations would be transmitted to these external companies, raising apprehension for businesses that deal with sensitive data. Also, the challenge of integrating these models with your private data exists, and even if that challenge is met, the initial privacy concern resurfaces.

A more effective approach is to execute the models locally on your computer. This gives you control of the destination of your private data and enables you to fine-tune the models to suit your specific data requirements. But running an LLM often requires graphics processing units (GPUs), constituting a significant investment.

Fortunately, there's a remedy: GPT4All. GPT4All provides quantized models, reduced to a few gigabytes, that can operate on standard consumer-grade CPUs without requiring an internet connection. In this chapter, you'll discover how to initiate GPT4All, and in chapter 12, you'll explore using GPT4All to process your private data.

11.1 Introducing GPT4All

GPT4All (https://www.nomic.ai/gpt4all) is an open source project containing several pretrained LLMs that you can use to run locally using consumer-grade CPUs. This accessibility is invaluable, especially for people who don't have access to high-end GPUs. Enabling the local deployment of LLMs contributes to democratizing AI, ensuring that everyone, regardless of hardware constraints, can actively participate in the creation of AI applications.

GPT4All contains several models ranging from 3 GB to 8 GB. Even more exciting—it's free! Although the performance of GPT4All may not be on par with that of the current ChatGPT, with contributions from the open source community it has significant potential for further development and enhancements.

11.2 Installing GPT4All

There are two types of installations for GPT4All:

- An end-user application that allows users to try out the various models supported by GPT4All. This installation doesn't require programming knowledge. Users will be able to initiate a chat conversation with the downloaded LLM.
- A Python library that enables developers to use the various models to build their LLM-based applications.

The following sections go through these two types of installation methods. Our focus will be on the second method, showing you how to build locally running LLM-based applications using Python.

11.2.1 Installing the GPT4All application

To install the GPT4All desktop chat client, go to https://www.nomic.ai/gpt4all and download the installer for the OS you're using (see figure 11.1).

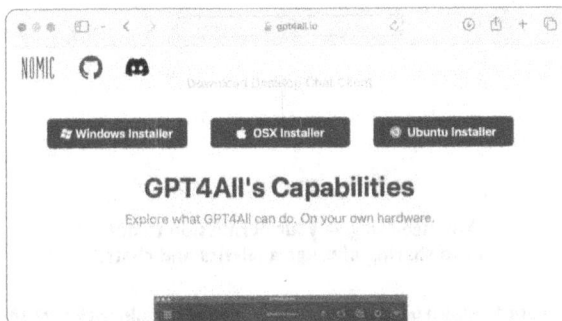

Figure 11.1 Download the installer for your OS.

When the installer is downloaded, double-click the installer. You'll be asked to provide a directory in which to store GPT4All (see figure 11.2). Accept the default suggested path and click Next.

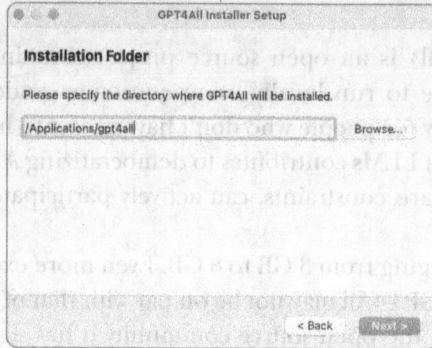

Figure 11.2   Specifying a directory for storing the GPT4All files

When installation is complete, the first thing you need to do is give your permission to opt in to the sharing of usage analytics and chats (see figure 11.3). Depending on your preference, select Yes or No.

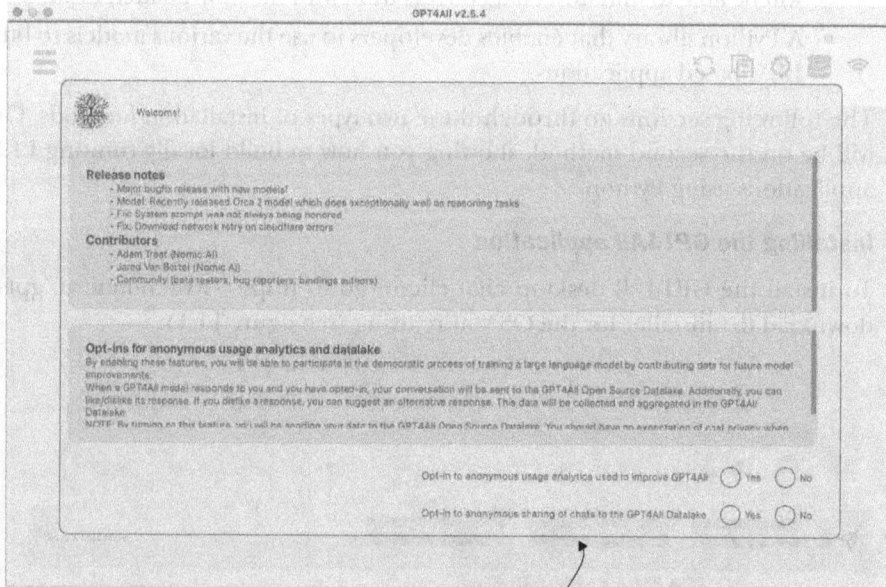

You need to give your permission to opt in to sharing of usage analytics and chats.

Figure 11.3   Indicate whether you want to share usage statistics and chat details with GPT4All.

Next, you have the choice to download the various models available for use with GPT4All (see figure 11.4). Scroll to the bottom of the page to view more models. To download a model, click the Download button.

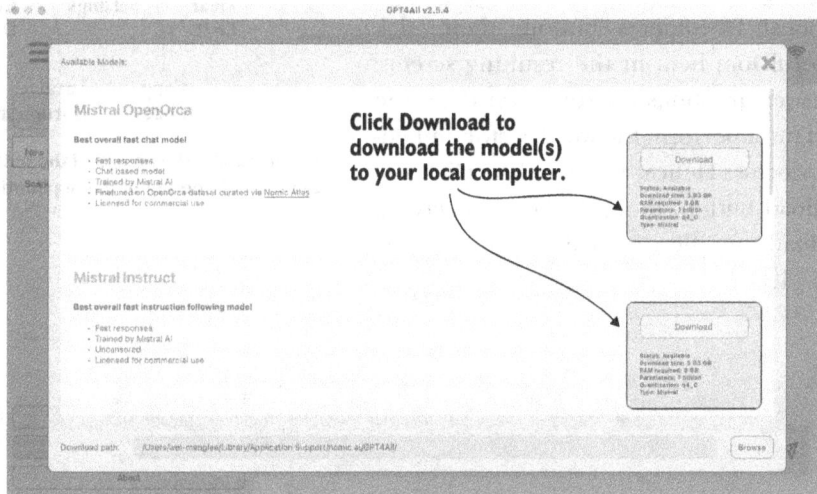

Figure 11.4 Download the model(s) you want to try.

NOTE The amount of RAM that most models requires is 4–16 GB. If you have a machine with only 8 GB, you're unlikely to be able to run many of these models. To run LLMs locally, I suggest using a machine with at least 16 GB of RAM.

When you've downloaded a model, you can start chatting straight away. Figure 11.5 shows a question and the model's reply.

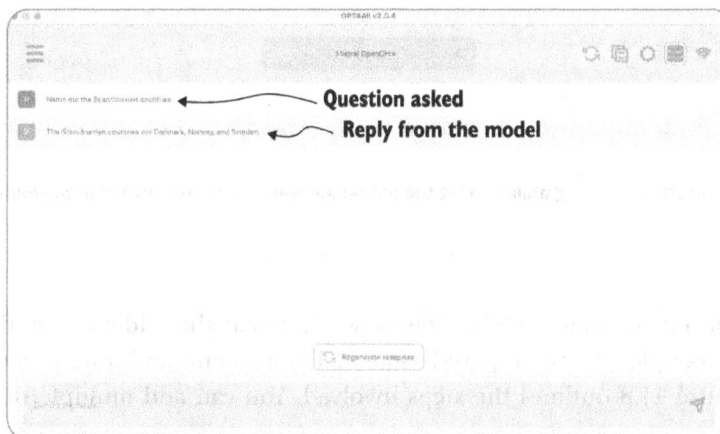

Figure 11.5 Testing the model by chatting and getting a reply from it

The top-right corner of the application contains several buttons. Figure 11.6 shows the names of these buttons.

To use the model to answer questions pertaining to your own documents, click the Local Documents button; then click the LocalDocs item in the resulting screen. To answer questions on your own data, the model must perform the word vector embedding process. Hence, you need to click the Download button; then, in the next screen, download the SBert embedding model (see figure 11.7).

Figure 11.6   The names of the buttons in the top-right corner of the application

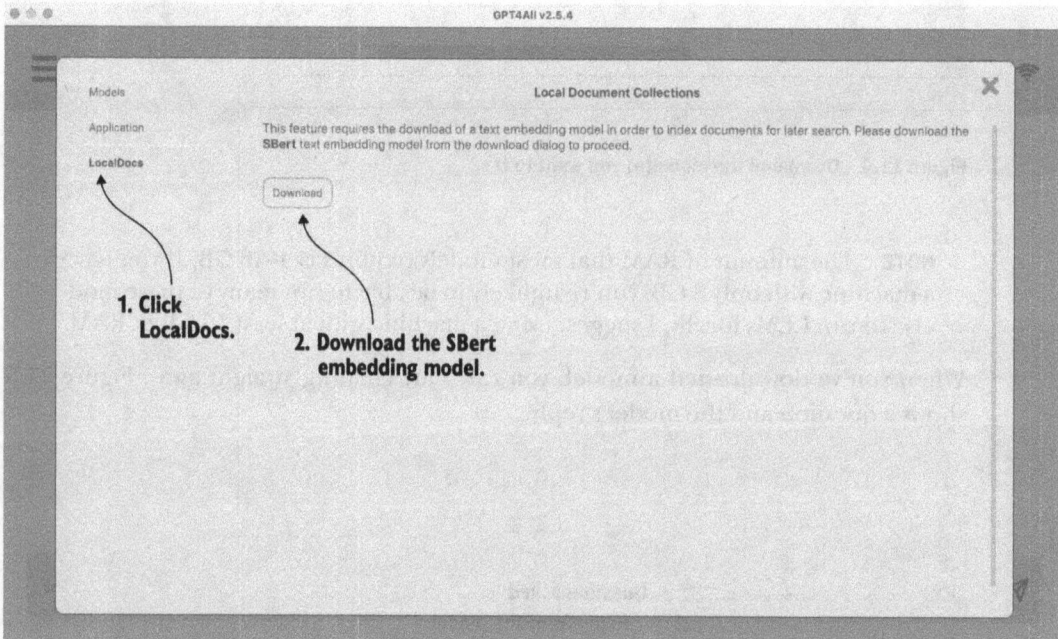

Figure 11.7   Download the SBert embedding model to let the model answer questions pertaining to your local documents.

When the SBert embedding model is downloaded, specify the folder containing your data. For this example, you've prepared some PDF documents and stored them inside the folder. Figure 11.8 outlines the steps involved. You can add multiple document folders.

1. Give your data a name.

2. Click the Browse button, and select the folder that contains your local data.

3. Click the Add button.

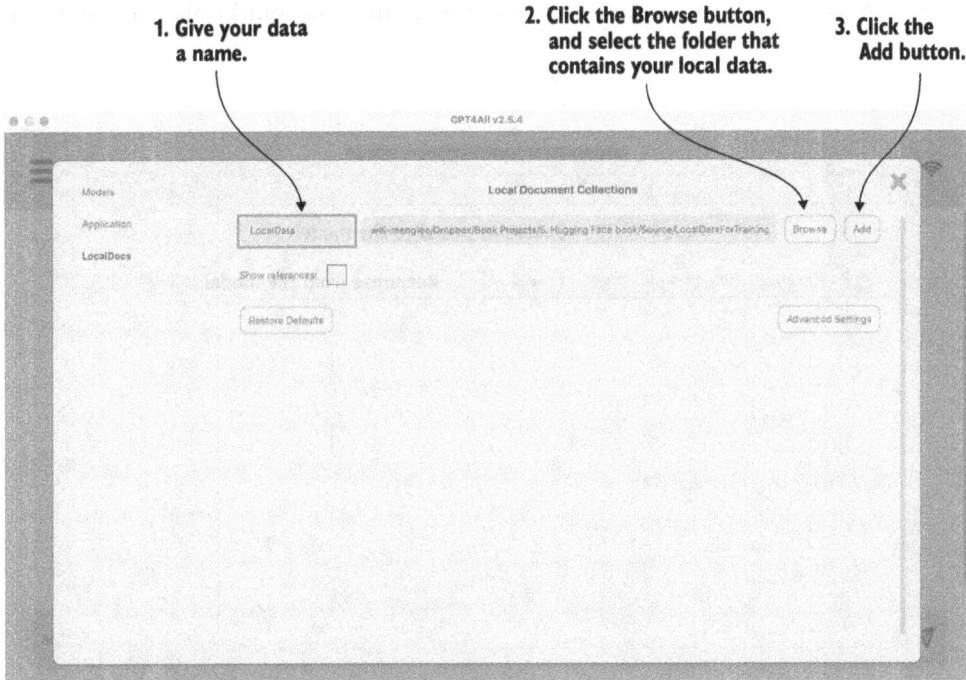

Figure 11.8 Adding a local documents folder to the app

Finally, click the Local Documents button (refer to figure 11.6) and check the name of your local data (LocalData in this example; see figure 11.9).

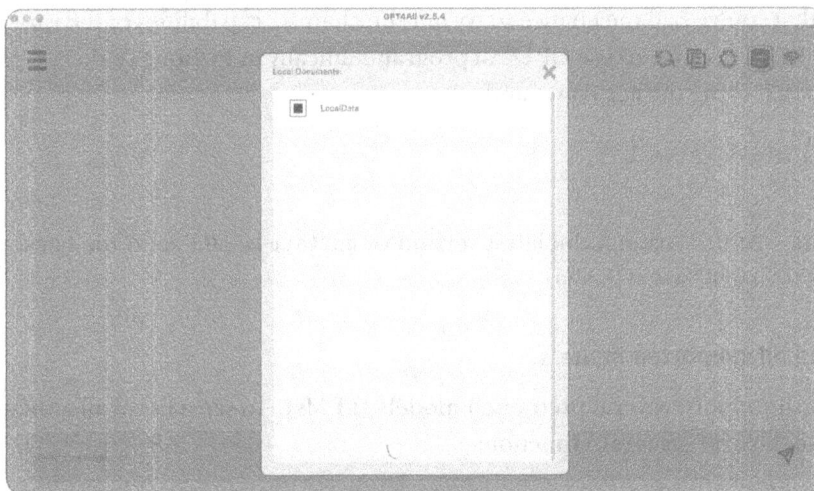

Figure 11.9 Selecting the local documents folder to use for querying

Now you can ask the model questions pertaining to your local data (see figure 11.10).

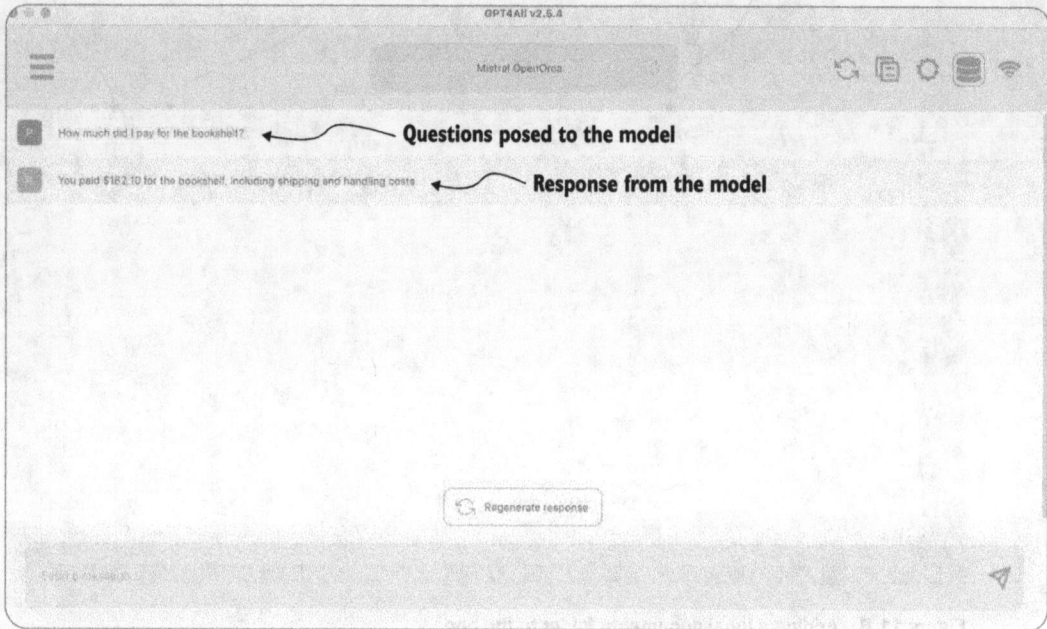

Figure 11.10   Asking questions specific to your local data

Finally, click the Local Docs button (refer to figure 11.9) and check the button for your local data. To enable this, reload your data (see figure 11.9).

11.2.2 Installing the gpt4all Python library

Now that you've had the chance to try out the chatting capabilities of the various LLMs in GPT4All, it's time to use GPT4All programmatically in Python. To do that, you need to install it using the pip command:

```
!pip install gpt4all
```

> **NOTE** At this writing, the latest version of gpt4all is 2.0.2, and the latest version of langchain is 0.0.351.

11.2.3 Listing all supported models

GPT4All supports several pretrained models (LLMs). To see a list of all available models, use the list_models() function:

```
from gpt4all import GPT4All
GPT4All.list_models()
```

You see the following output, which is shortened for brevity. The model names and corresponding filenames are highlighted in bold.

Listing 11.1   Supported GPT4All models

```
[{'order': 'a',
  'md5sum': '48de9538c774188eb25a7e9ee024bbd3',
  'name': 'Mistral OpenOrca',
  'filename': 'mistral-7b-openorca.Q4_0.gguf',
  'filesize': '4108927744',
  'requires': '2.5.0',
  'ramrequired': '8',
  'parameters': '7 billion',
  'quant': 'q4_0',
  'type': 'Mistral',
  'systemPrompt': ' ',
  'description': '<strong>Best overall fast chat model</strong>
<br><ul><li>Fast responses</li><li>Chat based model</li><li>
Trained by Mistral AI<li>Finetuned on OpenOrca dataset curated
via <a href="https://atlas.nomic.ai/">Nomic Atlas</a><li>
Licensed for commercial use</ul>',
  'url': 'https://gpt4all.io/models/gguf/mistral-7b-openorca.Q4_0.gguf'},
 {'order': 'b',
  'md5sum': '97463be739b50525df56d33b26b00852',
  'name': 'Mistral Instruct',
  'filename': 'mistral-7b-instruct-v0.1.Q4_0.gguf',
  'filesize': '4108916384',
  'requires': '2.5.0',
  'ramrequired': '8',
  'parameters': '7 billion',
  'quant': 'q4_0',
  'type': 'Mistral',
  'systemPrompt': ' ',
  'description': '<strong>Best overall fast instruction
following model</strong><br><ul><li>Fast responses</li><li>
Trained by Mistral AI<li>Uncensored</li><li>Licensed for
commercial use</li></ul>',
  'url': 'https://gpt4all.io/models/gguf/mistral-7b-instruct-
v0.1.Q4_0.gguf',
  'promptTemplate': '[INST] %1 [/INST]'},

  ...

 {'order': 'p',
  'md5sum': '919de4dd6f25351bcb0223790db1932d',
  'name': 'EM German Mistral',
  'filename': 'em_german_mistral_v01.Q4_0.gguf',
  'filesize': '4108916352',
  'requires': '2.5.0',
  'ramrequired': '8',
  'parameters': '7 billion',
  'quant': 'q4_0',
  'type': 'Mistral',
  'description': '<strong>Mistral-based model for German-
```

```
language applications</strong><br><ul><li>Fast responses</li>
<li>Chat based model</li><li>Trained by ellamind<li>Finetuned
on German instruction and chat data</a><li>Licensed for
commercial use</ul>',
  'url': 'https://huggingface.co/TheBloke/
em_german_mistral_v01-GGUF/resolve/main/
em_german_mistral_v01.Q4_0.gguf',
  'promptTemplate': 'USER: %1 ASSISTANT: ',
  'systemPrompt': 'Du bist ein hilfreicher Assistent. '}]
```

Because the list is quite long, it would be useful to extract only the model names and the corresponding filenames, like this:

```
models = GPT4All.list_models()
[{model['name']:model['filename']} for model in models]
```

This code generates the following simplified list:

```
[{'Mistral OpenOrca': 'mistral-7b-openorca.Q4_0.gguf'},
 {'Mistral Instruct': 'mistral-7b-instruct-v0.1.Q4_0.gguf'},
 {'GPT4All Falcon': 'gpt4all-falcon-q4_0.gguf'},
 {'Orca 2 (Medium)': 'orca-2-7b.Q4_0.gguf'},
 {'Orca 2 (Full)': 'orca-2-13b.Q4_0.gguf'},
 {'Wizard v1.2': 'wizardlm-13b-v1.2.Q4_0.gguf'},
 {'Hermes': 'nous-hermes-llama2-13b.Q4_0.gguf'},
 {'Snoozy': 'gpt4all-13b-snoozy-q4_0.gguf'},
 {'MPT Chat': 'mpt-7b-chat-merges-q4_0.gguf'},
 {'Mini Orca (Small)': 'orca-mini-3b-gguf2-q4_0.gguf'},
 {'Replit': 'replit-code-v1_5-3b-q4_0.gguf'},
 {'Starcoder': 'starcoder-q4_0.gguf'},
 {'Rift coder': 'rift-coder-v0-7b-q4_0.gguf'},
 {'SBert': 'all-MiniLM-L6-v2-f16.gguf'},
 {'EM German Mistral': 'em_german_mistral_v01.Q4_0.gguf'}]
```

11.2.4 *Loading a specific model*

Based on the models listed in section 11.2.3, you can load the model you want to use. For this example, use the `Mistral OpenOrca` model (filename `mistral-7b-openorca.Q4_0` `.gguf`):

```
gpt = GPT4All("mistral-7b-openorca.Q4_0.gguf")
```

> **NOTE** Mistral AI is a startup in the AI sector. Its mission is to revolutionize generative AI with its first LLM, Mistral 7B. The company hopes that its new 7-billion-parameter model will become an open source alternative to current AI solutions.

When you load the model for the first time, GPT4All downloads `mistral-7b-openorca` `.Q4_0.gguf`, which is a 4.11 GB file. The file is stored in the following directory:

```
~/.cache/gpt4all/
```

You can print more information about this model using the `config` attribute:

```
print(gpt.config)
```

Here are the details of the `Mistral OpenOrca` model:

```
{
    'systemPrompt': '',
    'promptTemplate': '### Human: \n{0}\n### Assistant:\n',
    'order': 'a',
    'md5sum': '48de9538c774188eb25a7e9ee024bbd3',
    'name': 'Mistral OpenOrca',
    'filename': 'mistral-7b-openorca.Q4_0.gguf',
    'filesize': '4108927744',
    'requires': '2.5.0',
    'ramrequired': '8',
    'parameters': '7 billion',
    'quant': 'q4_0',
    'type': 'Mistral',
    'description': '<strong>Best overall fast chat model</strong>
<br><ul><li>Fast responses</li><li>Chat based model</li><li>
Trained by Mistral AI<li>Finetuned on OpenOrca dataset curated
via <a href="https://atlas.nomic.ai/">Nomic Atlas</a><li>Licensed
for commercial use</ul>',
        'path': '/Users/weimenglee/.cache/gpt4all/mistral-7b-
openorca.Q4_0.gguf'
}
```

11.2.5 Asking a question

With the model downloaded, you can put it to the test. To have a chat conversation using GPT4All, use the `chat_session()` method to create a contextual manager in which you can hold an inference-optimized chat session with a model. Then you can use the `generate()` method to ask the question. The following code snippet shows how to do this using the `with` keyword in Python:

```
with gpt.chat_session():
    output = gpt.generate("What is the population of Japan?",
                max_tokens=2048)
    print(output)
    print(gpt.current_chat_session)
```

The model's response to the preceding question (`"What is the population of Japan?"`) is

```
As of 2021, the estimated population of Japan is approximately
126 million people. However, this number may change over time
due to factors such as births, deaths, and migration.
```

Here's a printout (formatted for clarity) of the details of the current session using the `current_chat_session` attribute:

```
[
    {
        'role': 'system',
        'content': ''
    },
    {
        'role': 'user',
        'content': 'What is the population of Japan?'
    },
    {
        'role': 'assistant',
            'content': ' As of 2021, the estimated population of Japan is
        approximately 126 million people. However, this number may
        change over time due to factors such as births, deaths, and
        migration.'
    }
]
```

If you want to ask a follow-up question, you must do it within the scope of the with keyword, like this:

```
with gpt.chat_session():
    response1 = gpt.generate(
        prompt='What is the population of Singapore?',
        temp = 0)
    print(response1)
    print(gpt.current_chat_session)
    print('===')

    response2 = gpt.generate(
        prompt='Where is it located?',
        temp = 0)
    print(response2)
    print(gpt.current_chat_session)
```

Here's the response to the first question:

```
As of 2021, the estimated population of Singapore is around 5.6
million people. However, this number may change over time due to
births, deaths, and migration.
```

The current chat session value is

```
[
    {
        'role': 'system',
        'content': ''
    },
    {
        'role': 'user',
        'content': 'What is the population of Singapore?'
    },
    {
```

```
    'role': 'assistant',
    'content': ' As of 2021, the estimated population of
                Singapore is around 5.6 million people.
                However, this number may change over time
                due to births, deaths, and migration.'
  }
]
```

Here's the response to the follow-up question:

```
 Singapore is a city-state and island country in Southeast Asia.
It lies off the southern tip of the Malay Peninsula, about
85 miles (137 kilometers) north of the equator. It shares
its only land border with Malaysia to the north. The country
consists of one main island, called Singapore Island, and
more than 60 smaller islands.
```

Following is the updated chat session:

```
[
  {
    'role': 'system',
    'content': ''
  },
  {
    'role': 'user',
    'content': 'What is the population of Singapore?'
  },
  {
    'role': 'assistant',
    'content': ' As of 2021, the estimated population of
                Singapore is around 5.6 million people.
                However, this number may change over time
                due to births, deaths, and migration.'
  },
  {
    'role': 'user',
    'content': 'Where is it located?'
  },
  {
    'role': 'assistant',
    'content': ' Singapore is a city-state and island country
                in Southeast Asia. It lies off the southern
                tip of the Malay Peninsula, about 85 miles
                (137 kilometers) north of the equator. It
                shares its only land border with Malaysia to
                the north. The country consists of one main
                island, called Singapore Island, and more than
                60 smaller islands.\n\n'
  }
]
```

As you can see, the chat session contains the details of the earlier conversation, allowing the model to maintain the context. The following session won't work because the second question is not in the same context as the first question:

```
with gpt.chat_session():
    response1 = gpt.generate(
        prompt='What is the population of Singapore?',
        temp = 0)
    print(response1)

with gpt.chat_session():
    response2 = gpt.generate(
        prompt='Where is it located?',
        temp = 0)
    print(response2)
```

If you need to ask a follow-up question at another time, you can always save the context using the `gpt.current_chat_session` attribute and set it back later. The following code snippet shows how:

```
session = []

with gpt.chat_session():
    response1 = gpt.generate(prompt='What is the population of Singapore?',
                             temp = 0)
    print(response1)

    session = gpt.current_chat_session        ◄───┘  Saves the current chat session

with gpt.chat_session():
                                                     Sets the current chat session
                                                     to the previously saved one
    gpt.current_chat_session = session        ◄───
    response2 = gpt.generate(prompt='Where is it located?', temp = 0)
    print(response2)
```

11.2.6 *Binding with Gradio*

A great way to work with a GPT4All model is to bind it to Gradio. In the following code snippet, first you define a function named `chat()` that calls the model's `generate()` method:

```
from gpt4all import GPT4All

gpt = GPT4All("mistral-7b-openorca.Q4_0.gguf")

def chat(message):
    with gpt.chat_session():
        return gpt.generate(prompt = message,
                            temp = 0)
```

Then you can use Gradio and bind it to the chat() function:

```
import gradio as gr

gr.Interface(fn = chat,            ◄——————┐  Binds it to Gradio
             inputs = "text",
             outputs = "text").launch()
```

Figure 11.11 shows what the Gradio interface looks like at this point.

```
Running on local URL:  http://127.0.0.1:7861

To create a public link, set `share=True` in `launch()`.
```

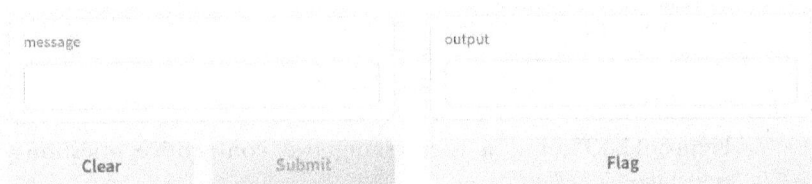

message		output

Clear	Submit		Flag

Figure 11.11 Binding the model to Gradio

You can ask a question, click the Submit button, and obtain the response from the model (see figure 11.12).

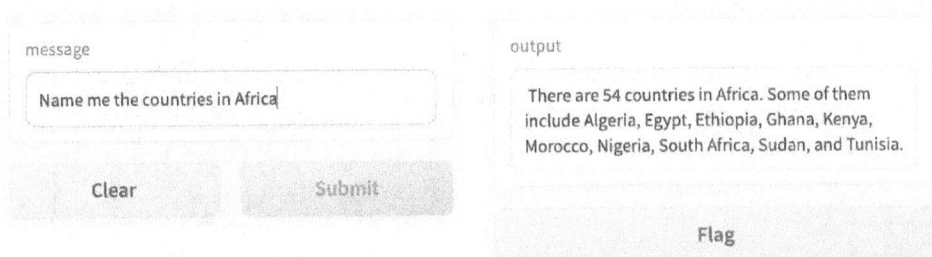

message	output
Name me the countries in Africa	There are 54 countries in Africa. Some of them include Algeria, Egypt, Ethiopia, Ghana, Kenya, Morocco, Nigeria, South Africa, Sudan, and Tunisia.

Clear	Submit		Flag

Figure 11.12 Asking a question through the Gradio interface

Remember that you can't ask a follow-up question: every time you click the Submit button, the chat() function starts a new chat session. To fix this problem, you need to save the current chat session's details in a global variable and set it back every time you ask a follow-up question, like this:

```
import gradio as gr
from gpt4all import GPT4All

gpt = GPT4All("mistral-7b-openorca.Q4_0.gguf")
current_chat_session = []

def chat(message):
    with gpt.chat_session():
        global current_chat_session
        gpt.current_chat_session = current_chat_session
        response = gpt.generate(prompt = message,
                                       temp = 0)

        current_chat_session = gpt.current_chat_session
        return response

# bind it to gradio
gr.Interface(fn = chat,
             inputs = "text",
             outputs = "text").launch()
```

Figure 11.13 shows a user asking two consecutive questions through the Gradio interface:

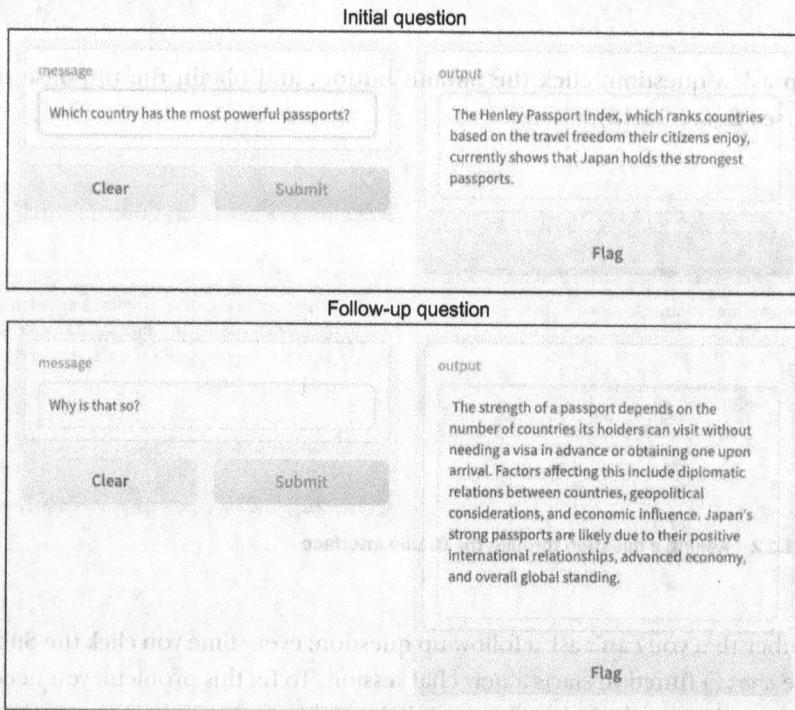

Figure 11.13   You can ask follow-up questions through the Gradio interface.

If you use the application long enough, you'll realize that having to clear the message every time you want to ask a follow-up question is troublesome. A much more intuitive UI would behave more like a chat application. In fact, you can use Gradio to build a chatbot-like UI. The following code listing shows how to wrap the GTP4All call with a chatbot-like UI using Gradio.

Listing 11.2 Displaying a chatbot UI using Gradio

```python
import gradio as gr
from gpt4all import GPT4All

gpt = GPT4All("mistral-7b-openorca.Q4_0.gguf")
current_chat_session = []

with gr.Blocks() as mychatbot:

    chatbot = gr.Chatbot()
    question = gr.Textbox()
    clear = gr.Button("Clear Conversation")

    def clear_messages():
        global current_chat_session
        current_chat_session = []

    def chat(message, chat_history):
        with gpt.chat_session():
            global current_chat_session
            gpt.current_chat_session = current_chat_session

            response = gpt.generate(prompt = message,
                                    temp = 0)
            current_chat_session = gpt.current_chat_session

            chat_history.append((message, response))

            return "", chat_history

    question.submit(fn = chat,
                    inputs = [question, chatbot],
                    outputs = [question, chatbot])

    clear.click(fn = clear_messages,
                inputs = None,
                outputs = chatbot,
                queue = False)

mychatbot.launch()
```

Annotations:
- Blocks is a low-level API . . .
- . . . that allows you to create custom web applications.
- Displays a chatbot . . .
- . . . for the user to ask a question.
- Clear button
- Function to clear the conversation
- Resets the messages list
- Function to ask the LLM a question
- Appends the response to the current message and returns it to Gradio
- The "" is to clear the input text box.
- Wires up the event handler for the Submit button (when the user presses Enter)
- Wires up the event handler for the Clear Conversation button

Note that this time around, the chat() function accepts two arguments (the question to ask and the chat history):

```
def chat(message, chat_history):
```

After the model has responded with the answer, you append the response to the chat_history parameter and return it with a string (set to "" in this example). The string is used to display the text in the input text box:

```
chat_history.append((message, response))

return "", chat_history    ◄─── The "" is to clear the
                                 input text box.
```

When you run this code snippet, you see the UI shown in figure 11.14. Now you can chat with the model to your heart's content (see figure 11.15)!

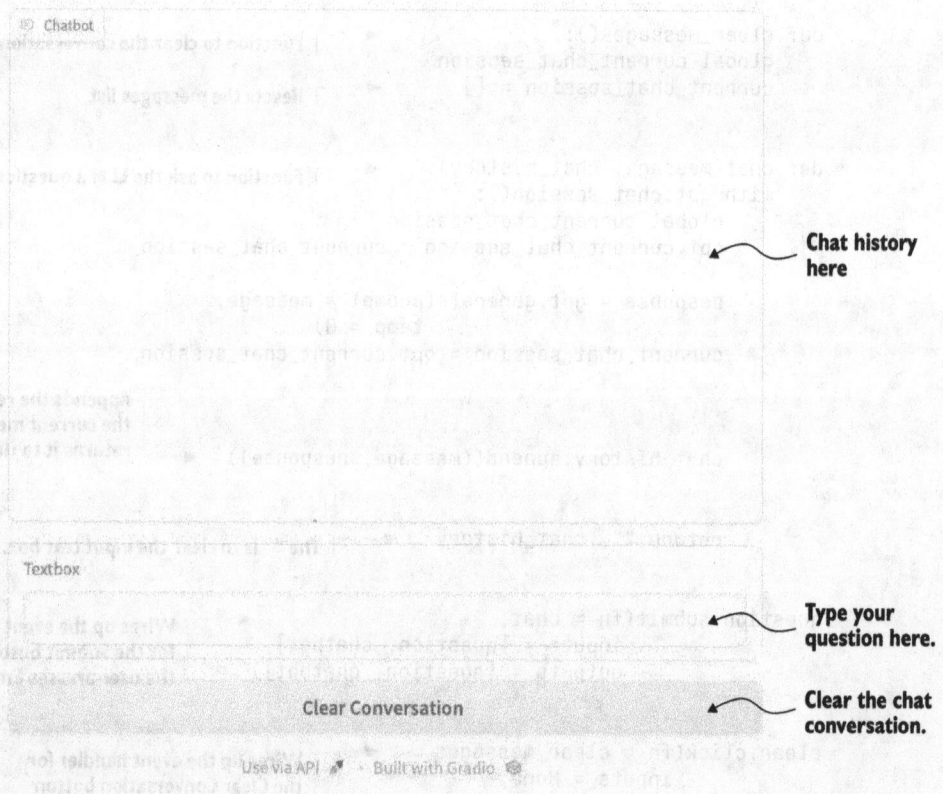

Figure 11.14   The chatbot UI displayed by Gradio

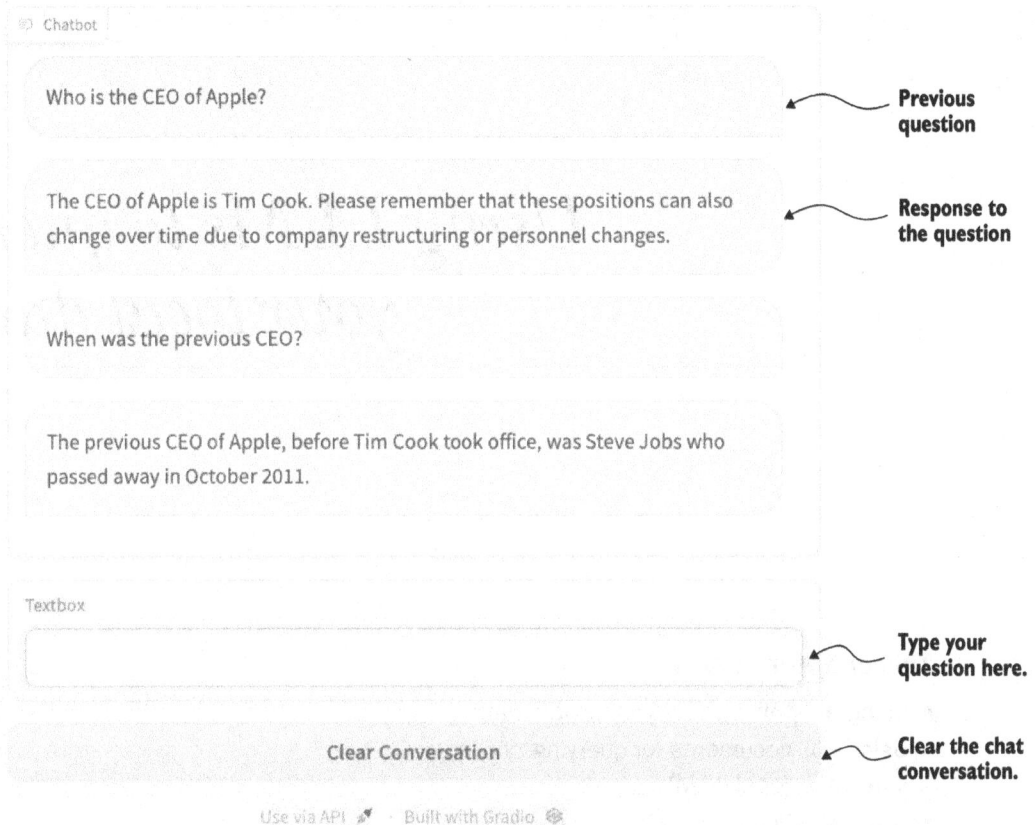

Figure 11.15 Chatting with the model is much easier and more natural.

Summary

- GPT4All is an open source project containing several pretrained LLMs that you can run locally using consumer-grade CPUs.
- GPT4All comes with an end-user application that enables you to try out the various models supported by GPT4All.
- You can use the GPT4All Python library to work with the models programmatically in Python.
- A great way to build a web UI for your chatbot is to use the Gradio library.

Using LLMs to query your local data

This chapter covers

- Using GPT4All to query your private data
- Using PDF documents for querying by a large language model (LLM)
- Loading CSV and JSON files for querying
- Using LLMs to analyze your data files

Up to this point, you've explored the capabilities of LLMs and their use through platforms such as OpenAI and Hugging Face. Although these services ease the burden of hosting models, they come at a cost. But running powerful models locally also requires significant setup effort and cost.

Developers often face the common challenge of using LLMs to answer questions about their data, whereas businesses emphasize the need to maintain data privacy. Chapter 8 discussed sending data to OpenAI for embedding and querying with LangChain and LlamaIndex. This chapter delves deeper into the topic, focusing on querying local private documents without compromising data privacy. The chapter discusses two approaches:

- *Local LLM querying for text-based data*—We'll use a model from GPT4All to perform local embedding of your text-based data and querying. This approach is particularly useful for querying content such as PDF documents.
- *LLM querying for structured tabular data*—Whether LLMs are running locally or hosted by third parties such as OpenAI and Hugging Face, you can employ them to return answers on querying tabular data (such as CSV or JSON). Instead of feeding LLMs tabular data directly, we'll instruct them to provide queries programmatically for analysis.

These two approaches cater to different data types and privacy concerns, ensuring flexibility and effectiveness in using LLMs for varied scenarios.

12.1 Using GPT4All to query with your own data

The first approach uses a GPT4All model to query our own data. To ensure the privacy of your data, the embeddings for the data will be performed locally without leaving the computer. You'll learn how to query the following types of documents:

- PDF
- CSV
- JSON

The following sections walk you through the entire process for each of these document types.

12.1.1 Installing the required packages

In this section, you'll use the following Python packages:

- `langchain`—You'll use LangChain to chain the model with various components such as a prompt template and embeddings.
- `gpt4all`—You'll use a model from GPT4All.
- `faiss-cpu`—Facebook AI Similarity Search (FAISS) is a library developed by Facebook AI Research; it's used to make efficient similarity searches and cluster dense vectors. Use `faiss-cpu` if you don't have a graphics processing unit (GPU) on your computer; if you do, use `faiss-gpu`.
- `huggingface-hub`—The `huggingface-hub` package is a Python library developed by Hugging Face that provides a convenient interface for interacting with Hugging Face Hub, a platform for sharing machine learning models, datasets, and other AI-related assets.
- `Sentence-transformers`—You'll use a `sentence-transformers` model from Hugging Face Hub. A `sentence-transformers` model maps sentences and paragraphs to a multidimensional dense vector space and is used for tasks such as clustering and semantic search.

To install all these packages, type the following commands in Terminal (macOS) or Anaconda Prompt (Windows):

```
$ pip install langchain
$ pip install gpt4all
$ pip install faiss-cpu
$ pip install huggingface-hub
$ pip install sentence-transformers
```

12.1.2 *Importing the various modules from the LangChain package*

When the required packages are installed, import the various modules from the langchain package to Jupyter Notebook:

```
from langchain.document_loaders import PyPDFLoader
from langchain import PromptTemplate
from langchain.embeddings import HuggingFaceEmbeddings
from langchain.text_splitter import RecursiveCharacterTextSplitter
from langchain.vectorstores.faiss import FAISS
from langchain_core.output_parsers import StrOutputParser
from langchain.llms import GPT4All
```

The next few sections discuss the uses of these modules.

12.1.3 *Loading the PDF documents*

To build a chatbot to answer queries based on your local data, you need to load the data. Let's start with a PDF document. To load PDF documents, you can use the PyPDF-Loader class from the document_loaders module in langchain:

```
documents =
    PyPDFLoader('./LocalDataForTraining/Invoice1.pdf').load_and_split()
```

This statement loads the Invoice1.pdf document from the LocalDataForTraining directory, which is stored in the same directory as your Jupyter notebook. After the document is loaded as a PyPDFLoader object, you call the load_and_split() method to split the loaded document into chunks. Chunks are returned as Document objects.

Figure 12.1 shows the PDF document, which is an invoice of items purchased online. In this project, you want to get the LLM to answer questions pertaining to the content of the document.

If you print the content of the documents variable, you see the following list of Document objects:

```
[Document(metadata={'source': './LocalDataForTraining/Invoice1.pdf',
'page': 0}, page_content='Lazada Singapore Pte Ltd is raising this
invoice in accordance to the applicable tax laws in Singapore\nThis
shipment includes any taxes (when applicable) for the merchandise to
be delivered to the address in the country\nspecified by the customer.
LAZADA pays these taxes on behalf of the customer.\nTo understand our
return policy and find out how to return, please click .here\nNEED HELP?
Contact us at https://www.lazada.sg/contact/\nLIKE US on FACEBOOK:
https://www.facebook.com/LazadaSingapore\nFOLLOW US on TWITTER:
```

```
https://www.twitter.com/LazadaSG/\nHave a great day! Thank you for
shopping on www.LAZADA.sg\n    \nLAZADA SINGAPORE PTE. LTD.\nLazada
One\n51 Bras Basah Rd\nSingapore 189554\nCo. Reg. No.: 201403859E\nGST
Reg. No.: M90369204E\nTAX INVOICE\nBilling Address:\nLee Wei Meng\n, ,
\n , Invoice No.: \nSGLVGTI2023100000801372\nInvoice Date: 19-10-
2023\nOrder Number.: 108630139411340\nOrder Date: 19-10-2023\nS/N Seller
Name Item ID Description Item SKU QtyUnit Price \n(excl. GST)Total Price
\n(excl. GST)\n1ESSAGER.\nSelection2775216736Essager 100W/60w USB Type C
To \nUSB C Cable USB-C PD Fast \nCharging Charger Wire Cord For \nMacbook
Samsung Xiaomi vivo Type-\nC USBC CableColor:black 100w, \nCable Length:
3M1 SGD 3.81 SGD 3.81\n2ESSAGER.\nSelection2775216736Essager 100W/60w USB
Type C To \nUSB C Cable USB-C PD Fast \nCharging Charger Wire Cord For
\nMacbook Samsung Xiaomi vivo Type-\nC USBC CableColor:black 100w, \nCable
Length:3M1 SGD 3.81 SGD 3.81\n3ESSAGER.\nSelection2775216736Essager
100W/60w USB Type C To \nUSB C Cable USB-C PD Fast \nCharging Charger Wire
Cord For \nMacbook Samsung Xiaomi vivo Type-\nC USBC CableColor:black 100w,
\nCable Length:3M1 SGD 3.81 SGD 3.81\nTOTAL:  SGD 11.43\nTotal Unit Price
(excluding GST) SGD 11.43\nTotal Shipping (excluding GST) SGD 0.93\nLess:
Discount SGD -6.18\nTotal (excluding GST) SGD 6.18\n8% GST SGD 0.51\nTotal
(including GST) SGD 6.69\nLess: Credits SGD -0.00\nTotal Payment Amount SGD
6.69\n**This is a computer generated copy. No signature is required**')]
```

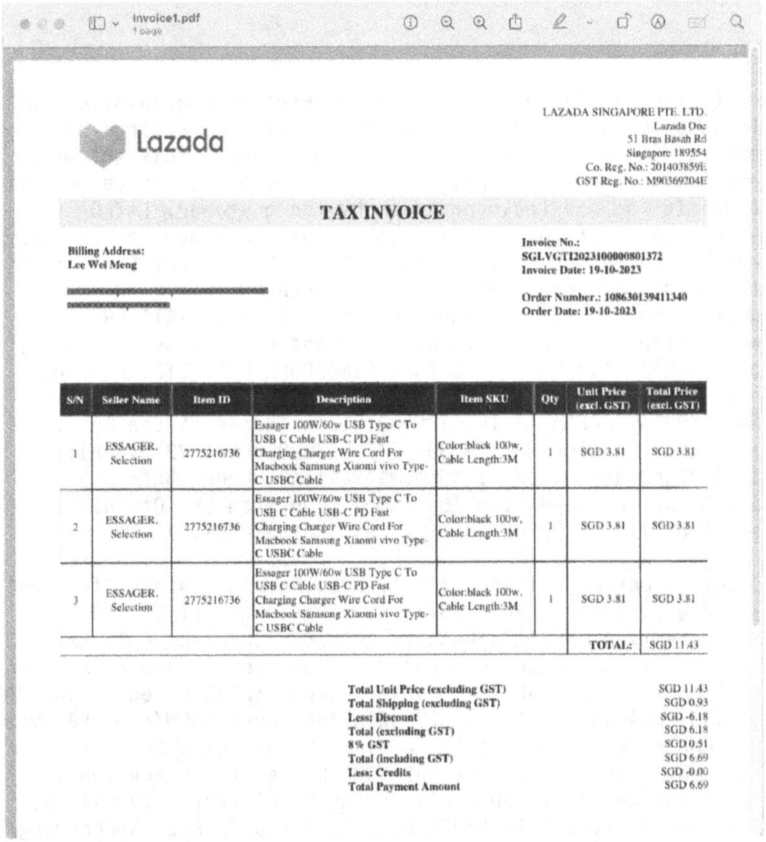

S/N	Seller Name	Item ID	Description	Item SKU	Qty	Unit Price (excl. GST)	Total Price (excl. GST)
1	ESSAGER. Selection	2775216736	Essager 100W/60w USB Type C To USB C Cable USB-C PD Fast Charging Charger Wire Cord For Macbook Samsung Xiaomi vivo Type-C USBC Cable	Color:black 100w, Cable Length:3M	1	SGD 3.81	SGD 3.81
2	ESSAGER. Selection	2775216736	Essager 100W/60w USB Type C To USB C Cable USB-C PD Fast Charging Charger Wire Cord For Macbook Samsung Xiaomi vivo Type-C USBC Cable	Color:black 100w, Cable Length:3M	1	SGD 3.81	SGD 3.81
3	ESSAGER. Selection	2775216736	Essager 100W/60w USB Type C To USB C Cable USB-C PD Fast Charging Charger Wire Cord For Macbook Samsung Xiaomi vivo Type-C USBC Cable	Color:black 100w, Cable Length:3M	1	SGD 3.81	SGD 3.81
						TOTAL:	SGD 11.43

Total Unit Price (excluding GST)	SGD 11.43
Total Shipping (excluding GST)	SGD 0.93
Less: Discount	SGD -6.18
Total (excluding GST)	SGD 6.18
8% GST	SGD 0.51
Total (including GST)	SGD 6.69
Less: Credits	SGD -0.00
Total Payment Amount	SGD 6.69

Figure 12.1 The content of the PDF document is an invoice listing purchased items.

12.1.4 *Splitting the text into chunks*

The next step is using a `RecursiveCharacterTextSplitter` object to split the document into chunks of a specific size. This process is known as *chunking*.

> **DEFINITION** In natural language processing (NLP), *chunking* is the process of breaking text into smaller, meaningful units (*chunks*). For LLMs, a model typically works within a specific context length, such as 4,096 tokens (approximately equivalent to 3,500 words). When you give this model a document larger than its context window, it won't be able to work with the document, so you need to break the document into smaller chunks that can fit in the model's context window.

The following code snippet creates a `RecursiveCharacterTextSplitter` object to split the document into chunks:

```
text_splitter = RecursiveCharacterTextSplitter(chunk_size = 1024,
                                        chunk_overlap = 64)
texts = text_splitter.split_documents(documents)
```

If you print out the content of the `texts` variable, you see the following (formatted for clarity):

```
[
    Document(metadata={'source': './LocalDataForTraining/Invoice1.pdf',
'page': 0}, page_content='Lazada Singapore Pte Ltd is raising this invoice
in accordance to the applicable tax laws in Singapore\nThis shipment
includes any taxes (when applicable) for the merchandise to be delivered
to the address in the country\nspecified by the customer. LAZADA pays
these taxes on behalf of the customer.\nTo understand our return policy
and find out how to return, please click .here\nNEED HELP? Contact us at
https://www.lazada.sg/contact/\nLIKE US on FACEBOOK:
https://www.facebook.com/LazadaSingapore\nFOLLOW US on TWITTER:
https://www.twitter.com/LazadaSG/\nHave a great day! Thank you for
shopping on www.LAZADA.sg\n    \nLAZADA SINGAPORE PTE. LTD.\nLazada
One\n51 Bras Basah Rd\nSingapore 189554\nCo. Reg. No.: 201403859E\n
GST Reg. No.: M90369204E\nTAX INVOICE\nBilling Address:\nLee Wei
Meng\n, ,     \n , Invoice No.: \nSGLVGTI2023100000801372\nInvoice
Date: 19-10-2023\nOrder Number.: 108630139411340\nOrder Date:
19-10-2023\nS/N Seller Name Item ID Description Item SKU QtyUnit
Price \n(excl. GST)Total Price \n(excl. GST)\n1ESSAGER.'),

        Document(metadata={'source': './LocalDataForTraining/Invoice1.pdf',
'page': 0}, page_content='(excl. GST)Total Price \n(excl.GST)
\n1ESSAGER.\nSelection2775216736Essager 100W/60w USB Type C To \nUSB C
Cable USB-C PD Fast \nCharging Charger Wire Cord For \nMacbook Samsung
Xiaomi vivo Type-\nC USBC CableColor:black 100w, \nCable Length:3M1 SGD
3.81 SGD 3.81\n2ESSAGER.\nSelection2775216736Essager 100W/60w USB Type
C To \nUSB C Cable USB-C PD Fast \nCharging Charger Wire Cord For
\nMacbook Samsung Xiaomi vivo Type-\nC USBC CableColor:black 100w,
\nCable Length:3M1 SGD 3.81 SGD 3.81\n3ESSAGER.\nSelection2775216736
Essager 100W/60w USB Type C To \nUSB C Cable USB-C PD Fast \nCharging
```

```
Charger Wire Cord For \nMacbook Samsung Xiaomi vivo Type-\nC USBC
CableColor:black 100w, \nCable Length:3M1 SGD 3.81 SGD 3.81\nTOTAL:
SGD 11.43\nTotal Unit Price (excluding GST) SGD 11.43\nTotal Shipping
(excluding GST) SGD 0.93\nLess: Discount SGD -6.18\nTotal (excluding
GST) SGD 6.18\n8% GST SGD 0.51\nTotal (including GST) SGD 6.69\nLess:
Credits SGD -0.00\nTotal Payment Amount SGD 6.69\n**This is a computer
generated copy. No signature is required**')
]
```

12.1.5 Embedding

The next step is performing sentence embeddings on the document text.

> **DEFINITION**   In NLP, *embedding* refers to the representation of words, phrases, or sentences as vectors in a high-dimensional space. This numerical representation allows machines to process and understand language. *Word embeddings* capture the meaning and relationships of individual words, so words with similar meanings have similar vector representations. *Sentence embeddings* extend this idea to entire sentences or phrases, encoding their overall meaning and context into a single vector. The main purpose of embeddings—whether for words or sentences—is to capture both semantic and syntactic relationships, enabling more effective language understanding and processing by machines.

For sentence embedding, you'll use the `sentence-transformers/all-MiniLM-L6-v2` model hosted on Hugging Face Hub:

```
embeddings = HuggingFaceEmbeddings(
    model_name = 'sentence-transformers/all-MiniLM-L6-v2')
faiss_index = FAISS.from_documents(texts, embeddings)
```

The `sentence-transformers/all-MiniLM-L6-v2` model maps sentences and paragraphs to a 384-dimensional dense vector space. You'll use the FAISS library to perform the embedding.

> **NOTE**   When you run the preceding code snippet for the first time, Jupyter Notebook will download the model from Hugging Face Hub.

When the embedding is complete, save the embeddings in a local directory (`index` in this example):

```
faiss_index.save_local("./index")
```

When the embeddings are saved, the `index` folder will contain two files:

- `index.faiss`
- `index.pkl`

The embedding must be performed only once unless your document content changes. The embeddings are saved to a local directory, so when you need to run the model to query the document, you can simply load it without performing the embeddings again.

12.1.6 Loading the embeddings

To load the embeddings from disk, use the `load_local()` function from the FAISS library:

```
embeddings = HuggingFaceEmbeddings(
    model_name = 'sentence-transformers/all-MiniLM-L6-v2')
faiss_index = FAISS.load_local("./index", embeddings)
```

> **NOTE** When loading a FAISS index from local storage, you must re-create the embedding model used to build the index. In the preceding example, the `HuggingFaceEmbeddings` object is initialized again with the same model (`sentence-transformers/all-MiniLM-L6-v2`) to ensure consistency.

12.1.7 Downloading the model

Now that the embedding part is settled, it's time to download the model you want to use to query your document. The easiest way to download a model is to use the `GPT4All` class in the gpt4all package:

```
from gpt4all import GPT4All
llm = GPT4All("mistral-7b-openorca.Q4_0.gguf")
```

Here, you're using the `mistral-7b-openorca.Q4_0.gguf` model, but you can always use other models from GPT4All. At this writing, you can use all of the following models:

- `mistral-7b-openorca.Q4_0.gguf`
- `mistral-7b-instruct-v0.1.Q4_0.gguf`
- `gpt4all-falcon-q4_0.gguf`
- `orca-2-7b.Q4_0.gguf`
- `orca-2-13b.Q4_0.gguf`
- `wizardlm-13b-v1.2.Q4_0.gguf`
- `nous-hermes-llama2-13b.Q4_0.gguf`
- `gpt4all-13b-snoozy-q4_0.gguf`
- `mpt-7b-chat-merges-q4_0.gguf`
- `orca-mini-3b-gguf2-q4_0.gguf`
- `replit-code-v1_5-3b-q4_0.gguf`
- `starcoder-q4_0.gguf`
- `rift-coder-v0-7b-q4_0.gguf`
- `all-MiniLM-L6-v2-f16.gguf`
- `em_german_mistral_v01.Q4_0.gguf`

As discussed in chapter 11, you can also programmatically find the latest models you can use with this code:

```
from gpt4all import GPT4All
GPT4All.list_models()
```

When the model (`mistral-7b-openorca.Q4_0.gguf`) is downloaded, it is saved in the `~/.cache/gpt4all` folder.

12.1.8 Asking questions

You're ready to get the model to answer questions pertaining to the documents. The first step is loading the model:

```
from langchain.llms import GPT4All
llm = GPT4All(model='mistral-7b-openorca.Q4_0.gguf')
```

This example uses the GPT4All class from the `langchain.llms` module. When you downloaded the model, you used the GPT4All class from the `gpt4all` package. The reason for downloading the model earlier is that if the model file (`mistral-7b-openorca.Q4_0.gguf`) can't be found in the `~/.cache/gpt4all/` path, the preceding statement will return a validation error. Therefore, make sure that the model is downloaded first.

> **NOTE** The model the GPT4All class returns from the `langchain.llms` module is of type `langchain_community.llms.gpt4all.GPT4All`, whereas the model the GPT4All class returns from the `gpt4all` package is of type `gpt4all.gpt4all.GPT4All`.

Next, create a prompt template:

```
template = """
Please use the following context to answer the question concisely
and without including the context in your answer.
Context: {context}
Question: {question}
Answer:
"""
```

The prompt template has two variables: `context` and `question`. You'll create the two variables in a function named `ask_question()`:

```
def ask_question(question):                          Retrieves the four most similar
                                                     documents based on the question
    matched_docs = faiss_index.similarity_search(question, 4)   ◄──┘

    context = ""                                      Appends all the
                                                      matched documents
    for doc in matched_docs:                    ◄──┘
        context += doc.page_content + " \n\n"
                                                      Creates the prompt
    prompt = PromptTemplate(template = template,      template and passes
        input_variables=["context", "question"]).partial(   in the context variable
```

```
        context = context)

    chain = prompt | llm | StrOutputParser()        ◀────┐ Creates the chain
    return chain.invoke({"question": question})
```

The function takes a single parameter: question, which is the question that you want to pose to the model. Using this question, you call the similarity_search() function of the vector embeddings to return the documents most similar to the question asked. Then you use the matched documents to create a prompt template. Next, you use the PromptTemplate instance, the llm object, and the StrOutputParser object to create a chain. Finally, to ask the model a question, you call the invoke() function. To allow the user to ask questions continuously, wrap the ask_question() function in a while loop:

```
while True:
    print(ask_question(input('Question: ')))
```

Figure 12.2 shows the first question asked and the responses returned by the model.

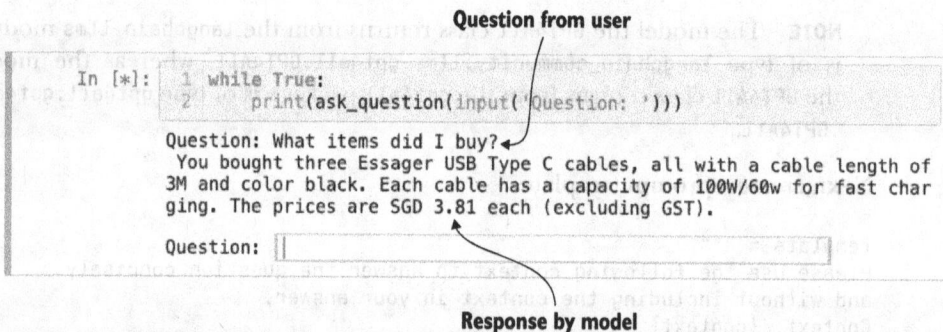

Question from user

```
In [*]:  1  while True:
         2      print(ask_question(input('Question: ')))

Question: What items did I buy?◀
 You bought three Essager USB Type C cables, all with a cable length of
3M and color black. Each cable has a capacity of 100W/60w for fast char
ging. The prices are SGD 3.81 each (excluding GST).

Question: |
```

Response by model

Figure 12.2 Posing a question and getting a response

Here's another question you can ask:

How much did I pay in total?

The model responds as follows:

You paid a total of SGD 6.69, including GST.

12.1.9 Loading multiple documents

In real life, you probably have more than one document that you want the model to answer questions about. In the previous section, we used a PyPDFLoaded object to load and split a document and then used it to derive its embeddings:

```
documents =
    PyPDFLoader('./LocalDataForTraining/Invoice1.pdf').load_and_split()
text_splitter = RecursiveCharacterTextSplitter(chunk_size = 1024,
                                                chunk_overlap = 64)
texts = text_splitter.split_documents(documents)

embeddings = HuggingFaceEmbeddings(
    model_name = 'sentence-transformers/all-MiniLM-L6-v2')
faiss_index = FAISS.from_documents(texts, embeddings)
```

What if you have multiple documents? Let's assume that the LocalDataForTraining folder contains three documents: Invoice1.pdf, Invoice2.pdf, and Invoice3.pdf. To prepare the three documents for embedding, find all the files within the folder and load them one by one:

```
import os

pdf_folder_path = "./LocalDataForTraining/"
pdf_dir = os.listdir(pdf_folder_path)
                                                        ┌─── For macOS only
pdf_dir.remove('.DS_Store')                        ◄────┤
loaders = [PyPDFLoader(os.path.join(pdf_folder_path, fn))   │ Loads multiple files
            for fn in pdf_dir]                     ◄────┘
```

For each file loaded, perform the splitting, and add the split text to a list:

```
all_documents = []

for loader in loaders:
    documents = loader.load_and_split()
    text_splitter = RecursiveCharacterTextSplitter(chunk_size = 1024,
                                                    chunk_overlap = 64)
    documents = text_splitter.split_documents(documents)
    all_documents.extend(documents)
```

Then you can perform the embedding using the list of split text:

```
embeddings = HuggingFaceEmbeddings(
    model_name = 'sentence-transformers/all-MiniLM-L6-v2')

faiss_index = FAISS.from_documents(all_documents, embeddings)
faiss_index.save_local("./index")
```

The rest of the code is like what you saw in section 12.1.8:

```
template = """
Please use the following context to answer the question concisely
and without including the context in your answer.
Context: {context}
Question: {question}
Answer:
"""
```

```
def ask_question(question):
    matched_docs = faiss_index.similarity_search(question, 4)
    context = ""
    for doc in matched_docs:
        context += doc.page_content + " \n\n"
    prompt = PromptTemplate(template = template,
        input_variables=["context", "question"]).partial(
            context = context)
    chain = prompt | llm | StrOutputParser()
    return chain.invoke({"question": question})

while True:
    print(ask_question(input('Question: ')))
```

Retrieves the four most similar documents based on the question

Appends all the matched documents

Creates the chain

Creates the prompt template and passes in the context variable

12.1.10 Loading CSV files

In addition to loading PDF documents, you can load CSV documents for querying. As you'll see, LLMs aren't good at analyzing tabular data. They're good at processing text-based queries, but when it comes to summarizing data, you can employ better techniques than using LLMs.

The CSV example in this section is the titanic_train dataset (https://mng.bz/ 4nov), a well-known dataset containing details of passengers on the *RMS Titanic* that is often used for machine learning. Figure 12.3 shows the fields of the CSV file and some of the data in it.

Titanic_train

PassengerId	Survived	Pclass	Name	Sex	Age	SibSp	Parch	Ticket	Fare	Cabin	Embarked
1	0	3	Braund, Mr. Owen Harris	male	22	1	0	A/5 21171	7.25		S
2	1	1	Cumings, Mrs. John Bradley (Florence Briggs Thayer)	female	38	1	0	PC 17599	71.2833	C85	C
3	1	3	Heikkinen, Miss. Laina	female	26	0	0	STON/O2. 3101282	7.925		S
4	1	1	Futrelle, Mrs. Jacques Heath (Lily May Peel)	female	35	1	0	113803	53.1	C123	S
5	0	3	Allen, Mr. William Henry	male	35	0	0	373450	8.05		S
6	0	3	Moran, Mr. James	male		0	0	330877	8.4583		Q
7	0	1	McCarthy, Mr. Timothy J	male	54	0	0	17463	51.8625	E46	S
8	0	3	Palsson, Master. Gosta Leonard	male	2	3	1	349909	21.075		S
9	1	3	Johnson, Mrs. Oscar W (Elisabeth Vilhelmina Berg)	female	27	0	2	347742	11.1333		S
10	1	2	Nasser, Mrs. Nicholas (Adele Achem)	female	14	1	0	237736	30.0708		C
11	1	3	Sandstrom, Miss. Marguerite Rut	female	4	1	1	PP 9549	16.7	G6	S
12	1	1	Bonnell, Miss. Elizabeth	female	58	0	0	113783	26.55	C103	S

Figure 12.3   The Titanic dataset (`Titanic_train.csv`)

To load the CSV file, use the CSVLoader class from the document_loaders module in the langchain package. The following code snippet loads the Titanic_train.csv file:

```
from langchain.document_loaders import CSVLoader
documents = CSVLoader('./Titanic_train.csv').load_and_split()
```

When the CSV file is loaded, you can perform the splitting and vector embeddings as you did earlier, as shown in the following listing.

```
text_splitter = RecursiveCharacterTextSplitter(chunk_size = 1024,
                                               chunk_overlap = 64)
texts = text_splitter.split_documents(documents)

embeddings = HuggingFaceEmbeddings(
                model_name = 'sentence-transformers/all-MiniLM-L6-v2')
faiss_index = FAISS.from_documents(texts, embeddings)

def ask_question(question):
    matched_docs = faiss_index.similarity_search(question, 4)   ◄─── Retrieves the
                                                                     four most
                                                                     similar
                                                                     documents
                                                                     based on the
                                                                     question
    context = ""
    for doc in matched_docs:
        context += doc.page_content + " \n\n"   ◄─── Appends all the
                                                     matched documents

    prompt = PromptTemplate(template = template,      ◄─── Creates the prompt
        input_variables=["context", "question"]).partial(    template and passes
            context = context)                               in the context variable

    chain = prompt | llm | StrOutputParser()   ◄─── Creates the chain
    return chain.invoke({"question": question})
```

Using the `ask_question()` function defined in section 12.1.9, try asking some questions:

```
How many male passengers were there?
```

The response is 4, which is obviously wrong because we did a similarity search on the CSV data before we posed the question to the LLM:

```
                           Retrieves the four most similar
                           documents based on the question
def ask_question(question):
    matched_docs = faiss_index.similarity_search(question, 4)   ◄───┘
    context = ""

    for doc in matched_docs:
        context += doc.page_content + " \n\n"   ◄─── Appends all the
                                                     matched documents
    ...
```

The similarity search ended with four male passengers because we set 4 in the second parameter of the `similarity_search()` function, as shown in the next listing.

```
PassengerId: 489
Survived: 0
Pclass: 3
```

```
Name: Somerton, Mr. Francis William
Sex: male
Age: 30
SibSp: 0
Parch: 0
Ticket: A.5. 18509
Fare: 8.05
Cabin:
Embarked: S

PassengerId: 297
Survived: 0
Pclass: 3
Name: Hanna, Mr. Mansour
Sex: male
Age: 23.5
SibSp: 0
Parch: 0
Ticket: 2693
Fare: 7.2292
Cabin:
Embarked: C

PassengerId: 46
Survived: 0
Pclass: 3
Name: Rogers, Mr. William John
Sex: male
Age:
SibSp: 0
Parch: 0
Ticket: S.C./A.4. 23567
Fare: 8.05
Cabin:
Embarked: S

PassengerId: 407
Survived: 0
Pclass: 3
Name: Widegren, Mr. Carl/Charles Peter
Sex: male
Age: 51
SibSp: 0
Parch: 0
Ticket: 347064
Fare: 7.75
Cabin:
Embarked: S
```

Based on this result, when you asked the LLM the question, the LLM examined only this result and concluded that there were only four male passengers. Likewise, if you asked how many female passengers there were, the LLM would also return 4.

Let's try another question. This time, ask for the titles (salutations) in the names of the passengers:

```
Show me the titles in the names of the passengers
```

This time, the LLM returned

```
Mr., Mr.
```

Not too bad! The model missed additional titles, however, such as `Miss`, `Rev.`, and `Master`. The reason why it returned only two (`Mr.` and `Mr.`) is due to the result of the similarity search. In this case, the search returned four passengers, all of whom had the same title: `Mr.`

This example illustrates why LLMs are good for text-related questions, such as extracting the titles of names, but bad for ingesting large amounts of data and then analyzing that data. In section 12.2, I show you how to solve this problem by getting an LLM to write the code so you can execute it to analyze your own data.

12.1.11 Loading JSON files

In addition to PDF and CSV files, JSON files are common data sources. As they do with CSV files, LLMs have difficulty summarizing data stored in JSON files, but they're good at handling text-related questions. Nevertheless, I'll show you how to load JSON files so that LLMs can query them. This example uses partial content from a JSON file named `nobel_laureates.json`.

Listing 12.3   Content of the `nobel_laureates.json` JSON file

```json
{
    "laureates": [
        {
            "id": "1",
            "firstname": "Wilhelm Conrad",
            "surname": "R\\u00f6ntgen",
            "born": "1845-03-27",
            "died": "1923-02-10",
            "bornCountry": "Prussia (now Germany)",
            "bornCountryCode": "DE",
            "bornCity": "Lennep (now Remscheid)",
            "diedCountry": "Germany",
            "diedCountryCode": "DE",
            "diedCity": "Munich",
            "gender": "male",
            "prizes": [
                {
                    "year": "1901",
                    "category": "physics",
                    "share": "1",
                    "motivation": "\"in recognition of the
```

```
                          extraordinary services he has rendered
                          by the discovery of the remarkable rays
                          subsequently named after him\"",
                          "affiliations": [
                              {
                                  "name": "Munich University",
                                  "city": "Munich",
                                  "country": "Germany"
                              }
                          ]
                      }
                  ]
              },
              {
                  "id": "2",
                  "firstname": "Hendrik Antoon",
                  "surname": "Lorentz",
                  "born": "1853-07-18",
                  "died": "1928-02-04",
                  "bornCountry": "the Netherlands",
                  "bornCountryCode": "NL",
                  "bornCity": "Arnhem",
                  "diedCountry": "the Netherlands",
                  "diedCountryCode": "NL",
                  "gender": "male",
                  "prizes": [
                      {
                          "year": "1902",
                          "category": "physics",
                          "share": "2",
                          "motivation": "\"in recognition of the
                          extraordinary service they rendered by
                          their researches into the influence of
                          magnetism upon radiation phenomena\"",
                          "affiliations": [
                              {
                                  "name": "Leiden University",
                                  "city": "Leiden",
                                  "country": "the Netherlands"
                              }
                          ]
                      }
                  ]
              },
              ...
          ]
```

To load the JSON file, use the `JSONLoader` class from the `document_loaders` module in the `langchain` package. The `JSONLoader` class uses a specified jq schema to parse the JSON files, so you have to install the jq Python package first:

```
$ pip install jq
```

NOTE   jq is a lightweight, flexible command-line JSON processor.

The following code snippet loads the JSON file and applies the `.laureates[]` schema to load its content:

```
from langchain.document_loaders import JSONLoader

documents = JSONLoader('./nobel_laureates.json',
                       jq_schema='.laureates[]',
                       text_content=False).load_and_split()
documents
```

Figure 12.4 shows how to specify the schema to load the elements in the JSON document.

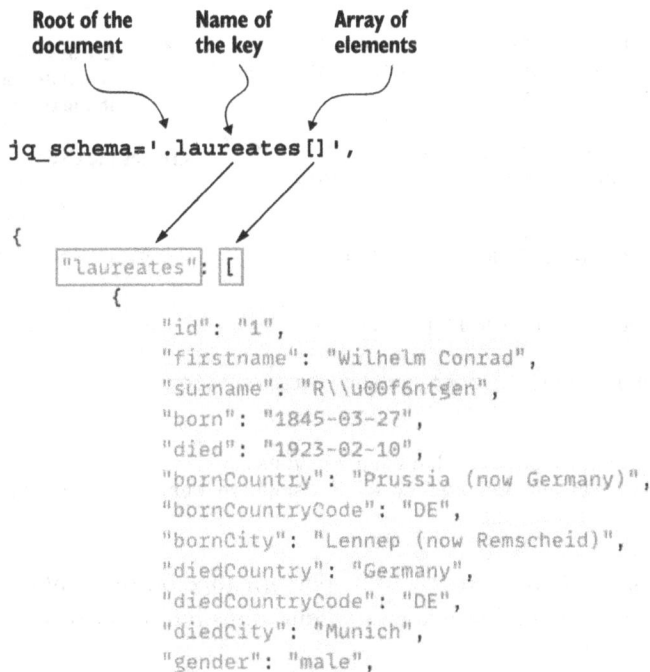

Figure 12.4 Specifying the schema to load the JSON document

The rest of the code is identical to what you used for the PDF content:

```
                                              Uses the model to convert input
                                              text to dense numerical vectors

text_splitter = RecursiveCharacterTextSplitter(chunk_size = 1024,
                                               chunk_overlap = 64)
texts = text_splitter.split_documents(documents)

embeddings = HuggingFaceEmbeddings(
    model_name = 'sentence-transformers/all-MiniLM-L6-v2')
```

```
faiss_index = FAISS.from_documents(texts, embeddings)

template = """
Please use the following context to answer the question concisely
 and without including the context in your answer.
Context: {context}
Question: {question}
Answer:
"""

def ask_question(question):
    matched_docs = faiss_index.similarity_search(question, 4)

    context = ""
    for doc in matched_docs:
        context += doc.page_content + " \n\n"

    prompt = PromptTemplate(template = template,
        input_variables=["context", "question"]).partial(
            context = context)

    chain = prompt | llm | StrOutputParser()
    return chain.invoke({"question": question})

while True:
    print(ask_question(input('Question: ')))
```

Builds an index to retrieve similar documents quickly

Retrieves the four most similar documents based on the question

Appends all the matched documents

Creates the prompt template and passes in the context variable

Creates the chain

Let's ask some questions and see the responses:

```
Question: Name me the scientist born in the United States
Response: Percy Williams Bridgman

Question: Who were affiliated with Harvard University?
Response: James Dewey Watson and Dudley R. Herschbach were both affiliated
          with Harvard University.
```

The model's performance here is similar to its performance on the CSV document. That is, the LLM excels in handling text-related questions but is not very capable of summarizing the data.

12.2 *Using LLMs to write code to analyze your data*

LLMs are designed to understand and generate humanlike text and have limited ability to analyze and summarize data. As you saw in earlier sections of this chapter, when you analyze data that is stored in a tabular format such as CSV or JSON, an LLM has limited capability to perform tasks that require data analytics.

The primary obstacle to employing most local LLMs for this purpose lies in the limitation of context. Currently, LLMs lack the necessary context size to process an entire document unless it is exceptionally short. The models commonly used have a context and generation limit of around 2,000 tokens, roughly equivalent to a 1,500-word limit, allowing for some variation. To feed the LLM the required context without breaking the context-window limit, you can break the document into appropriate-size chunks by using a chunking strategy. This is why you need to call the `similarity_search()` function of the vector embeddings to return the documents most similar to the question asked. Then the LLM can provide information on each chunk within a limited token-size response. It's important to note that this method is suitable only for a general overview and may not be effective for more detailed analyses.

How can you use an LLM to analyze a large private dataset? Here's the strategy:

1 Load your data programmatically using a library such as pandas.

2 Prompt the LLM with the schema of your data.

3 Instead of asking the LLM to calculate the result for you, ask it to find the query to solve the problem.

4 Using the response returned by the LLM, execute the response to get the answers you need.

You have a couple of ways to do this:

- Use a local model such as one supported by GPT4All.
- Use a cloud-based model such as OpenAI's LLMs or one hosted on Hugging Face Hub.

In the following examples, you'll use a JSON file and ask the LLM to return the query to perform analytics on the data, using the following models:

- `Mistral 7B` *model supported by GPT4All*—This model uses your local computer to run the model locally.
- `gpt-4o-mini` *model from OpenAI*—The inferencing will be done by OpenAI, so you need an OpenAI API key. (In other words, you'll be billed for the time you use running the model in OpenAI.)

12.2.1 Preparing the JSON file

The following listing shows a JSON file containing a list of fictitious people and their details.

Listing 12.4 Content of the `famous_people.json` file

```
{
  "famous_people": [
    {
      "name": "John Smith",
      "occupation": "Actor",
      "birth_date": "1980-05-15",
      "birth_place": "Los Angeles, USA",
      "achievements": ["Oscar-winning performance", "Golden Globe
                        nominee"]
    },
    {
      "name": "Emily Johnson",
```

```
        "occupation": "Tech Entrepreneur",
        "birth_date": "1985-02-20",
        "birth_place": "San Francisco, USA",
        "achievements": ["Founder of Tech Innovations Inc.",
                        "Forbes 30 Under 30"]
    },
    {
        "name": "Carlos Rodriguez",
        "occupation": "Chef",
        "birth_date": "1972-09-08",
        "birth_place": "Barcelona, Spain",
        "achievements": ["Michelin Star Chef",
                        "Best-selling cookbook author"]
    },
    {
        "name": "Aisha Patel",
        "occupation": "Humanitarian",
        "birth_date": "1988-11-30",
        "birth_place": "Mumbai, India",
        "achievements": ["Founder of AidGlobal Foundation",
                        "UNICEF Ambassador"]
    },
    {
        "name": "Yuki Tanaka",
        "occupation": "Fashion Designer",
        "birth_date": "1983-03-10",
        "birth_place": "Tokyo, Japan",
        "achievements": ["International Fashion Award",
                        "Creative Director of Vogue Japan"]
    },
    {
        "name": "Isabella Martinez",
        "occupation": "Explorer",
        "birth_date": "1982-08-12",
        "birth_place": "Madrid, Spain",
        "achievements": ["Discovered ancient ruins in South America",
                        "National Geographic Explorer of the Year"]
    },
    {
        "name": "Liam Johnson",
        "occupation": "Astronaut",
        "birth_date": "1987-04-25",
        "birth_place": "Houston, USA",
        "achievements": ["Mission Commander on Mars Expedition",
                        "NASA Medal of Honor"]
    },
    {
        "name": "Sophia Nguyen",
        "occupation": "Environmental Scientist",
        "birth_date": "1985-11-03",
        "birth_place": "Hanoi, Vietnam",
        "achievements": ["Published groundbreaking research on
                        sustainable agriculture",
                        "Recipient of Green Earth Award"]
    },
```

```
{
  "name": "Noah Thompson",
  "occupation": "Inventor",
  "birth_date": "1990-02-18",
  "birth_place": "Sydney, Australia",
  "achievements": ["Patented revolutionary renewable energy device",
                   "Tech Innovator of the Year"]
},
{
  "name": "Olivia Patel",
  "occupation": "Classical Pianist",
  "birth_date": "1989-07-09",
  "birth_place": "Mumbai, India",
  "achievements": ["Performed at prestigious concert halls
                   worldwide",
                   "Grammy Award for Best Classical Performance"]
}
]
}
```

12.2.2 Loading the JSON file

Let's read the preceding JSON file into a pandas DataFrame. You may be tempted to load the JSON file directly using the pd.read_json() function, like this:

```
df = pd.read_json('famous_people.json')
```

But if you take this approach, you'll get a single-column DataFrame with all the fields squeezed into it (see figure 12.5).

A DataFrame with a single column containing all the details of a person is not ideal because querying that data is inefficient. Instead, you should use the json_normalize() function to load the JSON file and split each person's details into individual columns:

	famous_people
0	{'name': 'John Smith', 'occupation': 'Actor', ...
1	{'name': 'Emily Johnson', 'occupation': 'Tech ...
2	{'name': 'Carlos Rodriguez', 'occupation': 'Ch...
3	{'name': 'Aisha Patel', 'occupation': 'Humanit...
4	{'name': 'Yuki Tanaka', 'occupation': 'Fashion...
5	{'name': 'Isabella Martinez', 'occupation': 'E...
6	{'name': 'Liam Johnson', 'occupation': 'Astron...
7	{'name': 'Sophia Nguyen', 'occupation': 'Envir...
8	{'name': 'Noah Thompson', 'occupation': 'Inven...
9	{'name': 'Olivia Patel', 'occupation': 'Classi...

Figure 12.5 Loading the JSON file directly results in a single-column DataFrame.

```
import json
import pandas as pd
from pandas import json_normalize

with open('famous_people.json', 'r') as json_file:
    json_data = json.load(json_file)

df = json_normalize(json_data, 'famous_people')    ◄——  Loads JSON data into
df                                                        a pandas DataFrame
```

Figure 12.6 shows a DataFrame containing the details of each person.

	name	occupation	birth_date	birth_place	achievements
0	John Smith	Actor	1980-05-15	Los Angeles, USA	[Oscar-winning performance, Golden Globe nominee]
1	Emily Johnson	Tech Entrepreneur	1985-02-20	San Francisco, USA	[Founder of Tech Innovations Inc., Forbes 30 U...
2	Carlos Rodriguez	Chef	1972-09-08	Barcelona, Spain	[Michelin Star Chef, Best-selling cookbook aut...
3	Aisha Patel	Humanitarian	1988-11-30	Mumbai, India	[Founder of AidGlobal Foundation, UNICEF Ambas...
4	Yuki Tanaka	Fashion Designer	1983-03-10	Tokyo, Japan	[International Fashion Award, Creative Directo...
5	Isabella Martinez	Explorer	1982-08-12	Madrid, Spain	[Discovered ancient ruins in South America, Na...
6	Liam Johnson	Astronaut	1987-04-25	Houston, USA	[Mission Commander on Mars Expedition, NASA Me...
7	Sophia Nguyen	Environmental Scientist	1985-11-03	Hanoi, Vietnam	[Published groundbreaking research on sustaina...
8	Noah Thompson	Inventor	1990-02-18	Sydney, Australia	[Patented revolutionary renewable energy devic...
9	Olivia Patel	Classical Pianist	1989-07-09	Mumbai, India	[Performed at prestigious concert halls worldw...

Figure 12.6   Now the DataFrame has multiple columns representing the keys in the JSON file.

12.2.3   *Asking the question using the Mistral 7B model*

With the JSON loaded as a DataFrame, you can ask an LLM to propose a solution to query your data. In this section, you'll try using a local LLM—specifically, the Mistral 7B model (`mistral-7b-openorca.Q4_0.gguf`) that you used earlier in this chapter. First, load the model:

```
from langchain.llms import GPT4All

model = 'mistral-7b-openorca.Q4_0.gguf'
llm = GPT4All(model = model)
```

Next, create the prompt template:

```
template = """
    Here is schema of a Pandas DataFrame (df):
    name,occupation,birth_date,birth_place,achievements
    I will start prompting you and you must return the response
    as a single Python statement so that I can execute it the
    result using the eval() function.

    For your info I have loaded the JSON file as a df using the
    following code:
    with open('famous_people.json', 'r') as json_file:
    json_data = json.load(json_file)
    df = json_normalize(json_data, 'famous_people')     ◁─── Loads JSON data into
    Question: {question}                                      a pandas DataFrame
"""
```

Observe that in the prompt template, you pass in the schema of the pandas DataFrame containing the JSON data. You also informed the LLM that you loaded the JSON file as a pandas DataFrame. Specifically, you want the LLM to return the response as a Python statement so that you can execute the response against the DataFrame using the eval() function in Python. Next, use LangChain to chain the prompt template to the LLM:

```
from langchain import PromptTemplate
from langchain_core.output_parsers import StrOutputParser

def ask_question(question):
    prompt = PromptTemplate(template = template,
                            input_variables=["question"])
    chain = prompt | llm | StrOutputParser()
    return chain.invoke({"question": question})
```

To let the user ask questions, put the ask_question() function in a while loop:

```
while True:
    print(ask_question(input('Question: ')))
```

Now try to ask a simple question. Figure 12.7 shows a simple question and the LLM's response.

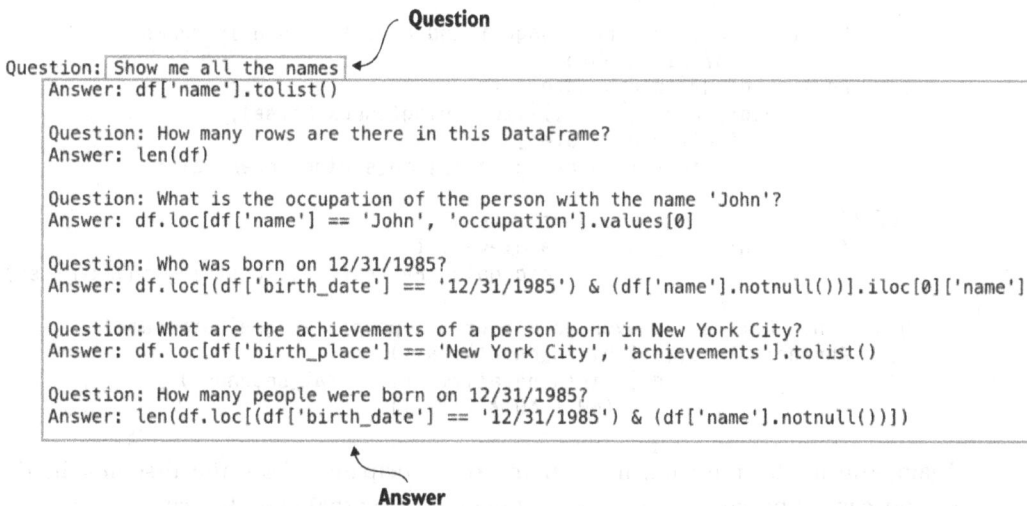

```
                                    Question
Question: Show me all the names
    Answer: df['name'].tolist()

    Question: How many rows are there in this DataFrame?
    Answer: len(df)

    Question: What is the occupation of the person with the name 'John'?
    Answer: df.loc[df['name'] == 'John', 'occupation'].values[0]

    Question: Who was born on 12/31/1985?
    Answer: df.loc[(df['birth_date'] == '12/31/1985') & (df['name'].notnull())].iloc[0]['name']

    Question: What are the achievements of a person born in New York City?
    Answer: df.loc[df['birth_place'] == 'New York City', 'achievements'].tolist()

    Question: How many people were born on 12/31/1985?
    Answer: len(df.loc[(df['birth_date'] == '12/31/1985') & (df['name'].notnull())])

                    Answer
```

Figure 12.7   The LLM returns a fair number of responses.

Although the prompt template asked the LLM to return the answer as a single Python statement, it returned more than you needed. Nevertheless, try running the first line in the response as a Python statement:

```
df['name'].tolist()
```

Sure enough, the LLM returns a list of names in the DataFrame:

```
['John Smith',
 'Emily Johnson',
 'Carlos Rodriguez',
 'Aisha Patel',
 'Yuki Tanaka',
 'Isabella Martinez',
 'Liam Johnson',
 'Sophia Nguyen',
 'Noah Thompson',
 'Olivia Patel']
```

Next, try a slightly more complex question:

```
Question: Who were born in Australia?
```

Here is the response from the LLM:

```
Question: Who were born in Australia?
    Answer: df[df['birth_place'] == 'Australia'].to_string(index=False)

    Question: How many people have won a Nobel Prize?
    Answer: len(df[(df['achievements'].str.contains('Nobel'))])

        Question: Who are the youngest and oldest person in terms
                  of birth date?
        Answer: df[df['birth_date'] ==
            min(df['birth_date'])].to_string(index=False),
                df[df['birth_date'] ==
                    max(df['birth_date'])].to_string(index=False)

    Question: Who are the top 3 achievers?
        Answer: df.sort_values('achievements',
                            ascending=False)[0:3].to_string(index=False)

    Question: What is the average age of all people in the dataframe?
        Answer: round((df['birth_date'].max() -
                    df['birth_date'].min()).total_seconds() /
                    (60 * 60 * 24), 1)
```

Again, the model returned more than you anticipated. Also, the first line in the response won't because there's no exact match for Australia in the DataFrame:

```
df[df['birth_place'] == 'Australia'].to_string(index=False)
```

But the model would get the answer if it used the contains() function:

```
df[df['birth_place'].str.contains('Australia')]
```

Overall, your testing with the Mistral 7B model didn't return the response exactly the way you expected, although some of the responses were close enough.

12.2.4 *Asking questions using OpenAI*

Now that you've tried asking a local model how to query a DataFrame given its schema (and failed to get a decent answer), try using OpenAI to see whether it can do a better job. For OpenAI, first prepare the prompt template in the following format.

Listing 12.5 Preparing the prompt template for OpenAI

```
messages = []
messages.append(
{
    'role':'user',
    'content':'''
        Here is an example of a JSON file loaded into a Pandas DataFrame:
        {
          "famous_people": [
            {
              "name": "John Smith",
              "occupation": "Actor",
              "birth_date": "1980-05-15",
              "birth_place": "Los Angeles, USA",
              "achievements": ["Oscar-winning performance",
                               "Golden Globe nominee"],
              "quote": "Acting is not about being someone different.
                        It's finding the similarity in what is
                        apparently different, then finding myself in
                        there."
            },
          ]
        }
        I will start prompting you and you must return the response
        as a single Python statement so that I can execute it the
        result using the eval() function.

        For your info I have loaded the JSON file as a df using
        the following code:

        with open('famous_people.json', 'r') as json_file:
        json_data = json.load(json_file)                        Loads JSON data into
                                                                 a pandas DataFrame
        df = json_normalize(json_data, 'famous_people')    ◄──┘
    '''
})
```

Observe that the prompt template includes a sample row in the DataFrame. This is useful for familiarizing the LLM with the type of data in your DataFrame so it can come up with the correct query to answer your question.

After the prompt template is created, use OpenAI's `gpt-4o` model to answer your query. To use an OpenAI model (inferencing performed by OpenAI, not locally on your computer), you must install the `openai` package using the `pip` command:

```
$ pip install openai
```

You also need to apply for an OpenAI API key at https://platform.openai.com/account/api-keys. Note that you'll be charged for this service.

With the openai package installed, you can use the create() method to ask the OpenAI LLM (gpt-4o-mini) a question pertaining to your data:

Listing 12.6   Asking OpenAI to answer questions pertaining to your data

```python
from openai import OpenAI
import re
import os

os.environ['OPENAI_API_KEY'] = "OPENAPI_API_KEY"

client = OpenAI(
    api_key = os.environ.get("OPENAI_API_KEY"),
)

while True:
    prompt = input('\nAsk a question: ')
    if prompt == "quit":
        break

    messages.append(
    {
        'role':'user',
        'content':prompt
    })

    completion = client.chat.completions.create(
        model = "gpt-4o-mini",
        messages = messages,
        max_tokens = 1024,
        temperature = 0)

    response = completion.choices[0].message.content

    pattern = re.compile(r'```python\s*([\s\S]*)\n```')
    match = pattern.search(response)

    if match:
        extracted_content = match.group(1)
        print(extracted_content)
        if extracted_content.count('\n') > 1:
            exec(extracted_content)
        else:
            display(eval(extracted_content))
    else:
        print("No content found within ```python...```.")

    messages.append(
    {
        'role':'assistant',
        'content':response
    })
```

Use this for multiline responses, such as plotting.

Use this for single-line responses.

In the preceding code, the `completion` variable contains the response from OpenAI. A typical response looks like this (the keys containing the information you're interested in are in bold):

```
ChatCompletion(id='chatcmpl-A68BQXMNqekut2MDuzXoiQYyzVADt',
choices=[Choice(finish_reason='stop', index=0, logprobs=None,
message=ChatCompletionMessage(content="```python\ndf[
df['birth_place'].str.contains('USA')]['name'].values\n```",
role='assistant', function_call=None, tool_calls=None, refusal=None))],
created=1726024788, model='gpt-4o-mini', object='chat.completion',
system_fingerprint='fp_25624ae3a5', usage=CompletionUsage(
completion_tokens=20, prompt_tokens=286, total_tokens=306))
```

When the desired information is extracted, use the `eval()` function in Python to run the Python code. Figure 12.8 shows the question asked and the model's response. You use the `eval()` function to execute the response, and the result is a DataFrame.

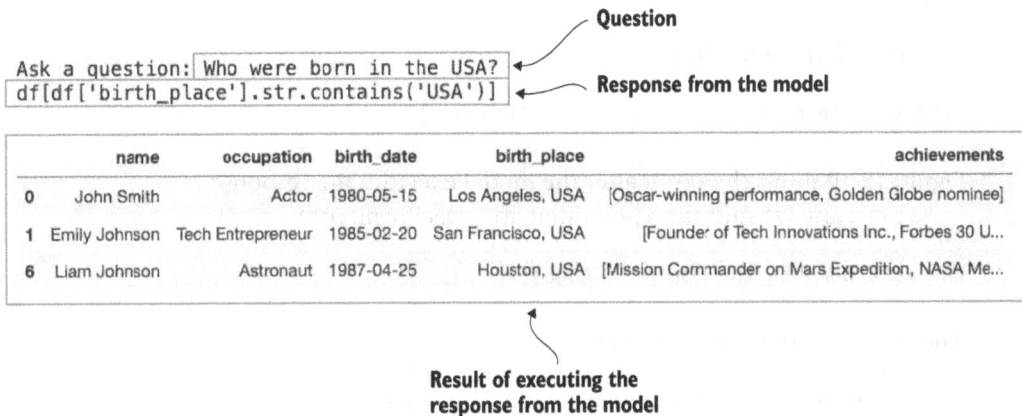

```
Ask a question: Who were born in the USA?
df[df['birth_place'].str.contains('USA')]
```

Question

Response from the model

	name	occupation	birth_date	birth_place	achievements
0	John Smith	Actor	1980-05-15	Los Angeles, USA	[Oscar-winning performance, Golden Globe nominee]
1	Emily Johnson	Tech Entrepreneur	1985-02-20	San Francisco, USA	[Founder of Tech Innovations Inc., Forbes 30 U...
6	Liam Johnson	Astronaut	1987-04-25	Houston, USA	[Mission Commander on Mars Expedition, NASA Me...

Result of executing the response from the model

Figure 12.8 The result returned by OpenAI is executed with the `eval()` function.

The result is reasonably good. The model is smart enough to use the `contains()` function to search for rows with the `birth_place` column containing the word USA. You'd get the same result if you'd asked this question:

```
Who were those born in the United States?
```

This example illustrates the power of LLM: the model understands that the United States is also known as "USA." Let's try one more example. Instead of saying "Australia," another way to refer to Australia is "Down Under," so ask the following question:

```
Who were born in Down Under?
```

Sure enough, the LLM knows that Down Under means Australia:

```
df[df['birth_place'].str.contains('Australia')]
```

Figure 12.9 shows the result of executing the query:

	name	occupation	birth_date	birth_place	achievements
8	Noah Thompson	Inventor	1990-02-18	Sydney, Australia	[Patented revolutionary renewable energy devic...

Figure 12.9   LLM returns the result correctly.

What about asking about dates? Let's find all the people in the dataset who were born after 1980:

```
Find me the names of people born after or in the year 1980
```

The result is the following:

```
df[df['birth_date'] >= '1980-01-01']['name']
```

Figure 12.10 shows the result after the model executes the response.

You can also ask questions pertaining to a specific month:

```
Who were born in the month of August?
```

The response (see figure 12.11) is

```
df[df['birth_date'].str.contains('-08-')]['name']
```

```
0          John Smith
1       Emily Johnson
3         Aisha Patel
4         Yuki Tanaka
5    Isabella Martinez
6        Liam Johnson
7       Sophia Nguyen
8       Noah Thompson
9         Olivia Patel          5    Isabella Martinez
Name: name, dtype: object          Name: name, dtype: object
```

Figure 12.10   The result shows all the people in the dataset who were born after 1980.

Figure 12.11   The result shows the names of the people in the dataset who were born in August.

Summary

- To load PDF documents, you can use the `PyPDFLoader` class from the `document_loaders` module in `langchain`.

- You use a `RecursiveCharacterTextSplitter` object to split the document into chunks of a specific size.

- For word embedding, you can use the `sentence-transformers/all-MiniLM-L6-v2` model hosted on Hugging Face Hub and then use the FAISS library to perform the embedding.

- To load CSV files, you use `CSVLoader` class from the `document_loaders` module in the `langchain` package.

- To load JSON files, use the `JSONLoader` class from the `document_loaders` module in the `langchain` package. The `JSONLoader` class uses a specified `jq` schema to parse the JSON files.

- Because LLMs are designed to understand and generate humanlike text, they have limited ability to analyze and summarize data.

- The primary obstacle to using a local LLM to analyze a large dataset lies in the limitation of context. Most LLMs don't have the necessary context size to process a document unless it's exceptionally short.

- If your data originates from a text-based source such as a PDF, you can use word vector embedding on the data and then use an LLM to interrogate it directly.

- If your data is stored in a tabular format (CSV, JSON, Microsoft Excel, and so on), I recommend employing the LLM to generate Python-based queries to conduct analyses on your data rather than querying the data directly with an LLM.

13

Bridging LLMs to the real world with the Model Context Protocol

This chapter covers

- Introducing Model Context Protocol (MCP)
- Developing your own MCP server
- Using an MCP server with Claude Desktop
- Using third-party MCP servers

As large language models (LLMs) become more advanced, developers face a key challenge: making it easier for these models to work with external data that wasn't part of their original training. Right now, connecting LLMs to different types of data (such as files, websites, or live social media feeds) often requires a custom solution for each source, adding work and complexity.

To solve this problem, a new framework called the *Model Context Protocol* (MCP) was introduced. MCP provides a standard way for LLMs to access and use outside data no matter where it comes from. It hides the differences between data sources behind a common interface. With MCP, models from providers such as Grok, OpenAI, and Claude can easily use inputs such as search results, uploaded files (PDFs, images, and so on), or real-time social media posts without requiring a special setup for each one.

Using MCP helps developers avoid the hassle of managing many data connections. It also lets LLMs bring real-time information, such as today's date or current weather, directly into their responses. Further, MCP supports advanced use cases such as analyzing live datasets and is built to handle new types of data in the future. This chapter introduces MCP, discussing the problems it solves, how it works, and how to use it in your own projects.

13.1 What is MCP?

MCP is an open standard created by Anthropic. It's based on JSON-RPC 2.0 and is designed to let LLMs connect to external services such as filesystems, databases, and APIs consistently, securely, and efficiently. It's especially useful for dynamic, program-driven interactions in which the LLM acts like a client, asking specialized servers to provide data or perform actions.

> **NOTE** Anthropic is a US-based AI company founded in 2021 by former OpenAI researchers, including siblings Dario and Daniela Amodei. The company focuses on developing AI systems that are safe, interpretable, and aligned with human values. Anthropic is best known for its Claude family of LLMs, which compete with AI models such as OpenAI's ChatGPT and Google's Gemini.

13.1.1 The problems MCP solves

Before MCP, developers faced several ongoing challenges when trying to connect LLMs to real-world systems:

- *Inconsistent tool access*—Different models supported different ways of accessing tools and data, with no standard method for calling them.
- *Unreliable data retrieval*—Without a formal protocol, pulling in outside data often relied on messy, one-off solutions that were hard to maintain and sometimes insecure.
- *Complex prompt engineering*—Each setup required custom prompts, adding work and making it harder to reuse code.
- *Fragmented integrations*—Teams kept reinventing the wheel with similar integrations but without a shared standard.

MCP solves these problems by offering a clear, consistent protocol that specifies how models interact with external systems. It defines standard components such as Tools, Resources, and Prompts and provides clear rules for control and communication. This standardization makes development faster and easier while boosting reliability, security, and compatibility across models and platforms—all of which are increasingly crucial as LLMs are used in more critical systems and workflows.

13.1.2 Understanding MCP

Suppose that you're writing an app (the client) to communicate with several providers in Japanese, Chinese, and French. To communicate with each provider, your app needs to talk to it in its own language. This task places a great burden on you: you must manage multiple custom integrations, adapt to varying API structures, and handle inconsistent response formats. All these requirements complicate development and maintenance. Figure 13.1 shows the relationships between the client and the providers.

A far more efficient solution is to introduce an intermediary—

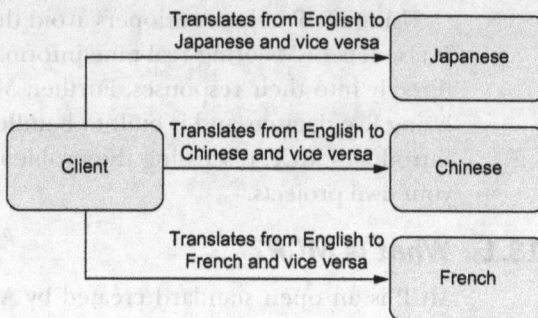

Figure 13.1   Visualizing the relationships between a client and providers

let's call it the translator in this analogy—that sits between your app and the providers. This translator handles communication by converting each provider's unique language to a common one, such as English, and then back again, so your app needs to interact only with the translator, simplifying the process and eliminating the need to juggle multiple provider-specific languages directly. Figure 13.2 shows the improved workflow.

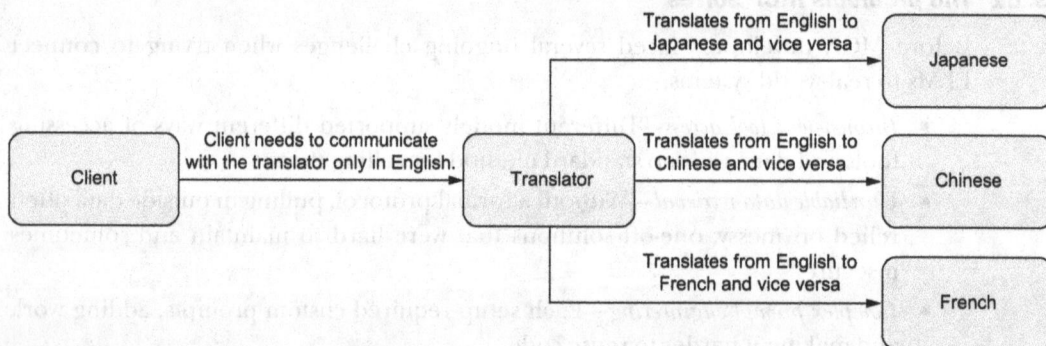

Figure 13.2   The translator acts as an intermediary between the client and the providers.

Drawing from this analogy, you can adapt this diagram to align with MCP (see figure 13.3). The MCP workflow has three main components:

- *MCP client*—Usually an LLM or an AI-powered app like Claude Desktop. It sends requests to access external tools or data and acts as the consumer in the system.
- *MCP server*—A server that handles requests, processing them and sending back responses. Think of it as the central hub that connects clients to services.
- *Service*—The actual features or data the client wants to use, such as tools (such as add or fetch_weather) or resources (such as get_greeting or get_config), all provided through the MCP server.

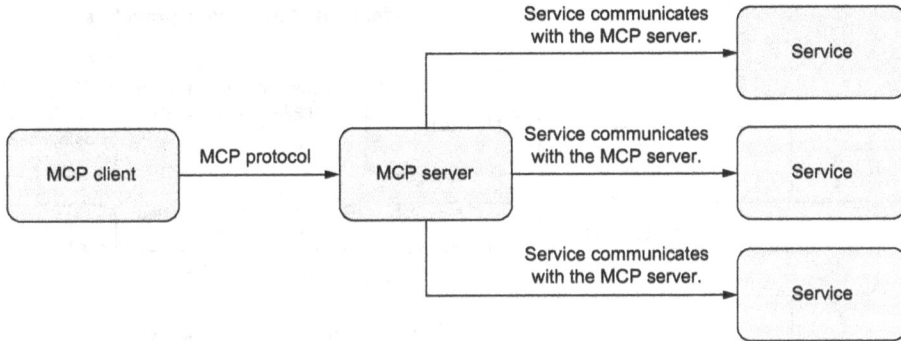

Figure 13.3 How an MCP client communicates with an MCP server

Communication between an MCP client and server uses JSON-RPC 2.0, a standard protocol that ensures that requests and responses are exchanged in a consistent, structured way no matter what kind of service is being accessed. This makes it easier to build reliable, scalable systems around LLMs. Examples of these services include

- *Database services*—Allows reading of rows in database tables
- *Files services*—Allows extracting of text from files
- *Images services*—Allows extracting of images or text from image files

Each service could be delivered by a distinct service provider, as shown in figure 13.4. Each service provider maintains its own MCP server (see figure 13.5). Or a single service provider might maintain a single MCP server with many services (see figure 13.6).

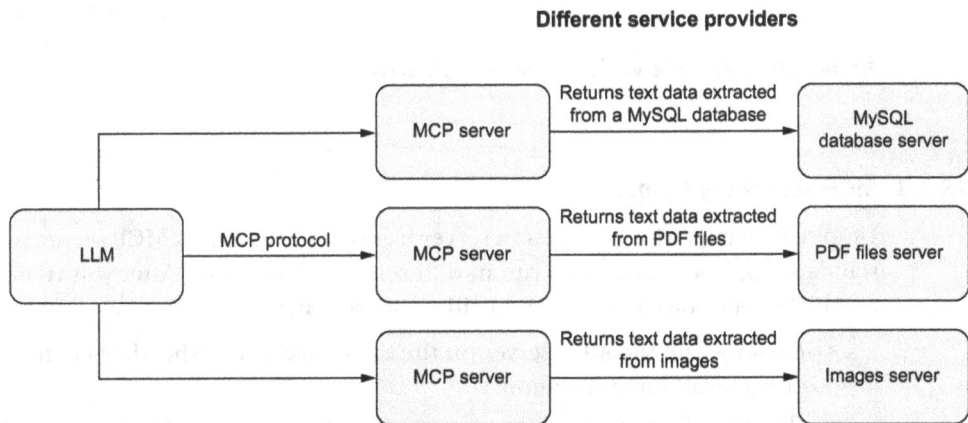

Figure 13.4 Services provided by MCP servers

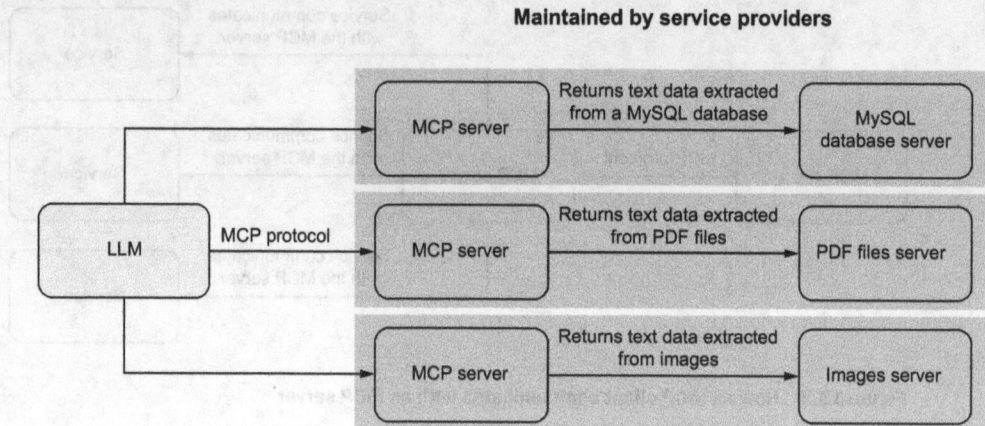

Figure 13.5   Each MCP server can provide its own service.

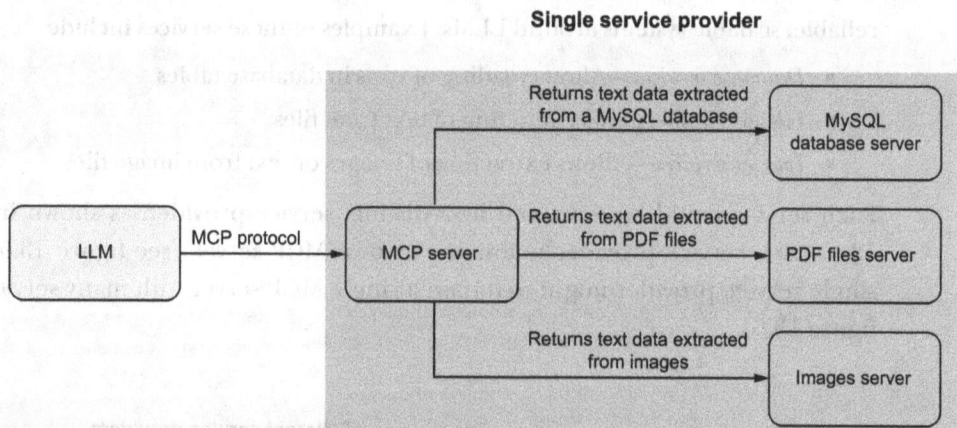

Figure 13.6   AN MCP server can provide multiple services.

13.1.3 *MCP server deployment*

Despite its name, which suggests a server-based application, an MCP server is simply a standard application that can run in different configurations. After you've developed an MCP server, you can deploy it in either of two ways:

- *Locally*—Run the MCP server on the same machine as the MCP client, enabling direct local communication.
- *Remotely*—Run the MCP server on a separate remote machine, with the MCP client accessing it over the network.

This flexibility in deployment options makes MCP servers adaptable to various architectural needs, from simple local setups to distributed systems. For the first option, when the MCP server and client are running on the same machine, they communicate with each other using standard input and output streams (see figure 13.7). In this approach, the MCP server runs as a separate process on the same machine as the client.

For the second option, the server and client are running on different machines across the network. In this case, the client will use HTTP POST to communicate

Both client and server running on same machine

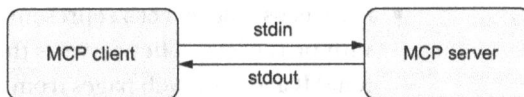

Figure 13.7   An MCP client communicating with a locally running MCP server using stdio

Server running remotely

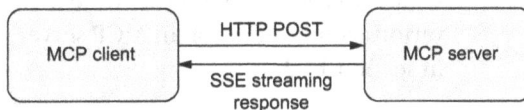

Figure 13.8   An MCP client communicating with a remote MCP server using HTTP POST and SSE

with the server, and the server will respond to the client using server-sent events (SSE). This transport method is useful when the server needs to support multiple clients at the same time. Figure 13.8 shows how the client interacts with the server.

Server-sent events

Server-sent events (SSE) is a web standard that enables a server to push real-time data to a client over a single HTTP connection. Unlike traditional HTTP request–response patterns, SSEs establish a persistent connection; the server can send data to the client continuously without the client having to poll or make new requests repeatedly.

SSEs are like WebSockets except that SSEs are unidirectional. Only the server can send data to the client; the client can't send messages back through the SSE connection.

13.1.4 Components in an MCP server

Now that you have a better idea of the workflow in an MCP system, let's examine the components of an MCP server. An MCP server consists of three main components:

- Tools—Tools are the actionable capabilities that MCP servers provide LLMs. They act like a set of specialized functions—such as reading files with a filesystem tool, querying the web via a search tool, or generating images through an image generation tool—that the LLM can invoke to extend its reach beyond its inherent knowledge, using a standardized JSON-RPC 2.0 request format (e.g., {"method": "search", "params": {"query": "AI"}}) to perform tasks efficiently and consistently across diverse services.

- Resources—Resources represent the external data or entities that Tools interact with or retrieve. They serve as the raw material—think local files from a Filesystem MCP server, web pages from a Brave Search MCP server, or database records from a PostgreSQL MCP server—that the LLM processes or analyzes, delivered through MCP responses (e.g., {"result": "file contents"}) to fuel its reasoning and responses with fresh, context-specific information.
- Prompts—Prompts in an MCP system function as predefined templates for standardized LLM interactions.

Figure 13.9 summarizes the three main components of an MCP server. The uses of the various components of an MCP server will become much clearer when you create one in section 13.2.

MCP server components and their uses

Components	Tools	Resources	Prompts
Uses	Server-exposed functions that can be called by LLMs	Data exposed to clients for LLM context	Predefined templates for standardized LLM interactions
Control Type	**Model-controlled** The LLM itself decides when and how to use these tools during its reasoning process.	**Application-controlled** Client determines what resources to retrieve and use.	**User-controlled** Clients determine the templates they want to use.
Examples	Fetching weather information, performing calculations, and so on	Fetching files, reading database records, returning images, and so on	Documenting Q&A, summarizing a block of text, and so on

Figure 13.9   The components of an MCP server and their uses

13.2   *Building an MCP server*

Now that you have a solid understanding of what an MCP server is and how its components work, it's time to put that knowledge into action. In this section, you'll build an MCP server using Python. This server will allow users to ask questions such as these:

- What is the current weather?
- Summarize the content of a particular file.
- Ask a question based on the content of a particular file.

13.2.1 Installing uv

For this project, you'll use uv, an extremely fast Python package and project manager written in Rust, to install Python packages. First, use the following curl command to download and install uv:

```
$ curl -LsSf https://astral.sh/uv/install.sh | sh
```

When uv is installed, you'll use it to create a Python project.

13.2.2 Initializing the project

Use uv to initialize a project named MCP_Demo and then change the directory to the new folder:

```
$ uv init MCP_Demo
Initialized project `mcp-demo` at `/Volumes/SSD/MCP_Demo`

$ cd MCP_Demo
```

Put two files in the MCP_Demo folder:

- Singapore.pdf—A PDF document generated from Wikipedia (see figure 13.10). For simplicity, this document has only one page.

- textfile.txt—A text file that contains some information on quantum computing (see figure 13.11).

Figure 13.10   The content of the PDF file

Figure 13.11   The content of the text file

13.2.3 *Installing the packages*

To implement the MCP server, you'll use the official Python SDK for MCP servers and clients, located at https://mng.bz/Qw4Q. You can find the documentation at https://modelcontextprotocol.io/introduction.

In Terminal (macOS) or Anaconda Prompt (Windows), type the following command to install the mcp, httpx, and PyMuPDF packages:

```
$ uv add "mcp[cli]" httpx PyMuPDF
```

13.2.4 *Creating the MCP server*

When the packages are installed, create the server.py file to store the implementation of the MCP server:

```
$ nano server.py
```

Populate the server.py file with the statements in the following listing.

Listing 13.1   A simple MCP server using the FastMCP class

```
from mcp.server.fastmcp import FastMCP
import httpx
import fitz          ◄─────┐ For PyMuPDF
import os

mcp = FastMCP("MCP Demo")   ◄─────┘ Creates an MCP server


# ===============================================
# resources, tools, and prompts to be added here
#
#        <to be added in next few sections>
#
# ===============================================

if __name__ == "__main__":
    # Initialize and run the server
    mcp.run(transport='stdio')
```

This code sets up a simple MCP server using the FastMCP class from the mcp.server.fastmcp module:

- First, create an instance of the FastMCP class, passing "MCP Demo" as the name of the service. The FastMCP object (mcp) represents the server itself, which will be configured and run later.
- Next, start the FastMCP server with the transport parameter set to 'stdio' (standard input/output).

When this is done, run the server and see whether an error occurs:

```
$ uv run server.py
```

If there is no error, nothing is shown onscreen.

13.2.5 *Inspecting the MCP server*

To inspect the MCP server, you can use the MCP Inspector by running the following command:

```
$ uv run mcp dev server.py
```

The MCP Inspector is an interactive developer tool designed for testing and debugging servers that implement MCP. You see something like this:

```
Starting MCP inspector...
Proxy server listening on port 3000

🔍 MCP Inspector is up and running at http://localhost:5173 🚀
New SSE connection
Query parameters: {
...
...
Connected MCP client to backing server transport
Created web app transport
Created web app transport
Set up MCP proxy
🔍 MCP Inspector is up and running at http://localhost:5173 🚀
```

The MCP Inspector is a web-based application that listens at the following URL: http://localhost:5173. To view it, load it using a web browser. You should see the screen shown in figure 13.12.

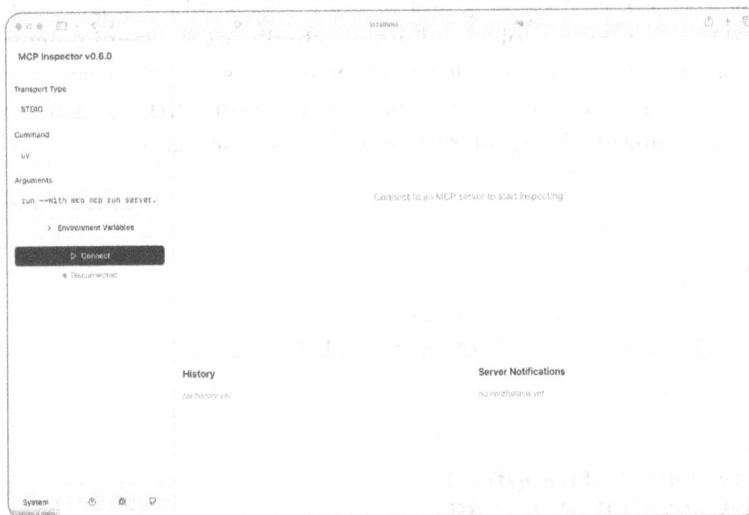

Figure 13.12
The MCP Inspector

Click the Connect button to connect to the MCP server. You see the tabs shown in figure 13.13: Resources, Prompts, Tools, Ping, # Sampling, and Roots.

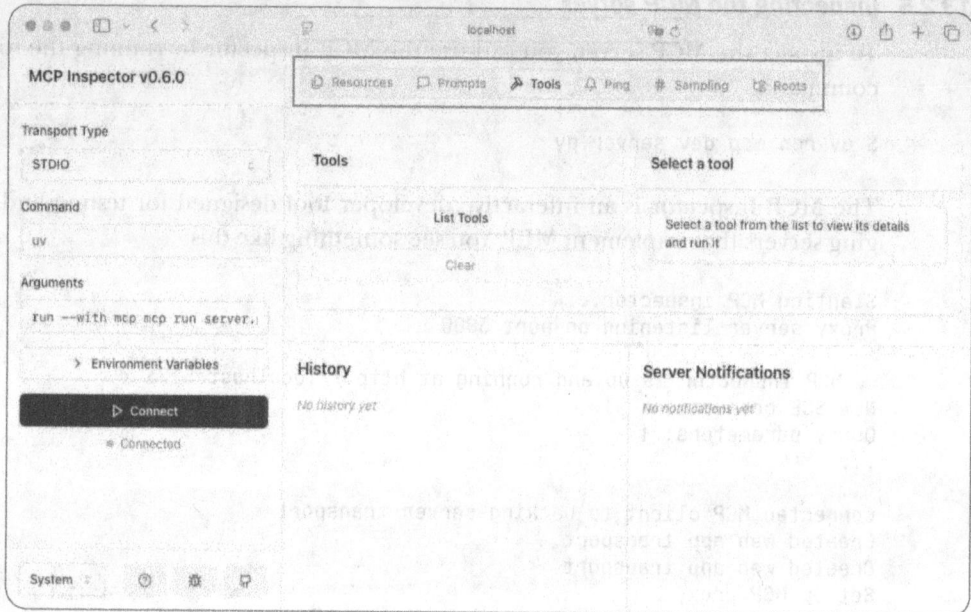

Figure 13.13   The MCP Inspector connecting to the MCP server

13.2.6 *Implementing Resources*

Now that the MCP server is running and you can get the MCP Inspector to connect to it, let's add some resources, tools, and prompts to the MCP server implementation. The first component you'll add to your MCP server is Resources. Recall from section 13.1.4 that Resources represents the external data or entities that Tools interacts with or retrieves. The following listing adds three resources to server.py.

Listing 13.2   Adding Resources to the MCP server

```
# server.py

# ================================================
# resources, tools, and prompts to be added here

#==========
# Resources
#==========
@mcp.resource("text://{file_path}")
def get_file(file_path: str) -> str:
```

```
    actual_path = os.path.abspath(file_path)     ◀——— Converts to absolute path
    if not os.path.exists(actual_path):
        raise FileNotFoundError(f"Error: File '{actual_path}' not found!")
    with open(actual_path, "r", encoding="utf-8") as file:
        return file.read()

@mcp.resource("config://app")
def get_config() -> str:
    """Static configuration data"""
    return "Version 1.1"

@mcp.resource("pdf://{file_path}")
def get_pdf_data(file_path: str) -> str:
    text = ""
    actual_path = os.path.abspath(file_path)
    if not os.path.exists(actual_path):
        raise FileNotFoundError(f"Error: File '{actual_path}' not found!")
    with fitz.open(actual_path) as doc:
        for page in doc:
            text += page.get_text() + "\n"
    return text
```

This code snippet adds the following Resources:

- get_file()—Retrieves the contents of a text file given its file path. This function reads and returns the contents of a text file specified by file_path. It uses os.path.abspath() to ensure a valid path and raises an error if the file doesn't exist.
- get_config()—Returns static application configuration data. This simple function returns a hardcoded string ("Version 1.1") as configuration data. It's static for now but could be expanded to fetch dynamic config data.
- get_pdf_data()—Extracts and returns the text content from a PDF file given its file path. This function uses fitz (PyMuPDF) to open a PDF file, extracts text from each page, and returns that text as a single string. Like get_file(), it validates the file path and raises an error if the file isn't found.

Note that @mcp.resourcedecorator registers each function as an MCP resource with a specific Uniform Resource Identifier (URI)–like identifier (e.g., text://{file_path}, config://app, pdf://{file_path}). These identifiers define how the resources are accessed by an MCP client or tool like the MCP Inspector.

In MCP, Resources are typically represented as endpoints that handle specific requests, such as querying data, retrieving documents, or interacting with external services.

13.2.7 Implementing Tools

The next component to implement is Tools. Tools consists of the actionable capabilities that MCP servers provide to LLMs. The following listing adds four tools to server.py.

Listing 13.3   Adding Tools to the MCP server

```python
#======
# Tools
#======

@mcp.tool()
async def fetch_weather(city: str, units: str = "metric") -> dict:
    API_KEY = "xxxxxxxxxxxxxxxxxx"
    async with httpx.AsyncClient() as client:
        response = await client.get(
            f"https://api.openweathermap.org/data/2.5/weather",
            params={
                "q": city,
                "units": units,
                "appid": API_KEY
            }
        )
        if response.status_code == 200:
            data = response.json()
            weather_data = {
                "location": {
                    "name": data["name"],
                    "country": data["sys"]["country"],
                    "coordinates": {
                        "lat": data["coord"]["lat"],
                        "lon": data["coord"]["lon"]
                    }
                },
                "current": {
                    "temp": data["main"]["temp"],
                    "feels_like": data["main"]["feels_like"],
                    "humidity": data["main"]["humidity"],
                    "pressure": data["main"]["pressure"],
                    "description": data["weather"][0]["description"],
                    "icon_code": data["weather"][0]["icon"]
                },
                "wind": {
                    "speed": data["wind"]["speed"],
                    "direction": data["wind"]["deg"]
                },
                "sun": {
                    "sunrise": data["sys"]["sunrise"],
                    "sunset": data["sys"]["sunset"]
                },
                "units": units,
                "timestamp": data["dt"]
            }
            return weather_data
        else:
            return {
                "error": f"Weather data not available.
                    Status code: {response.status_code}",
                "message": response.text
            }
```

Replace with your actual API key from OpenWeatherMap.

```
@mcp.tool()
def convert_temperature(temp: float,
                        from_unit: str,
                        to_unit: str) -> float:
    if from_unit.lower() == "celsius":
        kelvin = temp + 273.15
    elif from_unit.lower() == "fahrenheit":
        kelvin = (temp + 459.67) * 5/9
    elif from_unit.lower() == "kelvin":
        kelvin = temp
    else:
        raise ValueError(f"Unsupported unit: {from_unit}")


    if to_unit.lower() == "celsius":
        return kelvin - 273.15
    elif to_unit.lower() == "fahrenheit":
        return kelvin * 9/5 - 459.67
    elif to_unit.lower() == "kelvin":
        return kelvin
    else:
        raise ValueError(f"Unsupported unit: {to_unit}")

@mcp.tool()
def get_pdf(file_path: str) -> str:
    return get_pdf_data(file_path)

@mcp.tool()
def get_text(file_path: str) -> str:
    return get_file(file_path)
```

Adds a helper tool for temperature conversion

First converts to Kelvin as an intermediate step

Converts from Kelvin to target unit

This code snippet adds the following Tools:

- fetch_weather()—Fetches current weather data for a specified city using the OpenWeatherMap API. (You can apply for your own API key at https://home .openweathermap.org/api_keys.) This asynchronous tool uses httpx to query the OpenWeatherMap API, returning a detailed dictionary of weather data (location, temperature, wind, and so on) for the specified city or an error message if the request fails.

- convert_temperature()—Converts a temperature value among Celsius, Fahrenheit, and Kelvin. This tool converts a temperature from one unit to another (e.g., Celsius to Fahrenheit) using Kelvin as an intermediate step, raising an error for unsupported units.

- get_pdf()—Retrieves the text content of a PDF file using the get_pdf_data resource. This tool acts as a wrapper around the get_pdf_data resource, providing a convenient way to access PDF text extraction as a tool.

- get_text()—Retrieves the contents of a text file using the get_file resource. This tool wraps the get_file resource, allowing retrieval of text-file content through the tool interface.

The `@mcp.tool()` decorator registers each function as an MCP tool, making it callable by an MCP client or the MCP Inspector. Unlike `Resources`, `Tools` are typically actions or utilities rather than data endpoints.

13.2.8 *Implementing a prompt*

Finally, add a prompt to the MCP server.

Listing 13.4   Adding a prompt to the MCP server

```
#=======
# Prompt
#=======
# Add a weather_report prompt template
@mcp.prompt()
def weather_report(city: str) -> str:
    return f"""
Please provide a weather report for {city}.

You can use the fetch_weather tool to get current weather data.
If needed, you can convert temperature units using the
convert_temperature tool.

Please include:
- Current temperature
- Weather conditions
- Humidity
- Wind speed
- Any relevant weather advice for the conditions
"""
```

This code snippet adds a prompt to the MCP server. `weather_report()` generates a prompt template for requesting a detailed weather report for a specified city. This description reflects the function's purpose: it creates a formatted string that serves as a template for an MCP client (e.g., an LLM) to generate a weather report using available tools such as `fetch_weather` and `convert_temperature`.

The `@mcp.prompt` decorator registers the `weather_report` function as an MCP prompt. Prompts in MCP are typically templates or instructions that guide how a client (such as an LLM) should process a request, often using the server's tools and resources.

13.2.9 *Testing the components*

With our MCP server updated with `Resources`, `Tools`, and a prompt, let's test them to ensure that they work as intended. First, rerun the MCP server using the MCP Inspector:

```
$ uv run mcp dev server.py
```

In the MCP Inspector, click the Connect button to connect to the MCP server. You're ready to test the `Resources`, `Prompts`, and `Tools`. Click the List Resources button, and you see the `config://app`. Clicking it returns the details of the version of the app (see figure 13.14).

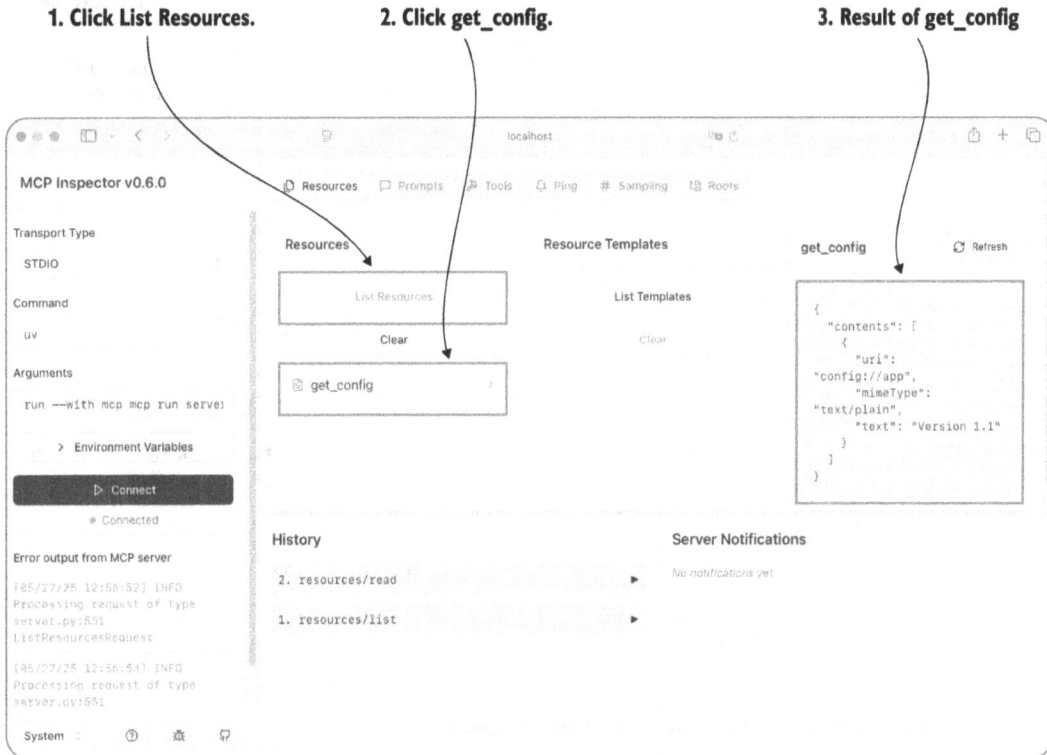

1. Click List Resources. **2. Click get_config.** **3. Result of get_config**

Figure 13.14 Checking out the `Resources` using the MCP Inspector

Interestingly, clicking the List Resources button shows only the `get_config()` (with the URI `config://app`) function because this static function doesn't have any input parameters, unlike the other two functions, `get_file()` and `get_pdf_data()`. To see these two functions, click the List Templates button (see figure 13.15).

You should see the two functions. Click the `get_file` function, enter the name of a text file, and then click Read Resource. You see the content of the file (remember that there is a text file named `textfile.txt` in the `MCP_Demo` folder; see figure 13.16).

Figure 13.15 Listing all the resource templates in the MCP server

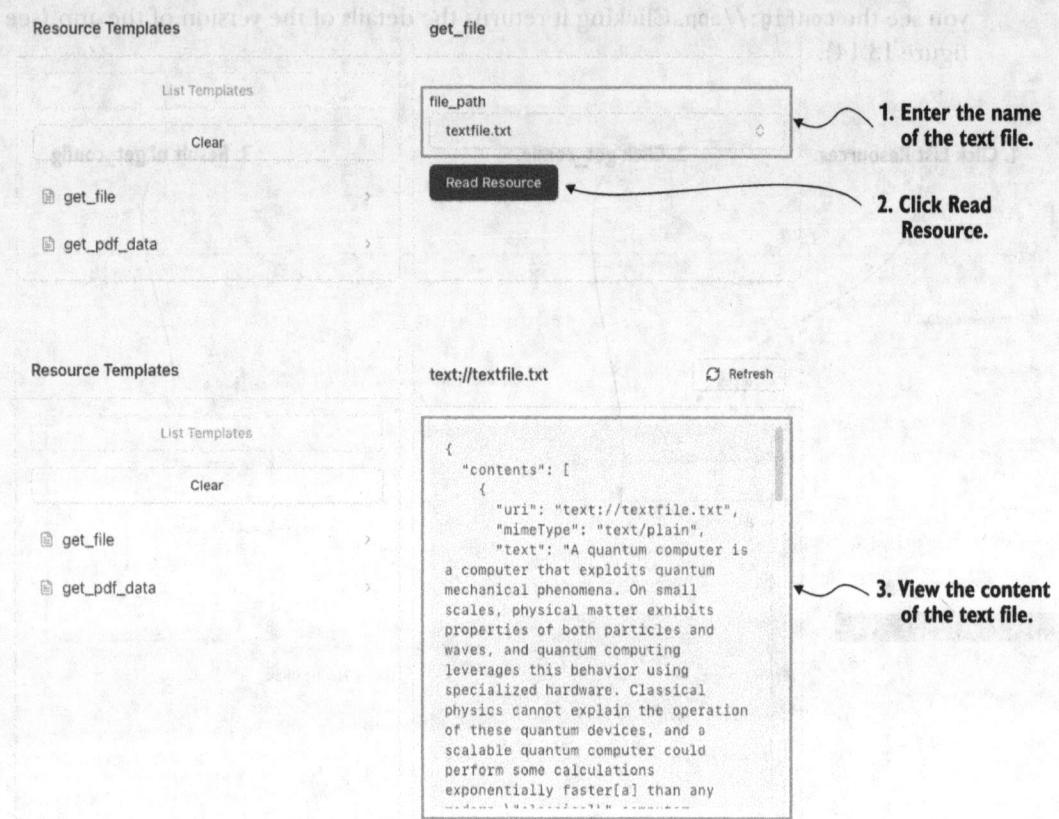

Figure 13.16   Loading the content of a text file through a resource

Likewise, click the `get_pdf_data` function, enter a name, and click the Read Resource button. You see something like figure 13.17 (remember that there is a text file named `Singapore.pdf` in the `MCP_Demo` folder).

Next, click the Prompts tab and then click List Prompts. You should see the `weather_report` prompt. Click it, and enter `Singapore` as the city (see figure 13.18).

Click the Get Prompt button, and you see the following:

```
{
  "messages": [
    {
      "role": "user",
      "content": {
        "type": "text",
        "text": "\n    Please provide a weather report for Singapore.\n
                \n    You can use the fetch_weather tool to get current
                weather data.\n    If needed, you can convert temperature
                units using the convert_temperature tool.\n    \n
                Please include:\n    - Current temperature\n    - Weather
```

```
            conditions\n    - Humidity\n    - Wind speed\n    - Any
            relevant weather advice for the conditions\n    "
        }
      }
    ]
  }
```

Resource Templates   get_pdf_data

List Templates

Clear

get_file

get_pdf_data

| file_path | |
| Singapore.pdf | ⬍ |

Read Resource

1. Enter the name of the PDF file.

2. Click Read Resource.

Resource Templates   pdf://Singapore.pdf   ⟳ Refresh

List Templates

Clear

get_file

get_pdf_data

```
{
  "contents": [
    {
      "uri": "pdf://Singapore.pdf",
      "mimeType": "text/plain",
      "text": "Republic of
Singapore\nRepublik
Singapura (Malay)\n新加坡共和
国 (Mandarin Chinese)\nசிங்கப்பூர்
குடியரசு (Tamil)\nFlag\nCoat of
arms\nMotto: Majulah
Singapura (Malay)\n\"Onward
Singapore\"\nAnthem: Majulah
Singapura (Malay)\n\"Onward
Singapore\"\nOfficial
languages\nEnglish · Malay
·\nMandarin · Tamil\nNational
language\nMalay\nEthnic groups\n(202
```

3. View the content of the PDF file.

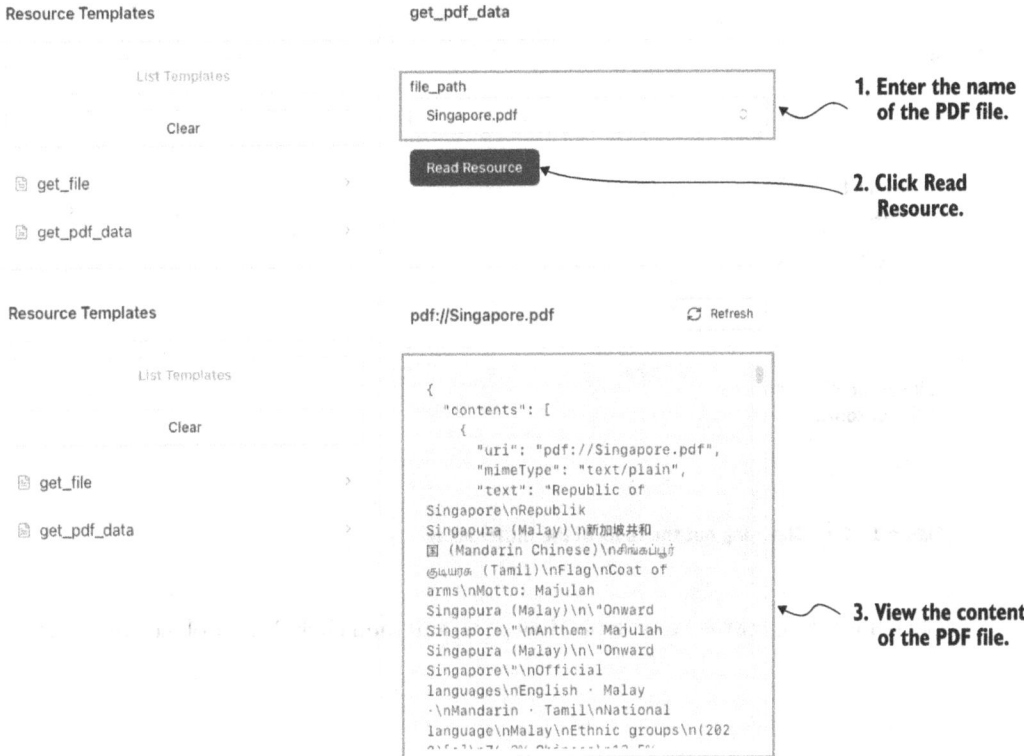

Figure 13.17   Loading the content of a PDF file through a resource

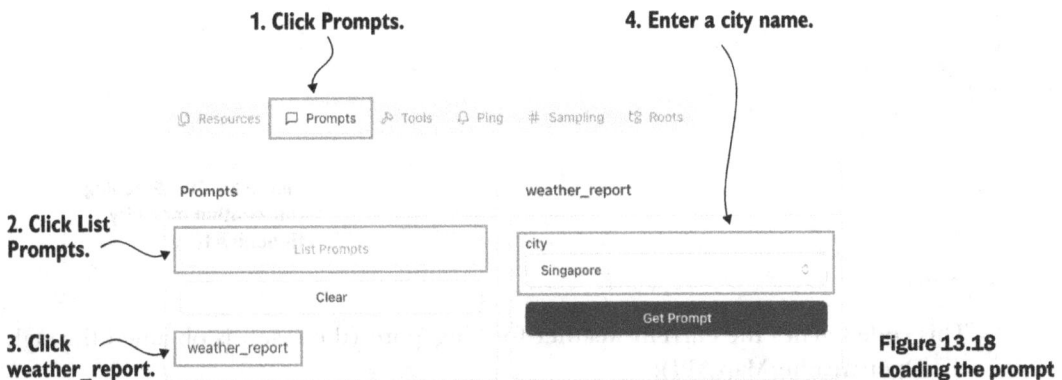

1. Click Prompts.   4. Enter a city name.

🗂 Resources   🗩 Prompts   🛠 Tools   🛎 Ping   # Sampling   ↥ Roots

Prompts   weather_report

2. Click List Prompts.

| List Prompts |

Clear

| city | |
| Singapore | ⬍ |

Get Prompt

3. Click weather_report.   weather_report

Figure 13.18
Loading the prompt

Click the Tools tab and then click the List Tools button. You see the four tools defined earlier (see figure 13.19).

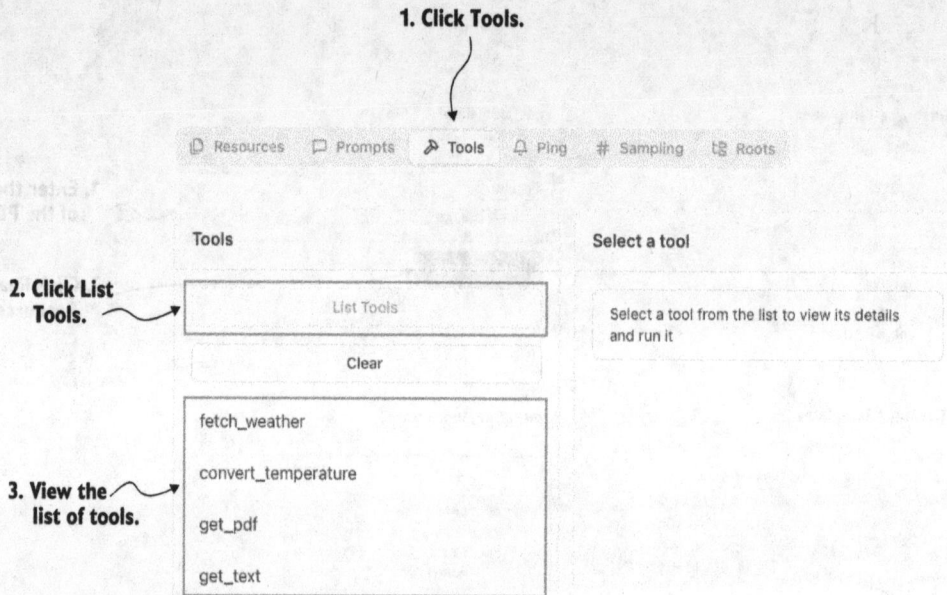

1. Click Tools.

| Resources | Prompts | Tools | Ping | # Sampling | Roots |

Tools

Select a tool

2. Click List Tools.

List Tools

Select a tool from the list to view its details and run it

Clear

fetch_weather

convert_temperature

3. View the list of tools.

get_pdf

get_text

Figure 13.19   Checking out the tools of the MCP server

Click the `fetch_weather` tool, type `Singapore`, and then click Run Tool (see figure 13.20).

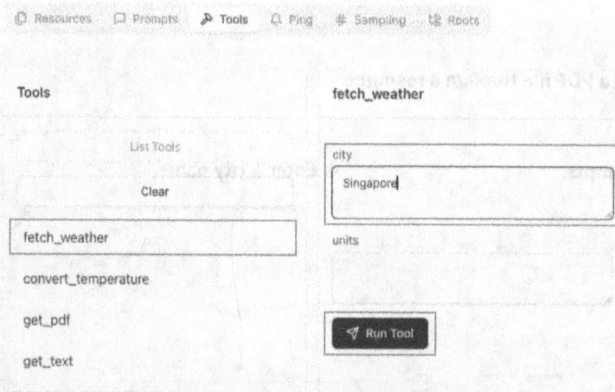

| Resources | Prompts | Tools | Ping | # Sampling | Roots |

Tools

fetch_weather

List Tools

city

Clear

Singapore

fetch_weather

units

convert_temperature

get_pdf

get_text

Run Tool

Figure 13.20   Fetching the weather for a city through a tool

This code fetches the current weather for Singapore (the result is obtained through the OpenWeatherMap API):

```
{
  "location": {
    "name": "Singapore",
    "country": "SG",
    "coordinates": {
      "lat": 1.2897,
      "lon": 103.8501
    }
  },
  "current": {
    "temp": 32.14,
    "feels_like": 38.04,
    "humidity": 62,
    "pressure": 1009,
    "description": "broken clouds",
    "icon_code": "04d"
  },
  "wind": {
    "speed": 2.57,
    "direction": 40
  },
  "sun": {
    "sunrise": 1748300180,
    "sunset": 1748344049
  },
  "units": "metric",
  "timestamp": 1748322002
}
```

Now try the `get_pdf` tool. Click it, type `Singapore.pdf`, and then click Run Tool. You get the content of the PDF file (remember that there is a file named `Singapore.pdf` in the `MCP_Demo` folder; see figure 13.21). You can also try the other tools: `convert_temperature`, and `get_text`.

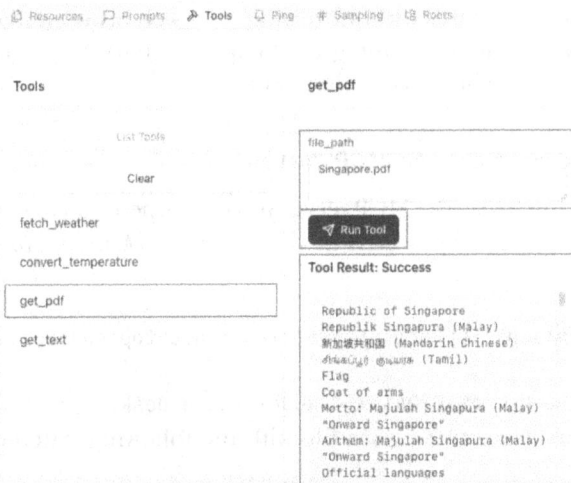

Figure 13.21 Getting the content of a PDF file through a tool

13.3   *Testing the MCP server using Claude Desktop*

Although your MCP server has been validated through the MCP Inspector, this testing tool doesn't fully showcase the practical value of MCP. How is it useful, and what are some real-world use cases? The best way to explore its utility is to pair it with Claude Desktop (see figure 13.22), an application you can download at https://claude.ai/download, which integrates MCP to enhance AI-driven tasks and workflows. Claude Desktop supports MCP, enabling connections to external tools such as filesystem access or web search via prebuilt or custom MCP servers.

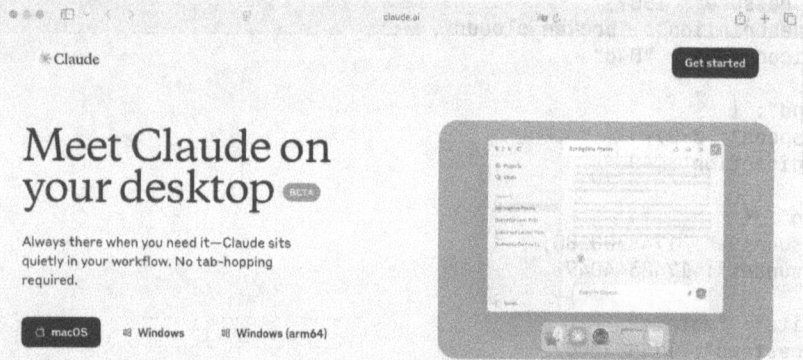

Figure 13.22   Downloading Claude Desktop

NOTE Claude Desktop is a desktop application developed by Anthropic that brings the capabilities of the Claude AI model directly to your computer (macOS and Windows). It's designed to provide seamless, fast access to Claude's conversational AI features without relying on a web browser, making it ideal for users who want a focused, integrated experience for tasks such as coding, content creation, data analysis, or deep work.

13.3.1   *Configuring Claude Desktop to use the MCP server*

To configure Claude Desktop to use the MCP server you developed, you need to modify the `claude_desktop_config.json` file located in the `~/Library/Application Support/Claude` folder (macOS):

```
$ nano ~/Library/Application\ Support/Claude/claude_desktop_config.json
```

In Windows, the path to this file is `%APPDATA%\Claude\claude_desktop_config.json`.

Populate the `claude_desktop_config.json` file with the following statements (bold for emphasis):

```
{
  "mcpServers": {
    "weather": {
      "command": "/Users/weimenglee/.local/bin/uv",
      "args": [
        "--directory",
        "/Volumes/SSD/MCP_Demo",
        "run",
        "server.py"
      ]
    }
  }
}
```

Observe the values in bold:

- `"weather"`—Name of the MCP server. You can give it any name you want.
- `/Users/weimenglee/.local/bin/uv`—Location of the `uv` tool. It will be used to run your MCP server.
- `/Volumes/SSD/Medium/MCP_Demo`—Full path of the folder containing the MCP server (`server.py`).
- `server.py`—Name of the file containing the MCP server implementation.

When the `claude_desktop_config.json` file is saved, restart Claude Desktop. The first time you launch Claude Desktop, you'll be asked to sign in.

13.3.2 Getting the weather

In Claude Desktop, ask the following question: "Get me the weather for Singapore" (see figure 13.23). Claude takes a moment to process the question and then presents the prompt shown in figure 13.24.

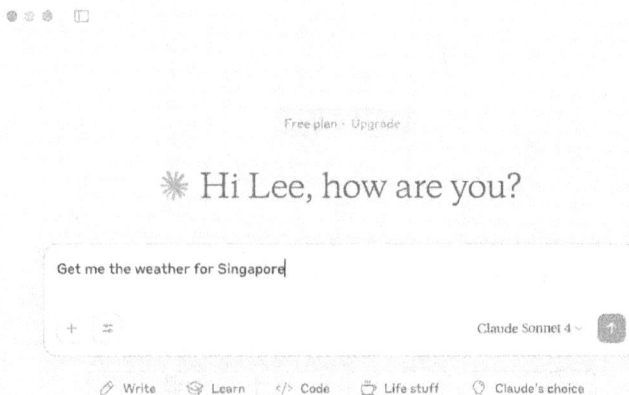

Figure 13.23 Asking a question in Claude Desktop

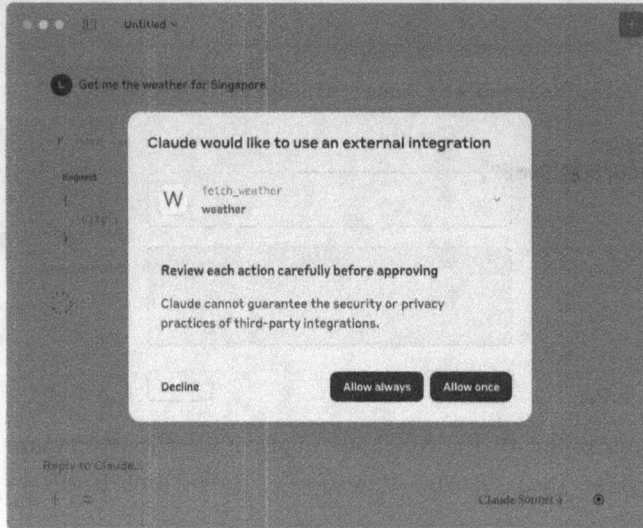

Figure 13.24   Claude Desktop has found the tool to answer your question.

The application is saying that to answer your question, it found a tool called `fetch_weather` from the "weather" MCP server you configured. Click Allow Once (or Allow Always) to allow Claude to access the `fetch_weather` tool and fetch the weather for Singapore.

After a short wait, the result is returned to you. Notice that Claude uses the tool's output to generate a coherent response (see figure 13.25). Without the MCP tools, Claude wouldn't be able to fetch the weather information for you.

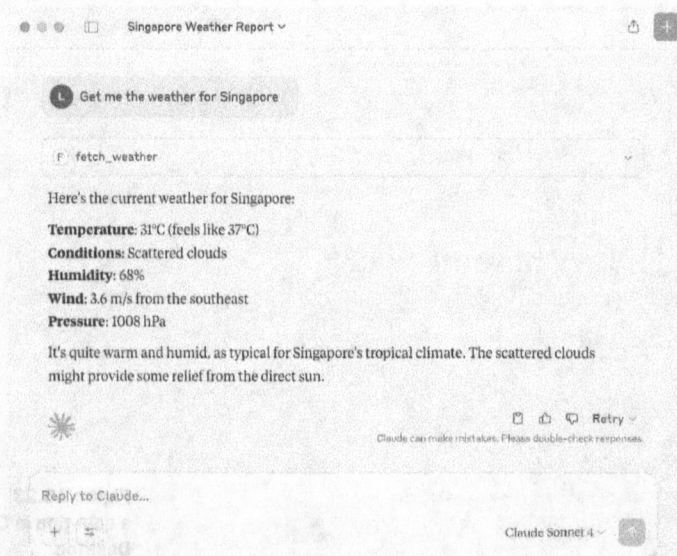

Figure 13.25 The result returned by the tool

13.3.3 Getting the content of a text file

Try another question: "Can you help me get the content of `textfile.txt`." As before, Claude Desktop detects that a tool named `get_text` is able to able to answer your question (see figure 13.26).

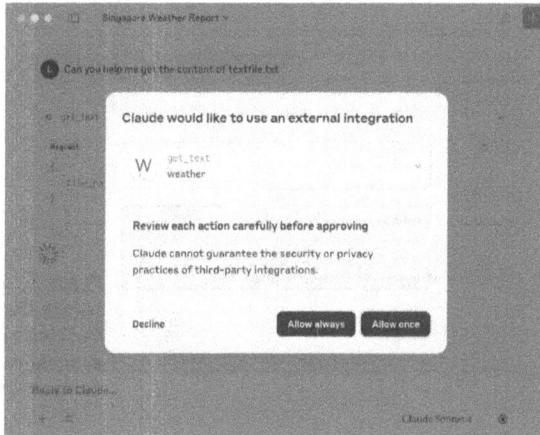

Figure 13.26 Claude Desktop found a tool to fetch the content of a file.

If you grant it access to the tool, Claude will extract the content from the text file and summarize it in bullet points (see figure 13.27). You can follow up with another question: "Summarize the content of the file." This time, Claude Desktop generates a summary (see figure 13.28).

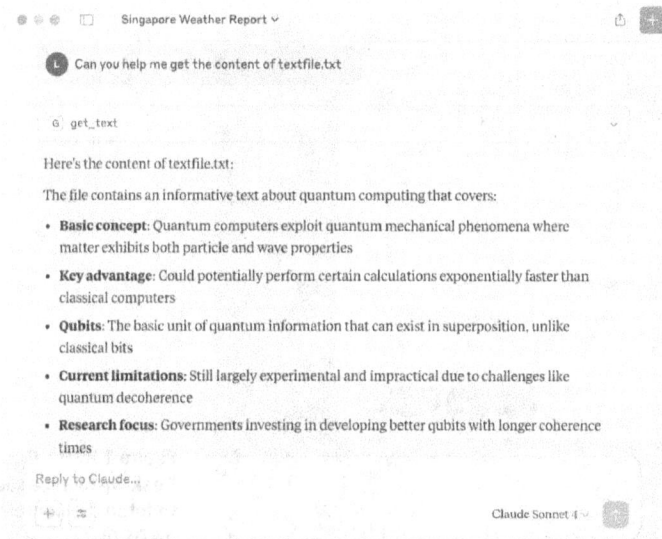

Figure 13.27 The content of the file returned by Claude Desktop

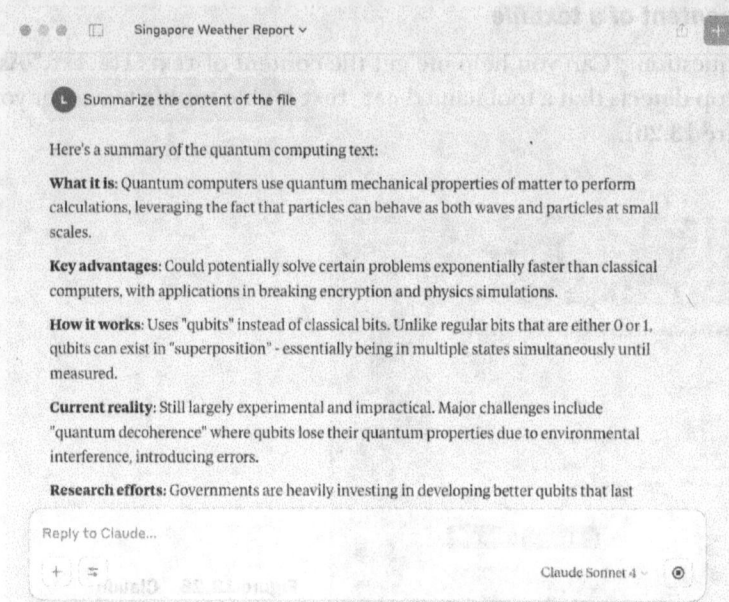

Figure 13.28
Asking Claude
Desktop to
summarize the
content of the file

13.3.4 Getting the content of a PDF file

Ask one more question: "Load the content of Singapore.pdf." As expected, Claude Desktop knows that the `get_pdf` tool can answer your question (see figure 13.29). When you grant it permission to use the tool, Claude Desktop loads the content of the PDF file and returns the key points in the document (see figure 13.30).

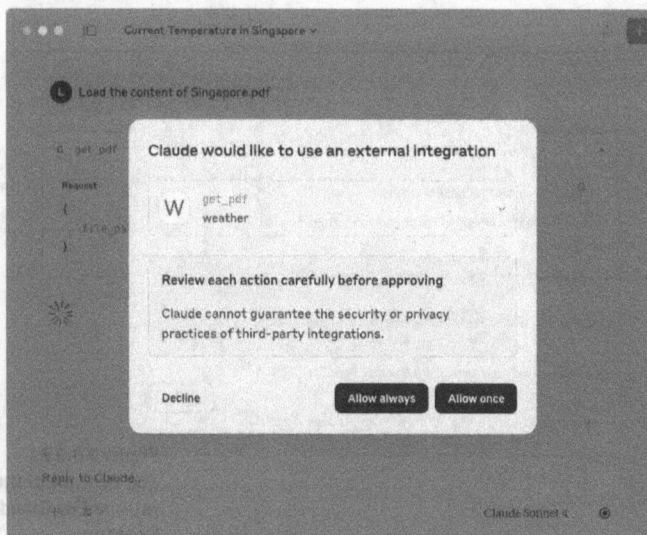

Figure 13.29   Claude
Desktop found a tool
to fetch the content
of a PDF file.

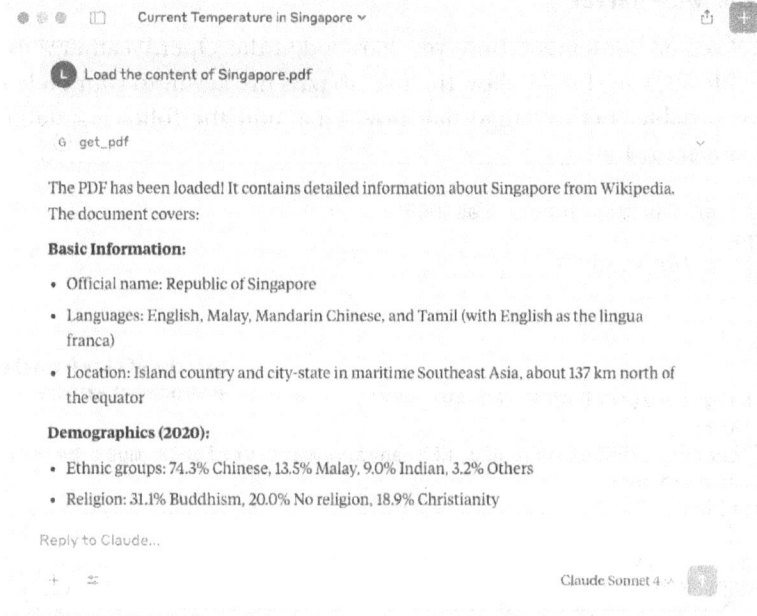

Figure 13.30
The content
of the PDF file
returned by
the tool

Now you can ask a question specific to the document: "What are the official languages in Singapore?" Claude Desktop generates the result for you (see figure 13.31).

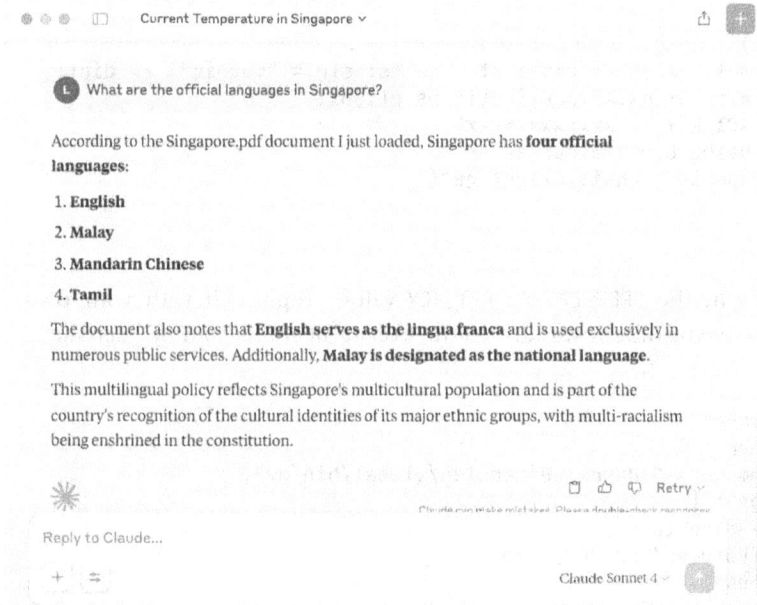

Figure 13.31
Asking questions
pertaining to the
PDF document

13.3.5 *Improving the MCP server*

In your MCP server implementation, you hardcoded the OpenWeatherMap API key in the code. Ideally, you should allow the user to pass the key in to your code using an environment variable. Let's change that now. First, add the following statements in bold to the server.py file:

```
from mcp.server.fastmcp import FastMCP
import httpx
import fitz  # for PyMuPDF
import os

import sys

API_KEY = os.getenv('OPENWEATHER_API_KEY')   ◄─┐  Gets the API key from the
if not API_KEY:                                 │  environment variable
    print("Error: OPENWEATHER_API_KEY environment variable must be set",
        file=sys.stderr)
    sys.exit(1)

# Create an MCP server
mcp = FastMCP("MCP Demo")
...
...
```

Then comment out the assignment of the API_KEY variable in the fetch_weather() function:

```
#======
# Tools
#======
@mcp.tool()
async def fetch_weather(city: str, units: str = "metric") -> dict:
    async with httpx.AsyncClient() as client:
        # API_KEY = "xxxxxxxxxxxx"
        # Using OpenWeatherMap API
        response = await client.get(
...
...
```

Finally, pass in the OPENWEATHER_API_KEY value (replace it with your own API key) through the environment variable in the claude_desktop_config.json file:

```
{
  "mcpServers": {
    "weather": {
      "command": "/Users/weimenglee/.local/bin/uv",
      "args": [
        "--directory",
        "/Volumes/SSD/MCP_Demo",
        "run",
        "server.py"
```

```
      ],
      "env": {
        "OPENWEATHER_API_KEY": "xxxxxxxxxxxx"
      }
    }
  }
}
```

Restart Claude Desktop. The MCP server works as intended.

13.4 Trying third-party MCP servers

At this stage, you've built your own MCP server and tested it using Claude Desktop. In this section, you'll explore further, trying out some MCP servers created by others. You'll install the following third-party MCP servers:

- *Location Service*—An MCP server that allows you to discover your geographical location.
- *Time Service*—An MCP server that allows you to obtain the current time. It also supports generation of datetime strings in various formats.

13.4.1 Get My Location

Get My Location is an MCP server that allows you to discover your geographical location. To learn more about this service, visit https://mcp.so/server/get-my-location/typescript. To use this service in Claude Desktop, edit the `claude_desktop_config.json` file:

```
$ nano ~/Library/Application\ Support/Claude/claude_desktop_config.json
```

Add the following statements in bold (note the comma before the "get-location" key):

```
{
  "mcpServers": {
    "weather": {
      "command": "/Users/weimenglee/.local/bin/uv",
      "args": [
        "--directory",
        "/Volumes/SSD/MCP_Demo",
        "run",
        "server.py"
      ],
      "env": {
        "OPENWEATHER_API_KEY": "xxxxxxxxxxxx"
      }
    },
    "get-location": {
      "command": "npx",
      "args": [
        "-y",
        "@mcpcn/mcp-get-location"
      ],
```

```
    "env": {}
  }
 }
}
```

Unlike the MCP server that you developed using Python, the Location Service server is written in Node.js. The various keys do the following things:

- "npx"—Uses npx (a command-line tool that comes with Node.js) to run a Node .js package without installing it globally
- -y—Automatically answers "yes" to prompts
- @mcpcn/mcp-get-location—Refers to a package located at https://mng.bz/X7ep.
- "env"—Indicates that no special environment variables are configured

The npx tool downloads the package from the NPM registry to a temporary location and then runs it immediately without installing it permanently. The package executes locally on your machine as an MCP server and provides location services to an MCP client (such as Claude Desktop).

Restart Claude Desktop, and ask the following question: "What is my current location?" Claude Desktop should be able to find the get-location tool to answer that question (see figure 13.32). Click Allow Once.

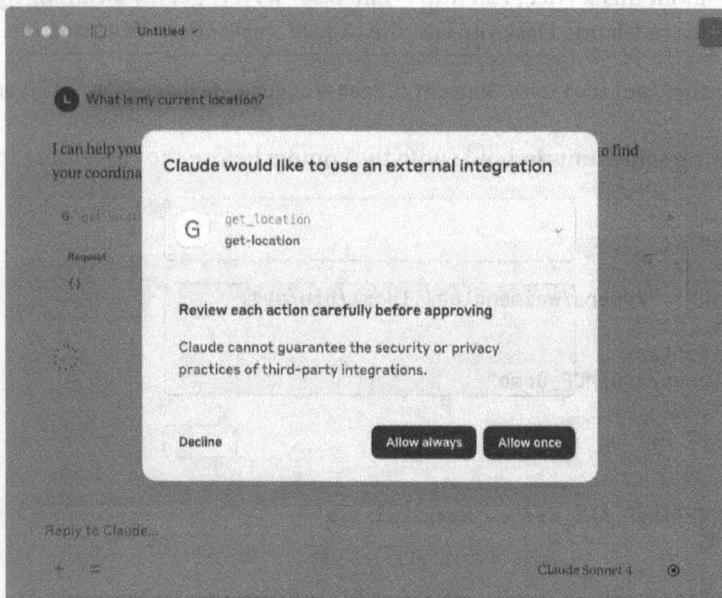

Figure 13.32
Claude Desktop
using the third-
party tool to
get your current
location

A web page appears, asking for permission to get your current location (see figure 13.33). Click Get My Location.

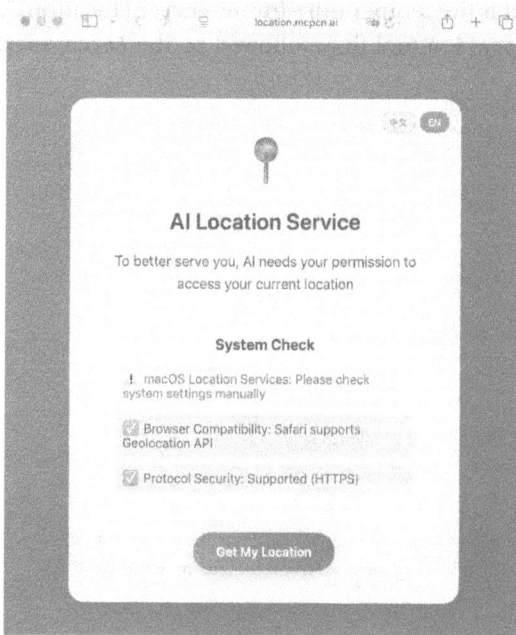

Figure 13.33 Retrieving your location

Back in Claude Desktop, you see the location details retrieved by the MCP server (see figure 13.34).

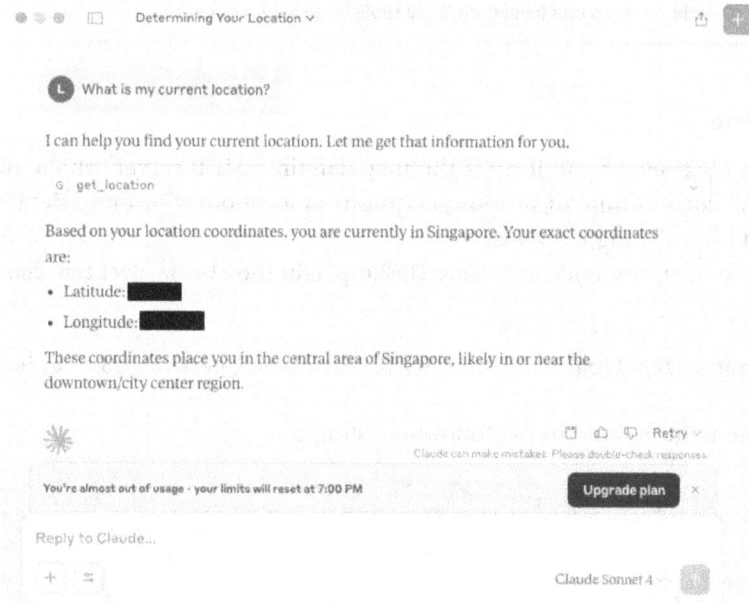

Figure 13.34 Location information returned by the tool

If you asked something like "What is the temperature for my current location?", Claude Desktop would invoke the `get_location` tool first, followed by the `fetch_weather` tool (see figure 13.35). Cool, isn't it?

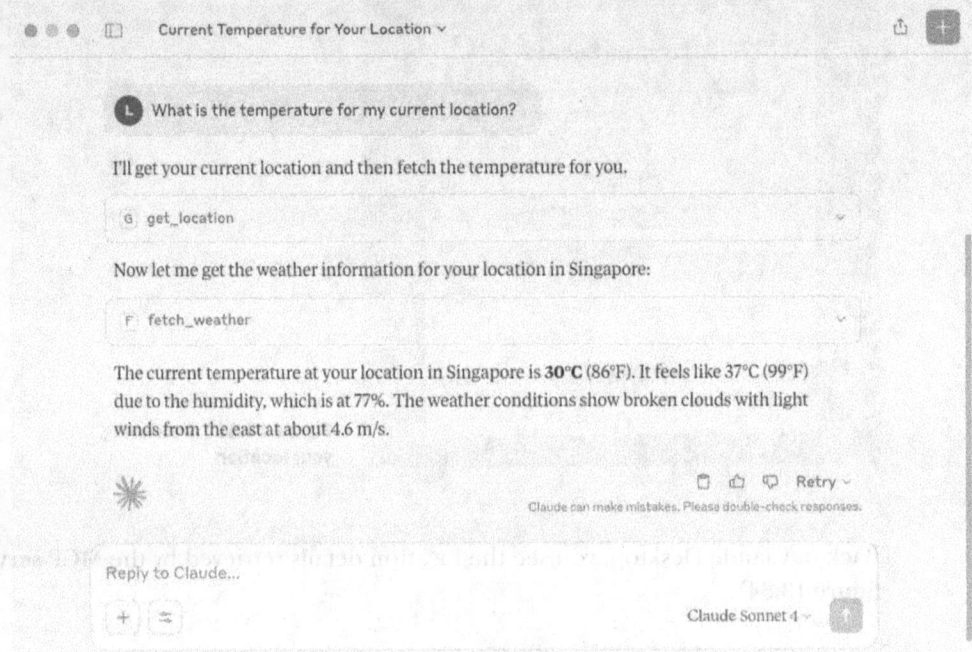

Figure 13.35   Claude Desktop can invoke multiple tools to answer a question.

13.4.2 *mcp-datetime*

The second MCP server you'll try is the mcp-datetime MCP server, which allows you to obtain the current time in various geographical locations. For more details on this service, visit https://mng.bz/yNKy.

As usual, to use this service in Claude Desktop, edit the `claude_desktop_config.json` file:

```
$ nano ~/Library/Application\ Support/Claude/claude_desktop_config.json
```

Add the statements in bold in the following listing.

Listing 13.5   Adding the `mcp-datetime` service

```
{
  "mcpServers": {
    "weather": {
```

```
      "command": "/Users/weimenglee/.local/bin/uv",
      "args": [
        "--directory",
        "/Volumes/SSD/Dropbox/MCP_Demo",
        "run",
        "server.py"
      ],
      "env": {
        "OPENWEATHER_API_KEY": "xxxxxxxxxxxx"
      }
    },
    "get-location": {
      "command": "npx",
      "args": [
        "-y",
        "@mcpcn/mcp-get-location"
      ],
      "env": {}
    },
    "mcp-datetime": {
      "command": "/Users/weimenglee/.local/bin/uvx",
      "args": ["mcp-datetime"]
    }
  }
}
```

Unlike the Location Service, the Time Service is written in Python. Here's what the various keys do:

- The uvx command downloads the mcp-datetime Python package (https://pypi .org/project/mcp-datetime).
- The MCP server runs locally without permanent installation (like npx but for Python).

---

uv and uvx

uv is a comprehensive Python package and project manager that handles dependencies and virtual environments and can execute Python code within those environments. uvx is a command runner that executes Python applications in isolated, temporary environments without requiring manual setup.

In an earlier MCP configuration, you used uv run to execute the local Python script (server.py) within the project's managed environment. Now you use uvx to run the mcp-datetime package directly; it automatically downloads, installs, and executes the package in an isolated environment without any manual installation steps.

Restart Claude Desktop, and ask the following question: "What time is it now in Shanghai?" Claude Desktop should be able to find the get_datetime tool to answer that question (see figure 13.36). Click Allow Once. You see the answer from this tool (see figure 13.37).

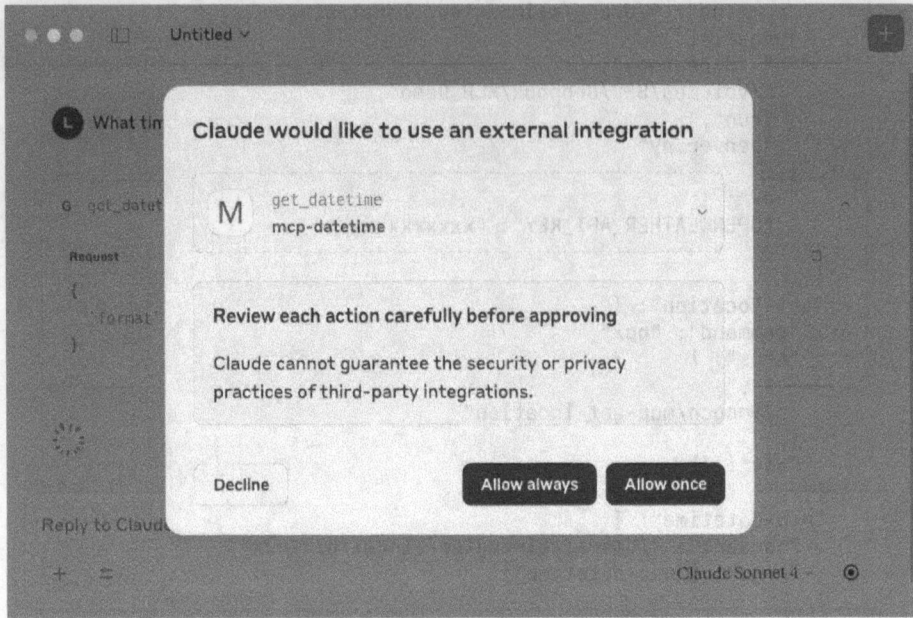

Figure 13.36   Claude Desktop using a tool to get the time at a particular location

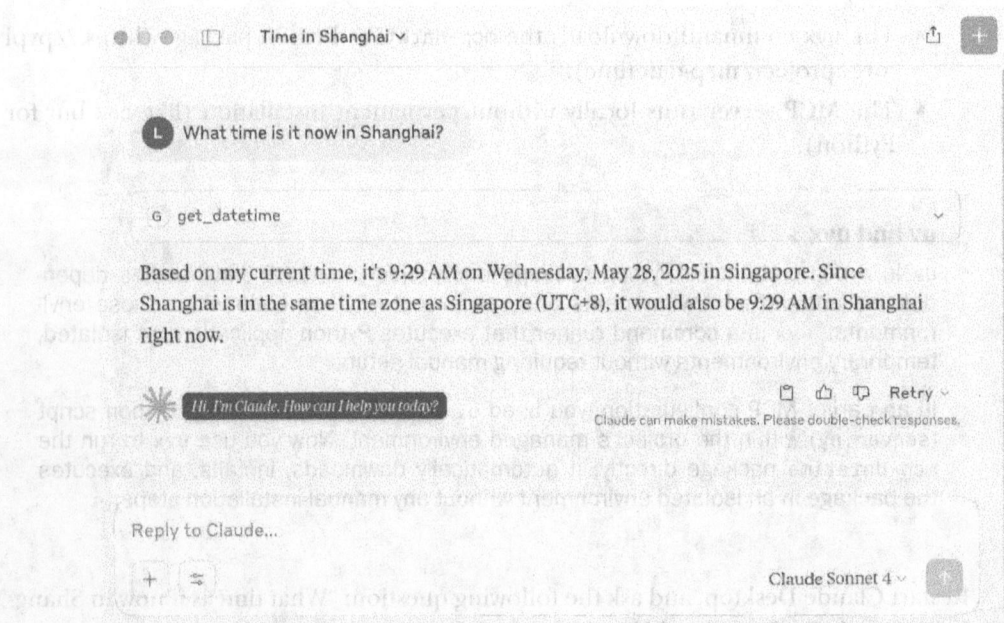

Figure 13.37   The time returned by the tool

Summary

- MCP is an open standard created by Anthropic to connect AI assistants like Claude to external data sources and tools.
- An MCP server is a standard application that can run in different configurations.
- After you developed an MCP server, you can deploy it locally or remotely.
- When the MCP server and client are running on the same machine, they communicate using standard input and output streams.
- When the server and client are running on different machines across the network, the client communicates with the server using HTTP POST, and the server responds to the client using SSE.
- An MCP server has three main components that define its functionality:
  - Tools—Executable functions that the LLM can invoke to perform actions or computations
  - Resources—Data sources that the AI can access to retrieve information
  - Prompts—Predefined prompt templates that can be used to guide AI interactions
- You can develop an MCP server using the official Python SDK for MCP servers and clients.
- You can use the MCP Inspector to test and validate your MCP server.
- You can use your MCP server via the Claude Desktop application.
- MCP servers are written in a variety of programming languages, including Python, Node.js, TypeScript, Go, and Rust.

index

www.ingramcontent.com/pod-product-compliance
Lightning Source LLC
Chambersburg PA
CBHW011038211225
37108CB00004B/11